Y0-BQD-182

THE UNDERGROUND ARMY

Fighters of the Bialystok Ghetto

by

CHAIKA GROSSMAN

Holocaust Library
New York

Translated from the Hebrew by Shmuel Beeri
Edited by Sol Lewis

Hebrew edition published in Israel in 1965

Library of Congress Catalogue Card No. 87-080905
ISBN: 0-89604-053-4 (Cloth)
0-89604-054-2 (Paper)

Cover design by Judith L. Anderson

Printed in the United States of America

Statement of Purpose

The Holocaust spread across the face of Europe almost fifty years ago. The brutality then unleashed is still nearly beyond comprehension. Millions of innocents, men, women and children, were consumed by its flames.

The goal of Holocaust Publications, a non-profit organization founded by survivors, is to publish and disseminate works on the Holocaust. These will include survivors' accounts, testimonies and memoirs, historical and regional analyses, anthologies, archival and source documents and other relevant materials that will help shed light on this cataclysmic era.

These books and studies will be made available to the general public, scholars, researchers, historians, teachers and students. They will be used in Holocaust Resource Centers, libraries and schools, synagogues and churches. They will help foster an increased awareness of the Holocaust and its implications. They will help to *preserve the memory* for posterity and to enable this awesome time to be better understood and comprehended.

Holocaust Library
216 West 18th Street
New York, NY 10011

POLAND UNDER THE GERMAN OCCUPATION

Table of Contents

Introduction

Chaika Grossman's book has, over the years, become a classic of Holocaust testimonials, unfortunately accessible only to readers of Hebrew. Its publication in English now makes available to a large audience first-hand evidence of one of the epics of Holocaust history: the organization and execution of a crazy and seemingly impossible plan of a group of Jewish youngers to stage an armed uprising against the tremendous might of the Nazi machine of destruction in the Bialystok ghetto. Chaika Grossman, now (1987) a Member of the Israeli Knesset, was then a young girl, member of the Hashomer Hatzair youth movement; after February, 1943, she became its effective leader in the Bialystok ghetto. After the end of the fighting in August, 1943, she became the leader of what remained of the Jewish resisters' group, and organized an underground Jewish anti-Nazi group active in supporting the forest partisans and in spying on and sabotaging the German machine in Bialystok.

If that were all, Chaika's book would have been an important element in any bibliography on the Holocaust. But the book is much more than that.

Its first version was written down not long after the war. Speeches by Chaika in the late 1940s and early 1950s repeat the descriptions found in the book — it is therefore not a late, but a very early testimony. The author has checked her memory against that of other survivors, most of whom are mentioned by name in the book, so that this is, in essence, a cross-checked memoir, not merely an individual's reminiscence.

One of the central problems raised in Holocaust historiography is that of the Jewish Councils (Judenraten) nominated by the Nazis in all European Jewish communities, their function as part of the Nazi machine of mass murder on the one hand, and their function as a legitimate Jewish leadership trying to protect their respective communities, on the other hand. The additional problem, directly addressed in this book, is the Judenrat's attitude to resistance. The case of the effective (not nominal) leader of the Bialystok Judenrat, Ephraim Barash, is a centrally important one in this respect. We have not only Chaika's account of Barash, his policies, his personality, and his actions, but we can compare it with the account given by Mordechai Tennenbaum, the commander of the rebellion, whose notes and letters survived the Holocaust though he himself did not. The two accounts tally. In effect, despite the sometimes bitter differences between the groups that made up the resistance organization in Bialystok — the reader will sense them in Chaika's description — the two accounts give much the same picture of Barash, and their evaluation of the Judenrat is to all intents and purposes the same: Barash was, personally, an honest, straightforward man, but he and his Council misled not only the ghetto but themselves as well into the deadly illusion that becoming slaves to the German war machine would save the life of the ghetto. Chaika's — and Tennenbaum's — answer was that as no one could be saved, the only decent human reaction was to attempt armed resistance. The motives are described in this book. They have little to do with the kind of idealizing, moralizing and sermonizing that has become an integral part of contemporary writing about the Holocaust. The motives were revenge, the desire to help, even in a very small way, in the destruction of the German war machine, and the desire to do that in the ghetto, to get the population to join in a last, desperate and totally hopeless struggle, whose purpose would be to leave what a resister in another ghetto, Cracow, called "three lines in history books." In this last endeavor the Bialystok resisters failed, and Chaika shows how and why the population did not join in; the resisters were alone. And yet, they succeeded; and the "three lines" are being written.

The real moral dilemmas are presented, openly, even sometimes brutally: the abandonment of one's closest family in order to fight; the problem of who should jump first from the train going to the death camp (those who jumped later stood less of a chance of survival); the terrible dilemma of whether to rebel without arms when part of the ghetto is shipped to death (in February, 1943), or whether to wait until there are arms and in effect join in the Judenrat's policy of passively looking on as thousands of helpless people are led to their deaths.

Chaika's book presents all these terrible problems in a matter-of-fact way, yet one is never unaware of the tremendous emotion she writes in. The tiny group that carried on the fight after August 1943 were almost all of them women. The fight of Jewish women, the pre-eminent place of the woman in the ghetto resistance movement, her specific role and her qualities of leadership all come out very clearly. It was so not only in Bialystok, and we need to look into this aspect more closely.

Lastly, that large majority among the resisters who were Zionists — there were Communists and Bundists too — especially left-wing Zionists of the

Dror, Hashomer Hatzair, Gordonia and other movements, is presented, again, without idealization. This devotion to a Zionist and collectivist ideal made for cohesion and for a pre-disposition to non-acceptance of a passive role; also, for a clear decision to identify with the Jewish people — hence the decision to fight in the ghetto. No bones were made about their identification with Jewish Palestine and with socialism. It was an important element in making for mistrust of Jewish communal authority, and hence for a rebellion of the young — they were all between sixteen and twenty-five years old.

We had to wait a long time before Chaika Grossman's story was published. Better late than never. It deserves to be read, studied and remembered.

Yehuda Bauer

Preface to the English Edition

In 1946 I made my first visit to the United States as a member of a group representing Polish Jewry, ninety percent of whom were destroyed by the Nazis. That was a year after the war had ended. During a meeting with a large Jewish community in the United States there grew deep within me the feeling that the people there did not fully understand what really happened in the Holocaust.

I was, at the time, a young woman, but old beyond my years with the weight of my experiences — both emotional and physical. It may be possible to forget the details of events, but it is virtually impossible to free one's self from feelings which have permeated the very depths of one's soul. There still echo in my ears the exaggerated statements made in our honor and in our presence. Everything said at that meeting induced in me feelings of sadness and depression. A tear, or two, would have given me more satisfaction than any of those words of praise which were bestowed on my compatriots generally, and on me in particular, as the youngest of the group and the only woman in it. When I saw the rich foods piled high on the dishes and trays but before us, I wanted to return to "my" Jews as quickly as possible, to the starving Jews of Warsaw, to those exhausted ones without roofs over their heads, to those who wandered from border to border desperately seeking emigration to the land of Israel.

When the first edition of my book, *People of the Underground*, appeared in 1949, I urgently wanted to publish an English language version for the United States. True, the story of Auschwitz is not told in the book. But, I wasn't in Auschwitz until after the liberation of that death-camp. And, this might be called a different kind of Auschwitz story. In other words: It is about the life and death struggle to circumvent the fate of those who could not avoid Auschwitz.

Almost forty years have gone by and this book has never had an English-language readership.

I have studied the literature on the subject that has appeared in the United States, and I have come to a sad conclusion: Holocaust researchers in the

United States seldom rely on original sources, especially those which are available in Hebrew only. This is occasioned by the fact that many of the historians and scholars of this fascinating and tragic subject have no knowledge of Hebrew. They rarely refer to the written Hebrew sources because they are unaware of their existence and much important material remains untranslated. It becomes a closed circle.

In Israel, too, a shortcoming exists among the historians: There is prevalent a certain disdain and avoidance of authentic witnesses and participants, and the reliance on the written word only. However, we cannot ignore the fact that writings during the Holocaust were not only lacking in detail but were, understandably, rare. In addition, the "documents", or what we refer to as documents, were written by humans. The unfortunate thing that happens is that certain documentary sources are used while others are discarded, selectively and uncritically. From this point of view, it might be preferable to give greater credence to personal testimony. This does have the disadvantage of limited scope, but it is reliable and it can be an important contribution to the overall picture.

I have therefore always dreamed of this translation and those of other worthwhile books. I hope that the publication of this English-language edition will signal the beginning of translations of other historical sources from Hebrew into English.

This book is appearing in English more than forty years after the defeat of Nazi Germany. During this period many additional sources have come to light — mainly German — and numerous valuable archives have since become available to researchers.

What seems most important to me is the information regarding the decisions reached about "the final solution to the Jewish problem," that is to say, the series of decisions and their implementation for the destruction of the Jews in all the conquered countries. This horrible phenomenon has been revealed in its entirety despite all the efforts of the Nazis to leave no documentation or trace of their perfidy.

The determination of the Nazis to totally and unconditionally destroy the Jews, even to their own disadvantage on their battlefronts and without considering the efficacy of their plan, has been proven. No logistic considerations halted the death-trains destined for the gas chambers in Auschwitz; no suffering of their soldiers at the front waiting for supplies; no interference from the various branches of the Wehrmacht prevented the transfer of the 70,000 Jews remaining in Lodz for their destruction on the very eve of the German retreat from that city. Nor were there any intercessions to prevent the destruction of the Hungarian Jews, when the Red Army was massed at the gates of Budapest. Today we know for certain that the fate of Bialystok's Jews was already sealed in the fall of 1942 when the destiny of 250,000 Jews of "Greater Bialystok" was determined. The destruction of the Bialystok ghetto was delayed for almost a year — a fact which did nothing to prevent their final sacrifice in August of 1943.

These facts are indisputable today, and all the German documents that have been discovered since testify to their validity.

Despite all of this, there surface from time to time renewed arguments about the attempts of certain of the Judenrats to save Jewish lives, more or less on the basis of serving the Germans with productive labor and in obedience to the commands of the Nazis. Now and then, there arises some doubt as to the wisdom and efficacy of the "ghetto uprisings".

It must be admitted that hardly anyone paid any serious attention to Hitler's "Mein Kampf" when it was first published. Even those who saw the handwriting on the wall took into account the fact that ideology and its realization are often at great variance, especially when the written theory seems to be insane and totally unrealistic. But we aren't talking about 1924 when "Mein Kampf" was written, or about 1933-34, or about the Nuremburg laws, or "Krystalnacht".

We are concerned with the years of the Holocaust and the more than forty years since. I must point out that to this very day there are many decent and respectable people who cannot conceive of the stark reality and enormity of the "final solution". Perhaps this is because of an inability to understand or for some other reason, despite the irrefutable facts and the testimony and historical documents available. The wonder is that there are historians who, even at this time, fail to grasp this reality, when just within one year of the occupation Jewish youth in the pioneering youth movements, especially Hashomer Hatzair (in the second half of 1941) understood the full meaning of the mass-murders in Ponar, near Vilna. Agreeing with the conclusion reached by these young people were Communists, some Bundists and a number of the Betar youth, among whom (except in Vilna) I was unable to find allies for the policy of armed defense of the ghetto.

I grow weary of trying to prove that the Jews of the ghetto had no choice between a humiliating survivial or an honorable death. The ghetto revolt offered a choice of death in Auschwitz or death in battle behind the ghetto walls.

This book was written one half-year after my arrival in Israel in 1948. Then, I was not obliged to argue with anyone and I did not have to prove anything. On that basis, this testimony is more credible than if I were to write it today. The memory of events at that time were fresh and accurate.

I must admit, that on this subject it is difficult to be wise after the fact. Yet, we must ask the question: From whence did the initiators of the revolt draw their self-confidence, realizing that already in 1941 the Nazis had all the necessary time to exterminate the Jews?

To deal with that question, we must accept the fact that even today there are those who possess all the documentation but who doubt that, under those circumstances, armed uprising in the ghetto may have been the only answer to "the final solution". Despite their knowledge they believe that armed revolt may have been the answer for only a few.

We must acknowledge that for the Nazis, the extermination of the Jews was their highest priority and "a sacred goal". Because of their rabid racism they pronounced that there could be no solution but the victory of the Nazis and the Aryan race and, of course, the total annihilation of the Jews. There were myriad reasons for this, which many Jews could not understand or were unable to come to terms with, especially at that time and under those circumstances. But to continue doubting, to this day, the missed opportunities for rescue and resistance seems to me to be espousing a false philosophy whose principles aren't always guided by the purest of motivations.

To the extent that this book bears a message for humankind in general, and for Jews in particular, it is written in the hope that these words will find an honored place among the testimonies of their times.

Finally, I should like to thank all those who contributed to this English language publication; my gratitude also to my comrade and friend, Shaika Weinberg of Tel Aviv, Sam Bloch of New York, Shmuel Beeri of Kibbutz Hatzor, Moshe Kagan of New York and Lennie Fritsch of Kibbutz Maabarot. Also, my deep appreciation to the publishers and editors.

Chaika Grossman

Childhood Ideas

"We are headed for war. It is hard to know what tomorrow will bring, but we know how we want to live, regardless of circumstances. Everybody is hiding in the cellars, afraid of what is coming, but we won't be frightened. We shall carry on despite the war."

These words were spoken at the last meeting of the "Tel-Amal" group, 15 and 16 year-olds who could not grasp the dangers of war.

Planes dropped their bombs. After the meeting we parted and went home. Passersby hurrying to take cover looked at us curiously: madmen walking quietly and happily in the streets!

I went to Rachel's house. We were the group leaders. There was no one in her apartment, on the fifth floor. Fear of the bombing had driven all of them down to the lower floors. We were 18-19 years old, and found it hard to imagine that the world was heading for catastrophe. We talked about the members of our group, many of whom were daring and intelligent students in the Polish gymnasium who had long since been absorbed in our society and were something of a social and intellectual nucleus.

That day I suffered the pangs of responsibility and individual decision-making for the first time. The *Hanhaga Rashit/ "B"* * whose first — and last — session had been held in Warsaw on August 20, 1939, days before the outbreak of war, had assigned me to prepare the groups in the Bialystok region for underground activity. I returned from Warsaw ten days later, with difficulty. I was the only girl among the few civilians in the train which was filled with conscripts, most of them peasants. A week later I had not yet succeeded in visiting the region. Once or twice I had packed my knapsack and gone to look for a bus, but there were no buses, and the trains had been taken over by the army to carry the conscripts: I had not fulfilled my first mission as a member of the emergency Hanhaga Rashit and my failure bothered me. Rachel cheered me up a little.

I realized that I had no one to turn to for help. There were no instructions,

* Underground leadership, formed from those exempt from conscription, especially girls.

there were no connections. For the first time I felt that I had no one to give me orders except my own conscience. My nineteenth year was coming to its close; behind me there was education in the movement. The leaders had each gone their own way — some to pioneering fulfillment and some to other lives. Before me there were only my conscience and my own strength.

On September 8, the terrible news reached the dead city and its empty streets: the Germans were nearby!

Doors and shutters were closed, gates were barred and the remaining passersby fled for their lives into the first houses they could find. The tenants all ran to rooms whose windows faced the back yard of the Great Synagogue. After the first rumble of cars there were shots, then silence, and sighs. Father ran to the entrance and looked out through a crack. For the first time I saw someone dying. A Jewish youth who had not managed to get inside had been shot. We bandaged his wounds and called the Red Cross and the city hospital. The answer from everywhere was the same: impossible to go out. Meanwhile, the young man was fighting for his life. We watched silently, unable to help him. Only in the evening was he taken to the hospital, where he died. The next day we learned that there were many victims; many people had been shot in the streets for no reason.

Most of the Jewish houses were locked. No one went out lest they encounter German soldiers. All day long we heard their voices, the clatter of their hobnailed boots. In the evening — loud knocking and the rumble of cars stopping in front of Jewish shops. They were breaking down the locked doors and looting. No one dared go to his shop to try to protect his property. Men hid in order not to be conscripted for all kinds of strange jobs, like washing the sidewalks, or carrying dirt from one place to another. Only women went into the city. They arose at four in the morning to line up at the bakery, but the bread went to the baker's family and friends.

The city seemed to hold its breath. True, there were stories of gentile girls who sold cigarettes, matches and other things to the Germans. There were also Jews who remembered "those Germans" of World War I, who had been received with bread and salt because they had saved the Jewish population from the oppression of the Tzarist army and the attacks of the local people. But these were different Germans, and the semi-modern city, half proletarian and half provincial, sat in fear and waited for a miracle. The thefts and robberies continued, but how strange — the Germans were not carrying out these acts in broad daylight like people who had the power and the law in their hands, but like thieves in the night, robbing the inhabitants of their possessions, looting goods and food.

I went out to the street with Rachel. The city was full of Germans and we walked almost alone. It was hard to bear their insolent looks and haughty manner. Where were the textile workers, the members of the PPS and the Communist underground? But workers were not armed in this country of arrogant officers, of false chivalry, of a police regime that was corrupt, anti-Semitic, anti-worker and hostile. If they had been given arms perhaps the Germans would not have chanted their jingle: "Es klingt wie eine Sage — Polen in achtzen Tage!"*

On the third day after the German occupation of the city, the radio announced that the Red Army had been ordered to cross the Soviet Union's western border and move westward. Jews stayed close to the radio. Every few hours the name of another city taken by the Red Army was announced.

Neighbors would come in the evening and crowd around the radio. One took out a map, another marked the supposed boundary line, and they decided unanimously that the Soviets would not give up an industrial town like ours, and there was no doubt they would arrive soon. Jews forgot their class differences. Storekeepers and craftsmen, workers and employers, all were united in their desire to get rid of the Germans. And it was clear to all that only the Red Army could save the Jews from the horrible fate they would suffer at the hands of the Germans. All the hopes we had in the Polish army disappeared swiftly, despite its heroic stand near Kutno, Hell, Warsaw and other places. The Jews of Bialystok like all the Jews of occupied Poland in 1939, had one fervent wish — for the Red Army to come and save them.

On the eighth day of the German occupation the first Red Army tanks began to appear on the eastern road from Volkovysk. The Germans were still in the western part of the city, along the Warsaw road, and the main street, formerly Pilsudsky Avenue, when Jewish children erupted in a stone throwing outbreak at German cars. The Jewish children felt very strong when the masses were demonstrating in Kostinshko Square and cheering their liberators.

The city was festive. The fears of the past two weeks disappeared completely. In the middle of the street, groups gathered around officers or soldiers.

"Will you stay here?" "Will you go on?" "Why can't you save all the Jews from the Germans?" "Are you hungry?" "Are there Jewish officers?" "Do you have enough food?" "When will there be war between you and the Germans?" The questions were endless. And the answers were both innocent and cunning at the same time, replete with the legendary good nature and

* "It sounds like a legend - Poland in 18 days!"

patience attributed to the Russians. They answer every one, encourage the Jews: "All are equal with use." "At home everything can be found in plenty," they say. But if you look more closely you can sense a touch of stubborn suspicion. They won't say where they are going; won't talk about the Germans, and in the end, they say "Of course, of course, not everything is so plentiful at home . . . we have also suffered, and because of that we will also triumph."

The answers implied more than they said. Jews understood the implications and remembered family and friends left on the other side, of the Bug River*.

On the morrow, a meeting of the Tel-Amal group under new circumstances. I remember every one of them, and how their minds tried to absorb and understand what was taking place around them.

There was Avraham, tall, blonde and blue-eyed — examining and probing; there was Yentele, black-haired, pretty, an expert organizer, clear-thinking and enlightened, the most talented of the girls; Israelke, the smallest and most mischievous of them all, clever and mocking, who grew up overnight and suddenly became serious and reserved. And plump Roshka, cunning, conscientious, courageous, and Sender and Chava. Dozens of children who matured on the threshold of death, who wanted to revolt against the philistinism of their parents and elders; who loved the Jewish street in which they grew up.

That meeting was a difficult one. They had learned to revere the October Revolution, had celebrated its anniversary and sung songs of the revolution. Now, suddenly, they had been asked a very real question: How to continue loving the revolution when the movement was banned by law? How to bridge the chasm that had opened? Innocently and with faith we repeated the old doctrines — that truth would ultimately triumph in a regime of social and national justice, that the day would come when this conflict would be no more.

Since they believed this with all their hearts, they decided to hold firm, not to disperse but to continue the life of Shomrim** together - underground.

Tens of thousands of refugees from western Poland, fleeing the German hell, bombed, hungry and weary, reduced to pauperism, were pouring into the city. Winter would soon arrive, and there were still many people who had no roof over their heads.

Many members of the movement were part of this refugee stream — com-

* The river that served as the boundary between the two parts of divided Poland as stipulated in the Molotov-Ribbentrop agreement.

** Members of Hashomer Hatzair organization.

plete pioneer training groups, active members seeking a movement focus, and routes to Palestine. Most of them arrived empty-handed, tired and weary, bringing with them their stories; of towns put to the torch, of people mowed down by rifles and machine guns, of refugees crowding the bombed roads, without shelter or help, relentlessly pursued by the mechanized German battalions. There were the stories of what had been done to the Jews in the Galician towns, of burning and killing, of women and children who were tortured. Comrades wandered from city to city, looking for friends they had lost on the road, looking for the movement and its institutions.

The movement was wandering too, seeking some way to re-organize and renew its activities, some way to make aliya.*

At Autumn's end the rumor spread that Vilna had been turned over to the Lithuanians. If this was true it would open some small window to the world and the road to Palestine could be found in Lithuania. Many tried to get to Rumania and were captured by the border guards; only a few succeeded in getting through. The road to Vilna, on the other hand, was an easier and more open route. Masses were streaming into Vilna and many comrades were crossing the border back and forth, bringing news, organizing groups, and preparing for the emigration.

The generally accepted solution to the collective problem of the Jews was through aliya, though there were those who imagined they could find personal solution in the Soviet regime.

The pioneering movement streamed to the aliya roads. Certain comrades were assigned to remain behind to keep the nationalistic flame alive, to transform the idea of a national solution from a vague ideal into an organized Jewish will.

I was 19 years old when I left the city of my birth with eight other haverim and boarded the train going north — to Lyda.

I still remember Tosya, back home. It was winter, the end of 1939. Tosya had returned from Vilna to occupied German Warsaw. She had come back to the hunger and cold to gather the youth of the movement. She crossed two borders at night in freezing temperatures, cold and exhausted. She toured the Soviet area, saw Jews walking erect, living and working without fear, feeling secure. She was a guest for two days in my father's house and then left in the dark and cold, with our blessings. After her went Mordechai (Anielevich), and after him Yosef (Kaplan) and then Shmuel Breslau.

We took risks, endangered our lives because we loved a different and better kind of life.

---

* Aliya: immigration to Palestine.

A New Name

It was the height of summer. The sun-drenched city, with its churches and famous cathedral, sparkled. The river flowed slowly. The Zareche forest was crowded with hikers.

A hot Sunday. A ripe summer's end. The typhus epidemic, that had raged for two weeks, subsided. Only yesterday the Soviet authorities had completed sending the last of the "unreliables" into the depths of Russia.*

"The rich man is lucky." The door of my room opened and the landlord, the famous Yiddish scientist Turbowich, stood angrily at the threshold. At first, I couldn't comprehend what he was saying but it soon became clear that the Germans had opened an offensive all along the Soviet borders. The War had entered a new phase. "And why was the rich man lucky?" I asked innocently. "Because the rich men have been exiled to Siberia and the Germans won't get there; not even with planes," my landlord explained.

I dressed quickly and went to look for the other members of the Hanhaga Rashit. We were six; an underground leadership. Pinhas** and Mordechai were living together on the next street. Edek was living with some members of his Kibbutz; Abba — with his family at the other end of the city, and Moshe Balosh lived in our neighborhood. Our main task, after the departure of the previous leadership for Palestine, was to settle the affairs involved in that emigration. There were no new prospects for further aliya. We maintained contact with part of the leadership in Lvov and Warsaw, but links to Warsaw had become much more tenuous lately.

We were liquidating the old and beginning new movement activity. We understood that the accord between the USSR and Germany had only been temporary, a prelude to war. Most of the "experts" forecast that the war would erupt in the fall after the grain harvest.

The war came as a surprise. A flight of aircraft was seen in the skies, flew overhead and disappeared. Nothing happened. We met in a restaurant with

* Many members of the bourgeois and petit-bourgeois classes, officials and Polish officers were exiled.

** Pinhas Stern, Mordechai Rosman, Edek Boraks, Abba Kovner.

Pinhas and Mordechai. It was difficult for us to decide what to do. We speculated on whether or not our members should join the army, and finally decided to wait and see what would happen.

We bought what food could be bought in some shops, especially jars of preserved tomatoes, and went home.

Toward evening we heard a tremendous explosion. Rivka and I stood at the window and watched the aerial combat. As the bombing intensified, we went to the basement. All our neighbors were already there. Strashun was amusing people with his popular jokes, in his Vilna Yiddish. An aged father was brought in on a stretcher, his eyes closed. We spent that night in the basement. Fires were burning all over the city and the flames lit up the darkness. Between bombings people went up to their flats to secure clothing and food.

On the next day we heard the sad news that the Germans had taken Kovno and were approaching Vilna. I ran to Pilsudsky street to consult with the comrades, and met them on their way toward me. Masses of people were running towards the railway station. Loaded down with sacks and suitcases, they were moving westward. According to rumor the last train was to leave in two hours.

"I am not going. You men go eastward. Not all the Jews are leaving the city; most are staying. I am a girl, and I look aryan. It will be easier for me."

Mordechai supported me: "We must divide our forces. Abba, Chaika, and perhaps also Moshe Balosh will remain. If you stay it will be easier for me to make my decision: I am going."

The debate was over. Pinhas was tense, and as a person of conscience was certainly asking himself: Is this an order? Is this why we gave up aliya, gave up our certificates? What does our organizational conscience say? Our organizational conscience tells us to accompany the Jewish masses in their troubles and to guide them.

At the time of parting you acted bravely, didn't you? What has happened to you now? What use is there in tears, foolish girl? With strangers you act like a stable, indomitable person who knows where she is going. Are the four walls so frightening? Is it so hard to be alone? The war has taken them all away . . . Comrades have gone to Palestine and now they are building "your homeland . . ." They are building a nest for themselves and the children yet to be born. And you are alone in a brutal world. Two days ago, on the last day of peace you received a letter from a comrade in Palestine. He misses you, is still waiting for you to come . . . Shalom, shalom to you! From this day on I am in the underground, underground to everything, to the German beast of prey, the far-away homeland. List me as dead . . . Tomorrow once again the hobnailed boots of the blonde soldiers will trample your Jewishness, your freedom, your youthful dream to go to Palestine . . .

But . . . perhaps we shall still meet . . . Perhaps it is better thus . . . Perhaps the iron will be better forged this way? It is good that you are there, good that you all are there. You, in my place, would act like me, wouldn't you?

During the first days of the occupation there was nothing to eat. I tried to stand in the queue at the bakery, at the grocery store. Someone shouted: "Aryans first; Jews last!" I left the queue. The gentiles looked at me in wonder. Why are they so surprised? Don't they understand that for a few groats it is not worthwhile to hide my Jewishness? Rivka and I were saved by the tomatoes. We sliced the ends of the bread (which are usually thrown away or given to some beggar), into tiny pieces, so they would last a little longer. Yesterday Rivka went to the factory in which she had worked for about half a year, and was told not to come back; Jews would no longer be employed. Some Polish working women, her former mates in the factory, offered her a little food. They had a small reserve. Rivka was an excellent housewife: She — and the tomatoes — saved us from real starvation.

I visited Moshe Balosh every day. He still had a radio, and there we could hear the news. Edek had come back, and Roshka was here, too, and Vitka. I am no longer alone.

Jews are permitted to be on the street only until six in the evening; they may shop in the market only from noon until one p.m. They had to walk on the sidewalk on the right side of the street, in single file, and only on certain streets. They had to avoid the main streets. On their left sleeve they had to wear a white band with a yellow Star-of-David. Until six I wore the band; after six I was an aryan. The doorkeeper watched me every day from the doorstep, angry and surprised: "A Jewess daring to leave her home after six!" From then on I attempted to avoid such meetings and sneaked into the house without being seen. Gentile boys in the street laughed at me: "Look, one of ours, a Christian, and she wears a band — crazy!" Rivka and I agreed that I would leave the house as a Jewess so that the doorkeeper wouldn't complain about me, and only on the next street would I take off my jacket and carry it on my arm, ostensibly because of the heat. It was difficult for a Jewess to move about in the streets, but with comrades scattered about the city it was necessary. We had to remain in touch.

Every day brought some new trouble . . . First came the mass kidnapping of men. Day and night Jewish men were led off to "work", and never returned. Some Jews worked in the army bases around the city. They had certificates requesting that the authorities not take the Jewish bearer to any other work. In less than a week we had stopped being people and had become "merchandise", available to every German. Some honored the certificates issued by the commander of an army unit; others snatched the "merchandise" despite its owners. Many of the kidnappers were Lithuanians. The Lithuanian girls with whom I had studied in the Vilna University (as a cover for my underground activity during the Soviet occupation), my acquaintances of yesterday, decorated their coats with the Lithuanian national colors. Student comradeship no longer existed. When had the Lithuanians managed to enlist in the German police? Travellers reported meeting Jews on the Minsk road burying war casualties. One day a peasant of the Ponar area, a railway station seven kilometers from Vilna, said that there were sounds of shooting and inhuman cries near his village: they were killing Jews there. But no one believed these stories. "Was it possible?" Killing people just like that?"

Edek roamed the streets gathering information. "They won't catch me" he would promise us. "I will always get away." Edek had become our source of cheer. He was always scheming, always planning. "There is nothing that does not have a solution," was the way he accepted the decrees.

Yandzia* lived in the center of the city, with his parents; in an artists' and sculptors' house. I don't recall whose idea it was, but it was Yandzia who carried it out: the forging of work certificates. Without serving the Germans we would be able to walk the streets, and most important of all — we would not be locked up in the cellars and attics. Mordcchai Tenenbaum brought a sample. He was a member of the Hechalutz** Central Committee before the war, and one of those who had remained behind. I don't know where he obtained the certificate. He did not, God forbid, work for the "unit". He always found an opportunity to take something, and then to return it without being seen. The laboratory began to work. We equipped most of the comrades with these certificates, but they did not always help. The certificate alone was not sufficient; its owner had to be swift and cunning in order to stand the test.

As usual I went to Moshe, to hear the news. I was feeling encouraged. Contact among comrades was intact, and we were no longer mere playthings in the hands of the occupiers.

The door was smashed in. The house was topsy-turvey; beds unmade; on the table, a half-eaten meal. It was all too clear: the men had been snatched, and the women had left the ruined house. The first victim was dear Moshe,

---

* Yandzia Lebieds, a native of Vilna, a veteran member of the movement, active in the cultural area.

** Pioneer.

the old comrade, wise, quiet and deliberate. I had to find the tenants and ask for details. Perhaps the women needed help and encouragement.

"I've brought you something," Yadwiga said, opening her bag and putting an identification card form on the table. She was still breathing hard from running up the stairs into my room. As usual, she spoke, quickly and tersely, in the underground style. She was short and stout, with a round face and snub nose. She was always occupied, brimming over with initiative and energy. She visited me often with her big bag in hand. I still remember Yadwiga Dudzetz, the "shikse", Yadwiga of the Z.H.P. command and the Polish scout movement, from the Shomer camps in the Carpathians. She had been a friend of Irena's and always friendly to the movement. A Pole, she believed in God and social justice, in Holy Mary and collective education, and above all — in human beings. It was apparently humanism that brought her to me in those difficult days. In front of the neighbors and the doorkeeper she would come to my house with news of our comrades she had visited and secret information of the invader's plans.

She put the identification card — of a refugee without citizenship — on the table, together with a Catholic birth certificate from the Warsaw Church of Saint Andziei. I refused to accept them. "I don't want to hide my Jewishness; I don't want to enjoy a fate different from that of the rest of the Jews", I argued.

"You can't move aound as an aryan without having the proper papers. It is an unnecessary risk. You must take them. I've heard that they are going to limit our movements on the streets even more. Who is going to maintain contact with the comrades? Who is going to help them?" She said she wouldn't budge from her place until I hid the certificate and gave her a photograph to paste on the identification card.

"How can I change my Jewish name? Would you hide your lineage?"

"If my movement demanded it, I would do it. In any case, talk about it with your comrades. I'll come back tomorrow to bring further instructions about the registration, and to stamp the picture."

She turned toward the door. Before going out she said: "I want to say something about the Star of David you are all carrying. They . . . I want to tell you . . . that I and all my comrades think that you should not be ashamed of your symbol. On the contrary, the Jews should wear it proudly." She left.

Edek agreed with Yadwiga. "We mustn't complicate obvious matters." We decided, however, to consult with Abba. Such things shouldn't be done without a leadership decision.

I found Abba locked-up at home, his ears glued to the radio. Since Moshe had been taken from us, all our sources of information had closed, and in our ceaseless running about the city — spurred by Jewish suffering — our contact with the outside world and the front had weakened. Abba had great sensitivity to what was happening. Every city, every piece of ground that fell to the invader seemed to cut into his very flesh. Abba agreed with Edek. What is more, he drew practical conclusions from Yadwiga's plan. "You must change your address immediately. You must register in some new place in another part of the city."

I left Abba depressed. The news was terrible. The front was rolling eastward. We could not assume that there would be any improvement soon. We had to make long-range plans.

We decided to meet with Mordechai. The first problem was that before we could start any action all our people would be taken in the endless kidnappings. Therefore — first and foremost we had to safeguard our people. Mordechai and I were given the task of determining what could be expected from the temporary Jewish community — the first "Judenrat". For security reasons we decided to visit the chairman, Mr. Werblinsky, at his home. We presented ourselves as representatives of the chalutzim in Vilna, who had come to determine the possibility of finding work for our "Hechalutz" members in the vicinity of the city so that they would not be kidnapped. Mr. Werblinsky, who was a veteran Zionist, received us warmly. There was a worried look in his wrinkled, tired face. He held out his hands and in a choking voice he explained:

"Such children! You think you are in Warsaw, but you are mistaken. The process of annihilation has already begun. No Jew from outside the city is taken to work. They want to destroy us all, all the Jews of eastern Poland. Remember that it is I who told you this. Let us hope you will be saved."

"But still don't you sometimes send Jews to work in the city, by German request?" Mordechai asked.

"True, sometimes the Germans ask the community for Jewish workers for their units. But I always send them sadly, fearful that they won't come back! I am not afraid for myself," he continued. "Tell everybody you meet, in my name, tell every Jew you meet, and especially your comrades: all those kidnapped are executed."

Here the conversation ended. We believed him. We had believed this even before. Would the other Jews believe? Some days after our conversation, Werblinsky was shot by the Germans.

According to Yadwiga's instructions I was to write an address on the blank side of the card in the same part of the city as Commissariat No. 111. It occurred to me to look for a bombed-out house in that area, one whose registration books had certainly been destroyed. In any case it would be harder to check whether I lived there or not. I found such a demolished house at No. 7 Kozla Street. Mordechai baptized me Halina Voronowich, daughter of Miechislav and Yosefa. From then on I was Chaika at home, and Halina on the outside.

The kidnappings increased, and harsher decrees followed. To my great surprise, Yadwiga offered to shelter a number of my men in the Vilna Colony, seven kilometers from the city, in the convent, until things quieted down and we could evaluate the new conditions. We had to do a lot of convincing and a lot of explaining that it was only for the good of the movement and not for his own personal benefit that he had to do this before he accepted our decision. Aryeh Wilner went with Abba, and in the course of time a group of 15 people was established in the convent. From then on the convent played an important role in our lives.

It was on that hill, surrounded by a high stone wall, cut off from the outside world within thick, cold walls repressing all human desire and the will to live, with the sounds of bells calling all to prayer and teaching the only right in life — to accept one's fate with love — that a plan of armed struggle and bloody revenge against the conquerer was developed.

Meanwhile the fear and depression of the Jews in the city increased. Armed Lithuanians, accompanied by Germans, broke into Nowogrodska Street and ran amok among the Jews. There was no one to help them. Jewish lives were free for the taking. They longed for only one thing: to flee the Gentile world, to lock themselves up among their own so that the murderers could not come within their four walls. There were rumors that they were shortly going to enclose the Jews in a ghetto. Some feared it, and some saw it as a door to salvation.

Summer was at its height. The green city suburbs were quiet. There was no sign or memory there of the war. I looked for an "aryan apartment". I found a room on Shenna street, owned by two old maids. They were prepared to rent, but demanded a permit from the housing department. By German order it was forbidden to rent to Poles even a corner in which to lie down, without a special permit. The Lithuanian official in the housing department informed me that he was not allowed to issue permits.

"But understand: my house was destroyed in the bombing. For weeks I have been sleeping in a different place every night." I handed him my papers. "Please look and see if a house was bombed at 7 Kozla Street, or not." He looked at the papers, and examined the address. My eyes followed his look. He turned toward me, and smiled cunningly. I thought that soon he would say that the papers were forged. But he folded them, gave them back to me calmly, and at the end he almost shouted in his rough voice, and in clumsy Polish: "Find yourself some hole; I'll give you a permit." I quietly gave him the address. I thought he would explode in anger; he had apparently thought that I wouldn't easily find a room, and he would be rid of me.

I received the permit that very same day, and became a proper aryan. Secure in the belief that no one knew me in the new neighborhood, and surprised at my easy success, I fixed the date for moving.

In those days the Germans carried out their first *aktzia**. For some time there had been no pogroms or kidnappings. Now the Germans bared their claws. This is what happened: On Lidska Street they allegedly found a murdered German. That street and those close to it were populated by Jews. The supposed logic of these facts was that the murder had been committed by Jews. Therefore, all the Jews of that street and the neighboring ones were driven out and herded into the Lukishki prison.

In order not to attract too much attention in the street and among the neighbors, I hired a porter to take my bundles to my new address. I walked some distance away from him. I had added to the number of bundles so that his handwagon would be full, and thus make an impression on my new landladies. The move succeeded. I went to the home of Roshka and Vitka. Their small room in a slum house on Stepfanska Street, in the Jewish section, was my merciful refuge in those days. All members of the Shomer family who were hungry went to this place; there, food was shared; the last slice of bread, the last plate of warmed-over groat soup — was the property of all, of all who came to find some small comfort.

On that day Jewish Stepfanska Street was empty and quiet, while in my comrades' home there was a great todo. Neighbors were running about and crowding into Roshka's and Vitka's room. I learned that the Jews had already been driven out of many streets. It was rumored that they were being taken to the ghetto. It became evident that the provocation on Lidska street had been only one of the incidents of a wider and more insidious program. The streets intended for the ghetto were being emptied of their Jewish inhabitants in order to make room for the rest of the Jews.

Two days earlier Strashun Street had been cleared of its residents, who were taken to Ponar. Jews of every street were ordered to take whatever they could carry and move out. It was done with surprising speed, and with many blows to accelerate the process.

Whole sections had been evacuated in this way, with people leaving empty-handed. Those whose turn had not yet come had better luck: they had time to pack the things they needed most.

---

* Raid on Jewish area.

In times of chaos people lose their wits; adults act like children. They came to the young people, our comrades, to ask what to take, and how to hide valuables from the police. Our comrades' room became the center of a closed court, as if in their helplessness, Jews found some support there, a ray of light. I sat quietly watching all the activity like someone from an alien world. They were going to the ghetto, to overcrowding and hunger, and I had settled among the Poles. I would not see their troubles. I would not live their lives.

How much I wanted at that moment to become part of that crowd, to stay close to these comrades and to let what happened to them, happen to me. But that was not a sensible solution. We did not have the choice of fleeing with the crowd.

In the ghetto, too, our comrades did not adopt the path of "let me die with the masses" but "let me live with our people." Being absorbed seemed an easier road, one free of responsibility, but was it not actually more difficult? After all, who said that easy lives awaited us, Jews and members of the movement?

For a long time I roamed the half-empty area. Here and there, at the ends of the street, groups of Jews were moving with their belongings on their backs, some of them pushing baby carriages. They moved slowly, dragging their feet, in a long line. Old people and children, tired and worn-out, with the Germans and Lithuanians spurring them on, shouting and threatening them with sticks and fists.

I arrived at my new home at sunset. The house stood on the high bank of the Vilia River, rocky but green. The lapping of water broke the suburban silence. Little children played in the middle of the street.

The sun set red and flaming. Twilight silence reigned in the house. The heavy old furniture cast a depressing darkness, its genteel splendor long since faded, with only torn and dusty velvet left.

The next morning I went to look for traces of the people I knew. The sad parades continued all day, although not in the direction of where the ghetto was supposed to be (as far as I knew, it was in the center of the city the ghetto of medieval times); it was moving along Mitzkevich Street, and coming closer to me. Along the walls of the Lukishki prison a barrier consisting of soldiers was stationed. Here, aryan passersby were stopped and directed to the nearby streets. I understood that not all the Jews were being sent into the ghetto. It was too small to hold them all. Whole streets, whole neighborhoods of Jewish inhabitants, were not "privileged" to see the ghetto: they were executed immediately.

There was no longer anyone in the house on Stepfanska street. The few

Polish neighbors in the area said that the Jews had already been evacuated the day before. They thought they had been taken to the ghetto. Mordechai, too, was no longer in his room in nearby Kiovska street.

Behind the gate to the right, at Kiovska 6, was a cellar, with two entrances; one from the street and the other from the courtyard. A Polish laundress about 40-50 years old lived in that cellar. All her life she had lived in this Jewish courtyard; all her life she had laundered linen. Sometimes, when the doorkeeper locked up early and it was urgent for me to see Mordechai, I would come through her cellar home. No matter how many times I woke her from her rest she never complained, and with the noble cordiality of a simple laboring woman she would accompany me with a kerosene lamp through the narrow corridor leading to the courtyard. When she saw me walking around the courtyard looking for Mordechai, she winked. I came into her home and she whispered in my ear: "Pani, everything is all right, Mordechai's wife was here. He and his comrades are already there. She went with them to the ghetto gates." Then she lowered her voice: "She is here; she will come tonight, to sleep here with me." This was my first knowledge, my first contact, with those who were already imprisoned "there".

I continued to roam the city without knowing where to turn. The time went slowly. Many hours would pass before Tema* came to the laundress. Where was she was wandering in the city streets, without papers? She was a nurse in the city hospital and many people knew her. There was nothing to do, and I had to pass the remaining hours. In the Ostrobramska market I bought half a kilo of tomatoes to appease my hunger. The streets were strewn with the remnants of discarded parcels: it was easy to trace the path along which the Jews were driven into slavery in the ghetto, to death in Ponar.

Evening came. Tema was already waiting for me in the laundress' flat. Her comrades had decided that she, too, would remain on the aryan side. I was extremely happy: I would no longer be so alone. Tema was a pretty girl, not a typical "shiksa" but also not typically Jewish. Her head was crowned with dark golden tresses, her eyes clear blue; she spoke eloquent Polish. However, my pleasure involved a great deal of concern. She still had to go through all the tiring stages before she "legally" won her new name.

After I convinced Yadwiga that she was one of "us", a member of Hechalutz, and that she looked aryan, Yadwiga supplied us with a blank form with the registration stamp. Only an aryan birth certificate was miss-

---

* Tema Schneiderman — Mordechai's girl friend.

ing, and this time she could not provide one. From that day on we were always together. We both registered in Shenna, at the old-maid landladies. Sometimes we would sleep in my room. Both of us were looking for a way into the ghetto. Almost despairingly, we roamed the streets, without success.

One morning we were awakened by a knocking at the window. I peered out, with a rapidly beating heart, frightened. It was Moshe Kopito. He resembled an aryan; blond, tall, open-faced and energetic. He brought the first news of the situation into the ghetto. He spoke tersely and fast, not wanting to endanger us. He had left the ghetto that morning with the first work brigade and in the middle of the street had slipped away. He had gone to look for milk for their baby — his and Sarenka's. According to him, Edek had gone out to work in order to contact us. He told us the place in the suburbs where Edek would wait for me during the afternoon break, between 12 and 1. Skillful Edek! We were overcome with joy. Contact would be renewed. A first, necessary step had been made. Otherwise we would have had to wait, doing nothing, among the old maids.

I went to the meeting alone, and I decided not to go empty-handed. In my bag I had fresh bread and tomatoes. I was "green" in ghetto affairs. My heart beat, as if I were 16 and going on my first date. I did not have to look very hard: Edek peeked out, saw me, and gestured for me to go straight ahead behind the green hill, where there were a few isolated trees. Without delay I climbed the hill. He came after me a few minutes later. We must conquer our emotions and get down to business. There is no time. Edek told me briefly what had happened. The moments passed; some Jews who worked there passed by, and so did some curious gentiles who lived in the neighborhood. They looked at us with surprise. "It is very overcrowded," Edek says. "Even now, many lie on their belongings under the open sky. People are so crowded that one couldn't put a pin between them. Filth and hunger are rampant. Many are alone, because their families did not get to the ghetto. Only a few of those taken to Lukishki return, and they tell stories of terrors we wouldn't have believed only a few days ago. People faint there from thirst and hunger; tens of thousands are crowded into the prison courtyard and the prison can't hold them any longer. Many die; people act like animals, they grab what they can from each other, and the stronger ones win. Everybody believes they are being led to their death."

We set another meeting for the next day at the same time. Until then I had to prepare food, especially bread. In the next few days I also had to establish contact with the convent. "Look within the city for new possibilities of establishing a network of contact outside the ghetto". Edek added: "We are locked up and it is doubtful whether we will be able to maintain any activity without securing some freedom of movement both in the city and outside of it. Don't be discouraged. Shalom."

The meeting ended. I slid down the hill to the other side, fixed my hair and clothes, and entered one of the suburban huts that resembled a farmer's house. I ordered a large quantity of bread for tomorrow at the same time. The woman immediately understood: "Trading with the Jews," and set a high price. In order to make a good impression I bargained vigorously.

In the afternoon Tema and I went to the nuns' restaurant, where meals were cheap and one could take food home. The customers were orthodox Catholics, pensioners, philanthropic ladies and all kinds of declassed persons who were trying to maintain their respectable status in society. Tema's alias was Wanda Mayevska. I told her that Mordechai was living in a room with our comrades Edek and Roshka, Vitka and Vitka's brother, and some others without family or home. Tema decided to go into the ghetto. She insisted, and I could not dissuade her. I had barely gotten used to this delicate girl. At first I believed that she was a spoiled child and would not be able to hold out. I don't know why I always thought her more fit for picking flowers than for the underground. After a few days I was ashamed of these ideas. I realized that she was stubborn, brave and firm in her views. The greater the difficulty, the greater her daring. Suddenly I saw in her innocent and gentle wide-open eyes a small flame that lit up. That was the center of gravity of her daring character. I discovered this on the day I reported what Edek had said about the ghetto. I suddenly saw that standing before me was an adult who knew how to love with all her heart, and who knew how to hate. She loved her movement, Hechalutz Hatzair,* with all her heart and all her might. She loved her people, and she had a special place in her heart for Mordechai, her guide, teacher and friend.

That same evening she went to the ghetto, and I went to look for Yadwiga. Yadwiga refused at first to bring me to the convent. "Wait a little, have patience! These are only the first days of the ghetto, and the whole population is tense over Jewish affairs." When I explained that the matter was urgent, that we might be too late, she promised to clarify the matter of contact with the convent, and give me an answer within two days. I urged her to ask her friends whether it was possible to fixup some people in the city, especially girls. Yadwiga was very interested in my situation. She wanted to know how my neighbors were behaving toward me. She wanted to visit me: "It is important that they see my face in your home."

---

* The young pioneers.

The days passed quickly. Moshe began to come and go in my home, and I presented him as my "Heniek". Sometimes he would bring information and instructions, and sometimes he would come just to visit with me. He would roam the courtyards looking for milk for his little daughter. I tried to warn him to be careful and suggested more than once that I or Tema supply what he needed. He did not agree. After all, he looked like a gentile, why should he not be our contact with the ghetto? Edek could not walk about as an aryan. Edek was responsible for the whole "business" and could not be responsible for one baby, Moshe would argue. One day he came to inform me that Edek had changed his place of work because in his former location they had begun to talk about him. "You see I am needed here. You would have walked into a trap if you had come to the old place." "If so, we must get you papers," I said. He did not take what I said seriously and left. I never saw him again. Moshe was a member of the Warsaw Hashomer *ken*,* belonged to Mordechai Anielevich's group and was one of his best friends.

Proud company! He was educated by the youth movement and the working class in Warsaw. When the civil war broke out in Spain, Moshe had gone there to help fight Franco. He had returned to Warsaw, smuggled across borders. He was faithful to the movement, to his desire to emigrate to Palestine and to his working class views. During the Soviet days he had worked in a factory and was highly regarded for his talents and simplicity. One of the factory men had recognized him and betrayed him to the Germans, not as a Jew, since he did not know him that well, but as a Communist. That morning Moshe left the ghetto, gave me information, fulfilled his Shomer and parental obligations and was apprehended in the market. The milk he had obtained would not get to Sarenka and his daughter. The man who shone like a bright star, the first to knock at my window, disappeared, and would never return. Only some days later did I learn quite by accident that he had been caught. One of the best of our comrades had been taken from us.

The days passed, dark and depressing. The Germans filled the city streets, parks and restaurants. They swilled beer and predicted a speedy victory. When the wine went to their heads, they would reduce their estimate of the number of days needed to get to Moscow.

Summer's end was beautiful, but the inhabitants of the city complained of the scarcity of food, of the bread ration that was enough for one meal, of the long queues at the shops, and especially of the Lithuanians, who lorded it over the former Polish masters of the country. And so the Poles became the natural allies of the totally disenfranchised Jews. "Excuse me madame, tell

* The unit or "cell" of the local youth movement.

me please, is your friend here a Catholic?" One of my landladies asked me when I passed her room. My heart beat swiftly; only I must not blush! The devil take her, that stupid old maid, who had managed so well to hit on our vulnerable point!

"What else? Do you think she belongs to the Orthodox Church?" I pretended not to comprehend her intention.

"Please understand, I didn't want to insult her, but she looks a little like a Jew."

The discussion ended. I wanted to laugh out loud over the strange suspicion, but I never remembered whether a real laugh emerged or only some hysterical screech. In any case the affair ended well.

On that same day I told Tema of the conversation. "We have to find the weak point in my conduct," she said. "How did that old maid sense that I am a Jew?" In any case we decided that Tema would continue to stay with me a few more days in order not to strengthen the suspicion. Meanwhile we would try to find some other place.

Yadwiga came and apparently corrected the impression. One day in my absence she came deliberately to talk with the landladies. How full of saving tricks she was!

The Emissary From Warsaw

I met with Edek every few days. He worked at the bottom of "Three Cross Hill," a beautiful hill, green and sundrenched. It was one of the city's romantic spots, where lovers met and where workers' families picnicked on Sundays after a hard week's work. It was here, too, perhaps, that the plans of the Communist underground were formulated and the youth movement's revolt was planned.

It was on the top of the hill, among some isolated trees in a romantic setting not in keeping with the circumstances, that we held our meetings. It was there that the threads between the ghetto and the outside world were woven, there that the underground activities against the occupation regime were developed.

The foundations of our lives had not been laid overnight. For years we cultivated our characters and gradually filled our hearts with a vision of a different world, one courageous and free of the dreadful remnants of the past. From our early youth we had learned to believe in historical necessity, in the day of judgment when violence, oppression and discrimination would disappear; the day of fulfillment for the selfless fighter. I can remember the dozens of books we read so avidly about the lives of fighters for freedom and justice who died in prison or on the scaffold for their principles.

The road led along the railway line. On one side there was a narrow path. In some places you thought you would slip and fall into the deep gully of the railroad bed. But you had to keep on going straight ahead with firm steps as if you were travelling to the neighboring village. Only those leaving the ghetto left with halting steps and failing feet.

The path led directly to the Vilna Colony, only seven kilometers from the city. When you got to the Colony you turned right. The Colony itself was a railroad workers' suburb, actually a village adjacent to the big city. Villagers stood in the doorways and looked at new faces. You behaved as if you had come to buy something: chickens, eggs, lard or the like. When you saw that no one was watching, you went up the hill, fast. Even from afar you could see the wall behind the bushes, covering the slope. The wall was high, and from outside you could not see in. You followed it around until you came to the door, pulled the bell on the right twice and then once more. Then a little window opened in the wall and a white-covered head appeared. You asked for sister Ada, and since you were expected they let you in right away. Green fields, scattered buildings — a church, a chapel, a dwelling, a barn — some calves, a barking dog, and around it all, the wall. That was the convent.

The nuns received me hospitably, fed me and then left us, Abba and myself, alone. The meeting had to be short this time since I had to return to the city the same day. Abba was dressed in a nun's robe. There were some other people in the convent, and two or three kilometers away, on other estates, were Aryeh Vilner and Yosef Ritter.

I found Abba in good spirits. He worked in the fields and it relaxed his troubled spirits and gave him confidence. Here he could ponder quietly over what was taking place outside. The situation of those imprisoned in the ghetto was clear to him. We set the order of our contacts and the date for a general consultation. Abba was deep in thought. I knew what he was thinking about. After all, we were all studying the same problem. He had not yet told me what his conclusions were. No one yet dared to voice his thoughts. Until the consultation we would attempt to make better plans for our comrades' existence, economically and legally. We did decide on the main issue. We had not yet passed the first stage. I returned to the city; on the morrow I would inform Edek of the date of the consultation.

My situation in the city deteriorated. First of all, I had no money. Secondly, the Germans had ordered all young people who were fit for work to register in the labor office. It was rumored that all those who came to register and were not employed were sent to Germany. Third, my landladies were watching and tried to find out how a young girl alone like me managed to support herself. The ground was eroding under my feet. Everybody had acquaintances, and some had a definite circle of friends. The average citizen's attitude toward you was not determined by your appearance but by your social status. If you were a stranger, not known to some respectable person, you had no right to exist in an occupation regime. You became one of the suspected, maybe a Jew or maybe a member of the underground.

My troubles increased. The registration order was repeated and from Monday next they would begin to examine not only passports but all work cards or registrations to go to Germany. First I tried to get a forged work card, but that alone would not have established my position in the quiet suburb. Once again I was saved by Yadwiga. This time she introduced me to a Polish woman in her fifties, Mrs. Skarzimska, who managed the ten orphanages in the city. Surprised by my aryan face, she declared that it was only because of her special attitude toward the Jewish scout movement that she was prepared to take the risk. In addition : "I am sure you will work well. The scouts have learned to work, right?" She laughed and suggested that I come to her home together with Yadwiga. I wasn't too happy about her offer. I would have to work long hours in the restaurant and would not be free. On the other hand, the work opened many possibilities. The restaurant was in the center of town, on Zawalna Street, three minutes from Rudnicka, the main street of the ghetto and the site of the ghetto gate. People visited the restaurant all day long and it was a good meeting place. I would have to do manual labor in order to continue to remain invisible.

Mrs. Skarzinska was an interesting woman. She was a Polish patriot, a lawyer by profession, a working woman who supported her family. I wondered about her political views. From her actions and attitude toward me I thought her to be a liberal democrat, one of those persons opposed to any form of oppression.

Mrs. Skarzinska was a woman who possessed great energy and initiative, a very active social worker. Perhaps it was thanks to her that the popular restaurants feeding wide circles of Polish intellectuals uprooted and unemployed under the occupation were able to last so long. Very often she would visit our restaurant, come into the kitchen and ask me about my situation. Her attitude toward me made me more respected by the other workers and improved my status as a Pole. Despite her sympathy and the risks she took, Mrs. Skarzinska was not free of the views prevailing in the middle classes of the provincial population. The chauvinistic Polish attitudes were, apparently, also hers. On one occasion when she wanted to express her satisfaction with my work, she could find no better compliment than: "You are a real Slav. You're really not a Jew at all. Jewish women don't know how to work like this." Mrs. Skarzinska was no worse than many other educated Polish women who had come only part, a small part, of the way. The restaurant workers were quite varied, but united by three things: the Catholic religion, their petit bourgeois concepts, and their hatred of Germans and Lithuanians. Their levels of anti-semitic feeling were not uniform. The restaurant manager, a teacher in the government high school, Mrs. Pardu, was later to become famous in the underground. She was a working woman who supported herself and her little daughter. She had a great deal of respect for religion but was not too observant in practice. She was an educated woman, good and wise, with her eyes open to the world around her. Her life was hard. In her world outlook, however, she had not managed to progress. She was the first to begin to wonder about my peculiar status.

"Why don't you take cleaner and better work?" she asked me one day. "You seem better educated than you would have us believe," she added in a whisper. I didn't reply and she repeated her question. At first I thought that she understood everything. Only after Vitka assumed an aryan lifestyle did it become evident that I had been mistaken

The head cook was a primitive nun, anti-Semitic and thoroughly superstitious, crossing herself constantly, blessing everybody with "Praised be the name of Jesus" whenever she came or left, and everybody would reply in unison, "Forever and forever, amen". My lot was bitter when she came into the kitchen in the morning and found me there alone. I had no choice but to recite the response in a loud voice, clearly and with feeling. To my great surprise I found that she was not honest at all, and that those lips that uttered holy words could also lie wonderfully. I hated her. Every Sunday she would ask me in what church I had said my Sunday prayers. In the course of time I learned to put on a good face and reply calmly. When she was not satisfied with something she would say curtly: "Just like the Jews." "The kitchen looked like a 'Jewish kitchen,' the pot was dirty like a 'Jewish pot' ", "It was noisy like a Jewish synagogue . . ."

All the other workers and waitresses were middle-class, educated or partially so. One even came from a family of barons.

No. 10 Zawalna. It had been a restaurant for Jewish refugees. Here hundreds of Jews would meet every day, to debate, to organize, to arrange emigration matters. Many of them went to Israel, others entered the ghetto, and still others, apparently, met German bullets. The windows of the house looked out on Zawalna street, one of the main thoroughfares of the city. Every evening through those windows you could see the long, sad parades of Jews coming back to the ghetto after a hard day's work. They were loaded down with pieces of wood, potatoes and other foods. There were days, however, when you didn't see any parades. Every morning when I went to work I worried: would I meet them or not? If I didn't meet them it was a bad omen, a very bad one. When the rainy days came I was constantly torn between hope and despair: would I meet them or not?

Very often I had visitors in the restaurant at 10 Zawalna Street. At noon, when the restaurant was busy, we would exchange words without anyone noticing. In that way we maintained contact between the ghetto and the aryan world. It was to this place that news was brought about the ghetto; here forged papers were brought and transferred to their destination. Here in whispers meetings were set in the ghetto and outside.

At dark, when work ended, I would leave every few days to go in the opposite direction, toward the ghetto. In my pocket I had a pass that was only valid for a large work battalion. My pass never matched a work group with which I could enter the ghetto. It was hard to know when some work group would return with which you could enter the ghetto or leave it. You therefore hoped that they would not examine the passes too closely at the gate. You tried to remain as unnoticeable as possible. The patch which by German order you had to sew on your clothes, on your breast and sleeve (these had replaced the white band on the sleeve) you prepared in advance; you mingled with the gray, slow and tired moving mass, pushed a little and in the confusion in front of the gate pinned on the front patch. If you had time you did the same in back . . . . Slowly, carefully, not by force. If you didn't manage, you took the risk and went in with one patch. At worst you would get a blow but afterwards you would be a free Jew in the ghetto . . .

Fall came, the High Holy Days approached. Strange rumors were rampant in the ghetto. Every morning people awoke with the question: would the day be quiet? And if the day passed and none of the evil rumors materialized, tensions relaxed.

The consultation of the Hanhaga Rashit and the cadres was set for Yom Kippur evening. We provided Abba with a pass so that he could enter the ghetto. He would be in danger, but we decided that he should come, nevertheless. We wanted all the cadres to participate in this consultation, and we could not hold it in the convent.

Jews were working along the railway line. On his way there Abba would pass the Vilna Colony before he came to the work group. He had to calculate precisely when they would finish their work, fool the German guard, and tell his story about working alone and his need to join them. My entry was simpler and more secure. With the card in my pocket I would enter directly from the aryan street, from the sidewalk near the Rudnicka corner. At first we were more careful, and Edek would slip out of the ghetto to meet us at the gate. He was known to the Jewish police. It was better, in any event, that somebody be there. That evening, Edek was supposed to meet both of us at the gate.

Edek did not come out to receive us. He apparently did not manage to get out, I thought, and pushed forward. Entry was simple. They hardly looked at the bundles and papers. When I came in I was met by a worried and angry group of people. "Why did you come in? Edek didn't come out and we had specified that without him you should not come in." A few moments later Abba appeared at the gate. The comrades began to think of how to get us out. We knew that tonight there was going to be an *aktzia*. The Germans were demanding 900 persons and the "Jews refused to go to their deaths willingly. They would surely search the houses and you, and without work cards, we would fall into their trap." The papers in our pockets were borrowed and we had to return them. Edek didn't come to meet us since even the police were not allowed to take a step away from the gate. We decided to remain inside. What happened to all the Jews would happen to us, too.

About ten persons lived in a small room on Strashun Street. They slept on broken down doors, on the table, and mostly on the floor. It was the last room in the house. The air was heavy, almost strangling. It was in that room that we met to discuss the situation. "We have behind us a short period of organization, of establishing contacts outside the ghetto. Before us — the annihilation of the Polish Jews." The main issue was a correct evaluation of the situation and clarification of our role as a movement.

At the outbreak of the war we knew that we had to combat the invaders. After the defeat, however, we remained behind the enemy lines, with the front moving further and further away.

Sixty-thousand Jews were imprisoned here within the alleys of the old medieval ghetto. They were dying of hunger, cold, without a roof over their heads, miserable slaves consigned to hard labor. Their lives had lost their purpose.

In the ghetto, people ran about helplessly. The "Shma Israel" prayer was heard in the courtyard on Strashun Street, the weeping, faithful accompaniment to Yom Kippur's Kol Nidre. It was Yom Kippur of 1941. Nearby flats were emptied of people and we were crowded into the last room. Roshka and Vitka moved a closet from the nearby room to block the entrance to our meeting.

That night the first 3,000 Jews were evacuated from the ghetto. Those remaining knew that they would be executed in Ponar. The survivors could, for the time being, stay calm, since the quota had been met and the evil was temporarily over.

That night one of our gentle and gracious comrades disappeared from the ghetto. She had been taken along with her mother. Two other young comrades were also grabbed without the ghetto hearing a sound of resistance. They had not fallen in Zawalna or Rudnicka streets but were secretly and quietly led to the Ponar hills.

Abba was the first to give voice to the bitterness. We had come to a place beyond the grasp of human imagination. We were not committed pessimists but young people, who were alive and who wanted to go on living.

We saw the Nazi in every soldier and officer, every official, every beer-swiller enjoying himself in the autumn sun, in the kicking boot, the thundering voice in the streets, the rifle barrel and pistol pointed at every one of us.

We saw the German in the officer's white hands and in the soldier's arrogant smile. Some of them murdered for sheer pleasure.

We saw fit to start with wisdom; to choose, of all the mad days, hours and minutes, the proper moment to utilize the full weight of our collective daring.

Afterwards came the precise calculations, to plan every step, every movement, to build an effective underground, and orderly organization.

The sense of responsibility grew deeper. We no longer assumed the burden of responsibility for our own actions alone, but for our people, and the movement. The fate of our people rested upon our shoulders.

We left the ghetto. Abba turned toward the convent, and I — to the aryan world.

From then on, every day there were the sad parades along Zawalna Street towards Lukishki, and from there to Ponar. Day after day I stood by the window looking into the street. Every few days the ghetto was closed and it was only from the parades that I learned how many were being led to death.

All that fall, in the dusk of the rainy mornings, those long lines continued. You saw them coming out of the grey mist, quiet, indifferent. Mothers with infants in their arms. You wondered — the infants weren't crying. Sometimes, when the guard looked the other way, you could see someone turning his head about, as though looking for help. We still wanted to live!

And I? How strange I felt. I would go to the restaurant to light the big stoves, to scrub floors and wash the dishes of placid citizens, confident that every day they'll have dinner to eat. I steal from the pots and dishes to the window of the big room facing Zawalna, choking back the shout wanting to break from my heart to my brothers going to die: "Don't go!" I bite my lips ferociously, until they bleed, and control myself. Will I be able to maintain my equilibrium? I must; I have no choice. My shout will not help in any way. I love that mass going down its last road; I believe in its strength and will to live; but revolt? That can only be brought about by an organized force. I believe in my people, but I trust only its organized and disciplined strength.

Comrades are building the organization, establishing its discipline, step by step, within the narrow confines of an enslaved ghetto lying in its own blood. We can rely upon them. I was ordered to go down into the cellar. There are thick logs there that must be chopped, one by one, and dragged back up. I must be a manual laborer, a laughing, pleasant aryan. If Edek manages to get out of the ghetto this evening I will go with him along the railroad line to visit Abba. We will consult and return at dawn. He will return to his battalion and will have to remain all day without occupation. By evening he will forget the fields in which we "strolled", the precise decisions, the plans for approaching actions. I will wash dishes, chop wood and peel potatoes endlessly. And so until dark.

Our consultation in the convent went well. We had walked along the railway like two strolling lovers. In the convent they fed us and left us alone. In Abba's "room", in his hut, by candlelight, we spent the night hours. Abba had prepared the program:

1. To establish the fighting organization and its cells. All members of the movement, upon the secretariat's ratification, would be mobilized into a fighting unit, and each one would know the members of his own cell only.

2. To look for allies in the other chalutz movements and among the Communists. The fighting organization would have to include all the organized anti-fascist forces within the ghetto.

3. To improve and expand the network on the aryan side. Its task was to look for allies outside the ghetto, to make contacts, and to obtain arms with their help. The problem of arms, the essential one, demanded the elaboration of a precise plan after examining all the possibilities in the German workplaces and among the Poles with whom we would widen our network of contacts.

4. To disseminate among the Jews, and especially the young people, the harsh truth about the Germans' plans for the total annihilation of all the Jews in Eastern Europe and to call upon them to defend themselves with arms, sticks, tools, and when there was no other choice — with bare fists.

This was the first consultation in which the problems facing us were discussed openly, clearly and practically. This time we raised our thoughts in an orderly fashion, to meet our work tomorrow, the next day and in the days to come. We also decided, at Abba's insistence, that he would return to the ghetto so that he could take the responsibility for the organization upon himself.

The implementation of the "aryan program" was my assignment.

The restaurant's manager, Mrs. Pardu, praised me. "In ordinary times," she sighed, and said to my great surprise, "you and your like would be the future of the Polish people." What she saw in me to make me the future of her people I do not know. I never took part in the numerous discussions about ghosts, about heavenly punishment, and Jesus and his sanctity. I never expressed my opinions in public. Perhaps that was why her educator's and teacher's sense saw the seriousness and depression that the German occupation brought out in me. In any case, all suspicions disappeared when she said that she knew my real situation. I understood that she considered my Polish patriotism as the reason for my unusual appearance in the limited company of 10 Zawalna Street.

When I was convinced that my status as an aryan was firm, I suggested to Mrs. Pardu that she take on my friend, a "student from Warsaw" (Vitka) as a teacher for her little daughter. I knew that she was looking for a tutor and guide for her child.

Vitka dyed her hair. Yandzia provided her with a forged certificate, and thereafter came and went in the ghetto, established herself in Mrs. Pardu's home and took care of her daughter.

The certificate-forging industry was quite developed. Yandzia had learned the trade thoroughly, and Rivkele, his little friend, helped him. She specialized in erasing the names and other details, and in putting the stamp on the replacement photograph of the newborn. The work was difficult, wearysome and nervewracking. A line not straight, a dot not in place, and the rare and precious document that had been obtained with such hardship was ruined and useless. The most difficult task was to change a Jewish certificate into an aryan one. Here a great deal of erasures and new writing was required. It wasn't the same when we received from the Poles with whom we were in contact the papers of some deceased young Pole. We could always find some comrade whose eyes, hair, height and age corresponded to those of the late owner of the certificate. These papers were doubly advantageous. Yandzia's work was then "standard", only requiring the stamp on the new photograph. It was easy to "revive" such a dead person some place else, far from his original dwelling place.

After Vitka we made arrangements for Liza Magon. Yadwiga established her in her own home. In addition, certificates were provided for all those living in the ghetto who, because of their work for the underground, had to leave the ghetto either for a whole day or for a few hours at a time. Edek was the most noteworthy of these certificate holders. He frequently left the ghetto.

Edek joined me in those meetings with the Poles that demanded more deliberation and closer investigation of the subject. Our first contacts with the Poles were established by Yadwiga and the Mother Superior, who also introduced us to a Pole who dealt in smuggling people abroad, a possibility that was very important to us. Our contacts with the world had ended with the outbreak of World War II, and renewing them meant access to news and, what was most important, the possibility of telling the world about the Germans' abominations and their plan to annihilate our people.

Our financial situation also demanded some contact with the outside. Our funds were depleted and new sources were nil. I went to such a meeting with Edek.

I was not able to see the man's face. The apartment, at the end of the long courtyard, lay in the darkness of autumn evening. His plan was both daring and simple. "We must get to the Libau port in Latvia. I can help you in arranging the papers, but the responsibility for the trip will be yours. The people (not many) will be received in the port and transferred in ferry boats to Sweden. The matter of the sea trip I take upon myself." He paused for a moment and then went on, as if deliberating: "That will, of course cost money, real money; gold coins."

That was one of our many meetings in those days with representatives of the civilian Polish underground which, according to all the information in our hands, had been in existence before the war between Germany and the USSR. We met people who offered us aid in supplying documents and in "arranging" people, and also those to whom we went with the hope that they would also help us obtain arms.

Our talks with Mother Superior lasted a long time. She would come to us on a bicycle and, in winter, on skis. She would inform us in advance of her coming via Yadwiga.

Her talks with Abba led her to accept some of the principles of our outlook. She had a sharp mind and an open heart and easily grasped our national problem. She also understood our socialistic and collectivist views, and only attempted to convince us that it was possible to bridge the gap between our views and her concepts about the godhead. She and Yadwiga helped us find sources of aid, contacts, and information, but not arms. With their help we succeeded in saving many Jewish children, and in establishing some more girls in the city. All the activities and negotiations, however, came to an end at the weak focal point — arms.

There was also no contact with the outside world then, since by the time we had gathered a small part of the necessary money the man who was supposed to carry out the plan had disappeared without a trace.

It was not, however, despair without end. First, ten wasted meetings, ten gropings in the dark, and suddenly there was an opening at a time, a place and in circumstances you had never expected to find. That is the way Heniek came to us.

One day Yadwiga came to me at 10 Zawalna, and told me that I had to come after work that evening to the Vorobelevsky Library: "Come exactly at ten, in front of the big building, from the Vilia side."

"Yadzia, what's happened? Some catastrophe?"

Yadzia waited like someone with a very important secret.

"Come, you'll see. I don't have time now." And finally, as if incidentally, "someone has come from Yosef."

She did not say who it was. The remaining time I bided impatiently. What news! There was no one I could tell, and I so much wanted one of the comrades to be with me, to be a partner in my secret.

Matters in the kitchen went on as usual. "Halina, give me a pot," "Halina, there aren't enough potatoes for dinner," "Halina, the stove is burning like a Jew stove; Is that what you call a fire?", and so on without end. Good, Edek was coming today; we had to consult on a number of matters; everything could wait for the new event. Contact with Warsaw! Do you understand what that means? Yosef has managed to send us an emissary. But I hadn't told Yadwiga that I was coming with Edek. I had simply forgotten.

After work I left Edek in my room and went excitedly to the meeting place. To my surprise there was a Warsaw non-Jew present and Yadwiga told me: "This is one of my kids from the scout movement." Heniek was a direct person who didn't need to have things spelled out in order for him to understand. It seems that he knew the names of some of the comrades. "I've brought you a little letter from Yosef," he said, "Everything is in order with us." Who is this "us"? I asked myself, but it very soon became clear: "with us" for Heniek meant "for us in the ghetto." Here I stopped him and told him that I wanted another comrade to be at the meeting. At first he showed signs of dissatisfaction, but when I told him that the comrade was Edek, his expression changed: "I know about him from Yosef's stories. Bring him."

Edek and Heniek immediately found their way to each others hearts. They were so alike in their conduct, in their fluent Polish with its suburban Warsaw accent, their innate folk humor and their direct and daring approaches to action and to people. I was astonished by them. Heniek told us some of the details of his coming:

"There, you understand, in the ghetto, especially Yosef, they are very worried about your fate. We have no news of what is happening here, you understand, and it is hard without this knowledge. We sit and think of things to do, how to get to you. So, I got up and went. I didn't want to take a lot with me, you understand, only this little letter, but Yosef spent some evenings telling me about the movement in Warsaw and I can repeat what he said exactly about the people, the movement groups, the movement seminar, and more. I know everything. I remember what he said. I am not so expert in all the details but Yosef explained them well and patiently, quietly. The main thing is I've been on the way for two weeks. I came on foot, and on bicycle which I left on the way. I had to concoct all kinds of stories in order to find some place to sleep. So, here I am whole and healthy, you understand. On the road I learned of the catastrophe that those murderers are preparing for you. I went past Troki, God in heaven — what a sight! To the devil, who am I to tell you? You know it yourself, why are you looking at me? It's hard to talk about it. If I hadn't seen with my own eyes those being led to death, I, too, wouldn't believe it. But what am I chattering about? I must hear from you. Write Yosef telling him what you want, describe the situation. No matter, it will still be alright."

He finished his story. He had a special talent of relating the most tragic things about his tribulations and troubles and about which he spoke little, in a simple, even a somewhat jocular style. In short, a "shegetz" from Cherniakovska.

We decided to show him the ghetto so that he could tell them about it in Warsaw. We made it Edek's task to explain the situation of the Jews of Vilna and of some other communities of which we had news, towns in the Vilna neighborhood, Kovno and its environs, where the situation was similar. Edek was also supposed to give him the complete picture. That could not be done in a letter, and if Yosef saw fit to send Heniek to us he could be trusted. We provided him with forged papers so that he could pass through Lithuanian territory. We met a few more times and then said goodbye to him in the convent. He listened quietly. He had seen the ghetto, looked at the remnants of the Jews that were left in Vilna's large Jewish community, sat in our comrades' cold room, saw the lines of those being led to their death. "You are real men," he finally said. "Don't accept what I say as flattery or as an expression of pity. The truth can be seen, do you understand?"

We few comrades who spent time with him grew fond of him. Heniek Grabovsky, a member of the Polish scout movement, far from being an ideologist he looked at us as human beings and friends. A worker since youth, a locksmith, he was endowed with native intelligence and could somehow sense the difference between evil and good, between truth and falsehood, cowardice and courage, slavery and freedom. We loved him for his good sense and clear mind, his courage and wisdom. We said goodbye with heavy hearts and with only a faint hope of ever seeing him again.

My old room was getting too small. In order to enter my old apartment I had had to disturb my landladies and enter through their large guest room. The situation was bad. On the opposite side of the street lived a Polish woman who knew me well from the Soviet period; we had both attended courses in the Vilna University. It was luck that played into my hands. I found a room on Vilna's main street, 59 Mitzkevich Street, that had a separate entrance. They had only to knock on the wall to call me. The landlady was an old woman who moved with difficulty, and who was slightly deaf.

The room was partially furnished, and the rent not too expensive. That very day I moved my belongings, and on the next day a second stamp was put into my identity card by the commisarion which certified that I was a legal tenant of 59 Mitzkevich Street.

From then on, my room was a center refuge. Anyone who left the ghetto towards evening on business and could not manage to return before curfew, could find a night's refuge there, a warm stove, and sometimes even dinner stolen from the restaurant on 10 Zawalna Street. That was no small matter. We were already in the midst of winter, the snow melted in the torn shoes and froze one's feet. How could one roam the streets on such a winter night? If you slept under the big bridge you might freeze to death, or the police might find you. To find a place to sleep, in my room, was no problem. There was a couch, and the broad backrest could be removed and laid across two chairs, to make a royal bed. A clean blanket could be found and if you added a coat or two and stretched your legs toward the heated stove, you could sleep soundly and rise early. If someone asked for a day's refuge until evening, when the Jews returned en masse from work, a key to the room was available. Only to remain silent, it was best to sleep. Even then you had to be careful not to sigh or talk and to turn from side to side very carefully. The old lady was indeed hard of hearing, but they say walls have ears, and there was another tenant in the same apartment. She was very seldom home but we still had to be very careful.

Once Edek was supposed to come toward evening. We were to go to what we thought would be an important meeting. I waited in my room until nine o'clock but he didn't come. In my despair I thought that they had caught him. It was hard to believe, however, that he could fail. Still, he apparently did that night. After nine o'clock, the curfew hour, I heard his secret knock on the wall. He was neither excited nor frightened, and with his mocking smile said that he had been caught by police at the second gate. They searched him carefully but did not find what they were looking for. Yandzia and Abba worked at night preparing papers to sell. We sold them to people we knew well, and used a go-between to hide the sources. We were strangled then by lack of means to maintain the movement, our apparatus and especially, the purchase of arms. We decided that this dirty money, the price of the modern Jewish right to live, would be devoted to arms. Our comrades were hungry in the ghetto, frozen because we lacked clothing and wood for the stove, but we did not take one penny of this money. I remember how we divided our par bread slice by slice, how we wanted to keep each other alive — Roshka, Vitka, Abba and also Edek. They lied about the bread's weight so that they would leave themselves less and add more to the others. When we came to their narrow room that winter the cold penetrated our bones. The walls were covered with snow to the ceiling; we would remove it with a broom, but it would always pile up again. Abba sat in his coat all night, bent over the table, his hands making the marvelous drawings on photographs in order to get money for arms.

That was the money that Edek wanted to carry to the aryan side. He got away from them after a long grilling. They wanted money from him as ransom for his life but he escaped, got back to the ghetto and still did not give it up. He had to bring the money to its destination.

That evening Edek left the ghetto a second time. He got past the always closed gate barred to Jewish use, and managed to get to me some minutes after nine.

Edek hadn't finished his story when there was a loud ringing; I was sure that the police or detectives had arrived. Who else would call during curfew and ring the doorbell so insistently? I opened the door before the landlady managed to get out of bed, and I was greeted by two blinding flash lights.

"Who lives here?"

"Please, that is the landlady's room," I pointed to the right. Maybe they would be satisfied with visiting her. I wanted to help Edek get away. I did not succeed. Only one went into the landlady's room, the second remained standing at the door. Both were in civilian clothes and spoke Polish with Lithuanian accents. I left them alone, as if I were not concerned, entered my room and closed the door behind me. A few minutes later they knocked at my door; this time more quietly without shouts.

"Please."

"Who lives here?"

"I do."

"What is your name?"

"Voronovich Halina."

"Show us your papers."

I handed them my identification certificate and work card. Edek sat and watched them silently, without lowering his eyes.

"Who is that?" pointing to Edek.

"That . . that is my fiance."

"May I see his papers?"

Edek did not hurry, he took out his wallet slowly searched for a moment, and said:

"My papers? Certainly! But perhaps I could know to whom I am showing my papers?

I sensed that his question had gained their trust. One of them handed over his certificate as a Gestapo employee.

"Please," Edek handed them his forged papers.

Edek's behavior saved us from trouble. They looked at his papers offhandedly, begged our pardon and went away.

Sarah Silber moved out of the ghetto. Now we had another address, another apartment and what was most important, another person for work. Her face was good, her Polish fluent; she was deliberate and was quick to understand. We decided to leave her alone until she was completely integrated into her new neighborhood. At first she served as the contact with the Polish institutions where we had put Jewish children.

One day on returning from work I found a postcard in my room with Edek's signature, announcing that Edek and two other men had gone to Yosef, that is — they were travelling to Yosef in Warsaw. They left suddenly, on short notice, and couldn't tell me or consult with me. He had put the postcard in a mail box in Vilna on the way out of the city. Edek with his Jewish face. He had to cross borders, and these crossings were not the same as crossing the street to the aryan side. At the border every Pole was examined and there was no doubt that they would discover his Jewishness. On the morrow Vitka returned from the ghetto and told the story.

"You know the Jewish couple from Germany, or Austria — the woman who was once a singer or something like that in Vienna. Imagine, one day she met a tall officer, Schmidt, who served in the Vilna occupation army, an acquaintance from former times. A decent man, a Viennese, he got along with people, and he was intelligent. He headed a collection station for soldiers who had lost their units. Cars and all kinds of papers were at his disposal. In short, the officer began a rescue operation. We had to find a contact. Mordechai Tenenbaum was already in touch with him in the ghetto and he would help you to contact him. In the meantime, something unexpected happened. They suddenly announced that he could send some men, Poles supposedly, to Warsaw. What road they would take he was not certain. He thought if he could bring them safely to Grodno, he would decide on the rest of the journey. The matter wasn't certain, but Edek seized the opportunity. His argument was short and convincing: we couldn't leave disseminating the news of the annihilation and the defense against it to Heniek alone, even if he was a good man. We had to convince not only our own comrades but also the public. That public was still complacent and knew nothing about the annihilation plans and they certainly wouldn't believe the stories of a Pole. Edek convinced the comrades, but why did he himself have to go? He decided that alone, and the others kept silent. With him went my brother, Yuzio the revisionist, and Solomon Entin from the Zionist Youth, the only one who looked like a gentile. If he managed to go the whole way without saying a word in Polish in his Jewish accent, maybe he would get to Warsaw safely.

"Fearful about the fate of the men who had gone, we waited for news and them. Meanwhile, the number of people fleeing the Vilna ghetto increased. Anybody with an opportunity, or with money in his pocket, set out to seek refuge in some other supposedly more stable, safer ghetto. The Jews wanted a moment's quiet, not to have to think of tomorrow for a while. Some went to Grodno, others to Bialystok and some even got to Warsaw. Schmidt, the German officer, didn't ask too many questions. With the help of his two Jewish friends, he organized groups that were sent to various ghettos, without guidance from any public body. His apartment was a refuge for these people, who often had to wait a day or two until the rest of the refugees were assembled, with their families and bundles, in Schmidt's apartment, opposite the railroad station. This method of moving people without any organization or ruling did not improve the secrecy of his activities.

"Unwittingly, Schmidt was moving his refugees out of the frying pan into the fire. This imaginary salvation deadened Jewish resolve, gave him illusions and dulled any desire for revolt and opposition.

"We found a connection with Schmidt. Mordechai brought us to him. The Sabbath was coming to an end. After work I entered the ghetto as usual. On Saturday they were generally stricter at the gate. That day I had gathered more food than usual. On Saturday everybody was in a hurry to go home and I was able to fill my bag with all kinds of goodies: fried potatoes which, if heated, tasted like a gourmet treat, a considerable number of broken meatballs which couldn't be served at the table; boiled beets and carrots — altogether a royal feast. At the end of Rudnicka Street, on the right, before the gate, there was a Catholic church. The church's alternate exit was on Zawalna Street. In order not to be seen when you turned into Rudnicka Street, you had to go through the church from Zawalna to Rudnicka Street. In the dark you could see the approaching work battalion; you had to stop, kneeling near the door, to hurry but not too fast so they wouldn't see you waiting for the Jews, but not too late: you had to mix with them in time to enter the ghetto. The comrades would be happy to see that you were well. There, a little of the tension of my aryan days would ease; I would be among friends.

"That evening, a little before nine, we reached the ghetto gate: Mordechai, Esther (from the Revisionists), and I. Everything had been arranged in advance with the police at the gate. We left; Schmidt lived nearby. We crossed two courtyards, one street, and came out on Ostrobramska opposite the railroad station. The code knock at the door, and we were in Schmidt's home. There were three not overly large rooms, one, his bedroom. A bed, a closet and a table: In the other two rooms utter confusion. There were beds along the walls and thin blankets on the bare mattresses. The remnants of all kinds of foods littered the floor. Here, apparently, was where the refugees stayed. I saw Schmidt: tall, handsome, with a kind face. He looked at me with penetrating eyes:

'You are from Hashomer Hatzair? Mordecai told me. Yes, I still remember the Zionists in Vienna.'

"From Schmidt's words I learned that he was informed on the matters of the Jewish parties. My first surprise. Around the table were seated a number of other guests from the ghetto. The landlord, Schmidt, filled the glasses, and the discussion at the table was a second surprise: Those seated had maintained contacts with Schmidt for some time but the nature of these contacts and their purposes were not clear to me. In the ghetto binding decisions had been adopted by the various public bodies with whom we were connected. Abba was the coordinator of these people together with the Revisionist, Glazman, and Mordechai from Hechalutz.

"How did it happen that there were deals being made with Schmidt, involving valuable furs and precious stones? Where did these come from and why were they being deposited with Schmidt?

"Among our comrades there was not a memory or hint of such articles. The only ones who owned them were the policemen who collected the money and jewelry from the Jews being led to their death. I knew that many of the Revisionists participated in the *aktzias* as policemen. Was it possible that Glazman and his people, the only group of the revisionists that had joined us in planning the armed revolt, was also partaking in the spoils? I knew that many of Glazman's people had betrayed him, but it seemed to me that Esther was one of his loyal comrades. None of these seated at the table drew Schmidt's attention to the subject of arms. They all spoke of going away, transfer, flight. It was for these purposes that the means had been mobilized and this was the reason for the contacts with Schmidt.

"All this was in conflict with everything we were doing. We decided to exploit any remaining possibilities connected with Schmidt in the interest of defense. Here views were divided, to our sorrow, even with the members of "Dror"*, Mordechai at their head. We were surprised by Mordechai's declaration that in his opinion the connections with Schmidt should be utilized to help us move all of our people to Bialystok.

'How? Is that what you still think after the defense decision? Where will you go if the Bialystok ghetto is endangered?'

"Mordechai, however, persisted:

'In Vilna there are altogether eighteen thousand helpless, broken and tired Jews left. We must go to some place where we will have the strength to

* Labor Zionist youth movement.

fight. Let us concentrate our limited forces, not divide them. Here I don't see any possibility of recuperating.' "

"We must defend ourselves where we are": that was our rule and our guiding principle. It was upon this basis that we wanted to establish our program of action. Vilna is a symbol of Jewish life in Poland. Should we abandon Vilna, give up the heroic symbol? Who knows where we will find greater possibilities? It was here, for the first time, that the decision for armed defense was made. Abandoning Vilna was like deserting a sinking ship.

The situation of the "Dror" members was more difficult than ours. Most of their comrades were scattered throughout Lithuania's provincial towns. Their numbers in the Vilna ghetto were small. Without any support from the loyal people, the Vilnaites, were without any central and authoritative leadership except for Mordechai, whose ties and past were with the leadership in Warsaw. Perhaps this situation impelled them to transfer the center of gravity of their movement's life to Greater Bialystok, still tranquil then.

Courageous and dynamic Mordechai, so marvelously alive to everything that was happening, possessed a most active mind. He planned great things and blamed himself for every failure. He made plans, and in his great innocence believed that with his strong will, his immense energy, they would succeed. But harsh reality proved otherwise.

I can still remember his decision not to become one of the prisoners in the ghetto. He was determined to be free, outside the high walls where they wanted to bury him alive. I remember his long nose burning, his black eyes, his thick black eyebrows. He wanted to deceive the enemy, so he passed himself off as a Karaite and gave his gentle Tema his made-up name — Tamarot the Karaite. He failed a number of times, but he did not give up. He sent his comrades by car with Schmidt, and he himself took the train to Bialystok.

We decided to move a small organizing group to Bialystok, to include Yandzia, Rivka Madeiska, his girl friend, and Sarah Dabeltoff. The team was a small one, but we did not have the means to move it without Schmidt's help. It was important to establish a fighting organization in that Jewish city, in the Bialystok ghetto of 60,000 Jews. We did not want to use the money we had for the move, and we therefore decided to send those who looked more aryan by railroad, with forged papers. Where, however, were we to find that kind of paper which was used in the printing of a special permit to cross the Lithuanian border to the Bialystok province that had been annexed to the Third Reich?

At that time Tema returned from Warsaw bringing with her a typical light blonde "shiksa", called Lonka. Three days later Tosya also came.

Tosya and the Joys of Life

Tosya arrived by train with false papers. Even Warsaw had not known whether they were good for the passage between Warsaw and Bialystok and between Bialystok and Vilna.

Frozen and tired by the trip's tribulations as she was, I found it hard to recognize her. How she had aged in the two years since I last saw her. She was no longer the mischievous little Tosya who had worked with the younger children in our movement. Only her hair was still in disarray as it had been, and her eyes still sparkled. Her movements, however, were now slower and more deliberate. The day she came to be my guest in my warm room, by the lighted fire, I recognized the young Tosya only for a few minutes, once she had stretched her aching bones and bathed in a basin of hot water. For a while, her natural mischievousness and joy returned. This was her first stop in Vilna, a one-night sojourn quieter, warmer and more comfortable than all the others. Tosya knew how to talk, and when she talked about Warsaw everything else stopped. The pleasant warmth faded, as did the silence enveloping the house. Instead of the white bed we suddenly saw a street in the Warsaw ghetto, and I could see hungry Jews running about as long as they were alive. The thin man and the one inflated by hunger hold out their hands and shout: "Give charity, give me a penny, only a penny!" You could almost hear their voices. The door to the room is gone, instead there is a gate. The gate is big, and there they play, shoot, do whatever they like. Tosya's eyes take on their own special softness and she tells of the children, the Jewish children. I could visualize what Tosya was describing. They were sneaking through some opening, going through the barbed wire, running along the cemetery, loaded with potatoes, bread and vegetables. I could hear the crying of the beaten child, the sighs of some miserable man who had been hit by a Nazi bullet. Tosya lived through these things with all her being. She told many stories: a story of a violinist and a writer who had become beggars, standing with their plates in the long line before the charity kitchen to get their watery soup; stories of underground speculators who had become fabulously wealthy and devoured roast duck in splendid restaurants. One of these came out of the restaurant with a package under his arm — cakes and cookies and other good things, and a five-year old boy ran towards him, grabbed the package and sank his teeth into it. The owner shouted, called for the police — but what will the blows rained on his thin shoulders accomplish when the goodies are already in his mouth? The price was worth it — cakes and cookies for some light blows!

For hours on end Tosya went on telling her stories.

The next evening Tosya, Vitka and I entered the ghetto. When Tosya spoke about Warsaw and the General-Government, there was deathly silence in the ghetto room. The "shomrim"* sat on the floor, beds, doors, broken chairs borrowed from a neighbor, crowded and silent, listening to every word, every sound. We weren't hungry then for stories of troubles, we had our own troubles aplenty. However, when Tosya related the story of how the Warsaw Jews had existed during the past two years things fell into place. How would our movement have held out in all of this? Still, it was renewing its life as much as possible.

Secretly we knocked on doors, looked for our young people. We were the first to call on them to rise up, to organize, to preserve what had been. In that way we organized our branches and training groups. We had two agricultural kibbutz training groups in the ghettoes of Warsaw and Chenstokova. We didn't allow the youth to sink into despair. We guarded our people against the worst evils which erode the will to live, leading to beggary and starvation and abject poverty. We were determined to give no rest to the scoundrels and traitors. The pioneering youth movements, and our movement in particular, used their inspiring moral powers to put Jewish public life, with its parties and institutions, back on its feet. Our movement's paper called for a renewal of the young people's revolt, told the truth about the front and the Nazis' actions, and the opposition by even the still weak fighting forces. Our paper reflected our firm belief in a German defeat and a Soviet Russian victory.

Tosya pulled out of her bag a copy of our scout paper, "El-Al". It told of a movement seminar, normal activities of the various sections and groups in which the doctrines of Marx and Borochov were taught. It was hard to believe.

Tosya continued: "If you meet young, vibrant people, singing their songs in the ghetto to the wonderment of the bereft people running about, singing the songs of life and non-surrender, you know that is our youth. There are

* Members of Hashomer Hatzair.

many young people who have joined us, even in the ghetto. They are attracted to us because of our vitality."

Tosya paused for a moment and then continued: "Look, Aryeh Vilner, who recently left Vilna as an aryan, is working with the kibbutz in the Warsaw ghetto, helping them to prepare themselves for independent action." Tosya's words still echoed in the air, the story remained unfinished; the climax was yet to come. Everybody understood that; it was what Tosya meant: action had not yet finished; it had only now begun.

The people dispersed in the dark. A guard stood at the door, another in the courtyard near the gate, and a third near the staircase, directing those who were leaving. By nine the room was empty and quiet. A small group remained; Tosya was silent, listening to our talk, carefully following everything we said.

"Listen Tosya," we told her, one after the other, "you say that you are prepared to receive all of us in Warsaw with open arms, that you will be happy to be with us and for us to reinforce your activists. You and Yosef, and all the other comrades, are prepared to care for us, to accept us. That is good. What is especially encouraging is that you understood that you don't abandon a place without weighing this step conscientiously, and as a group. It is good that you leave the decision to us; good that you have grasped the great principle of the movement. We here are already at the bottom of the pit of evil, while you are still on the slope. The worst is still to come — total annihilation. We have already tasted it. Your situation is better but at the same time more dangerous. Better, because you have time to prepare for the contest one step at a time. We have to do everything at once in one step. But they are liable to disrupt everything you have accumulated in two years of underground work. It might seem that you are preparing yourselves for a long road and that your plans are leading to a solution — while in truth you will not be given the time to carry out your long range plans. Tomorrow you may have to face the fact of annihilation, like us."

That was the crux of what we said and Tosya listened tensely, her face very serious.

"I don't have the right or authorization to tell you what to do. You have lived with death; seen it with your own eyes. You have the right to decide. We are in a different situation. I will report everything to Warsaw, including your comments on Warsaw and its environs. I confess that you have raised a question that we never faced so directly. I will allow myself only to say something in my own name . . ." Here Tosya reflected for a moment: "I think that we would do as you do; I think that we, too, would not abandon our city."

Tosya told us about Edek. "He reached Warsaw; and it is good that he came. We had him meet the representatives of the Jewish public in the ghetto, the Joint people, the party representatives. His words made a tremendous impression. After all, he was the first emissary to bring us the terrible truth. In his simple language he described what had happened. Of course, most did not believe him, or believed and declared that it could not happen in Warsaw, that the Germans would be afraid of Europe. He was waiting in Warsaw for two things: the money promised him by the Joint, and some kind of transport pass."

During the evening meal, this time a festive one, with potato pancakes, Tosya told us about Edek's experiences. "His road had been long and tiring, with its adventures, hurdles and mistakes. But I'll tell you about it in brief. He and his two fellow travelling companions arrived in Grodno safely. In Grodno they were caught by the police, who suspected they were Jews. But when they were brought to a street that had been bombed they escaped in the darkness and fled through the ruins. That trouble was one of the lighter ones. They found the car in which they had come and arrived safely in Warsaw. There, however, while they were looking for some way into the ghetto, they were caught again. This time, I think, only Edek and Yuzio. Luckily, Yuzio had a little money. The Polish policeman let them go, but then they fell into the hands of the Germans, who said they were Jews. Edek denied it, of course. On the way they attempted to escape, but they were caught again, and their hands were chained. I don't know exactly what happened next. Really, it is hard to understand how they got to the ghetto. Anyway, they did arrive, in their chains, without coats or hats, at night, in freezing cold. Now Edek is with us. He's fast and cunning, as you know. It's hard to believe that he went all that way with his Jewish face. He's in a hurry to get back, but how? We're trying to make him wait until he gets some sort of papers."

We spent that night with Tosya. It was a meeting that was both cheering and sad. Tosya had imbued us with a fresh, invigorating spirit; she brought us the message from places and spaces that had disappeared at that time because of the troubles. By coming, she broke the siege under which we lived. We raised the problem of coordinating the activities of the scattered movement; of joint action, of learning each other's experience. Abba told his tragi-comic stories of the Judenrat and the traitorous police. Roshka talked about the Vilna youth, the little ones who only yesterday had been children in the movement and were today seeking answers for what was happening. Vitka related her stories about her employer, Mrs. Pandu, and about her nun neighbors, who wanted to know what a girl did who was not a nun.

We lay down to sleep very late and rose early to leave the ghetto, each to his own affairs.

Tosya spent a few more days in my home between visits to the ghetto, and I learned much from her. I learned to be sensitive to things that seemed to have no connection to our work: nice weather, soft, white snow, a good meeting with a comrade, a pleasant warm room and sometimes even the taste of candy.

She admonished me not to see only the ugliness of life, the Germans, the occupation. "If you see these things only, you won't succeed as a fighter," she said to me.

"You are so strange . . . Why don't you understand that we have had a great privilege, a privilege not given to many: to enjoy life and to suffer, to suffer without end. We also have the right to hunger. Ordinary citizens don't have that right. When they are hungry they complain bitterly. It is our privilege to be hungry, to suffer and not to complain; that is a great privilege. So — don't worry. Here is life before you, take of it in plenty.

"The underground person always faces the danger of beginning to hate people as people. You look so gloomy, so tight and dry. Stop it, stop it Chaika! It only makes it harder, wears you out."

She gave me my first lessons in the art of living. I revolted against these lessons, because I did not understand them too well. How foolish I was then.

Those were great days in our "aryan" lives. Tosya, Lonka, Tema and I would gather in the evenings at Vitka's and amuse ourselves. Vitka's room was small with a curtain setting off the kitchen. Surrounding the house were churches and monasteries. Wherever one turned there were crucifixes. If you came from University Street through Napoleon Square, to the right of her street, you thought that only the very devout lived there. It was not wise for us to gather in this religious courtyard, but the desire to be together prevailed over intelligence and common sense. We were not yet sufficiently immunized against loneliness and the fear of it. These meetings were one of the reasons that the neighbors began whispering about Vitka, until one day an open argument took place between her and her neighbor; who cursed her vehemently. In any case, at first we did not pay much attention to this superfluous risk and to the fact that we relied too much on an address that seemed to us to be secure.

Mrs. Pardu, Vitka's employer and the manager of the restaurant where she worked, readily accepted the "aryans from Warsaw", as Vitka introduced us. After her first conversation with them, she told Vitka: "Interesting, in the many years that I taught and educated our Polish youth, I never met young people like these, so intelligent and so brave. Especially I never met girls like these." She used to talk with Vitka a great deal in the evenings. They discussed literature and art and beautiful, occupied Poland. "You know, your friend is very intelligent and wise," she once said to me in the restaurant kitchen. She made similar remarks to both of us, so that we began to consider the situation. We understood that she suspected something but we didn't know what. Vitka was impressed by her character, patience and sensitivity and in one of her talks could not restrain from telling Mrs. Pardu that we were Jews. We became angry with her, and told her that she had been too careless, but Vitka insisted: I couldn't fool her anymore. The following days proved her correct. From then on, Mrs. Pardu never tired of helping us. She sought every opportunity to aid us with her small means. "You have become even bigger in my eyes," she told Vitka. "If Jewish youth imprisoned in the ghetto is capable of organizing for action in days like these, to sneak across borders — and don't tell me Vitka; you don't take risks of going to Warsaw and Vilna for pleasure, but some specific purpose . . . Where is our youth, the Polish youth I educated?" Very interestingly, after Vitka told her our secret, Mrs. Pardu never gave me the slightest hint that she knew my secret. She avoided meeting me alone, apparently not to make us both feel uncomfortable.

Tosya and Lonka brought forged transit papers with which they crossed the frontiers. Now Yandzia was making similar documents for their return. We knew that these papers would not be sufficient. One of the members of the ghetto underground worked in a German printshop and was making border transit papers printed in gothic letters. Where could we find gothic print? Our papers were printed in latin script on an ordinary typewriter. The bearers were in danger of being caught at the very first station. In Vilna's railway station all permits were examined. You couldn't leave without a permit. Poles were forbidden to travel even to the next station nearby without a permit, let alone crossing borders.

One morning little Rivkele brought me the permit forged by Yandzia. I asked for half an hour off from work supposedly to visit a sick friend, and we both went to the station. It was very cold, the white snow crunched under our feet. The sun's rays glinted like shining sparks. On a day like this there was no desire to be imprisoned in Lukishki, the prison from which one never survived. In the ghetto they believed that you shouldn't send one man alone on a dangerous operation. But we talked it over: I was established in the city, legally registered, and had a work card in my pocket. I would therefore go. Rivkele would stand near the entrance as though she didn't know me and would watch carefully. An old plan. "Wait a minute," Rivkele said and paled when I left her near the station and walked with swift steps towards the guard standing near the platform approach. At that moment everything around me was quiet, as if the station were abandoned, and I heard only my own steps on the stone floor of the large waiting room.

"I have received permission from my employer to go to my family in Warsaw for the holiday. Will you look please; can I go with this permit?"

He read the permit and said:

"Of course, of course, but I'll ask the station officer anyway."

He saw a passing officer, handed him the papers without asking me anything further, and pointed to me. I saw Rivkele arranging her long braid. She must have been very nervous. The sentry returned and gave me back the paper: "Your papers are in order. If you want to go now — please."

I thanked him and returned, to Rivkele's joy. We went out enthusiastically. "Simpletons," I whispered to my friend, "but that test doesn't prove anything. That was a soldier, not a detective. Every round stamp with a swastika is valid for him; he is easy to fool."

We were happy and sad at the same time. We knew that this was not the end of the matter. We would not defeat our enemies by deceit, by forging documents and by acting "aryan". In those days, however, the railroad was still under the supervision of the army and that eased our movement and travel.

Our comrades laughed when they heard our story. We laughed and joked but we knew that the enemy was still there. It was still a long way to the last laugh.

It was with this paper, with the round stamp on it testifying that the bearer worked in Vilna in a German unit and was traveling to Warsaw for work, that Tosya left us, with the intention of visiting Grodno and Bialystok on the way. Following her to Bialystok were Sarah Dabeltoff and Rivkele Madeiska. Yandzia was the last to leave them. He was also the last of Schmidt's passengers.

One day we found Schmidt's door locked. No one opened it in response to the coded knocks. No one answered in the evening either. The house looked the same as always. It was quiet on the staircase, the blinds were not drawn, the door was not locked from the outside. We understood that something had happened. But if something did, why hadn't they caught me when I knocked at the door? Why were there no guards around the house? At the front of the house, facing the station, on the second floor there was a big sign: "Station for Soldiers Who Have Lost Their Units". The house had been under Schmidt's supervision. Here he had been the master. Maybe we should ask about him there? Only two days later one of his chauffeurs, who had helped him move Jews, told us that it was a good thing we didn't go to look for

Schmidt and that we hadn't stayed near the house. An hour or two before we came Schmidt had been arrested, and it was fortunate that we did not try to visit him during the past two days, because his house was under surveillance. Since Schmidt had been arrested in front of his house, they left, intending to return at night to make a search. We had apparently been at the house in the hours between his arrest and the search. Schmidt was lost. In his house, and in the military station he ran, they found forged stamps, and bills for fuel expenditures and other valuables. What was most important, they had found the fabricated permits allowing workers to make long trips to places which had no connection with their work.

Two days later Gens, the chairman of the Judenrat, called Glazman and told him: "You are lucky; Schmidt was caught and shot; killed because of you and the deals you made with him without telling me about them. You are lucky he didn't betray you. I myself would have punished you for such childish behavior." Glazman, of course, did not reply to this attack. Our staff, however, examined the matter closely. A fine German had failed because of Jews and because he had been connected not with the ghetto's fighting organization but with private persons. We were unable to find out who had betrayed him. We didn't know with whom he had been linked, and on whose advice he had worked. A first failure in an action without plan or discipline. A German saviour — a sign that all the lights had not gone out.

The mass *aktzias* in the ghetto died down. Normal living progressed as usual in cold, hunger, and hard labor. The Germans posted their daily battle orders on the walls in three languages: German, Polish and Lithuanian, told the inhabitants of cities taken in the Russian interior.

"Yesterday we took Oriol by storm."

Ten days later the Germans announced, in big headlines: "We have taken Odessa", and even before that, Kiev, Taganrov, Kharkov, and they were already fighting at Rostov on the Don, and battling for Moscow.

Between the lines one read of cities defending themselves, of citizens going out in the north Russian frost to defend their homes, their properties and their homeland.

It was the end of 1941. The life and death struggle was getting on our nerves. "We are at the outskirts of Moscow," the loudspeakers blared, but still the battle went on, day after day, without the capital being taken.

There was no news all that winter: Yesterday we took . . . The day before some other place fell . . . Every day the same style, the same expressions, the same words. The city's inhabitants grew indifferent to the white proclamations. The O.K.W. news (the Wehrmacht Command) came over the loudspeakers in all parts of the city three times a day.

In addition to the military orders of the day there were frightening bans and warnings, that dampened any desire to stand up to the Germans. "Anyone extending aid to a Jew, concealing him in his house, or selling him food — takes his life in his hands." "Because of their opposition to the new German regime, the following . . . (25 Polish citizens) have been executed by order of the city's military governor." "Because of acts of sabotage . . . ", etc., etc. The city's residents, however, never knew what acts of opposition and sabotage those executed unfortunates had committed.

One day we found a new order posted. To teach the inhabitants law and order, and to obviate disobedience to the laws, three citizens who had aided Jews and violated orders had been hung in Cathedral Square. "Go, citizens, and look at these criminals; the same will happen to anyone breaking the law, giving shelter to a Jew, or disturbing the accepted and necessary order."

The hanged men swayed in the winter wind. I didn't know who they were, or who was now mourning for them. I wanted to run away from the terror, but my legs were paralyzed, and my body had become very heavy! As I dragged my feet through the twisted streets, a new, strange, thought suddenly came to my mind: perhaps I would be hanged tomorrow. What was I to do? Instead of death I thought of the cold, the damp and the wind, which would show no pity to me either, if that were my end. Unwittingly I hastened, and by the time I reached 10 Zawalna Street I found that I was running as if pursued. Perhaps I should flee to the ghetto; leave everything and find refuge in the company of friends? Hide in my comrades' cold room on Strashun Street?

I was not the first one in the restaurant that day. Some of the workers apparently sensed my agitation.

"What's happened to you, Halina?" they asked.

"Nothing. I saw the hanged men near the Cathedral."

"Why did you go there, foolish girl? You didn't have to look." That was their answer.

They were all good Poles, but they did not have the same sense of identification with the hanged men that I did.

Meanwhile, the scope of our activity on the aryan side became more and more restricted. We found that we had erred in relying upon a fighting underground outside the ghetto and believing that it would support us with organization and equipment. We still did not realize that we would have to establish the underground against the fascist terror in Vilna by our own strength and daring. The Vilna Communists had, perhaps, preceded their comrades in other places in foregoing the tendency to act according to instructions from one center. As soon as we discovered our error, the fighting organization began to spread its wings with greater momentum and courage. Our searches outside the ghetto were not crowned with hoped-for success. By the end of that winter we still had not obtained a single pistol from outside the ghetto, not to speak of heavier arms. We had not found a single group planning armed struggle behind the lines, and ready to cooperate with us to that end. The links we made had helped us a great deal because we had managed to exploit the aryan side for the activity of some cadres and through them to obtain papers and apartments for the organization and provide for secure people to aid us in future actions. Most important: we established contacts with the other ghettoes. These activities, however, had not gone beyond assistance; they had not led to coordination and cooperation between the ghetto and the aryan side. Imprisoned within the ghetto, we did not imagine that we could obtain arms without the assistance of a Polish fighting organization, without some approach to the villages, the forest, and the outside world. At that time there were freedom-seeking Polish circles, but they never flourished. We established contact with them mainly with the help of Yadwiga and the Mother Superior. These were more liberal-democratic than the old Sanacia had been, but after a while they merged into Sikorsky's underground organization and the special liberal tone of some of those with whom we had contact no longer had any effect.What was decisive was the general line that was hostile to our aim to fight the Nazis. It is interesting to note that in that first period in Vilna, when we were making contacts with circles that had crystallized into links in the chain of the Polish civilian underground, our demands to fight already came up against a blank wall.

Our organization dug itself in. After analyzing our relationships with the outside we concluded that the main objective had not been and could not be achieved. The first arms were brought into the ghetto by our own boys. With great care and greater daring they stole them from the German units in which they worked, piece by piece, without any help from anyone. We also had a kind of civilian apparatus, consisting of people whose task it was to nose around in their non-military places of work and to provide us with information. We also succeeded in producing papers and documents which were better than those first printings on the typewriter that Glazman had stolen for a little while from the Judenrat. We were now producing printed documents, even with gothic lettering. We stopped the production of stamps by hand and improved our craftsmanship: someone created a "real" forged stamp. Of course, all these skills were at the disposal of headquarters alone, and no document was made except by joint decision.

We improved our primitive tools, but our work improved slowly and became more dangerous.

At that time headquarters decided to transfer me to other work.

Headquarters consisted of three people: Yitzhak Vittenberg, representative of the Communists in the ghetto, who was elected commander, Glazman, from the Revisionists, and Abba. We decided to organize other ghettoes, that had still not felt the danger, along Vilna's lines. Headquarters assigned me to organize a fighting center in Bialystok, since I knew the city and its conditions, and in some measure I was known there. Since Bialystok was situated half way between Vilna and Warsaw, I was also asked to establish a communications center between the two regions, now separated administratively.

I liquidated my affairs in Vilna speedily. Vitka already shared my contacts with the Poles. Luckily, the restaurant on Zavalna street, together with other Polish restaurants in the city, were closed at that time by German order. The food that fell to my share on the restaurant's closing, I moved to the ghetto. Vitka and I decided to grasp the opportunity, and suggested to the manager that she sell us the potatoes in the cellar. There weren't many buyers for those frozen, rotten potatoes, so we bought them for pennies. Vitka arranged their transfer to the ghetto. The Christmas holidays were nearing and in the ghetto the hunger and cold were increasing. We both spent Christmas in the ghetto, we ate those potatoes in all kinds of ways: fried, with oil and without, cut into little pieces and baked in the iron stove. They left a kind of strange sweetness in our mouths, making us forget our appetite and hunger for just a moment. We spent our last days in Vilna that way, and during that time Frumka also came, bringing part of the money that the Joint had promised in the negotiations with Edek. The money was intended for Vilna, to help the needy, the hungry and sick, and its official address was the pioneering movement. The Joint people had decided then to ignore the fact that the money was going to be used by the fighting underground. Frumka and Edek had assured them that they didn't know how the money would be used, that only Gitterman (one of the Joint directors — C.G.) knew.

I recall the Frumka of those days, with her dark blonde hair, longish nose and beautiful eyes. She seemed to me then like a noble Jew whose every movement, every word was imbued with love of Jews and care for their suffering. I recall her sitting in the dark, empty room of the charity restaurant run by Nissim Resnick, smoking and listening attentively, and weighing what she heard. The debate centered around the use of the money she had brought with her. It wasn't an argument over money, but over the verities of our lives. Frumka had encountered a problem she hadn't known in Warsaw. It was the new slogan: all our funds and all our resources for arms; no movement activity except self-defense.

Frumka loved the movement and cared for it like a mother. The money was meager, the Joint had been tight-fisted. How could she not help her comrades in their sufferings?

Frumka, however, did not differ with us. She was depressed and worn out. Seeing Vilna destroyed had plowed new lines in her face, saddened her and deepened her reflections.

Bialystok, My City

Armed with a transit pass from Lithuania to the Bialystok region and from the Bialystok region to Congress Poland and back, and with four similar blank forms sewn into my belt, I left the Vilna ghetto. From Wittenberg I had received a letter to a Bialystok Communist, Lolek Mintz, a cobbler by trade. After looking into his behavior in the ghetto I was supposed to ask him, in the name of his Vilna comrades, to assist me in establishing a united fighting front with his Communist comrades.

Dressed in an embroidered peasant fur with a bulging bag under my arm, in possession of the documents and with the fighting organization's first call to the Vilna Jewish youth for armed resistance, all sewn and hidden in various parts of my undergarments, I sat in the train which was taking me to my home city, Bialystok.

It was snowing again that day. It was the beginning of January 1942. The train crawled along, stopping at every station, and at every other station travel permits were examined. I was supposed to reach Bialystok toward morning of the following day. If the snow increased the train would be delayed because it would have to be cleared from the tracks. I had at least a whole day's trip before me, and a thorough examination at the Lithuanian-German border. I mustn't think only about that border inspection. I should also sleep a little if I could, if my tension was eased.

The car was almost empty, and it was very cold. I didn't pay much attention to that. There were two railway workers on board, a peasant and his wife and three other Poles of uncertain occupation. All, except the railway workers were going to stations near the border. They talked, argued about the high prices, about the amount of snow that had fallen that winter that had closed the roads, about the fuel that had not been distributed. The villagers argued with the city people. The latter proved that the villagers were "sucking the blood" from the city people. "They are getting rich while we hunger for bread," they shouted. When the German policeman came in to examine the permits the arguments ended only to resume again when he left, reaching their peak when one of the travelers mentioned the Jewish problem.

"That's just what they deserved! They bled us and ruled us together with the Bolsheviks," said one of them, the most elegant of the Poles.

"No, what they're doing to them is really too much," said the second one. "I can understand — punish them; but Pani, (sirs — C.G.), they're killing all of them."

I looked around, there was no disagreements, but not all of the passengers were taking part in the argument over the Jews. One kept quiet, another shook his head, and it was hard to understand whether that head-shaking meant pity or agreement.

Meanwhile the passengers changed and I stopped listening to their talk. My thoughts leaped from one thing to another, and I wanted to stop for a moment and concentrate on one subject. I recalled walking in my childhood, with my mother, or my nurse, my hand in theirs, and jumping on the side-walk, skipping and jumping over the holes and cracks in the asphalt.

The train's steady noise grew louder. It was growing dark and I was again changing from one subject to another. The proximity of the border and the lonely night awaiting me made it difficult to concentrate. Soon I would arrive in the city, to the streets I knew, to dear people whose faces I hadn't seen for two years. Every time I came back even after only a short absence, my heart filled with joy. True, I was a little strange at home, always busy with affairs that were not understood by my father and mother, but I was drawn towards the warmth that only a mother can bestow.

This time . . . this time my heart was filled with fear. Our house had been burned down, my father had disappeared into the Nazis' hands and my brother had not returned from the army. How was I going to meet my penniless and lonely mother and sister? To maintain self-restraint, to overcome, no matter what! Now there was another examination of travel permits and identification cards.

At the last station before the border, Marcinkantze, green-uniformed officials surrounded the cars. There was no leaving or entering. The examination took some time, and then, two by two, the border police entered the cars. They took my permit and identification card and left without saying a word. I did not understand their conduct yet I had no choice but to wait, patiently. Perhaps, they had taken the papers in order to inquire by telephone if the permit had really been issued me by the Vilna security police. Maybe I still had time to escape? After they took the papers they went into the station building, and now there were no police near the cars. Was this last moment to pass without action?

That is what I thought, as I sat quietly, waiting. The time passed quickly, and gendarmes returned. One of them handed me my papers. A stamp on the reverse side of the travel permit testified that on a certain date I had crossed the border between Lithuania and the Bialystok province. That stamp would make it easier for me to cross the second border to Warsaw, since it was proof that my papers had already been examined by the German border police. In any case the success was encouraging. It showed that they were not omniscient.

We arrived in Bialystok after waiting for hours in some isolated stations in the heart of the heavy snowfall. It was an hour before noon when I left the Bialystok railway station and turned toward the city. Once again my feet were treading the familiar sidewalks and the rough cobblestones of the Bialystok streets. This time I would look in vain for the Jews who used to crowd the ticket booth and waiting room of the station before and after every trip. In vain I would look for the old path, the life that I had left that first winter of the war. Now, I was a stranger here. I would not turn my steps toward my father's house. I would find neither the house nor its tenants. Opposite the station there was a large building that the Soviet Russians had begun to build for the railway workers. Now there were German officers there, supervising the work of Jewish girls. The latter hauled out wooden boards, washed floors and carried piles of refuse out to the street. Here I would find Rivka, my friend and roommate in Vilna. She had left Vilna on foot in order to help her aged parents in Bialystok when I moved to my first aryan apartment. After our first emotional meeting in one of the rooms, she pushed her work card into my hand and helped me attach two yellow patches on breast and back. I would have to give her back her papers early, otherwise she would not be able to return to the ghetto or to remain outside. In this city Jews were still permitted to wear furs, an exceptional privilege that long since had been taken from the Vilna Jews. In Vilna the Germans had confiscated even cheap collars that had some trace of fur upon them. I put my aryan papers in the fur and set out toward the ghetto. It was hard walking on the cobblestones all alone, with all the passersby looking at me. At that hour there were no Jewish faces to be seen in the street. These were working hours, and any Jew walking in the street without his group was suspect. I crossed the high bridge over the railway and continued along Sivientego Rohos Street. There was a German guard opposite the high church. This was apparently one of their institutions. If I had known, I would have avoided that street: I had papers that must not fall into their hands. Should I turn back? I was deliberating when a terrifying shout stopped me:

"Halt!"

I stood still.

"Where are you coming from?"

I hand over Rivka's work card.

"What do you have in your bag?"

I answered swiftly: "My boss gave me linen to launder."

"Open the bag!" Apparently my clothing and bag did not fit the yellow patches.

I opened the bag. He saw linens, and did not look into them. Now he measured me from head to toe. I cannot remember his face, I remember only his angry searching eyes. Perhaps he was disappointed. Maybe he had hoped a reward to catch some criminal. Here everything seemed to be in order. However, he did not take his eyes from me. They peered into the clothing where the false inter-city travel permits, intended to free Edek from his imprisonment, were sewn. Once more he looked at the bag. I thought. In a minute he would look into the side pocket and discover the hidden aryan papers. Suddenly his hand touched my breast. The sentry had discovered that the two ends of the Star of David were not sewn properly, and I felt a hard slap on my cheek. The patch on my back was sewn even worse, and again I received a slap, and then another. When he saw that I was still standing erect he let me go.

"Raus! Get away from here."

My blood boiled. I had not expected this. In my fearful nightmares I had seen Germans shooting at me, chasing me. But slapping my face? I had not expected that. I considered that an insult, a mockery of my goal. My cheeks burned. I was ashamed of myself. For the first time I wished I had a pistol.

That was the way my home city received me.

I reached the ghetto without any trouble. I was not stopped at the gate. With accelerated steps I arrived at the street where our comrades lived. That was the only address I had. Where my mother was I still did not know.

From that street gate it was only a few steps to where our comrades were living. Our training kibbutz had once been located in that court and on the side, near the doorway, were stairs. It was there that Malka Shapira, a veteran movement member, lived. The house was a "Shomer" one. In the attic there was a small apartment, with a smaller room near the entry, then a larger one, and a tiny kitchen. I arrived during the common noon meal. I found it strange, but this ghetto seemed warmer, with more light than the Vilna ghetto. I breathed freely among my comrades. I found them all sitting at the table, talking loudly, making jokes. When I entered they surrounded me with concern and questions until one of them, chased the others, took my bag, and my peasant fur, and sat me down on the old couch near the table with a plate of hot soup. That was Chaika Ribak. In addition, there were Yandzia, Rivkele, Sarah Gabeltof and three members of the Shomer concentration in Vilna, who had come back after fleeing the Germans when the army sealed the road. The movement veterans and activists were here, members of kibbutz "Lamivhan"*; Zerah Silberberg, Gedalya Shayak and Ephraim Strikovsky. This was a Shomer family living in total communality. My first fear that I would not find active members evaporated. The presence of such a group of people was a pleasant surprise.

"How did the trip go?"

"Fine."

"How did you get into the ghetto?"

I told them of Rivka's help, and that I had to give her back her papers right away.

There were two meetings I was afraid of in the Bialystok ghetto. The first — with my mother. How would I find her? I was afraid that I would not be able to bear seeing her hungry and cold. I feared I would disappoint her; she probably believed that I was all-powerful, and how would I be able to continue my dangerous work before her all seeing eyes?

I was also afraid of my meeting with my kids, the members of the Tel-Amal group. It was on these youngsters whom I had left in a prosperous Soviet situation that I put my hopes and that I sought support. What had happened to them?

Mother I found, aged and weak, unlike her natural self. How much she had changed. It was only two years since I had seen her. Her hair was completely white and her cheeks had sunk. She was wearing a summer coat in the middle of the hard winter. She lived in someone else's home, without clothes or cover. Everything had been burned on that catastrophic night. I was amazed to find that her spirit had not been broken. And my sister was just like her. Both worked hard to support themselves, somehow to hold out against their distress. My sister smuggled things out of the ghetto and sold them to her gentile friends. With the money she bought half a kilo of butter, a little cheese, and especially vegetables. She hid them all in her basket and sold them in the ghetto. That was an honorable living, if somewhat risky. She had enough for bread and sometimes also was able to smear it with butter and cheese. How grateful I was to them for not even hinting that I must help them. Without understanding why I was outside the ghetto, they believed that my work was devoted to some great purpose, they never sought to investigate or ask about that high purpose. They asked no questions and did not question my actions. Only from their deep and understand-

* Hebrew — "To the Test!"

ing silence did I guess how many sleepless nights they spent worrying about me in my days and weeks of absence from the ghetto.

Dear mother, how pure you became in those days: Always a simple woman, loving your children and husband and seeking only their welfare and happiness. You did not understand much about the aspirations of the new age, the new trends at work in literature, art and science. You left the big world to father, for him to judge, you relied upon his intelligence. In our movement's direction, however, you sensed, with your mother's intuition, the new trends in society and culture, which not having read about them in books, you read in our hearts. I never told you, when I left the house, where I was going. I always strove to save you and myself the pain of the long hours between decision and deed.

No, my meeting with my mother did not disappoint me. I was shocked at the sight of her weak and withered body, though her mother's heart was as brave as ever.

I was to remain in Bialystok a week or two, and then return after a short visit to Warsaw. That evening, my first in the ghetto, we sat together to share our first reports — I of Vilna, and they of Bialystok.

During their short stay in Bialystok the members of the Vilna group had managed to establish a movement center in the ghetto. That was not an insignificant matter. Now there was an address, a meeting place for our comrades in the evening even without a formal meeting. Here they came to receive encouragement, to advise on work affairs and matters of the movement membership, to seek answers for their many questions, to tell and hear about the fronts and to bring information about ghetto institutions, the police and their traitorous hirelings. Most important — it was here they came in time of trouble. The house was like a mother and father, caring for their children. Here anyone who hungered for bread came, anyone who did not have shoes for work and also those with means who did not want to help a hungry friend directly. Here all the movement's values were joined in its social work. Here there were no rich and no poor, all were equal. Here views and thoughts were argued, for better organization. All this was not done without a great deal of effort. First of all, there was the matter of the apartment. It had been necessary to seek and find it despite the ghetto crowds. Second, funds were required to maintain the communal kitchen, and lastly, some "legal" cover was needed for the presence of the "immigrants". All these had cost large sums of money which had been obtained only by the vigorous insistence of our comrades, of Yandzia among them, appearing before the ghetto institutions as representatives of an organized group that knew what it wanted to do. Either because they still did not know to whom they were giving all that money, or because they believed that "it did not pay" to get involved with these people, the ghetto institutions yielded to our demands. True, they did so with difficulty and only in part, but still they were the first who — unwittingly — helped to lay the foundations of the fighting underground.

That work had only begun. The young people were drawn to the movement but they still had not been told clearly what new tasks the times had imposed upon them. What is more, our own comrades had as yet not been organized in the strict form demanded by a militant underground.

Meanwhile the city sights passed before my eyes. The scenes followed one another, one harsher than the next. I drove them away but they reappeared. The city center where the town clock had been — the heart of a population of 120,000 persons, half of them Jews. Here there had been a small dry goods store where mother used to buy the cloth for my khaki scout uniforms. A short distance from there lived Reb Sender the "smith", whose forefathers once had been blacksmiths and who himself owned a decent shop, with laborers working for him, and had even built himself a house. There, too, at the top of Suraska Street, stood a fine building on whose second floor was the apartment where I had lived and dreamed my youthful dreams. There my movement trainees had come to consult with me, and to pour out their young hearts.

There were streets here, winding, narrow and littered, the homes of impoverished and oppressed Jews. It was from these streets that the Jewish revolt originated, and the Jewish self-defense, in 1905. Here the Bund and the Russian S. D. parties had come into being. When the socialist Zionist movement developed, it too spilled over into these streets. In the center there was a square, not large, and in that square was a synagogue, that had given its name to all this strange maze: "Der Shulhoif." Some distance away there was a street called "Shmuel Schmidt's Gessel", that I always unthinkingly identified with Reb Sender, who owned a shop there. Here there was everything: big and small shopkeepers, peddlers, wagon-drivers, craftsmen, "heder melameds" and school teachers, scholars, Hassidim and Misnagdim, revolutionaries and petite bourgeoisie. Behind that "main" street and the alleys was the Jewish market, before the city markets were built.

It was dense a Jewish community, varied, crowded and pressed together, oppressed, and involved in its internal conflicts, accepting its fate and the burden of anti-Semitism submissively. Everything was here, the whole life of a generation living between two eras and under two regimes. Now these lives had been erased as if they never existed. Fields of snow stretched from the town clock to the forest. Where were the houses, the shops, the draftsmen? Where were the peddlers and the wagoners? Where was the

Great Synagogue? A community razed, crushed into the ghetto. Narrow, foot-trodden paths crossed the fields and led directly from Kostiushko Square, where the clock had been, from the center of Jewish Bialystok, to the forest. They had shortened the road. The streets no more. Only the rusty iron skeleton of the Great Synagogue remained, lying on its side like an uprooted giant tree. The remains had dwindled, and the iron columns, the tiny frame of lives that had once been, were all twisted.

On June 27, 1941 the Germans had occupied the city a second time[1]*; this time — during their invasion of the USSR. Their first task was to kill, and to burn Jews alive, together with their possessions. First they set fire to the synagogue and threw every man who fell into their hands into the fire. They picked up everyone they found who had a Jewish nose. Anyone trying to escape was shot. About a thousand Jewish men were burned to death. The fire spread from the synagogue to the Jewish neighborhood. The little wooden houses in the "Shulhoif" alleys went up in flames like matchboxes. The Germans threw grenades into the houses. Some managed to escape; the others were burned alive. Germans collected the men in groups and shot them. They went from house to house, skipping only the Polish ones. A Polish "guide" showed them the way, and he never made a single mistake. They completed the work of annihilation to the very end, to the last stone, to the last wall. About two thousand people, mostly men, young and old, were shot, burned or tortured to death. The survivors of that Friday slaughter later said — women of their husbands and children of their fathers — "He was one of the Fridayers."

They went on to relate that on these streets they had kidnapped Jews on Thursday; 300 Jews who never returned. Then on Saturday about 4,000 more Jews were kidnapped, and they too did not return. Just outside of the city, in Pietrashy, where I used to go on hikes with youngsters, they were all shot. Since they had all been kidnapped, and killed — their debts had to be paid and so they imposed a tax on the city's remaining Jews payable in gold and silver: five kilograms of gold and 20 kilograms of silver. The Jews took out their old silver candlesticks, their gold earings and sabbath vessels and paid the required amounts. Then the city quieted down and matters proceeded "normally". They imprisoned the Jews in the ghetto, made them wear yellow patches front and back. The "Judenrat" was set up, and "all's well with Israel."[2]

Here was the ghetto: busy, noisy and alive; living as best it could. In the ghetto — the surviving remnants, symbols of another life, were the youth.

* Numbered notes refer to Notes beginning on page 400.

These were the young whose senses had not been dulled, and whose memory had not failed. It was to them I was going today. It was to them I would come with demands and encouragement, a militant consciousness and a warm heart. I remembered how I had left them during the Soviet period, and had gone to wander, and steal across border. I remembered our last meeting, my last remarks: "It is hard to know what tomorrow will bring. But we know how we want to live, whatever the conditions." I had added, in my naivete and ignorance of what was to come: "They will not frighten us, we shall hold out even under wartime conditions." Then I had left them to their fates. Perhaps I had thought that they would organize by themselves? Do I know what they are like today, what has happened to them? After all, life had shown its ugliness and brutality to them, too. Had they remained the same good, clear-eyed children of two years ago? Perhaps they despaired and turned away? Only a few days ago 5,000 Jews had been driven out of the ghetto to Prushany[3]. The weak, the poor, the refugees had been driven out, all those who had no patrons in the Judenrat. Perhaps my "kids", too, had come to the conclusion that it was preferable to belong to the "establishment" — the police or the Judenrat? Life was hard and brutal. One had to fight for existence. Here young people were liable to despair easily, to have their spirits broken in one blow: It's all words, life isn't literature. I would have to prepare a program for the meeting, to arrange it properly, with the purpose clearly in mind.

I finally decided not to make any decision. After all, these were living people. I had left them two years ago when they were still boys and girls, virtually children, and now they were persons who the times had quickly matured. I would wait, see and then decide.

That evening there was to be a meeting of the Tel Amal group. Only those who had remained together clinging to each other were invited.

It was already dark in the ghetto. At 10 Bialostochanska Street, tall, blonde and bright-eyed Avraham lived with his family. He had a small side room, with a separate entrance. The blinds were drawn, the doors closed, and only after using the secret knock was it possible to enter. They had done their work well. In the ghetto they still weren't too strict with the young. They weren't forbidden to have a little fun in their rooms, to talk about anything they liked. The Germans didn't pay much attention to trifles like that. Jewish talk didn't concern them. Still, caution was preferable. This was not a regular meeting: a secret emissary had come to them. They had, therefore, prepared carefully. Zerach and I found them all seated — on the bed, on the floor, on the small table. What joy was in their faces! They were happy at the meeting and looked forward to the future,whatever it might bring.

That meeting was one of our most profound experiences. It demanded activity, disturbed our rest, reminded us that we had still done very little, that we could do much more. It was our credo. Here we had young people who didn't want to compromise. Until now we had taught them theory — now we had to turn to deeds.

Skipping the usual opening explanations, I took out the Call that Abba had written to the Vilna youth. When I finished reading it I added: "Our youth in Vilna has decided to act in keeping with the Call."

The room was very quiet. The 35 young people crowded around me. They sat expectantly, waiting patiently, for some one to tell them what they had to do, this very evening, tomorrow, the day after — on all the coming days. What were they to do immediately in response to the call?

"So, what are we to do?", Avramele's eyes lit up. His long arms, stretching out of his too-short sleeves, moved in the air as if seeking something to grasp.

Only Yentel remained sunk in thought. Suddenly, she spoke up:

"Wait! I want to think carefully. We learned and read so much about heroism, self-sacrifice and daring. The movement educated us to live without petty egoism, about communal living, pioneering, and some greater social goals. What, then, are we going to do now? Break up the group? We can no longer educate for communal Shomer life; that has no point now, it is no longer the main end. We are not going to get to Eretz Yisrael nor be privileged to live in a kibbutz. So, perhaps we must abandon all those fine things which seem so childish today and turn our attention to weapons and live like an army? The way we decide will determine how we organize."

"The movement comes first," said Chava, always extreme, sometimes to the point of blindness.

"What do you mean, movement? It doesn't mean anything if it does not lead us along the right road. The movement isn't an abstract concept, some first principle."

"You are denying the main idea, Yentel," Chava called out.

Sender, who had been sitting in a corner where I couldn't see him, suddenly stood up. How tall he had grown:

"I don't think the discussion is going properly. If I have to die tomorrow I want to die as I lived, as a Shomer, with all that it implies."

Blonde Roshka added:

"Correct."

Then I spoke. I said a great deal; about what awaited us, about the catastrophe that had befallen the Lithuanian Jews, about fascism, whose true nature had only now been revealed to us, about the ghetto the Nazis had created, which we must see as a function of Nazi doctrines for the destruction of all the achievements of the 20th century and of 20th century Marxist theory, of humanity, honesty and justice. The ghetto was not a form of Jewish autonomy, as many believed, but an instrument with which first to kill our spirits, and then our bodies. The ghetto was intended to annihilate our people, to wipe it off the face of the earth. I spoke of the great illusion, of the "scheins" the Germans had inaugurated in the Vilna ghetto, of their intention of creating new social classes, new division, all leading to destruction and death but giving the Jew the illusion that he was of a special rank and immune to death, since the Germans had granted him a special "schein". In that way they were killing our people's souls, draining essential logic and common sense, corrupting the healthy instincts of an organized public. I showed them that it would also happen here, otherwise the Germans would not have created the ghetto and set up the police and the Judenrat. The Germans were not seeking to help the Jews, but to harm them. Why had they granted them autonomy, ostensible self-government? So they would fight each other, undermine the simple human solidarity of suffering people.

They sat tense, absorbing every word. Suddenly, one of them said:

"I thought, better to have the "Judenrat" than German rule within the ghetto; better a Jewish police than the Gestapo standing at the gate and keeping order within the ghetto."

"Yes comrades, we'll come back to these problems and discuss them. In our work we will come up against those whose ways of acting and different concepts conflict with ours. To all these we will have to know how to reply properly. First of all, to ourselves, so that we can direct our actions toward the essentials. We cannot make mistakes! Remember that — neither as individuals nor all of us together as a group.

The meeting began to break up. "First comrades, the first step toward our goal: Sealed lips!"

When Zerach and I returned from the meeting we were exhilarated. We kept quiet, but we were happy and relieved. The main point, the essential ingredient was there — we had people!

The Bialystok ghetto was different from the other ghettoes we had seen or head about. The Bialystok ghetto was relatively quiet and comfortable. It had many streets, the crowding was not dangerous, the dirt wasn't as widespread and there was a greater feeling of freedom there than in the other ghettoes. In the ghetto center there were a number of parks and large empty lots. The space and the greenery gave this ghetto a different kind of look. The watch over it was not too strict either, and it was possible to obtain entry and exit permits. That is: Jews could come in and go out by special permit, without their work group or a German guard. Jews sometimes even obtained permission to travel by train. These were, of course, a few persons with good luck. Internal government in the ghetto was completely in the hands of the Judenrat Vice-Chairman, the engineer Barash, and his assistants. When Germans did come into the ghetto they were only there as inspectors of health, work, employment, economics, cleanliness and the like. They only saw what Barash showed them. The Jews in there were tranquil at that time, they trusted their leader and thought him all-powerful. Barash looked for and found solutions for all the problems. Throughout the ghetto it was whispered that Barash knocked on the doors of the German institutions, that he promised great things, wriggled between their avaricious fingers, and played on their greed for valuables[4]. He filled the Germans with promises, and saved the Jews from harmful new decrees. Jews had seen Barash's carriage returning to the ghetto, he had been seen in the palace housing the supreme civilian bodies, the "Zivilverwaltung", talking freely with the "Chief" himself. Barash was not afraid of the officials; every Jew could tell miraculous stories about that. He was wise and intelligent, he was a good Jew, and most important — the Jews were peacefully occupied in their jobs. The ghetto was working, all the Jews, big and little, men and women. The factories were humming, producing shoes, soldiers' winter-boots, hats for the army, warm clothing and linen for the front. Women were knitting, by hand or machine, gloves and ear-muffs of warm wool. The warehouses were filled with raw materials; emptied every day and filled anew. Barash didn't like lazy people: "We need working people, we'll buy our lives with work.[5]" Every day Jews saw his carriage hitched to the black horse galloping from the ghetto and back. His gray head rocked, disappeared and an hour later reappeared. He disappeared into the Judenrat building and once again left the ghetto. Barash's office was not open to all. Only people involved with work, heads of the Judenrat departments, factory heads, his secretaries and assistants came to him. Others saw him only in movement. Sometimes Jews saw him laugh and then the rumor spread throughout the ghetto: our situation was apparently going to improve. Barash was generally busy, and it was hard even to catch his eye in passing. His vehicle, therefore, had become a hero, an "important person" whom the Jews plied with their questions. It was necessary to know what the situation was.

The Jews lived with their illusions, and there was no one to shake them loose. The ghetto was productive, there was no room for fear. And still . . . Jews did not feel secure. Every day they sought proof that danger was not impending. Every day they wanted new proof, to strengthen their faith. A few refugees had arrived from Slonim. All there had been executed in

November 1941, and only a small number escaped to the forests and fought. Most had been killed, and only a few survived to reach Bialystok. What of Bielorussia and Lithuania? A strange document was passed from hand to hand, the testimony of a woman who had fled from the execution pit in Ponar; those who didn't read it heard fragments. But here, too, matters had not always gone well: where were those who had been incinerated that Friday in the synagogue? And what about those taken Saturday and on Thursday? No, they had not returned, and as a kind of hymn to their suffering Jews sang the sad song of "Rivkele die Shabbasdike", that is — Rivke who had been widowed on that Saturday. Why, too, were high-ranking Germans coming every day to demand more and more? Jews were compelled to hand over the last of their savings and treasures, all their belongings, their coats, their furs, and furniture that they had planned to sell in time of need in order to buy bread. Many of the Jews wanted to see in Barash, in his smile and pride, their dwindling strength and dissipating security, the last remnant of Jewish pride, trampled day by day. Yes, things were different here, many said, and thought of Barash as their omnipotent savior.

There was a debate among our comrades: should I appear before Barash? If so, how? The matter was not simple. Barash himself was a loyal Jew; he wouldn't betray me to the Gestapo. He was not an informer; but he believed that he would save the ghetto by his intercession, or by bribery, and by our being "good Jews," and diligent workers. Unwittingly, he was carrying out a hopeless mission and inevitably would betray us if some radical change did not take place in time. What change, however, could he make? His path was a slippery one and it was easy to fall. He was deluding the Jews and lulling them to sleep. Was it worth trying to win Barash over? Was it worthwhile, with such dismal prospects, logically almost impossible, to try to convince him to change his ways? Was it worthwhile to reveal ourselves to him?

It was decided, in the end, that I would go to him, not to tell him about the movement, but to let him know the truth about the annihilation. It was also important to look him over. Perhaps we could succeed in extracting from him some administrative relaxations for our work. In any case, we believed that it was worth exploiting every opportunity and every resource, without revealing our aims. We knew he believed that I was only a refugee. The friendly discussion made me realize that he thought I was an emissary from the Zionist movement in Vilna[6], and that suited me very well. Barash was a veteran General Zionist and even in the ghetto he had not concealed his views. In order for us to be able to talk freely he invited me to come to his home at 8 o'clock.

"How will I return after curfew?"

"Everything will be all right," he smiled at me, accompanied me to the door and pressed my hand firmly. When I left his room all those waiting their turn stared at me. Anybody that Barash received was not just a nobody in the ghetto. The looks of those sitting there waiting reminded me once again: *Look into their eyes and you will see how mistaken and misleading Barash is. The day will come, there is no doubt, when they will turn against their leader and no longer give him their trust; you and your comrades (it is not hard to know who they are in the ghetto) will be considered his confederates and you, too, will not be trusted any longer.*

I came to Barash at the appointed hour. I was received by his wife, who knew of my visit. She was a simple woman who could not find words to express her surprise at my aryan appearance. She was especially excited when she learned that I had come "all the way from Vilna." She was a dentist, a likable Jew, devoted to her husband and overly concerned for him. Barash arrived after a few minutes. He came into the room in a rush. In the ghetto, too, as well as in his office, he was always in the same hurry. His apartment was pleasantly warm. He lived in one room of a spacious apartment. The formal chairman of the Judenrat, the aged Rabbi Rosman, lived in the other rooms. Except for courtesy visits and meetings, he did not appear in the Judenrat and did not deal with public affairs. His deputy was the real chairman.

After the hostess served tea, Barash began to talk with us as though we were old acquaintances. He told me of thousands of decrees which he had hidden from the public and fought alone to have them rescinded. He told me of the praise and compliments given him by high-ranking Germans for his exemplary organization of the ghetto.

"Do you know, every day we produce 300 full sets of military clothing," he said with pride[7].

"That is, you clothe 300 Nazi soldiers on the front," I blurted out and immediately regretted my carelessness.

Barash's face clouded. I saw that I had hit his weak point, and this was further proven during the discussion. I tried to correct the mistake but I did not succeed. From then on, the thread of the discussion was cut every few moments and I could not change it. I told him all about Vilna, about the annihilation and its methods, the compulsory labor, the hunger and sickness. In the end I told him of the betrayal of the Judenrat in helping in the liquidation of the little ghetto, and about the police going through the houses to help roust Jews out of their hiding places.

"It is our opinion that that is not only a Vilnaite or Lithuanian phenomenon, or Bielorussian. We Vilnaites believe that it is not a regional problem but a national one, and that the annihilation which began in our city will eventually be general and total. What do you think?"

"Now it becomes difficult for me to answer. You are shaking my security. Still, that won't happen here, without it becoming known to me a long time in advance."

"And then?"

"Then I will hurry to alert all the Jews so that they may be able to save their lives."

"But they don't kill all of them at once."

"I don't believe that what happened in Vilna will take place in Bialystok. The Germans I know will not dare to act that way. Only if they send executioners from Berlin . . . Then . . ." Here he stopped for a moment, "They will inform me then. No! No! They will not use the Vilna methods here. They need us. In any case, for the time being we can live in peace. I would like to tell your people about what is happening in the ghetto. You should know about it. But I am afraid of the young people, they are liable to do foolish things. You absolutely must not take responsibility into your hands. I will always know in advance if something is going to happen. Don't do things on your own."

After that Barash would tell me many things that weren't known within the ghetto. There was a Jew working there at that time, named Zelikovich[8]. He was a Gestapo man, and it was well known, although they didn't know who might be the victim of his treachery. Zelikovich was more of a businessman than a traitor. He was apparently more afraid of the political people than of the wealthy, and the smugglers. When a Jew dealt in smuggling cattle Zelikovich would inform on him, and then ransom him for money which he shared with his German confederates. He occupied himself with extortion and his house was filled with valuable objects. Zelikovich was not alone in his occupation. He gathered about himself a group of dark characters who served him and enjoyed his generosity. He worked against Barash, spied on him and frustrated many of his plans. When Barash bribed a German of one of the institutions Zelikovich would inform another institution about it. He stirred up trouble and served everybody in turn. When pressed to the wall he would admit everything. When "illegal refugees"[9] who, according to German plans, had been supposed to die like their brothers in Vilna or Slonim or Volkovysk arrived, Zelikovich felt Volkovysk's duty to betray them to the authorities. We, too, had become objects of interest to him. He also used to move around outside the ghetto without the yellow patches, in order to discover Jews daring to pass as aryans. It was Barash who warned us when Zelikovich began to show interest in us.

Barash used to tell us about all the questions the officals of the German institutions asked him about the ghetto and especially about those of us who had come from Vilna. He gave us the names of traitors who were still unknown to the ghetto. At that first meeting I had asked Barash for a number of things: legalization for our comrades, their formal registration in the ghetto register and in work, and permits for some of us to move about the ghetto after curfew. We also wanted to be able to leave the ghetto during the day (we would remove the patches and pose as aryans; the problem was getting out) and legalization for the kibbutz as a charity kitchen.

Barash granted all our requests. Some things depended upon other Judenrat officals, and he therefore asked that I return the next day. He would issue the instructions. Throughout the meeting I sensed that Barash was eager to maintain contact with us, since he wanted to know what we were doing. He was too clever to ask direct questions. It was on that basis that our relationship developed. He wanted to know what we were doing and we exploited his potentialities. Neither side was ever fully satisfied.

Later on, things did not always work out as we had hoped and planned. We were not the only ones maintaining contact with him. Our relationship was not organized for a long time, just as the underground movements were not organized.

The following day the exit permit for all hours of the day was in my pocket. Barash knew that I was moving about the city but didn't fear that I would betray him if I was caught. I wondered why he acted in that way, without any hesitation. For a long time I wondered at his courage in not hesitating to take great risk when he thought it important. He also gave me exit permits for other comrades. He did not ask me for what purpose, and his silence spoke for itself. It also raised the question: why? Was it only because of his esteem for us that he did so? No, he was too clever to be sentimental toward the youth. The matter of the kitchen would also be settled, he said. He only had to apply to the head of the economic department and receive his agreement.

The head of the department was one of the city's well-known Zionist personalities, Goldberg, the father of a young girl, a member of the ken (Hashomer Hatzair branch) who had studied in Moscow during the Soviet era and had remained there. I knew him, and he knew me. He was not too enthusiastic about Hashomer Hatzair but he thought its members nice children who, in the course of time, would awaken from their childish dreams. He related to his splendid daughter in the same way. He received me hospitably and I entered without waiting my turn and thought the matter arranged. To my great surprise he began to speak to me seriously.

"You know that I know you and your family, and I trust you. I will therefore speak frankly. I have been a Zionist and remain a Zionist. The chalutz movements are very precious to me. I think we must help the chalutzim to maintain themselves . . . True, I was never very enthusiastic about all kinds of foolishness and the communist ideas you taught my Estusha. I am sure, however, that you are good Jews. But all kinds of rumors have reached me to the effect that you are publicizing mistaken information and calling on the Jews to act stupidly and irresponsibly, to make war. Is that true? Have you become Communists and partisans? Are you waiting for the Red Army, eh?"

Blood rushed to my face. I wanted to answer him properly, to prove that he was suffering from blindness and did not see what was in store. Here he was, sitting in his imaginary kingdom, distributing food rations to the Jews and believing that the government was in his hands. His narrow-mindedness, stubbornness and blind hatred of communism were all leading him astray. He apparently believed that the Germans were not really so bad. I should throw the German rations, the hunger rations he was distributing to the Jews, at his feet. He was satisfied, too satisfied. I controlled myself, kept my self-restraint. Let that little man, so important in his own eyes, even proud of his Zionism, think that we are "only" chalutzim. Did he know what a chalutz was? He was apparently a Zionist, but he had never really grasped what a chalutz was. He had never known or understood his own Shomeret daughter. I couldn't change him. To the end he would consider himself one of the elect and forget that it was the Nazis who had chosen him and granted him his imaginary power. He was actually only the emissary, their small and despicable servant. To the end of his days and to the last Jew, he would think that someone could hide himself from the Jewish tragedy and continue to live after the great holocaust. People like that should be exploited. They should unknowingly serve the war against the Nazis, serve the needs of the underground. It was right to exploit people like that.

He was not like Barash, nor like the tens of others we met in the course of our struggle for places to live, places to hide, for pennies and for food.

"Who told you such foolishness?" I asked him, "Do I look like a partisan?"

"Of course I trust you; you are the daughter of Nachum Grossman."

I received all the documents, the permits and the slips of paper, and from then on we ran our economy at his expense. The addresses we later obtained in the ghetto, the meetings we held, all these were accomplished with the help of the documents he had signed with his own hand, certifying that our house was a restaurant for the poor.

In the ghetto the poor were not few in number. The ghetto also consisted of a whole new aristocracy, wealthy persons — speculators and large-scale smugglers, middle-men, dealers in precious stones and currency. There were also working people, the largest section, maintaining themselves with difficulty and struggling for their living. At the bottom were the beggars, the eaters in the charity restaurants, the street nomads, sick and slowly melting away, like wax candles. These were a varied and well-known group, every one with his own illness, his own madness.

The most famous of the madmen, who was allowed to say anything he wanted, was Feingold. He used to walk the streets and tell the passersby in a loud voice about the corruption of the Judenrat Jews and in a joking manner would tell "secrets" about their lives of luxury at the expense of the hungry Jews; about their wine and women. Suddenly he shouted out loud. He was asked why he shouted that way: "Everyone says that Sobotnik has two lovers, and I must convince them that he has only one," he replied, and continued his shouting. Sobotnik was the ghetto "minister" of finances and we later came up against him, too. In the course of the flood of seemingly foolish talk, Feingold would repeat the names of communities on the eastern front where the Red Army was heroically holding out in its struggle against the Nazis, places that were unknown to the Jews imprisoned in the ghetto, thousands of kilometers away. That was the time of the Soviet's first stand at the front, of the first encirclement of General Kleist's regiments, and later of Schmidt's.

The ghetto lived its life, struggled, looked for some light in the darkness around it. Outwardly it was placid, laboring and submissive.

One day our comrades were caught for compulsory labor. Zerach, Gedalya and Yandzia had to go. The work was hard, unbearable. They had to push wagons full of peat for kilometers, and when they became too tired they were beaten bloody. When the Germans saw that our comrades didn't bow their heads, they intensified their blows.

That evening we were deeply depressed. The day's experiences were most recognizable in Yandzia. A number of times he started to say something but then kept silent. We discovered a reason the next day. Yandzia hadn't been able to stand the test and had begged for mercy, and that plea for mercy was apparently the reason for his depression.

Warsaw — Groping in the Dark and Looking for Allies

I had a letter in my pocket to a Communist, Lolek Mintz. How was I to find him among the 50,000 Jews? Among the members of the Tel-Amal group there was a girl who had joined them in the ghetto; her name was Chanka. Her mother who came from the well-known Patt family, was the sister of Jacob Patt, and close to leftist and communist circles. Before the war she had lived in Warsaw and had worked in the Soviet legation as a teacher for the children of the staff. The information I gathered indicated that it would be worthwhile to know that woman. She was a well-known educator, and, politically, a member of Left Poalei Zion*. She was in charge of the big orphan asylum in the ghetto. When I told Chanka that I wanted to meet her mother she didn't ask many questions, and arranged a meeting.

Sheina Patt-Levine was a frail woman with streaks of grey in her black hair. She had deep, dark eyes covered by heavy lashes with sunken cheeks, and tight lips. She was very interesting in a discussion, but when she walked in the street one hardly noticed her; she looked like an ordinary working woman. I told her that I was looking for a fellow who had been a member of the Communist Party, called Lolek Mintz, a shoemaker by trade.

"I don't know him. Maybe you'd like to meet somebody from the Communists?"

"I'd like it very much," I replied, "maybe they can find Mintz."

Sheina laughed; her smile was swallowed up in her live eyes, her heavy brows. She invited me to the orphan asylum. "At this opportunity I will introduce you to someone who, I think, is one of their central personalities." Later I learned that Sheina had found places as teachers in the asylum for many women who the Gestapo was seeking. One of these was Chaya.

The asylum was situated on the second floor of a large building, opposite the ghetto hospital, on Fabrychna Street. I found Sheina in a white robe,

* Left-wing Labor political party.

walking among the little beds and the crying, shouting, laughing children. How much love and courage emanated from her thin tired face. Sheina was mother and educator to more than 100 children in the orphanage, and the head of the institution. She moved about the narrow passages between the beds, saying a good word, smiling, or humming a song the children liked. It was afternoon and the children had awakened. Only slowly did I become accustomed to the sight of their big sad, adult eyes looking at me fearfully. Even Sheina was unable to dissipate that fear. The despairing efforts of the workers were also of no avail; there were shortages of linen, clothing, diapers; there was a lack of food that could not be replaced by a caress. Sheina could tell dozens of stories about each child. She took me into the storeroom.

A few minutes later Chaya came in.

"I am looking for Lolek Mintz. Can you help me?"

"Yes. Come to number 2 on this street; in Frieda Feld's room we will be able to talk. Frieda will be there, and also Mintz." The meeting was a short one. Chaya was no longer young. I do not remember her face, we met only twice. She wasn't a member of the organization's cadres at the time of the occupation. Perhaps she had been given some internal function. The third and last time I saw her was on August 16, 1943, among the fighters along the fence on Smolna Street.

Frieda, too, was an educator in the asylum. They worked different shifts so as not to appear together in public. The evening meeting was well prepared. Tea was served in Frieda's room, and no uninvited persons came in. Their caution seemed to me to be exaggerated. Apparently, they were unable to free themselves from the memory of past experiences that did not match the new situation.

When I gave Lolek the letter the tension eased, and the discussion flowed freely. I told them about Vilna. Some of the things sounded strange to them:

"Vittenberg has united with the Zionist parties, even with the Revisionists?"

"Yes, in order to fight the invader together. You have heard about the methods of total annihilation. Without fighting we will not be able to exist as Jews, as a people, and especially as members of revolutionary parties."

"Yes, we have heard about Hashomer Hatzair. You are more progressive; but what about the others?"

"Comrades, let us put aside our political differences. Are we going to establish a united front to fight the invader or not? Are you prepared for a principled and practical discussion? On the Vilna pattern, of course."

After we left the tension disappeared. We spoke as friends. Lolek Mintz was unable to control his emotions over receiving the letter and the greeting and also at hearing of my adventures: how I had sneaked across borders to get here, how I had come all the way from Vilna to look for him so that he could be the link between us and his party comrades. He was a simple worker who was eager for action, he was moderate, deliberate and energetic.

"I'll tell you the truth," Frieda said, "first of all, I want to congratulate you on your courageous and militant initiative. We admire you for the daring of your ideas. We, here, however, are not a deciding body. We shall consult and find some way. Perhaps we can meet tomorrow. Can you?"

"Yes, but you will have to hurry. I have been looking for you for almost two weeks. I am going to Warsaw shortly and I would like to hear something from you before my trip."

Frieda replied: "You are not correct, Chaika. Look, first of all we weren't a separate Jewish party in the Soviet period, but members of the great big party of the Soviet Union. Most of the cadres fled eastward and the Gestapo did its work on the rest. We were the first ones the Gestapo looked for by name. We were the only ones looked for by name. Do you understand what that fact means? Second, after we come to know each other more closely we will also tell you about our present activities."

I understood what she was saying. The conclusion I drew was simple, and worrying. They were still not organized as a party and were still only circles of members and sympathizers. There was as yet no underground Communist Party in the ghetto, unlike Vilna with its dynamic Vittenberg, Hiena Barowsky, Shershavsky and other comrades.

After I told them that I was going to Warsaw a new possibility arose. One of their comrades had recently been called to Warsaw and was there now. This very day they would look into all the details.

On the morrow I received the following answer: the program for a united front to fight against the invader was acceptable to them. They welcomed our initiative but they could not make any move toward cooperation with movements they had always combatted without instructions from on high. I would be fulfilling an important function if I would carry a letter to Warsaw, to a Yosef Lewartowsky, outlining the program I had suggested here, and bring back an answer in writing. I agreed. Sheina herself told me about Lewartowsky, and after that we would consult her on all matters. She was our older counsellor, and she knew the Communists. I told her of my first talk with Frieda and her response was:

"If Yosef were here we wouldn't need any long negotiations. He would decide and then convince his comrades." After I had received the letter I asked Sheina once more about Lewartowsky. "He was called to Warsaw directly by the organization, she said. "We do not know exactly where he is, or what he is doing. We have no communicatons with Warsaw, and if you succeed in linking them to the capital maybe they will succeed in liberating themselves from their isolation and adapt their views of the new situation. Many of them do not understand that their experiences do not exactly fit the present situation."

It was hard for me to understand where Sheina the educator, locked up in the asylum, had gained her knowledge of the experiences and complications of the present. Only later did she reveal her secret to Edek. In any case, we relied upon her, her understanding and resourcefulness.

I made my way to Warsaw safely. At Malkinia, half way to Warsaw, the train was once again surrounded and its passengers ordered out. Once again the cars were inspected to see whether anyone was hidden within. At the customs station they searched through our papers and belongings. One woman in front of me was taken out of line and to a side room. The police apparently suspected her and would undress her and search her from head to foot. I approached the high counter. Ahead of me was a peasant. He handed over his papers, and I looked over his shoulder at his permit: it had a long stamp.

Yes, I thought, he won't pass. The railway police like round stamps. Indeed, he was taken aside and I was called. The police were not courteous. I handed over my transit pass and attempted to turn it over so that the stamp from the Lithuanian-Bialystok border would be seen.

"Look," the policeman said to the peasant, and showed him the paper, "that is the kind of document you need. Do you understand?"

The peasant apparently did not understand completely, and only stared enviously. I, however, did understand and smiled at the policeman's stupidity. Thinking that I was smiling at him, he smiled back and investigated me no further.

Now I had to wait a whole night in the Malkinia railroad station. The town was in ruins, and some distance from the station. I knew no one there, and there was no place where I could warm my body. The station was on the other side of the Congress Poland border, and there was no need for a special pass to get to it from Warsaw. Generally, the Poles travelled without permits within the Warsaw district, what was called the General-Government. The crowding was beyond imagination. Potatoes, milk, butter, hams were smuggled from the village to the city and there was a police check at almost every other station. It was here that you could accidently fall into a trap. Here the Germans used to conduct sudden searches: surrounding the train, making the passengers leave and leading them to the police station for identification. In order to avoid these unpleasant encounters it was wise to get away from the crowd, from the market, the train, and the tramway . . . That is what Tosya had advised me. But how?

In the Malkinia station were hordes of people lying on the stone floor on their bundles, suitcases and sacks. There was no place to sit. If you found a polite traveller he might find you a place on a sack of potatoes. Generally, however, people demanded payment for giving you a place. If the Polish or German police came, you had to promise to say that the sack was yours. One sack of potatoes was allowed. "You see how many I still have," the man tried to convince me. Most of those who stretched out on their belongings were filthy from the long trip, from dragging the sacks, from the war itself. They looked around fearfully, and kept trying to settle themselves comfortably — one on his stomach, another on his back and a third on his behind, stuffed as they were in front and back and also underneath their clothes. You could see the nervous types, the deliberate ones, the women who were always better in "arranging" things. Malkinia station was a nightmare for every one of our people who were compelled to take to the road during the occupation.

I arrived in Warsaw in the morning, rumpled, shivering with cold, lack of sleep and hours of standing in the train "for Poles." I entered the city. Warsaw was strange to me and cold, without any house or street that I knew. Traffic seemed normal, the ruins were not too apparent to the eye; electric trams came and went.

Where to go? I shivered with cold. I knew only the address of the chalutz farm in Cherniakov. I had been told that to reach Cherniakov I had to go by tram to the last station, get off and go left along a village street to its end. I did so and arrived safely. It was the only Jewish refuge in the city that one could enter and leave without a permit.

I cannot really describe the farm. Like a distant and unclear dream I saw young men and women dragging cans and work tools, working in the winter cold, in fields that were not theirs, of course, but they were happy and singing. I can recall a dilapidated stone house with wooden posts supporting its roof. There were beds in two crowded tiers, and there was also a long, rough table.

In one of the beds I found Lonka. She had returned that morning from a long trip and had remained here to rest and warm up, to sit a little among friends and to tell them what she had heard and seen on the way. Tomorrow she was going to return to the ghetto. Leah, the farm director, was involved in everything and also took care of the guests. I was moved by the poverty, that was relieved only through the people's generosity. My sister's splendid coat seemed incongruous in this place. Leah helped me sew a piece of cloth on the fur collar (in Warsaw too, Jews were forbidden to wear furs), instructed me to wait until half past three or four and then go to a certain place where I would meet Jews returning from their work to the ghetto. I was to give the appointed Jewish leader 10 gulden, and he would "arrange" for the Polish policeman to take me into the ghetto.

Following Leah's instructions, I found the Jewish work brigade on Cherniakovska Street. There were altogether about 10 to 15 persons there. Every one of them was carrying some kind of goods in his clothing: some potatoes, bread or a little milk. They were all hungry for crumbs, but they weren't smuggling for themselves. I went into the shed where the Jews were waiting, gave the 10 gulden to the leader and received from him a white band with a blue star of David to tie to my sleeve. After he stepped aside with the "blue" Polish policeman, I joined the line. My heart beat wildly. I prepared myself for my first view of the capital of all the ghettoes. I recalled my first meeting with Edek on the hill outside the Vilna ghetto, the meeting where my first ties to the ghetto were made. This approaching contact with the most important ghetto of all, upon which everything depended — the future of the movement, the end of the struggle — made my heart race. I was entering the holy of holies.

The road from Cherniakovska Street to the ghetto was interminable.

I thought of the meeting with Yosef, with Mordcchai and Tosya, and with Edek, and of my comrades in the sad procession. I did not have to guess what they were thinking; I knew that very well from the other ghettoes: of hungry families waiting for their return, of those waiting to buy the smuggled goods, and mainly of the German at the ghetto gate — would he be good or bad, would he look under the dresses and in the pockets or not?

Suddenly I stopped short. A roll had fallen on the pavement, small and round. It rolled to my feet. One of the passersby had thrown it. I was sure that he had done so in contempt and mockery: here, take this and choke! There was a tumult in the file, they all fell upon the little roll. Some of those who passed by laughed; some shook their heads in pity.

We arrived at the ghetto. This time we went through the gate without any trouble. At the corner of Zelazna and Leshno Streets there was a strange odor, one that I had not smelled in any other ghetto; a compound of cold, congestion, poverty and above all, of carbide. Strange sounds filled the heavy air, the odor of bodies rotting alive. It seemed as if a deaf man was dying and all his house was crying to the heaven and praying for salvation and a miracle. I still had some minutes before curfew. The noise and traffic increased at this time and it reached a crescendo. Beggars shouted as loudly as they could, as if afraid to waste the last few minutes. The stench and the beggars' shouts enveloped me, and penetrated my bones. Very slowly my tension eased and I was left with only one desire — to faint, to sink into oblivion, not to hear, not to feel, not to live with all this.

I reached 23 Nalevky with difficulty. I had known these streets long ago before the war. I had one good sign: Leshno 6 where the Hanhaga Rashit (national leadership) was located and from where I knew the way to the Jewish quarter.

At the gate I met Mordechai Anielewich. He was running fast. The day was passing and there was still a lot of work to finish. He recognized me immediately. The gate closed behind us and I didn't know what to say. I was very excited and as usual in such moments, I only asked : "What's new?" Mordechai took me to the kibbutz.

The kibbutz apartment was divided in two. In the two rooms to the right was a group meeting. Aryeh Wilner closed the session hurriedly. Only some fragments of the discussion reached my ears: a seminar, a wall newspaper. His last words were swallowed up in the noise of the departing people. The two rooms to the left comprised the kibbutz. In the middle was a smoky kitchen and a sign which read: "Refugee Home."

Tosya and Edek came out of a corner. Yosef was not in Warsaw and Tosya had returned that day from Chenstowova, from a visit to the kibbutz there. I found Shmuel; he hadn't changed at all since the leadership camp during the summer before the war. We had both lectured then, on literature and education.

That evening the comrades did not leave for their homes. The meeting assembled in Yosef's room. He wasn't there but everybody knew where to find some food. They all hurried to introduce themselves; they all wanted to receive me well. In the middle of the room, between the sofa and the bookcase, stood an iron stove. Tosya added some wood that had been purchased by the kilogram.

I told them about Vilna. Since Edek had left the movement had developed considerably. A united and consolidated underground movement had been organized. Foundations had been laid for cells of five persons each. The main difficulty was the lack of weapons and money. There simply was not a penny to spend. The aim of my coming, by decision of the F.P.O. in addition to receiving information and public opinion, was to obtain money. In Vilna there was no Joint, no institutions, no connections with the outside world. I was also supposed to bring Edek back; Abba was complaining about his absence.

The situation in Bialystok was much sadder. People there were only taking their first steps. There was no unity. We had found the way to individuals and organized groups but still had not found an approach to the parties and movements. Prospects were greater there than anywhere else. I told of the "Judenrat" and of the benefits which might be gained from it. There, too, there was no money, but there was no hunger on the proportions of Vilna. I had made the first connections with the Communists and here we needed help — the help of someone who knew their representatives in Warsaw. Our relationship with "Dror" had still to be settled; despite our cooperaion we still did not understand each other. In this area, too, Warsaw had to use its influence in deciding the issues.

It appeared that in Warsaw there was still no definite decision concerning the organizaion of a joint fighting defense organization from all the political bodies. My stories of the F.P.O. made a great though strange impression. Public life in the Warsaw ghetto existed in the customary routines, and it was difficult to arouse them to revolution. On the other hand I was greatly surprised and impressed by the underground organs, the network of papers expressing opinion of all shades. The newspapers were debating and changing views, and were providing precise information about the front, the world struggle against Germany and distant places throughout Europe that had not yet yielded to the Nazis.

The Warsaw ghetto was not cut off from the world; it had a busy public, cultural and educational life. These were the deeper ghetto streams, rather than the smugglers, the speculators, the peddlars and beggars. In the ghetto depths men helped each other, took risks and preserved their human Jewish countenances. Poems were being written — poetry of revolt; children were being taught to love beauty, daring, justice, history and science, to hate the enemy and his lackeys. In Warsaw there was an underground movement that had been built one step at a time in the midst of the two year battle against hunger and despair. The revolutionary awakening, the fundamental change in values, was, however, hard to find. As compared to what had happened in Lithuania and Bielorussia, matters in Warsaw were wearying, without content or focal point and it would be most unfortunate if the last brick was not added to the building of the underground: the unification of forces and preparation for armed battle. At that time we still could not decide when and how we were to begin the armed defense, whether it was to be a single act at the time of the ghetto's liquidation, or prior to that. We still were studying the matter, but in the course of time the answer appeared of itself, under the pressure of experience and magnitude of our sacrifices during the Nazi occupation.

There were then half a million Jews confined in the Warsaw ghetto. In the course of the two years of occupation there had been, except for occasional brutalities against individuals, no organized action aimed at liquidating the ghetto. True, calculations were made that every day from 300 to 400 Jews died of sicknesses, hunger and cold, and it would take only a few years to liquidate Warsaw's 500,000 Jews "peacefully." That calculation was a remote one, however. What had started in Vilna would inevitably conclude in Warsaw. I did not have to convince our comrades; they understood very well. I admired the national leadership for its ability to think and act, in ideological matters also. I saw Mordechai Anielewicz, planner and activist.

What were we, then, to do tomorrow to move matters forward?

"I suggest organizing a meeting at Kirshenbaum's, and inviting all the parties. You will speak there of the situation in Vilna, Bialystok and Bielorussia. Press them to the wall so that they themselves draw their own conclusions. Shmuel, you will call a meeting with the Joint. Describe the social conditions and the sanitary ones, so that they will contribute money right away, but there we have to be more careful. I suggest that Tosya first see Gitterman and arrange a meeting in his home. With him, I think we can speak about everything including arms. What do you think? I will introduce you to the communists. By the way, I would like to go to Vilna and Bialystok. I grasp the matters but you can discover new aspects when you see them at first hand," Mordechai concluded.

"It would be worthwhile, too, to exchange ideas on political questions. We are in dispute with almost all the parties who put out the underground newspapers. Except for the "Dror" people and the Left Poalei-Zion, we have no partners. To this very day they spoil everything with their fear and hatred of the Soviet Union. Tomorrow Shmuel will bring you a bundle to look at." He laughed. "Maybe it is foolish in your view to deal with such things today; still, they are apparently important." Mordechai stopped reflectively.

Shmuel was lively and talkative, as usual. It was he that edited the newspapers and listened to the radio. "Tomorrow I will take you where you will listen a little by yourself," he boasted. Shmuel and Mordechai, two comrades, both alike and yet different. Shmuel loved classical music, beautiful pictures and poetry. He was a bit of an esthete in his attitude toward both cultural values and people. His thinking was clear and quick, sometimes too much so. He was versed in pure Marxist ideology, most of which had been obtained from books and only a little from life itself. Not always did we all agree with the political line set forth in the press. However, all believed in the movement's clearly defined allegiance toward the Soviet Union. They argued with him and opposed the extremism of his formulations and political definitions. I heard many comments about this from Tosya and Aryeh Wilner.

Mordechai, on the other hand, combined in himself two important necessary traits of a representative of a fighting public: his clear and unequivocal thinking grounded in study, and his decisive, courageous and deliberate proletarian character. Practicality in thinking and thinking put into practice — that was Mordechai.

After the meeting everyone returned to the kibbutz, and only the three of us, Tosya, Edek and myself remained. Our discussion was as weary as we were. Only Edek was wide awake. He joked endlessly, and while doing so, formulated his ideas. With enthusiasm and imagination he told us about his plan to get out of the ghetto, where he would go, when he would get to the railroad, and how he would get to Bialystok and Vilna. "A madman," I thought to myself, "doesn't he know how many difficulties he will encounter before he arrives?" His face is "typically Jewish". Of him it was said that he did not look like a Jew, but that all Jews looked like him.

Edek left Warsaw a few days later. Under no circumstaces did he agree to wait for me. "It's a waste for both of us to do the same work at the same time," he said. Actually, he did not want to travel with me because he did not want to endanger me by his appearance. Extortionists apprehended him at the border. Edek did not answer their questions and they called the "blue" policeman.

"Where did you get the transit-pass? Did you get it from the Judenrat?" the policeman asked him sarcastically.

Edek who didn't lose his sharp wit, shouted at them and in his vernacular Polish replied: "Panie, what kind of 'rat', where is that 'rat', is there such a city in Poland? I got it in Grodno and not in any of your rats!" They left him.

The next morning I observed the ghetto in broad daylight. The courtyard of 23 Nalevky Street was like all the courts in these streets. All day long they were filled with beggars and ragged and tattered street singers, and for all they sang the same song: "Good people throw me a piece of bread . . . A crust of bread at least . . . " Slowly I became accustomed to this singing, too. At the courtyard gate there was a small store. Here it was possible to obtain a few grams of white bread, herring, jam (without coupons) and pieces of wood, by weight. At the first entry to the right was a charity kitchen. Here they cooked the same dish every day: a thin broth they called soup. Jews were always standing in line near the kitchen, waiting from morning for their dinner. On the top floor, over the kitchen, was the kibbutz. Here young people would meet in the evenings and sing their songs. Within the courtyard itself was the underground. In Yosef's room the linking threads among the ghettoes were tied. Within these narrow walls were printed the informational bulletins. The day planted new hopes in Jewish hearts. Here announcements were prepared destroying the illusions of life without battle.

Yosef returned from a tour of the "Government". He was my guide and through him I learned to recognize the passersby and the beggars. He could tell the story of a lonely child in the street, of a singer, and of their families; how they had transposed their lives from the "decent home" to beggary; how they had buried their families in a common grave after they had perished in the street. Lonely, abandoned, beggars without number, every day hundreds of whom died with no one taking notice.

Yosef was tired and thin and looked tubercular. There was, however, a fire burning in that thin body. Was it the fire of the love of Israel? He shared the lives of all the miserable people on the street, of all those swollen by sickness and hunger. Everybody knew Yosef; public leaders and the street waifs, the movement and its friends, opponents and sympathizers. Everyone respected him, appreciated his great soul and courage; Yosef the man and Yosef the fighter.

My visits to the institutions began. At the meeting with the public representatives I described the situation. It was held in the home of Kirshenbaum, a General Zionist and head of the Jewish National Fund. Around the table sat representatives of all the Zionist parties, and non-Zionists, as well. Actually, they had learned of the situation in Vilna from Edek, but I added some of the latest developments, and details about Bialystok.

I did not have any good news to bring and my stories seemed a little strange at the long table and the upholstered chairs. It was a rainy and cold January day. Our host's home was warm and comfortable. When tea was served a lively debate started. Only a few attempted to draw logical conclusions from my words. I was surprised at the position of the "Bund" people, at their representative Ozech's declaration, stated with complete confidence, that it would not happen in Warsaw.

"You understand, Warsaw is after all Warsaw, a big metropolis in the middle of Europe, with half a million Jews. The world would be shocked and would protest. Warsaw is not like Vilna, nor is it remote and isolated like Bialystok. The Germans won't want to anger the western world because of the Jews . . . "

I would not have been surprised at such talk if these words had been spoken reflectively, with the reservations of "maybe" or "perhaps". It was the desire to convince others in blind confidence that filled me with concern for the fate of alert, fermenting and conservative Warsaw.

They were not all of one view, but what I was waiting for did not happen: The necessary conclusion was not drawn, neither by the Poalei Zion representatives nor the other Zionists.

Additional meetings were held subsequently in the big building on Tlumaeka Street, and then outside the ghetto. Zivia participated in one of these meetings and it was at these meetings that I found support in the presence of Zivia and one of our comrades. This was a natural front, united in its decisions and in its power to make them.

The meeting with the members of "Dror" seemed to us to be superfluous. The latter had gone through the same development as our movement. True, the barriers between us had not yet dissappeared, and we still had to find a common language that would leave no room for doubts. At that time every one still feared that his allies were not being completely frank. It seemed to each side that the other was still concealing something, plotting secretly. It was a race against time, and every one wanted to win.

I learned some things about the deep crisis the members of "Dror" were experiencing because of the events in Lithuania and Bielorussia. They were, like us, a united and organized movement with its own institutions. I am sure that I will not be falsifying history if I say that Hashomer Hatzair and Dror were the only two large chalutz movements that preserved their integrity, coordinated activity and learned from the experiences of the various geographically isolated parts of their movements. We were the only ones to heed the great commandment of the underground movement: to plan and to coordinate our actions. We were the only ones that knew how to change course when necessary.

Why were so many public persons, the members of the parties and institutions, misled by the maze of "possibilities" during the occupation? Why did they find so many possibilities of getting through the dark times, and of holding out to the end? Why was it that the representatives of certain parties, especially, were so prone to believe this delusion? The Bund, the bourgeois Zionists and the right wing of Labor Zionism? If one wants to study the history of the parties, their aspirations and mistakes, he or she must go back to those days; go to the ghetto and the answer will be found. Read what was written then, by Shmuel and his colleagues. Ideological foundations are crystallized in times of peace; they are tested in time of war.

Those who believed before the war, that it was possible to attain socialism peacefully, to "grow into socialism", to bring workers to power by indirect means, without a direct clash, those who believed that it was possible to achieve complete national liberation without sacrifice, without pioneering action, without a deep, internal national revolution, were those who led our people astray and deluded them insisting that the Nazi occupation, the murders and oppression, could be evaded. They were the ones who channelled their own and the people's actions into smuggling and evading reality at a time of desperate battle between two conflicting worlds; as though a whole people could escape through the cracks in history. There were individuals who did escape through the cracks. But a whole people? We did not want to, and could not, understand the national and social leaders. We did not wish to make it easier for them. We refused to compromise. Those meetings were very bitter, for them and for us. The differences were not psychological ones among young people and older ones, as some commentators think, or the difference between pessimists like ourselves who saw the holocaust coming and did not want to hide that fear from the public, and the optimists who believed that humanity would rise and save us in our time of distress. We did not demand then that the horrible information about Ponar be published because that would lead to public apathy and despair. "In any case the S.S. is going to kill us." If we did that, we would be criminals. We demanded that the truth about what awaited us be published, to show what we could expect so that we might defend ourselves. We demanded organization, to stand in the breach, to poise our weapons while there was still time.

Our opponents apparently did not have the strength to organize for that great action; they were apparently afraid and deterred from acting. They just refused to see what was coming. Their faces reflected the fears engendered by their world outlooks. They feared history.

Our meeting with Gitterman, one of the Joint directors, was unexpectedly encouraging. He did his best, so that I would not leave Warsaw empty-handed. He decided on a grant, the amount of which I do not remember, but I do recall that it was by no means small. The money had to be collected and the method was a difficult one indeed. It was necessary to find some Jew who would agree to deposit his money until . . . after the war, in Joint hands. In any case, I received an advance, and that was a great day in our lives. Not because of the money alone, but because we had received it from Gitterman to buy arms. The other Joint directors believed that the grant was to be used for "social relief in Vilna". Its real purpose was known only to Gitterman and one other Joint director, Gozik.

The excuse for the hesitancy of the public leaders concerning armed defense was "collective responsibility". The problem had already been raised in Vilna. We did not want to arrogate to ourselves the right, in the smallest degree to decide on the date of the annihilation of thousands of people. Even though we knew that masses of Jews were destined to die helplessly, we did not want to bring that end closer. We knew that five minutes before their last hour Hitler's battalions would complete their total annihilation of the Jews. We also knew that despite the various rumors and calculations concerning the early termination of the war, it was certain to be a long and difficult one with the Red Army victory coming only after years of battle. That was why Shmuel sat locked up in his room for hours glued to the little radio. We eagerly sought news from the front. We knew that the second front would be slow in appearing, that salvation would not come soon, and that annihilation was the ghetto's end. But we did not want to hasten that eventuality. Already in Vilna we had been troubled by the central and responsible question of when to begin the armed resistance. Furthermore, if we fought in Vilna, would that not affect the Jews in Warsaw? On the other hand, we knew that if we did not defend ourselves in time we would not be able to resist at all. We knew that the Germans' method was to "divide and conquer"; cut off only one limb, separate one part from another, intensify the desire to live among those remaining, destroy their souls and instincts, break that spirit and you have broken his power to resist. Meanwhile the masses will go to their slaughter believing to the end in some miracle, the miracle of those who remained alive.

We knew there was no escape from responsibility. It was with that responsibility for the public over whose fate we were struggling, that we lived. We had determined not to desert the collective, and that decisiion strengthened us, spirit and body.

Moreover, we had seen that the collective responsibility upon which the Germans insisted was but a small detail of a grand program. It was a way to instill fear, to paralyze thought. It bred another kind of illusion, that if you did not fight, and did not revolt, your situation would improve and your security was assured. The "public responsibility" remedy proved to be a mistake but too late. It became evident that it could not change the situation. It was like the political prisoner who was promised freedom if he would betray his comrades. No political prisoner was freed for his betrayal. He either died like his friends, or became a slave of the Gestapo.

However, we did not take that responsibility upon ourselves. We attempted to carry out our actions in a way that would not endanger the ghetto prematurely. We decided to carry out one concentrated action at the decisive hour and not to waste our forces in frequent skirmishes. We left the crucial effort for the day of revolt.

We continued with difficulty to the corner of Nalevki and Hovolipki. Here the passage opposite the wall and the ghetto's big gate was very narrow. Before we came to Dluga Street we passed through some of the long twisting courtyards of Jewish Warsaw. Suddenly we heard a tumult in the street. Before I knew what was happening Mordechai pulled me by the sleeve into one of the courtyards, pushed me to the staircase and wordlessly dragged me to the top floor. Here he explained: "Didn't you hear? Shots? Right near us? Another S.S. patrol has come into the ghetto. Remember, when you walk alone in the street and you hear shouts and the noise of running, you run, too!"

The ghetto already knew the infamous S.S. patrol that from time to time would come to "have fun" with the Jews. They shot at random. They went through the streets with sharpened sticks, hitting out left and right. The Jews generally managed to escape into the courtyards and the nearby staircases. The S.S. didn't trouble to chase those running away, they weren't as interested in Jewish victims as they were in having fun.

The most popular German game was to cause fear.

When we came out of the court we found a woman who had been shot near the gate. The unfortunate was quickly removed, the body taken to the place reserved for such victims, and life went on with its customary noises.

In the hidden room in Dluga Street, Modechai introduced me to Yosef Lewartowsky. The meeting had been decided upon in advance. Mordechai was quiet; he was by nature not one to rush ahead. It was a good trait, comforting and helpful.

Yosef was older than we were, middle aged, and he wore dark-framed glasses. I do not remember too many details of his face, but the impression was of seriousness. He received me like a comrade, without too many preliminaries. He expressed his happiness at the greetings I brought him, and created a calm and comfortable atmosphere for the discussion. Neither in his conduct, or his words or in the slightest suggestion of a smile did I feel the condescension of a man claiming "revolutionary experience", like his Bialystok comrades. There was no trace of prejudice from the past, or suspicion and lack of trust of others who were not communists.

After I spoke of the Bialystok matter and gave him the letter, Yosef said: "I am surprised that they are turning to me for instructions. I cannot give any instructions, either in writing or verbally. I am not authorized to give any instructions for an area that was Soviet until the war. I am active within the area of Congress Poland; in that region, surely there are authorized institutions. However, I can express my personal opinion in thinking you are correct. The establishment of a united Jewish front to fight the invaders is the order of the hour. This is not the time to consider past accounts. Any approach that does not answer the needs of our time is barren and must fail. I am confident that our cadres in Bialystok who are numerous and strong will find the correct path. I understand their hesitation and I know its source, but they must not wait for instructions. They must act according to their communist understanding, and they will find the right way."

"Are you prepared to express that opinion in writing?" I asked.

"I see no reason to hide it. I will write briefly and give the proper hints. So, shake their hands for me, I have many very close friends there." I received the letter the next day through Mordechai, together with good wishes.

We were with the Communists. Mordechai replied: "I see that you have not fully grasped the facts of life. Society is a sick man on the operating table. Today there is no special need for the sharp, theoretical scalpel of history. Today the sick man himself can teach us some of the lessons of society Jewish and non-Jewish." As Mordechai explained it, our views differ from those of the Communists. The differences are not a matter of more open or sharper minds or the moral value of humanity. They are a matter of our conception of the present situation. There is no doubt in our minds that Yosef Lewartowsky and his comrades honestly want to fight the Nazis. That is self-evident, unlike in other cases where it is not so clear. They also appreciate the importance of the Jewish war against the Nazis. You have certainly heard from Shmuel that they sent representatives into the ghetto. Yosef is one of the two who went. One of them was even parachuted in. To them, however, the ghetto is to this day just one of the city quarters. A geographical entity — do you understand what that means? For them the ghetto is not a group of people living a different life, fighting a special kind of fight under circumstances and conditions that do not adopt the accepted slogans of fighting the invader; to them it is just another part of the city. The ghetto's high wall makes their underground work physically difficult, but that wall, to them, is only a physical structure. Do you understand the historical implications of that approach? Don't you see here a hint of the entire past of the Jewish communists? It is only one little detail, revealing the whole. Since the Jews are in Warsaw, the capital of Poland, the Jewish anti-fascist underground is not compelled to adopt special methods of fighting, and there are no circumstances obliging them to do so. They therefore see the wall as only a geographical concept, and so they are calling upon us not to wage a national anti-Nazi war, as people being annihilated by the Nazis, but to go in to the forests as partisans and join the other antifascist forces. You will learn," Mordechai concluded, "that it isn't only a Bialystok problem."

Mordechai's sense of objectivity did not, however, allow him to criticize only the Communists. He also valued partnership with them historically, looking tonderstood the intention of our Warsaw comrades, Mordechai and Shmuel, when they applied their historical analyses to the distant future, distant because that future would come only after we were all dead. I can still recall their articles in the underground press on the Zionist solution to the Jewish problem after the war, and specifically in partnership with the Soviet Union. From this standpoint, too, Mordechai appreciated the joint antifascist front with the Communists.

Shmuel once showed me a pistol. "This is the only Jewish pistol in the ghetto," he laughed. I don't know whether he said it in sorrow that there weren't more pistols, or in satisfaction that the only one was his. Shmuel, in addition to his concern for the general welfare, also possessed a kind of childish mien that was not without a certain grace. With that presence he would express his criticisms of parties and movements. Shmuel was capable, however, of negating an opinion he held yesterday. His light-hearted boasting about the movement derived from his enthusiasm for its great values. Sometimes it seemed as if he was carried away by the flight of his thinking, instead of restraining and channeling it. Sometimes he could not control it. Still, he was a good editor, publisher, printer, collector of information, and writer of rich, daring and inspired prose.

Shmuel was not always correct. Almost all of us criticized him, except Mordechai who was able to appreciate his closest friend "historically". We took objection to Shmuel's lack of self-criticism, his hasty, youthful impression of parties and movements, and his arbitrary way of classifying people and organized forces. In his youthful thinking he did not know the necessity for soul searching before despairing of persons, parties or whole communities. Shmuel had to be taught to question, to battle, to win over forces and people and to believe that what reason could not do would be accomplished by time. "In public life and a battle as difficult as ours, we cannot give up on anybody," Yosef Kaplan would say. "We would do well to examine both ourselves and others. Perhaps we do not really know the "Dror" people. Maybe we are exaggerating our criticism, and perhaps in our blindness we are not seeing the real and moral strength of others." Yosef was the oldest of them all and apparently had the most mature concept of the importance of the hour and of the task. The popular fighting front, the Z.O.B. in Warsaw, like the broad antifascist underground in Bialystok, was born out of internal conflict, but in that conflict it was firmly forged.

Frumka

I returned to Bialystok encouraged. I was bringing both money and news of some progress in the matter of the popular front.

I found Edek in the Bialystok ghetto. According to our plan he was supposed to go on to Vilna some days later. However, though he was there for only a few days, Edek was incapable of sitting idle, and he found himself becoming involved in affairs here, too. Those were still very tiring, with whole days of running about and a beginning still not in sight. The hours went by in meetings, discussions and more meetings; in the evening you summed up the day and found a lot of talk and nothing accomplished.

Edek met with Zerah and Gedalyahu and also with Frank and Yoshko, from Volkowysk, all his kibbutz comrades. Closest to him was Zerah. They grew up together in the Kalish *ken*, had played together, read books together, matured. Edek was drawn by these attachments and suddenly realized that he could not leave Bialystok. A military commander was lacking here, and Edek was the only one of the comrades who had any real military training. He decided to wait until I returned. I agreed with him. There was no one here to fill Edek's place. Moreover, what about Vilna? Edek found it difficult to decide. We all believed that Edek should stay, since Vilna already had an organized underground, a broad united front. Preparations for fighting were being made and arming had begun. Here in Bialystok there was virgin soil. On the other hand, Edek had been sent on a specific mission and was expected to return. It was only for lack of choice that he had been delayed in Warsaw. He therefore did not feel free of the duty to fulfill his mission.

I suggested to Edek that he stay. Since I was leaving for Vilna within a few days I promised to clarify the matter there.

Edek, however, remained adamant. He did not want to set a precedent for other comrades to do things on their own. It would not set a good example if a member of the national leadership broke discipline with arguments about logic, he said. However, before he left, he decided that he would not go empty-handed:

"If we are stealing across the borders with forged papers, especially as aryans, we might as well benefit from it." Once again we argued against this but in vain.

In the ghetto Edek found a Jew who had recently come from Vilna as a refugee. He questioned him about the prices of dollars, gold, and gold rubles in Vilna. According to his figures it was worthwhile to smuggle gold coins to Vilna and to sell them there. He would try; maybe he could make money for arms. With part of the money I had brought from Warsaw he bought gold coins; if he succeeded in selling them at a profit he would telegraph a code sentence. Then I would do the same. We sewed the coins in the shoulder padding of his jacket and fearfully waited for his announcement.

My sister had friends outside the ghetto, Polish women with whom she had worked in the Soviet period. One of them, Stefa, a young woman living with her mother at the top of Senkevich Street, agreed to receive mail for me at her address. After Edek's departure I began to visit her every day. I left the ghetto with the permit I had received from Barash, took off the patch after turning the first corner, and got on the sidewalk. It was the beginning of spring, a little misty, more like a fall morning. Stefa received me courteously, looked at me through her lowered eyelashes, and from her greeting I learned whether a letter had come or not. Her mother would try to cheer me: "It will come, maybe tomorrow." I wondered why she did this. She didn't know what kind of news I was waiting for. Apparently it was just simple humanity, knowing how important the letter was to me.

Meanwhile life in the ghetto went on as usual, without any extraordinary shocks. Once they had relaxed from the tensions of the early days Jews began to take an interest in what was being written in the newspapers.

Bialystok did not have a single newspaper in Polish. The local German-language paper, the "Bialystoker Zeitung" was a cheap German rag without too much to read. More was learned from reading between the lines in the "Algemeine Zeitung" and the "Volkischev Beobachter" than was printed in them. True, Jews were forbidden to read German papers, a ban that was published in special announcements by the city police and the S.S. Nonetheless, they could buy the papers on the ghetto's main street. Not only potatoes, bread and meat but newspapers too, were smuggled into the ghetto, and the newspaper vendor had many customers. Sometimes the newspaper vendor felt like playing a morbid joke.

"Give me 'Das Reich'."

"There is no Das Reich."

"But you're holding it in your hand!"

"And I tell you that Das Reich is finished." The purchaser gave up and went, but came back in a hurry. The vendor was teasing him.

"Give it to me, mister! Have you gone mad? You're holding 'Das Reich' and say you don't have any."

Between the lines of the newspapers Jews read that Moscow had not fallen and that the Soviet Union was holding out. If the German paper wrote that "O.K.W. reports that we have taken Staraya Rossa (or some other place) in a counter-attack", the Jews knew that the Russians had attacked and the Germans had to counter-attack. That was a good sign. At the beginning of that spring it slowly became evident that the USSR was holding out. They had cut off the 16th Army in the vicinity of Staraya Rossa and begun to liberate many places in the Smolensk area. The news was like a refreshing spring which revived hopes.

Immediately after coming to Bialystok I met Frumka. She was occupied in organizing the Bialystok Dror. I met her on the bridge over the muddy Bialka River crossing the ghetto. I recognized her from afar by her slightly bowed back and her head sunk into her shoulders. Frumka was engaged in important work here, establishing the Hechalutz organization in a new place. Our hurried discussion immediately got down to the essentials:

"Frumka, what is going to happen? You alone and we alone?"

"What do our comrades in Warsaw say about the defense?"

"I did not clarify the matter with your comrades. Our Warsaw people will do that but, from what I heard, it is Yizhak who is pushing it."

"Believe me, Chaika, it does not leave my mind. I am doing things which are little concerned with defense. I am dealing with rooms, employment and other such matters. But my heart isn't in them. It is difficult to grasp the greatness of the revolution before us and the responsibility it involves. Believe me, I am overwhelmed by these daily tasks. I dare not decide by myself even though I know that the Vilna people are correct. I cannot, it is beyond my power to do so. Chaika, I am struggling and seaching and I cannot leave what I am doing and begin with that. Within a few days I will be going to Warsaw."

The negotiations with the Communists were tiring, unlike what I had expected after bringing Yosef's answer. I had pinned great hopes in Edek's return. Perhaps he could press them to the wall. He would also have more time; he wouldn't travel, be busy crossing borders, and could devote himself completely to organization. But where was Edek?

A week after Edek's departure a letter arrived for me at Stefa's address: "I have received a position, would like to consult with you. Edward."

My joy knew no bounds. Edek had arrived safely. We could earn money to buy arms. I packed my bag; this time we decided to work on a larger scale. Yandzia knew many Jews in the ghetto. From one he took ten-ruble gold coins and I sewed them into the buttons of my sweater. That was not a very difficult job. You took off the wool-covered wooden buttons and in their place sewed coins. It was a large sum of money and the danger involved was great. The risks, however, were worth taking. We heard that the mark was worth more than the ruble, and was the general currency. It was, therefore, worthwhile to bring marks from Bialystok. Marks, however, were not silver or gold coins but bills, and it was hard to conceal large bundles of bills. They were sewn into my belt and I thought they would not be noticed. My papers were only cursorily examined at the border after having already been stamped by the border police at Marcinkance.

"How much money do you have?" They had decided to find out whether I had money, nonetheless.

"Right away," I replied, and opened the purse in my hand. The policeman counted the money and shook his head angrily as if to say: what are you showing us, is that what you call money?

I had about 15 marks.

I arrived in Vilna during the daytime. Yadwiga was still living at her place on the street adjacent to Viliya. I didn't find her at home and I therefore had to look for some place to stay after two o'clock. I met her the following day. When she heard that I was the woman who had looked for her she expressed surprise.

"The landlady explicitly told me that a pregnant woman was looking for me!"

I told her that yesterday I had been pregnant but I had not expected anyone to notice. I was mistaken, and it was a good thing that the border police had not thought of examining my suspicious belly. We both laughed. The money was already in the ghetto.

The deliberations in the ghetto were fatiguing and bitter. Edek and I tried to convince Abba that Edek's place was in Bialystok. But Abba, was adamant; Edek had to stay in Vilna. Vilna was the symbol, the first victim that had arisen before its death — could we take the risk of the fighting organization not succeeding there?

I still recall the twilight of that dreary day. We almost lost control of ourselves, and almost said things to each other we would later regret, just to prove a point.

We decided that Edek would return to Bialystok to assume the military command.

I was given the task of centralizing the political work and of maintaining the connections between the three large centers — Vilna-Bialystok-Warsaw.

The Debate

It was then that I spent a great deal of time on trains moving between borders and the barbed wire of the Polish ghettoes. Between trips I participated in organizing the Jewish underground in Bialystok. The Bialystok ghetto was the only one in which I concentrated on local matters, both political and organizational. I clarified fundamentals with comrades, exchanged information and experiences and dealt with financial problems. The method we adopted for ongoing consultations and exchanges of information between the underground leadership of the separated ghettoes and regions involved great risk, but its real value was so high that we agreed to maintain it at all costs. We decided to expand our communications apparatus. At first we were very careful, even over-cautious, implying some doubt, regarding the ability of the rank and file membership. We were especially afraid of first attempts. We knew that any mistake, even the smallest, could lead to catastrophe. We were afraid to put people to the test, since we knew the price we would have to pay for failure. Underground life is serious and complicated, with one mistake leading to another if you do not know how to combine caution and daring. But how do you manage that combination? Many revolutionary movements and parties wavered between the two. Out of caution, revolutionary leaderships sometimes hesitated before assigning tasks to new people. That fear accompanied them even when they came to power or in open activity in peace time, when the failures of the inexperienced could still be corrected. How much more careful were we, then, in those years. Some tyro's failure would be a catastrophe. Once the Gestapo got hold of you, you never got out. Therefore the leading comrades, positioned commanders and front commanders (and every ghetto was a front in itself) took on a lot of the most dangerous work, sometimes only technical in nature, which did not require any special training and ability, instead of delegating it to rank and file members thirsty for action.Today it is clear to me that it was a mistake for Edek to occupy himself with smuggling money, it was a mistake for me to travel in order to carry materials. The techniques of travel and communications could be taught to the novice. True, Tosya risked her life to get to

Vilna, but that was the first link we made, and it was a decisive, fateful issue that had to be discussed.

When we found that we had erred, we sent Rivkele to Vilna and Sarah and Roshka to transmit printed materials, money and information. We were surprised at Rivkele's cleverness, her talent for appearing innocent, and her workmanlike precision. We were also surprised by Sarah's mature deliberateness, the calm reflected in her movements and actions, her mature seriousness when working on a job. She was also adept at concealing the printed materials by sewing those on the Ponar massacre, the documents on the abominations in Kovno, the testimonies and first-hand manuscripts from Minsk and other Lithuanian and Bielorussian cities, into her clothing; using her purse's double lining in order to conceal the F. P. O. proclamations, the money and the code. We were astonished at all this, and new surprises awaited us.

There was also another accepted method of communications: short postcards by mail. Edek had invented the "code". A five-man cell was a "shop", arms — "furniture" long rifles — "closets", pistols — "chairs", heavy arms — "tables", dollars — "stephens" (in honor of Stephen Wise), false papers — all kinds of work tools, every paper its own tool. Imprisonment was "sickness" of course, and so on. I cannot recall all of them. The code in small letters on a few square centimeters of thin paper, which Edek, Yosef Kaplan and Roshka Korehak and I held, has not been preserved. The specialists in writing the secret postcards were Edek and Roshka. Edek was most adept at putting a wealth of information on a single card, and that would sometimes save dangerous communications trips.

It was spring when Edek returned to Bialystok. There was a great deal of work awaiting him but he had to be patient. Whenever we were in the city, Edek, Zerah, Gedalyahu and I served as the local secretariat. Negotiations with the parties, organizing our own cells and beginning arms acquisitions had to be carried out carefully and persistently. You imagine that tomorrow something is going to be decided and that tomorrow your partner will come and say "let's go!", but when tomorrow came, what should have been decided was put off to the next day and the day after that, and so on, from one day to the next. The same was true for obtaining arms. Someone promised to put you in contact with someone else, who would bring you to someone who was selling arms. Suddenly the thread was cut. One of those "someones" did not appear, disappeared, or was arrested. Once again the matter was put off.

The first sign of progress was the formation of the cells — the fives. Edek, Zerah and Yoshko worked out the plan. Individuals were accepted into the cells one by one. After one, two or three face-to-face talks, and sometimes more, the candidate was allowed to attend his first meeting with his cell which had no connection with the existing educational framework. In the group there was no talking about the cell. It was as if they didn't exist. They mixed according to sex and age. The separation, educationally, practically and organizationally was necessary in those days. The youth movement groups, their rank and file and its leaders were well known. The groups lived together even in the ghetto and their existence was actually semi-legal. The parties, their mutual aid, the frequent meetings in the kibbutz at 11 Kupiecka Street, all these could not be concealed, and disbanding the groups would not have helped much, nor did we want to. They continued in their educational function, one which the cell could not take over. Their open existence also served as a partial camouflage for the Judenrat and other elements flourishing in the ghetto. The Judenrat members believed that a pioneering and socialist movement like Hashomer Hatzair, in its earlier form, could not be dangerous, especially when it was quasi-legal and public. They did not grasp the significance of a youth or pioneering movement.

In that way we maintained the kibbutz and our public status. It was important that the Jews know that there was a force that had not fallen apart like everything else. Indeed, Jews did know that we existed, and looked upon us as a united force.

The work in the groups and our adult society was both educational and political. It was there that we discussed the fundamentals. In that way we also hoped to maintain the internal democracy so necessary for an underground movement. In order to enhance further that democracy, and collective responsibility, we also maintained a cadres circle which decided questions of basic guidelines. These were the two elements that shaped the democratic regime of our movement as a whole. However, one must not think that these problems lent themselves to solutions by absolute preconceived formulas. Sometimes it was necessary to limit democracy, especially in order to avoid its denigration. At times we suffered from loosening the reins and giving voice to the weaknesses of even the best of comrades.

Not all members were recruited into the cells, and those who weren't sometimes protested in a very unpleasant way. They wanted to know why they were being kept out of the action.

Since the laws of the underground were also among the principles discussed in the meetings, comrades knew that such a question should not be asked, that they would have to wait patiently. There were comrades who observed this rule; there were also more than a few impatient ones who suffered such a seeming affront. Then a very dangerous phenomenon took place — the attempts to ferret out secrets, and ill-considered criticism charging an internal dictatorship, oppression of the individual and denial of the right to act. There were personal charges against the cadres suggesting that while they were not doing anything they did not permit others to act. These complaints within the movement, however, were never more than marginal. The positive predominated.

There was one adult member, Aryeh Weinstein,[10] whom we knew from the Vilna concentration. He had studied Judaism in the university and was noted for his literary talent. He was careless, however, and tended to speak of anything that came to mind. Edek decided to delay his recruitment. Aryeh gave expression to the era, the ghetto, and our vision of the future. I still remember his poem which we often recited in our home in Kupiecka Street. It has not been preserved, but I can remember its theme: the voice of a crying child in the chaos of slaughtered Jewry. I can still hear the soft weeping voice coming from the poem, the voice of the living child among the ruins. It was sober reflection of our hard lives. His poems expressed at one and the same time a lyrical tenderness and a combatant spirit. We could not, however, put him into a fighting cell. Aryeh had a younger brother, Koppel, a pianist with a talent for composing, who belonged to the younger Tel-Amal group. In his music he expressed the thoughts and feeling that his brother did in his poetry. I can still recall the "Stalingrad" march he composed during the battle for Stalingrad. It reflected not only the tragic, despairing battle we were waging in those days, but also victory. I can still remember the great program performed by the children of the ghetto school, more about which I shall write later. Aryeh's brother played at the end of the concert. Koppel was recruited into a cell. He was different from his brother, talked less, was more moderate and deliberate, reserved, but aggressive in moments of decision. Aryeh was older, but it was Koppel, the younger, who entered a cell.

I remember the meeting of the adult movement members on defense and its methods. Aryeh demanded clarification concerning the construction of the underground. Edek insisted that the meeting was convened only to decide upon the general system; the internal construction of an underground was not something to be discussed in such a broad framework. For that purpose authorized institutions were elected and "they must decide what elements the unit will include, who will belong and what function he will perform."

In the course of his tirade Aryeh lost control and blurted out, "But who made you the authorized institutions?"

We knew that it was a slip of the tongue. All those present said that he knew that he had erred, but had not found the courage to admit his weakness.

Aryeh never did belong to an underground cell, though we did give him the important task of gathering historic material and documents, of editing the ghetto daily, together with Yandzia, and of organizing the movement's archives. The conflicts with Aryeh, however, were repeated and interestingly enough, he always found something to say in the most difficult days and hours of failure.

Aryeh was a man of extremes. He showed many of the weaknesses of an underground movement, and also served as the voice for the hesitant who did not dare say what they thought.

Yandzia was different, but with him, also, we had difficult debates. These were about the forest, the partisans and fighting in the ghetto. After we had finished this argument amongst ourselves, it raged bitterly between us and opponents.

It had begun in Vilna. Yandzia had not opposed the resistance but had hesitated more than the others; he was the last to accept it as movement doctrine. He had argued that revolt in one ghetto meant suicide. "We have to save people, to save as many as we can." The debate in Vilna had died down when action began. In Bialystok it surfaced again, and there, too, at an adult members meeting, one that was open and decisive.

I recall that Franek argued that we had to decide what was more worthwhile, what would cause the Germans more damage — war in the ghetto or in the forest. It seemed to him that there were more possibilities for harming the Germans in the forest, where we could strike at them from ambush. Did we have enough strength to do this in the ghetto?

When Yandzia raised the subject of saving Jews, Franek exploded:

"I don't care a fig for your salvation!" (The Polish word was an obscene one, and he immediately apologized.)

"What kind of salvation are you thinking about? Of saving slaves?" He made an effort to end his short speech in a more restrained fashion, without blurting obscenities from between his clenched teeth.

The discussion returned to its quieter form after that explosion. Everybody spoke: Sarah Dabeltoff and Chaika Rybak, who did not tend to express their views publicly but were known to be good comrades. Zippora Kruglak, too, of whom we knew so little, a Bialystok girl who did not make many demands. All of them together said: "Edek is right; our Vilna comrades are right. If we fight we'll fight as Jews."

Zerah's quiet fashion always produced a stillness within the room. What made Zerah so respected by his comrades, who always paid attention to what he said I do not know.

Zerah used to think out loud. With his special emphasis on the "I" he would eke out the words very carefully, without any evident emotion. "Franek is right. If we have to weigh the problem we must do it from the standpoint of the war against the Nazis. Any other approach, no matter how embellished with ideologies of saving Jews, or of saving ones own life, is treason. Anyone talking of saving masses in the forest is either wrong himself, or misleading others. How are you going to save masses in the forest. Is that the way to rescue the old people, the women, the children in the ghetto? Will you wage the war against the Nazis without Jews? I see that there are people here who want to bring us back to a discussion we finished a long time ago. First of all, there is no possibility of saving masses. That is utopia, a dangerous illusion leading us to accept our fate. You can only save individuals, and even those who speak of saving masses do not intend to save more than some individuals, knowingly or not. And maybe among those he is including himself."

Yandzia was insulted and bowed his head. We all felt that Zerah had gone too far, but he continued slowly:

"It is not important if anyone has been hurt by my remarks. Maybe I hurt him unknowingly, but the matter is not a personal one. Among ourselves, perhaps, we could come to an agreement. But we have to decide on how to educate the masses and a movement, how to demand and what to demand. We have a bitter argument with many; let us at least be in agreement among ourselves. Let us ascertain, first of all, whether everything is in order in our own ranks. As far as the ghetto and the partisans are concerned, I am of the same opinion as our Vilna comrades, Edek and Chaika."

Edek spoke after him:

"Comrades, I would like once again to make clear our position on the ghetto. Perhaps in the forest there are better prospects for effective warfare. Are we, however, going to be satisfied with that, and leave the masses to their fate, to be led, here too, as in Vilna, like sheep to the slaughter, so that we may seek effective battle in the forest? I do not minimize sabotage activities: so many bridges destroyed, so many munitions trains blown-up, so many telegraph lines cut. All these things are very important, but do they provide an answer to the central question: how do you organize a mass response, how do you bring a whole people's resistance to fruition, how do you lead the Jewish forces, locked in the ghetto, to their fate — to keep them from being annihilated? Are we going to fight in the forest and disclaim any responsibility? Will we have done our duty? The forest is a solution for individuals who want to help in the war against nazism, but where is the collective, national solution? Are we to desert the disorganized ghetto, with its old people, women and children and say: we have saved our lives? Where is our movement's vanguard? I see the head of the rebelling masses. The war must be carried out in the ghetto, and we must be in the vanguard together with those others who agree with us. We are being killed as Jews, and it is as Jews that we must fight back; not as individuals but as an organized community."

Yandzia remained hesitant. We knew that he was suffering from the pains of love and concern for his people. What would the end be, he asked; are we going to be satisfied with showing how brave we are? Yandzia had begun to study history, to lock himself in the Judenrat attic which contained many old and precious works of history, the remainder of the former library of the Bialystok community. He assembled the testimonies of the Jews who had been destroyed.

Then, suddenly, all his repressed revolt burst out, and Yandzia then became the voice of the entire underground.

What happened was this. In the ghetto was a school, legally authorized, for Jewish children. The school principal was a former teacher in the Hebrew gymnasium (high school). There were six elementary classes but it was more of a social institution than an institution of learning. There were a few hundred pupils. Yandzia was invited to organize a party for the children, just an ordinary one to help relieve the bleak atmosphere prevailing in the big building at the end of Fabrychna Street, at the end of the ghetto. Yandzia absented himself for whole days. We knew that he was organizing a party; had he gone out of his mind? A party in the ghetto? Weren't there more important and useful things to do? Yandzia, however, did not say anything. One day he invited us to the party, and we went, out of curiosity. The large hall was full. It was five o'clock in the afternoon and ghetto curiosity was great: a children's party! Many people came, even those who were not parents of children there. They crowded into the narrow corridors and classroom doorways.

What we heard and saw that afternoon is hard to describe. The adults sat, stunned. No one applauded at the end of the play. No one turned to his neighbor. It was not the children who had performed on the stage, but Yandzia's soul. We saw a dramatization of Bialik's "A Freilich's" (A Merry Tune), and we heard not the young, somewhat hoarse voices of the children, but the beating of our own hearts. didn't the words fit our situation.

. . .Nishtgenasht fun olam-hazeh, olam habah oich noch veit,
Vus zhe shvaigt ihr? . . .
(Not yet tasted of this world and the other world so far . . .
Why then are you silent . . .) And the repeated refrain:
Zoll akrenk der soneh vissen, vos in hartzen brott und brennt . . .
(And then the powerful hasidic dance of courage, despair and revolt.)

A kappuro hundert veltn, far ein shoh fun dreist und mut . . .

('No need of a hundred worlds, only an hour of courage and strength'.)

The party ended and we left quietly, the adults stirred and reflective, the children wondering at the seriousness and silence that had prevailed in the hall.

It was in that way that Yandzia revealed himself . . .

Because of the difficulty in acquiring firearms we decided to accumulate other kinds of weapons and to manufacture arms, if only primitive ones. "Cold" weapons were more easily obtainable. We knew that a German "action" in the ghetto might come at any moment and we did not want to face it with clenched fists alone.

The "national" weapon at that time was an electric bulb filled with sulphuric and other acids. The cells were occupied in accumulating the burnt-out bulbs, and in preparing the acid, pouring it into the bulbs then sealing them. Every cell worked separately without knowing what the other cells were doing. Preparing the bulbs was a delicate and precise task. One had to be careful of the acids and of the thin glass. Any careless move could bring catastrophe to the workers and to the whole underground. After the tasks were completed the bulbs were carefully packed in straw and in boxes which which were stored away. The storerooms had to be kept dry and since they were dispersed throughout the ghetto, guarded. They were placed in attics, walls, and the ceilings of comrades' homes. The location of the storeroom was known only to the one who had established it, and to his cell-leader. The bulbs were supposed to blind the Germans and burn them. You had to be able to aim at the enemy's delicate parts, for the action of the acid to be effective.

Another weapon was a long knife, this too a "home product," made not by the cells but by more professional experts, generally metal-workers. Collecting the material; rusty iron rods scattered in the courtyards, was the work of the cell members. After a time we began to accumulate ordinary explosives and other chemical materials which could serve as weapons.

Production was directed by Franek. It was said that he had "golden hands". He would compound materials and find ways of improving the product, reducing work hours and exploiting existing shops. Franck never rested; was never still for a moment. If he saw a rusty wire in the street he would not pass without examining it carefully. He always looked for assistants. He would examine every bypasser, look at his hands, follow his movements, ask questions about his occupation, where he had worked, who his teachers were. He would consult with Edek on comrades' character and trustworthiness, and in that way he mobilized helpers. After the meeting at 6

New World Street Franek swore not to deal with "politics", as he called it, any longer. "My task is to do something." And he was, therefore, in a good state of mind. If he did become gloomy, something that did not happen often, we knew that Franek was facing some great difficulty, that there had been some failure. When Franek did not sing, it was a bad sign. He would rock on his slightly bowed legs and whistle and sing loudly. He had a good voice. After a while he went to work as a carpenter outside the ghetto; he was skilled in all the building crafts. He would return every day loaded with all kinds of scrap, and the German sentry would look in surprise at the "filthy Jew" dragging trash. Franek, however, knew what he was doing. After returning from work towards evening, tired and weary, he would begin a new day's work that continued until midnight. The next day he would rise at about five o'clock and once again leave the ghetto, to return in the evening loaded, rocking and whistling or singing. That was Franek. He played with the idea of stopping the production of the bulbs, and making grenades, instead. He only started on that project, some months later. He directed the work and together with Edek, was responsible for the storerooms.

At the time one of the boys, Sender, I think, brought the first rifle into the ghetto. The rifle was not a very modern one but good enough for training. Since it served that purpose and had to be moved from one cell to another, we removed the wooden stock. We used to call that rifle an "otryez" (cripple.) Carrying the rifle from one cell to another was Edek's job. The operation was considered an underground action of prime importance, and we would not have entrusted it to just any comrade.

The date and location of the cell meetings were transmitted to members of the cell on the day of the meeting, and always at a different time. A permanent communications chain had been organized, to also serve, for alarm and mobilization. Edek was then responsible for the cells (he also led the leaders' one composed of Zerah, Yosko and Franek). After a short while all the other members of the leaders' cell also directed individual ones. These were Yentel, Avremele, Srulik, Sender and Yaakov, the first four from the younger Tel-Amal group, Yaakov from the adult group. They were 19 years old, the young guard of our movement in the underground. The veterans at that time were 21 to 23; the oldest of us was Yandzia.

We understood that cold weapons would be good only for self-defense, and that with them we would not be able to repulse the attackers even once. The only kind of weapon that could make the Germans retreat was firearms, and not pistols, either, but longer weapons, rifles and bigger.

The lessons in the cells, held in attics and securely locked rooms began with underground doctrine and continued with Judo exercises, studying the map of the ghetto (courts, passages, parks, empty fields), careful study of the wall, with its gates and passages, dismantling and assembling the rifle and using it. We learned to throw grenades by tossing stones at night in the Judenrat's green parks where our comrades guarded against thieves. The scouting-game geography exercises were carried out within the ghetto walls. Edek would first ouline the strategic plans, which were carried out by the cell heads. Every cell was given a specific exercise for a specific time; in due course the cell leaders also learned planning.

Slowly, very slowly, summer came, hot and beautiful. The parks gradually turned green and the trees blossomed even in the ghetto. Summer brought growing hopes despite the desperate situation at the front. The Germans were taking the Crimea, the Karch peninsula was under fire. German terror was growing stronger. There were shootings and kidnappings among the aryan population. In Warsaw and Minsk, Ivov and Krakow, were public hangings. The Nazis were intensifying their vengeance against those people who did not submit. At the same time rumors were spreading about Chelmno, although only a few were ready to believe them. From Warsaw came the testimony of a refugee who had worked in the furnaces. Chelmno was the scene of the first attempt to use gas in sealed buses. The description was precise, and left no room for doubt. And the front was moving deeper into Russian territory.

In May, Karch yielded, in June, Sebastopol was put under siege and bitter battles were continuing on the Kharkov and Kursk fronts. Still, Jewish hopes grew stronger. The ghetto Jews improved their situations, attempted to ease the suffering, poverty and despair. The slogan of constructivism prevailed everywhere, in life, work, thinking. "With our own hands, the sweat of our brows we will help ourselves."[11] The slogan made its way from the Judenrat on Kupiecka Street to the broad strata of the population and, worthy to note, public institutions as well, including social and political ones. In those peaceful summer days of 1942, in that summer of "constructive building" and the development of industries, we in the ghetto were Don Quixotes looking for windmills to charge. True, those targets were Chelmno and Ponar, Volkovysk and Slonim and Kovno's 9th "port"* the total annihilation of Minsk and Kiev, but Bialystok was still living in peace. The factory for woolen clothing headed by the Jewish manager, Wachs, worked three shifts. Stefan's** large shops opened new departments for chemical production and precise weapons parts in addition to the existing manufacture of

* The fortress near which the Nazis carried out the first murder of Jews in Kovno.

** A German industrialist; Goering was one of his stockholders.

military garments. The shoe factory increased production. True, entering or leaving the ghetto was not as easy as it formerly was; the main gate at Kupiecka had been closed;[12] food, bread[13] and meat rations had been cut,[14] but one day the Jews were given happy news: workers' bread rations would be increased.[15] That was another good omen, and everybody rejoiced. Actually, the food rations were constantly being cut though in camouflaged form: a little more, then a little less, a little added, and then greatly reduced. But anyone who had been satisfied with the rations ended up begging; these, however, did not matter. The majority struggled, supported themselves with great effort and tried to stay alive.

People began to grow vegetables in the parks. These would remain within the ghetto, and supply vitamins. When you work the soil and eat its fruits you also gain confidence. People grew cucumbers, beets, carrots; they even had milk cows. All these were subject to the supervision of the Judenrat's economic department. We thought it better to work in the Judenrat gardens and to add to Jewish food than to work in the factories for the benefit of the German front.

Among the Judenrat members were Zionists who were very enthusiastic about the idea of teaching the youth agriculture, especially the members of Poalei Zion (Right).

Many of the Dror members were also enthused. This activity was headed by Mersik, a gentle and moderate man. He never raised his voice, never complained. He listened to your words but never understood them completely. And he had not understood them when he died of typhus. He could not understand why we should not maintain the chalutz movement. In his view it should be protected from the degeneration prevalent among the youth, from unemployment, the hopes for easy lives, speculation and deceit. The chalutz movement must not fail, it would still have a future. It should be protected from the evil of these mad days, from the Germans and the treacherous Gestapo lackeys.

"Mersik, don't tell Goldberg everything; don't send people to work for him or for the other Judenrat departments. That isn't the right way!" He did not reply.

In the early ghetto days we had cooperated with the Dror members in money matters, work, housing, certificates, in renewing contacts that had been cut, with addresses. We helped each other. There was a necessity for these secondary occupations which served to achieve the main goal. To the Dror members, in that spring and summer of 1942 in Bialystok, these activities were their occupations. We knew that our comrades in Warsaw would bring the change to Bialystok too. Mordechai and Frumka, Tema and Lonka had been in Warsaw from the beginning of spring. Mordechai Tenenbaum reached Bialystok only at the end of summer. On his arrival he united all the active forces among his comrades and directed their scattered and unorganized activities toward resistance against the enemy, and cooperation with us.

After my first return from Warsaw I passed on Yosef Levantowsky's letter to the Communists. Edek, on his arrival, concentrated on the establishment of a fighting front with the participation of all the existing movements tending toward the tactic of fighting. The easiest road led us to the communists. With Sheina's aid the first meetings were set up between Edek and their representative.

After some time, a meeting was also arranged with the Bund representative. The latter did not speak for all the Bund members in the ghetto. Some Bundists sat in the Judenrat and participated in all its activities. Shlomo Poportz represented one section, which was the most radical. These three — Edek, Leibus Mandelblit, the Communists' first representative (later to be replaced by Yoshko Kawe), and Poportz, formed the command of the Shomer-Communist-Bundist union. That was the foundation of the greater front that was realized later.

Very slowly it became obvious to them that we were intent on a fighting underground, a national front to defend the helpless Jewish masses againt total annihilation, a united front of all progressive forces for the purpose of fighting the invader from the rear.

It is impossible to define our relationships with them within the simple framework of positive or negative. This group, the most consolidated and best organized, was also subject to inner conflicts over ideologies, varying conceptions of the problems of the time, difficulties of a political underground, and, most important, subject to internal conflict against prejudice and distrust. The distrust of the past was still prevalent. Sometimes it seemed as if all the barriers had fallen and that our two sides had reached full understanding, and then suddenly, without knowing why, after days of cooperation, the old suspicions arose to divide us. Hashomer Hatzair, as a youth movement, was more dynamic. In addition to the positive world outlook that the movement had implanted in our hearts, it had also cultivated physical agility and dynamic thinking. The Communists, on the other hand, often retreated after making a giant step forward. There were days when they seemed drawn into their shells and disappeared only to return the next day to march with us. Two steps forward, and one back. We began to fear whether we would have time. Edek was troubled, consulted after with Sheina, deliberated and thought aloud, but moved the cause forward.

Two problems that were really one never were absent from the agenda in the history of our joint activity; two problems that remained with us to the end, to August 16, when we all went to the ghetto wall to break through in battle. The first one was that of the goal of the antifascist organization in the ghetto; the second concerned the identity of our partners. Here we actually encountered the same Communist conception that was prevalent in Warsaw which took on a slightly different form in Bialystok because of different conditions. They said: we must defend ourselves, but they sent those who knew how to use weapons to the forest to join the general partisan movement. What that meant was that the defense of the 60,000[16] Bialystok Jews, including the aged, the ill, the women and children, the defense intended to be the expression of our people's soul and its national honor, would be left to others, to the unorganized masses and we could, therefore, not understand what they said. For them the ghetto was a period of suffering which had to be endured, a geographical concept. They did not see that the lives of the people were coming to an end. They did not understand that within the ghetto were imprisoned years of national creativity, an entire history that was going to be wiped off the face of the earth. For them, the walls of the ghetto erected by the Germans were analogous to the anti-Semitism created by capitalism or fascism. It was this doctrine that was the basis of their method. It was also difficult for them to comprehend how men who had never been Communists suddenly became devoted antifascists. Was it possible, without their party tradition, to be loyal, and not to be tempted to betrayal? They couldn't see the changes, nor could they understand that they had to examine their past positions in the light of the new reality. "You have good intentions," they said, "we believe you. We believe that you are antifascists, but how can we believe the others."

We did not ask for immediate unification with Dror within one underground. We battled bitterly over their character in the early Bialystok era, and demanded that they set a clear goal, a real popular front of all those forces able and prepared to join the war against the invader and for the defense of the Jews. While this debate took place we and the communists built our cells, and cooperated exchanging tools, consulting, planning through our joint command, and coordinating our armament efforts. Edek was sent to the command's military center. The military advisor was Alexander, an elderly man with some military knowledge. Franck, as production head, would meet with the engineer Hanoh Farber of the Communists, to exchange views, discuss possibilities. In the course of time successful production was coordinated, leading to the final amalgamation of all the tools and stores.

That summer the united organization decided to place one of our men in the police. We were not completely satisfied with the connections with Barash, or at least could not trust them completely. We chose Gedalyahu. In my whole life I never saw Gedalyahu so miserable and unwilling as he was at that time. Barash arranged the matter that same day and on the morrow Gedalyahu wore the dark blue hat with the "Judische Ordnungsdienst" inscription on it. He did not want to accept the task, but he obeyed nonetheless. From then on we learned many things about the police, Jewish criminals, the Germans' demands, and especially about the behavior of the various public representatives and their relationships with the Germans. We greatly appreciated this information. We wanted to know who the ferrets, the speculators, and the traitors were. It was also easy for a policeman to move about the streets at night, to carry material, to arrange communications during curfew, sometimes also to help others to get out and to come back in. The hat and stick made up for any misbehavior, but Gedalyahu was apparently either the only — or one of the few policemen — in the ghetto who never used his stick on a Jew.

Lublin

Once agan I was on the road. Travel was getting more difficult. The examinations were becoming stricter. Especially so was travel in the "Government" area because of the greater crowding and the smuggling in village and town.

Most of the travellers were smugglers and peddler women carrying forbidden goods. Children played a special role in the struggle for existence during the occupation. They were skillful smugglers, sometimes even better than the adults. They hung on to the steps and during an inspection were able to jump off even while the train was moving. They would sing songs in their hoarse voices, and beg. Most of the songs were patriotic, of little poetic value but speaking to the listeners' hearts. sometimes one even heard satiric songs about the Germans.

By the time I reached Warsaw I was exhausted from lack of sleep, the crowding between Malkinia and Warsaw, and the tension in crossing the borders. It was easier for me to shove my way into and find a place in the car because I was not loaded down with bundles. I was not smuggling. Our merchandise was invisible, and did not take up much room. There was one thing however, from which there was no escape, and which we had no choice but to smuggle: the lice.

In Warsaw I had two addresses on the aryan side. The situation at the farm in Cherniakov was tense, and it was not a good place for a day's refuge. Every sojourner was examined at the farm. The neighbors already recognized the people there and you did not go unless there was no choice. My first address was at 33 Zelazna, at the home of the Zaionchkovsky family. From there it was possible to contact Haniek (who had been the first emissary to Vilna) and Irena. There I could look into the situation at the gates and outside the walls. The Zaionchkovskys were a somewhat proletarian family, working intellectuals. He had been a teacher before the war and now he and his family lived on modest "shmuggle". They devoted their spare time to negotiations with the Polish liberation movement (apparently Sikorsky's). Over and above everything else, they helped Jews. Their apartment was one of our contact points on the aryan side. The second address was Heniek's. He lived with his wife, their small daughter and his wife's mother in a suburban wooden house where he raised vegetables and chickens. If we didn't find him at home he could be found not too far away at his father's grocery store on Cherniakovska Street. It couldn't really be called a store, one couldn't find very much there. What was interesting was the storekeeper himself: he was a typical Pole with a long mustache, cursing the Germans in a hoarse voice. He always received me very courteously.

This time I had not come to Warsaw by myself. I had brought Sarenka, from Vilna with me. After the tragedy that had overtaken her friend Moshe Kopito, we decided to move her to her family in Warsaw and to enlist her in our activities. Sarenka was short and thin. She had a tiny pale face and a short nose, the face of a child. Her hair was light. But we could do nothing about her black, burning eyes, the eyes of a Jewish child. We dressed her as a little girl, her tangled and slightly wild hair we wove into braids, and tied them with red ribbons. In my forged transit pass we wrote that Halina Woronowich "und Kind" were going to Warsaw for . . . etc. We passed the border examinations safely. Sarenka, who was a year older than I, travelled as a little girl in my care (we had not written that she was my daughter!). In any case, the Germans did not notice. This time my sister had dressed me properly. I wore a big hat that made me look older by about five years at least. My lips were painted. I wore a fancy coat and had an expensive leather purse (which I had borrowed from a friend, who had taken it from her mother). Trouble, however, appeared at the border. At Malkinia it was necessary to wait all night in the station. Here they watched you all the time. Polish policemen and German border-police were stationed there. Here someone might suspect you and turn you in and there was no escape. The night was rainy and the station was open to the wind. We were both shivering. Sarenka showed extraordinary courage, and was not frightened by suspicious looks or afraid that someone might bother her. Still, our situation was difficult. We decided to seek shelter. Some railway workers standing near the exit were offering passengers a night's lodging. I begain to bargain with them, when suddenly a stout German officer in the uniform of the German transportation service appeared and suggested: "Opposite here I have an apartment; I am on duty now. You can rest there." The German's apartment appealed to me more than did some Polish one whose occupants I did not know. I called Sarenka and we followed the German. We crossed the tracks and the stout man opened the door. We entered a small apartment; one room and a kitchen. We felt a pleasant warmth.

"You can sleep here," he pointed to the two beds along the walls.

"We shall sleep together, don't bother making up both beds, " I said in my fluent German (I was able to make up and speak some sentences in a mimicked accent).

"But the child can sleep there, it will be more comfortable for us; you will sleep here with me, you understand? " he whispered in my ear.

"Excuse me sir, you have made a mistake. We will pay for a night's lodging with money and with nothing else. You said you were on duty now."

"Hmm . . . you're strange. Why don't you want to?"

"You've made a mistake, sir, come child, put your coat on and we'll leave," I said to Sarenka in Polish, but loudly. Sarenka had not heard the conversation.

The pot-bellied German stood riveted in his place. He looked at me in surprise:

"But why are you going?" I explained once again that we had sought a night's lodging and nothing more. I thought that he might change his mind and go back to his work, but he still insisted: "What does it matter," he asked in astonishment, "why are you so hard-hearted?"

We left. Silent, we shrank into a corner of the cold, stinking station. Sarenka lowered her head into her collar, closed her eyes and tried to sleep.

We arrived in Warsaw before noon. I left Sarenka in the Zaionchkovsky home on Zelazna Street, near the main station, and went to look for Heniek. In the evening Heniek led us to the wire fence on Shenna Street (also near Zalazna). He went up to the Polish policeman on duty (I don't know whether he was guarding against smuggling across the ghetto border in general, or against smuggling that did not earn him anything), whispered something into his ear and gave him 10 zloty, five zloty per person. (The price for Jews was higher: 10 zloty per person.) The policeman turned his back then Heinek raised the wire from below and motioned Sarenka to creep through. Sarenka was small and got in quickly. I crawled in after her. Heniek waved to us, and disappeared in the darkness.

The Germans patrolled the whole length of the ghetto walls and fences on motorcycles. (Only Shenna Street and Zelazna Street still had wire fences instead of the thick ghetto walls). They would roar by, and fire their submachine guns at anybody approaching the border. They would appear suddenly at tremendous speed, and woe to anyone they found. Almost every day corpses of those they shot, mostly children, were brought from the ghetto border. We entered the ghetto and were surrounded by Jewish policemen. Here the price was five zloty per person. Once you were rid of the policemen you went to the first band-vendor, and for 50 pennies bought the bands to put on your sleeves, and you were home. Once again the days were filled with running to the institutions, command workers and parties. Sarenka was swallowed up in the ghetto tumult, and I did not see her again.

This time I was asked to visit our kibbutzes in Chenstohova and the farm in Zarky. Tosya and I left the ghetto through the hole in the wall on Orla Street. The wall was quite high, but with some effort you could climb up and reach it. After giving the Jewish policeman a few zloty, you jumped right through into the aryan side. You had to get away without being seen from neighboring streets. You made some extra turns in the streets near the Bank Square and then you could rest until the train left, or wander about the streets to kill time. You could not get away from people in the station. They were always there, whispering in your ear: "I buy and sell dollars, gold . . . I buy . . . I sell . . . "

Not all the buyers and sellers were really occupied at what they said. Many of them were government spies. It was better to get to the station just before the train was to leave. True, you would not find a place to sit or even to stand, but you would be safer. It was better to spend the waiting time in a cafe, and if you suspected that strange eyes were watching you, had better hurry to another cafe. In each, drink a coffee, and eat a cake. The saccharine in the cakes left a bitter taste that lingered.

Once again the crowded trains, and the anti-Semitic jokes. You pushed into the perspiring, dirty crowd. The train stopped at certain stations for examination. You met the nasty looks of the police: let them pass without moving your eyes or lowering them to the ground. On the way to Chenstohova you went through Kolushky, a crossroads station, and a place to be feared. Here they beat people, broke jars of milk and cream, turned over baskets of eggs, looked under the women's dresses, kidnapped people and took them to Auschwitz.

The Chenstohova ghetto was not fenced in. Poles were allowed to go through the Jewish quarter; Jews were forbidden to leave without a permit. In any case, the situation was easier. We entered the streets of the Jewish quarter as aryans, put on the bands we had bought in the street and were soon at the kibbutz on a side street. The comrades surrounded us and avidly asked questions about what was happening in the world, in the other ghettoes, and what was happening to their friends and acquaintances in Warsaw.

Tosya felt at home here. She knew everyone by name and past history. One had a relative in the Pawiak, the large Warsaw ghetto prison; another had a sister in the Warsaw ghetto, a third - a family that had been deported from a town near Warsaw. Everyone was waiting for news, and Tosya usually was able to relate authentic information. It was this wonderful combination of concern for the important cause and interest in the comrades' personal troubles that permeated the work of the movement's central personalities. May we not pity the roses because the forest is burning?

We found many who were sick in the Chenstohova kibbutz. The comrades worked in the German factories, and at whatever other jobs they could find. The danger of being sent to a work camp was very real; the battle for existence fatiguing. They received a great deal of help from the agricultural farm near Chenstohova, where some of the kibbutz members worked. The purpose of Tosya's visit was to prepare the kibbutz for the organization of fighting cells. Aryeh Vilner would succeed her in guiding the kibbutz. Tosya fulfilled her mission at meetings and in talks with comrades. I looked on, weary and depressed. On the train from Chenstohova to our farm at Zarky, I blamed myself for my depression, for the narrow, dirty apartment, for allowing the sickness and hunger to affect my judgment and my ability to concentrate on action. Tosya was not depressed, though it was she and not I who had dealt with the problems of the Chenstohova people.

Once again we were on the train. This time it was not very crowded. From the window we saw the silvery, sun-lit fields. Tosya put her head out of the window, her big dressy hat fell aside, her curls waved in the breeze, her clear eyes shone. We rode to a side station called "Zloty Potok". From there we continued by peasant cart to Zarky. The road wound through wooded hills; waterfalls glinted in the sun's rays. Tosya sang all the way.

The sight of the farm made a strange impression on me. It all seemed so odd in view of what was going to happen. I looked on silently. Tosya said:

"Don't worry, they will leave all this in time and turn their 'ploughshares into swords'. See how Jews are living here."

For the first time I saw a village without a ghetto, and without its bans. Jews dwelt in all the parts of the village without limited movement. The Jewish shops were open, and the Polish farmers bargained with the Jewish shop-keepers. Only two weeks ago the doors of Jewish homes were first marked with the Star of David. That was an ill omen. They neither knew nor had heard anything about what was happening in the Jewish world, in Vilna or Bielorussia or even in nearby Chelmno. The only links to the outside world were maintained by the shomrim at the farm, who were visited by people from Warsaw. Here they could obtain everything cheaply, including forged papers. The infamous "Kenn-Karte" (identification card) was sold at bargain prices. Instead of paying 50 or 100 zloty demanded in Warsaw for the photograph and form, they paid only 20 zloty here. Indeed, this had been the first source of "Kenn-Kartes" for our "aryan" activists.

We returned to Warsaw after a few days. Tosya communicated with the ghetto by telephone. The safest way to enter the ghetto, she thought, was an "arrangement" with the police stationed at one of the ghetto entrances, and by doing "business" with the Jewish police. The police enjoyed a thriving trade. One kind of merchandise smuggled in and out of the ghetto was people. These events, however, had to be arranged in advance by telephone with our comrade in the police, Aryeh Grabobski, or his comrade Engelman.

We found the ghetto in panic.

The night before, 60 Jews had been taken out of their beds and shot, not far from their homes. The action had obviously been planned in advance. The Jews who were shot came from various strata of the population: a speculator, together with a community worker, printers, publishers and financial supporters of the underground press. Among those slain was a young scientist and statistician named Linder, who had maintained close ties with the underground. He had been gathering documentary and statistical material about the Polish Jews under the occupation, and had been one of the closest cooperators with the underground organizations. He was one of the public and scientific figures supporting revolt and armed resistance. Linder had also been a central figure in the group of archivists headed by Ringelblum. In the morning it became known that they were also seeking Yitzhak Zuckerman. Obviously, the action had been carried out based on detailed information. The death of these 60 Jews, who represented all sections of the underground, was evidence that the Gestapo knew what was taking place in the ghetto. The execution of the 60 was one example of the prevailing methods of instilling fear in the ghetto. Perhaps they hoped in this way to frustrate the resistance plans, and to warn us this would happen to any person who dared to disobey, or participate in the underground.

When I visited Linder's widow I was impressed by the silence and seriousness prevailing in the house. She moved about in her black clothes on tiptoe, spoke in a whisper, and did not cry. She was happy to receive a greeting I had brought her, thanked me and in the end said reflectively:

"Are they going to draw the correct conclusions from my husband's death?" I could only keep silent in the face of her self-restraint and moral strength. Did it not, in some way, reflect the stubbornness of Warsaw's Jews? This was not the petty trade, the peddling and smuggling of the ghetto — this was another Warsaw, the united strength of Jewish Warsaw. At that time the "Antifascist Committee" was formed, the first organization of all the militant progressive forces within the ghetto.

On my return I found that matters in Warsaw were progressing, but not at the necessary pace. We were extremely tense; the ground was already burning under our feet. And still, in my running between ZTOS (Jewish Social Relief) and the Joint, I wasted whole days.

I do not recall the order of the last visits and I may be confused about the chronology. The meetings took place more frequently, but were often stopped in mid-discussion. Sarah Silber's travels did, indeed, help me a great deal; she brought material and newspapers, as well as money. The negotiations over money, and the meetings, were my assignment. The institutions did not want new faces, they did not want to negotiate with different people, and perhaps they were right. If our cooperation with Dror had been closer we might, perhaps, have avoided superfluous trips and unnecessary risks. Of course, we never really succeeded in attaining the complete coordination of underground activities, a situation of "not one superfluous step". We did progress however, and we learned from our mistakes.

I seem to recall that this was my last visit to the Warsaw ghetto. This time the trip took three and a half hours. I rode in a train barred to Poles, an express for high-ranking Germans; ordinary soldiers were excluded. I boarded by accident. The train, marked with the letter "D", left Bialystok a few minutes after the regular, two-car train left on its slow trip, scheduled to reach Warsaw after 24-hours and a long stop at the Malkinia station. When I asked, in German, what train was going to Warsaw the clerk pointed to the express. He apparently thought me a German. Upon entering I saw that I had made a mistake but decided to try my luck. There were upholstered chairs, almost empty cars, polite Germans sitting at their ease, smoking fat cigars, high officials, businessmen, officers and some stout ladies in fashionable German dresses, with me in the middle. I thought of leaving this "pleasant" company, and I don't know why I hesitated. Some feeling of spite moved me to stay.

The trip was wonderful. The examination at Malkinia was perfunctory, with courteous, smiling functionaries in charge. They hardly looked at my travel permit. I took it out of my fancy purse (long live Sonka, who had taken it from her mother!) in a careless manner and spat out a curt "bitte".

The official did not even ask for my identification card. The train moved on immediately. I did not speak much with the German sitting opposite, and rested, satisfied with alternating "jawohls" and extended "neins". It was not a good idea to put my German to an unnecessary test. This was not Malkinia, here you did not lie on a stone floor; here it was not crowded, and no one was smuggling potatoes and cream. The car was clean and well ventilated, and there were no lice.

Success sometimes induces courage. I decided to enter the ghetto without a guide. Must I always trouble Heniek? I went up to the fence at the ghetto border. I would attempt to imitate his familiar tones, his suburban Warsaw "nerve":

"Panie," I apply to the "blue", "I want to go into this Jewish paradise."

"What do you have in your bag? Eh? Fine goods?"

"Well, panie, a person has to live!"

"Well, creep through! Give me a gural (ten zloty)."

"Why a gural? The Jews pay a gural?"

I gave him five zloty and crawled through. The policeman turned his back and marched slowly along the wire fence.

We heard news in the ghetto: citizens of neutral countries, living in the ghetto, would be returned to their native countries. Gitterman, the Joint officer and our sworn friend, offered to add me to his family, since his Argentinian passport included his daughter who was already in America. The situation was critical and since the world did not know what was happening in Poland, we had to send someone abroad to mobilize world public opinion so that it could adopt measures to compel Hitler to cease his annihilation of the Jews.

At the Hanhaga meeting in Warsaw it was decided to give Gitterman my papers. I wanted to consult on this matter with our comrades in Bialystok and Vilna. Meanwhile, I was waiting for the money that Gitterman had promised to provide before leaving. It seemed strange to me that there were still those who believed that it was possible to leave this hell safely, and that it was the Germans who were providing the opportunity.

In the ghetto there was already some progress made in acquiring weapons, and cells for military training had already been established. These too, were in groups of five, I think, and they were already seeking weapons outside the ghetto. Tomorrow there was to be a consultation with Irena, Heniek and Walter. Walter was a German living in Poland with his family. He had grown up and was educated there. He had been one of Irena's members in the Polish scout movement, and when Poland had been occupied he'd been drafted into the German army, against his will. He had fought on the Leningrad front, and two days ago had come home on leave. Walter was tall, broad-shouldered and blond, a typical German. The band with the Star of David on his sleeve looked strange. Irena would generally come in with the permit of one of her workmates, and the two men would push their way in through some opening.

The ghetto had not changed. It was summer in the malodorous streets with little air to breathe. We walked through the streets on the way to Nalevwki. On Leshno Street there was a great deal of movement. Apparently, it was a good time to leave. Every few minutes a large opening was made in the wall on Leshno Street (some bricks had been taken out) and full sacks rolled in and fell to the sidewalk. The work was done with great speed; the hole was opened and closed again immediately. Hands pulled the sacks to one side, and they immediately disappeared. That was one of the paths for contraband coming into the ghetto that gave a livelihood to hundreds of smugglers, middlemen and shopkeepers. Unrationed food was also brought in that way.

We pushed him ahead. Suddenly there was a commotion on Leshno Street. We were passing the church of the converted Jews, and could not see where the noise was coming from. Little boys pulled us aside.

"Run, they're looking for gentiles in the ghetto!"

We had barely managed to enter a nearby courtyard when two tattered boys began to fight, pushing us back and forth. When we left the gate Heniek's wallet was missing from his breast pocket. Now we understood why the commotion.

The situation was serious. In addition to the fifteen zloty, the wallet contained Heniek's papers, including his identificaion card. It was risky to take a single step without papers in the occupation area. Yosef Kaplan went to look for the thieves, at their market, on Nowolipie Street. If you had "the right connections" there you could redeem your stolen property at a reasonable price. There was a "company" whose messenger-agents were little children. Find the "banker", you no longer had to look for the thieves themselves. A business like all others. If you tried to call the police you never regained your loss. The bargaining went on all day. They remained firm, and so did Yosef. They thought they had made a great find and demanded an exorbitant sum: "only 50 zloty". Heniek, however, announced that for 50 zloty he could get a new and better forged certificate. It seemed that the stolen certificate had also been forged. In that case, the loss was not so great. On the contrary, he could change his name again, and feel even more secure. Thus, the affair ended.

Walter was willing to help in everything during his stay in Warsaw: in the risky travels, and in activities outside the ghetto involved in acquiring weapons. During those days "something" was brought into the ghetto; not too much or too heavy, but it was a good beginning. If I am not mistaken that was when we brought in grenades.

Suddenly the rumor spread that in Lublin there had been an *aktzia* aimed at liquidating the entire ghetto and its 40,000 Jews. After some time it became known that Himmler himself had been there before the *aktzia* to give final instructions. That was the first total liquidation of a Jewish community in the General-Government.

Since I had to wait for the money another few days I was asked to go to

Lublin to see what had happened, the methods used, and the overall plan (in Warsaw we heard nothing except the rumor itself) and to help existing organizations as far as possible with money, if anything could still be done. Resistance apparently was now out of the question. No preparations had been made, no cells established, no weapons accumulated, and the *aktzia* was amost over.

I had never been in Lublin. The trip was long and tiring. Once again crowding, sacks of potatoes, shouts, screams, police, examinations and searches with the help of dogs. This time there was an added difficulty: since the day earlier special travel permits were being demanded from all those seeking to go anywhere from Warsaw. There were long queues at the booths, question upon question: why? where? Even these difficulties, however did not lessen the crowding on the trains, or the smuggling. This stubborn people wanted to live, even under this harsh regime. With good reason it has been said that there is some similarity between the Poles and the Jews. Suffering, apparently, actually intensifies one's will to live.

Upon reaching Lublin I looked first for some shelter: a place where I could rest from the trip, wash, eat and feel human again. When an *aktzia* took place in any city it affected everybody, and all new faces were suspect. I asked a Polish woman in the street where I could find a hotel. There were none for Poles, she said, but I could wash, eat and rest in her home. I accepted her invitation. She lived near the station, and that was convenient for me. On the way she told me what was happening in the ghetto. I did not ask; she just talked about it. This was the fifth consecutive day that they were removing Jews from the ghetto. There were Jews who had lived outside the area (until recently Lublin had not had a closed ghetto), but today these, too, had been taken. One Jew remained. He lived not far from here, and was an engineer or a doctor. Abominable things were happening in the ghetto. Anyone who could not get up and walk was shot on the spot, and in the ghetto there were sick and aged who could not move. The city was full of Ukrainians, Lithuanians and Latvians who were assigned to guard the barbed wire fences. Poles sometimes wanted to throw food over, but the guards did not let them. This was the fifth or sixth day that no one had left or entered. Inside they were dying, being killed by the thousands. All this was in clear view from the outside, through the barbed wire.

The Polish woman's house was small and warm and sparklingly clean. Her husband, a railway worker, earned good wages. This was the third day that she had not cooked; she was simply unable to do anything. She talked and talked, and wept. I don't know why she trusted me; in times like these every person hid his feelings from his neighbor. I heard her story, and stored all the details in my memory.

I wandered about the city. Wherever I looked for a Jewish address on the aryan side I found barred doors. I decided to go to the ghetto, no matter what happened: I could not return empty-handed. I was afraid to ask the ghetto location and just followed my instincts, and the movements of the S.S. units. When I reached the streets leading to the ghetto a terrible sight was revealed. On the other side of the barbed wire there was a deadly silence, not a single living being, not even a dog. Broken doors gaped like black pits. Nothing stirred. Here and there Poles were leaning toward the fence, looking for a living soul to whom they could throw some package. Out of that valley of death some creature would appear, grab something and flee. One managed, a second did not get away and was shot on the spot. And again silence.

Near the ghetto, outside the fence, there was a big brick building where the Judenrat offices, the social institutions and the charity kitchen were housed.

"Panie, there are still some Jews there. There is the Jewish woman who used to manage the social relief for the aged and poor people."

I seized on this news: that was what I was looking for. In Warsaw I had been told that if I found her I would have a contact. It was forbidden to enter the building or to leave it. Police were marching around the building. When the guard at the door made a turn, I leaped in and raced to the top floor. I found the social relief head immediately. I do not recall her name. She could not hide her surprise when I told her that I had come from Warsaw to help, that I was an emissary of the public and of the institutions. I asked her to assist me in contacting the ghetto. It became clear that this was not possible. She, too, was isolated, and forbidden to leave the building. There was no longer anybody in the ghetto. There was also no way to get in. The 7,000 Jews who were left would apparently remain as members of a work camp. That was what she had heard. However, it was entirely possible that they too would be taken from the city. All those not included among the seven thousand "legals", and who had succeeded in hiding, could not be found in any case. No organization remained, and anyone attempting to flee was shot. The whole area was wide open.

"Where did they take the 33,000 Jews? How did they take them?"

It appeared that exactly as in the other places, they had first demanded 12,000, then another 3,000, and then more. The Judenrat had not been consulted. The Jewish police had not, and could not, intervene. Everything had been done by the Latvians. Here they had done their job simply: they either shot and killed them, or drove the people out. Special units for that purpose had been brought in from outside. Before the *aktzia* no one had known anything, Jews and non-Jews. The holocaust happened suddenly. It was reported that Himmler himself had visited here a week ago and given instructions. Where were they being taken? Certainly to execution. In sealed freight cars, horribly overcrowded, without bread or water, going southeast. From later information we learned that the Lublin Jews had been taken to Majdanek or Belzec.

"It is no longer possible to do anything. It is the end. Why didn't they make preparations earlier, for rescue, resistance or revolt?" She spoke without bitterness, as if talking to herself. In my mind, too, the question was insistent.

I gave her the money and told her that she could do with it as she wished, perhaps she could still save somebody, or try to escape herself. I would help her.

"I am not going to run away. I will stay here to the end. First of all, I am being guarded. Second, there are still some Jews here, and I am responsible for them. In any case, I won't run away now, maybe at the end."

I stayed with her for a number of hours knowing that I would be leaving someone sentenced to death. She gave me the addresses of some Jews outside the ghetto. Perhaps they needed assistance. I left the building safely, and succeeded in escaping the eyes of the guards. I wandered about the city, looking for the addresses, and found only one Jew, who thanked me for my good heart but said he had Polish friends who were helping him and that he lacked nothing.

I returned at a late hour to the Polish woman's house near the railway station, and left Lublin on the night train.

When I returned to Warsaw to relate my bitter tale and tell all that I had seen, the assembled leaders to whom I made my report were silent. Gitterman gave me part of the money and promised to give me the rest in the next few days. I decided to go to Bialystok, and to return later for the balance of the funds.

I left the ghetto through Muranovska Street, whispering the code word to the guard, knowing that Aryeh, our policeman, would later pay my head tax.

I turned right and came to the no. 3 tram station leading directly to the central railway station on Yerosalimska Avenue. Near the ghetto gate, on the aryan side, various suspicious persons were moving about, children, boys of 15-16, their hands in their pockets, hats drawn down and their eyes looking in all directions. For the first time I saw the persons popularly called

"Shmalcovnik", that is extortionists. That was their livelihood, to prey on Jews sneaking out of the ghetto and to demand ransom in money or valuables, to prevent their betrayal to the Gestapo.

"Maybe you want to get into ghetto, I can show you where," one man said to me, pretending that he knew my secret. He was older than the other hoodlums. It was evident that he was not sure of what he had discovered. The "Shmalcovnik" had a sixth sense in ferreting out a Jew.

This one had seen me coming out of the ghetto, but was not certan that I was Jewish. Gentiles, too, sometimes went there. He therefore wanted to see what impression his offer to show me the way into the ghetto made. I saw his hesitation and resolved not to respond. The no. 3 tram that had meanwhile arrived was my lifesaver. When I went to the ticket booth I saw the fellow standing behind me without lowering his eyes. Apparently I flushed. When the tram slowed down I leaped to the sidewalk on Marshalkovska Street and began to walk slowly. Suddenly I heard steps behind me. It was noon, a clear, warm day. The street was almost empty. I crossed to the other side and stood near a shop window. Very slowly my nerves quieted. What angered me most was my bag filled with canned food, the gift the Warsaw comrades had insisted on sending to the comrades in Bialystok. In my pocket were documents and pictures of the camps where Jews were dying of torture and beatings, of Chelmno where Jews had been gassed. Dr. Ringelblum had put these documents and pictures in my pocket before my departure, so that I could show them to the people in Bialystok, especially Barash. These precious preserves were to be used in Warsaw only for sale, to obtain money for the movement's needs. Why had I agreed to take them with me to Bialystok? Had I lost my senses? Maybe I became intoxicated by the success of my previous trip on the D train? Not every day is a holiday!

The fellow followed me, step by step. When I stopped, he stopped. I went into a court supposedly to tie my shoelace: he waited until I came out. He apparently was not in a hurry : he had time and was sure that his victim would not escape. Maybe I should give him money? Foolishness. The money I had been given by Gitterman was sacred to the movement, and it was hidden. My bag was heavy, and I felt the pictures and papers in my coat pocket. My hand in my pocket was sweating. I became furious.

"Paie, psia krew! Why are you creeping behind me like a smelly dog?"

He straightened up and replied, first in a courteous and quiet voice:

"Excuse me, madame, but you are not going to get to the railway station . . ."

"And why won't I get there?"

"You're Jewish!" Now he stopped being courteous. His voice was quiet but threatening.

"Are you going to get away from here or not you stinking dog?"

"Oh, how nervous we are! Look, there is a Polish policeman, let's see who wins . . . "

"So . . . what policeman did you say? Wait, look a little further . . . at the top of the street there is a German. Do you see the S.S. unform? Let's go to him . . . "

He looked around, the German's uniform gleamed greenly from afar. Slowly, slowly, he turned aside and left.

It was over. This time I came out safely. My nerves were ragged and I was angry at myself, at this crow in human form, at the policeman, the gendarme — at the whole world.

The sentry examining papers at the border asked me if I was a teacher going on vacation. I nodded my head, and unintentionally smiled. Let me be a teacher, on vacation, only not to stand together with this idiot here in the Malkinia border station! Praise the Lord! You only had to press the button, and the smile came. Where was that button? It's all the same, anywhere in the body, in the head or the nerve center.

That is how I went to Bialystok from Warsaw for the last time during the occupation.

In the Bialystok ghetto I met Solomon Entin, who was about to leave for Warsaw. I aked him to wait for me since I would also be returning in another few days.

"There's no time; they're waiting for me in Warsaw."

Solomon was what we called a "wonderful fellow". He was born in Pinsk, and was a member of the Noar Hatzioni Zionist youth movement. They always said of him that he was not like the ordinary members of the Noar, that he was "too revolutionary". Actually, the truth was otherwise. Most of the Noar Hatzioni members, perhaps because of the very fact that they were members of a youth movement, and perhaps because they had been educated according to the experience and example of another, revolutionary, youth movement, were like Solomon. Tall, broad-shouldered, a typical athletic type, he was blond, with a mustache he had grown because of his task, blue-eyed: a handsome and healthy "sheigetz" (gentile boy). He also travelled the road from Warsaw to Bialystok and Vilna. Since he was a native of Pinsk he didn't speak Polish fluently; what need for Polish in Jewish Pinsk? On the road he chose to keep silent. His aryan face preceded him and that would have been sufficient, if not for the Polish girls who wanted to amuse themselves on the train in the company of this handsome fellow.

Solomon left. Two days later Sarah Silber and her sister Roshka went the same way, loaded with papers and reports. On the third day, a day or two before my regular trip to Warsaw, I went to my friend Stefa, outside the ghetto. I found a telegram there: "Don't come, Lonia and Solomon are ill."

Explanations were unnecessary. They had fallen into a trap on the border, and since they had gone before Sarah and Roshka, the latter two had probably fallen into the same trap.

About that time, just before I received the telegram, the Communists had asked us to give them one permit so that their comrade Yakubovsky could get to Warsaw for consultation. We did so willingly. Antony Yakubovsky was one of their veteran comrades, and according to reports, a militant and moral person, one of their best. He had stayed in the ghetto for a long time with his Jewish party-comrades. There he had hidden from the Gestapo, and participated in the Jew's battle.

He, too, left and did not return.

What was happening? Solomon and Lonia had gone together but each in a different train; why had they become partners in disaster?

"Are you a teacher; are you going on vacation?" I remembered the sentry's questions. That question had been asked five days ago. Then the permits had been valid. For some weeks we had known, however, that the old permits had been invalidated and new ones introduced: they were green on fine, cross-ruled paper, in gothic script. These permits were almost impossible to obtain. We had had no choice: either we stop the trips or take the risk. Since we had chanced it a number of times and succeeded, we believed that there was no danger. According to the dictates of common sense we should have given up, gathered our last remnants and stopped. It was no longer possible to take a single step. The siege was suffocating, the isolation and separation brought despair. The world was silent. I would not go with Gitterman to help arouse the placid west . . . It was the end!

A lie. We kept trying.

The First Weapons

It was summer, 1942. I found Edek head over heels in work. The group had coalesced, the links were tight. Tension bound us together. The young people were working, some outside, others within the ghetto itself, in the Judenrat gardens and the German factories. Any service performed for the Germans and the front had only one aim: it was an evil that had to be transformed to good. Many Jews and non-Jews were concentrated in the factories. We had to influence these masses, directly and indirectly, and organize them for internal resistance, to sabotage production. What is more, we had to exploit these workplaces not only morally but practically. There it was possible to steal, to "pick up" material for our own arms production. Here it was possible to organize, to incite, to encourage and to educate. It was both a meeting place and a hiding place. Members of the underground served the Nazi's war production for only one purpose: sabotage. Anyone who forgets this even for a moment would never be absolved. It was in that way that Franck worked and changed work places when the possibilities for sabotage were obviated. It was in that way that Avremele and Sender worked outside the ghetto; Yentel and Roshka in the knitwool factory inside where Zerah carried the heavy sacks, bricks and stones. In the evenings we would meet in Kupiecka Street, or 6 New World Street.

At 6 New World Street there was a room in a formerly splendid apartment in which some of the poorest now lived. Dirty children in rags ran between our feet in the dark, damp corridors, black from the smoke of the makeshift stove in the middle of the room. There were hardly any men here, just women and children. The children begged in the streets and the women sold vegetables in the market. In any event, they paid no attention to their neighbors in the side room, where we lived. It was our hiding place. There the members of the secretariat, Franck, Zerah, Gedalyahu, Edek and I lived, all in one room. At night we would take two folding beds from under the ones standing in the room and the entire place became a bedroom. During the day order and cleanliness prevailed. That was the concern of Chaika Rybak, our commune mother. Only her understanding, and the fact that she worked at night, made it possible for her to keep the place clean. 6 New Work Street was a haven for rest and inspiration in our mad world. Sitting together, joking, consulting with each other, we would relieve the tensions and gain new strength. Experts in this area were Franck and Gedalyahu; good-hearted and gentle Franek with his merry songs, and Gedalyahu with his Russian obscenities and his mocking hatred of his job as a Jewish policeman in the ghetto. Edek and Zerah were soul-mates, friends who hid nothing from each other. I never saw them in intimate discussion and wondered how they maintained that friendship. Edek would reply: "by a quiet look." How much I absorbed from that mature male friendship, at once worrying and restrained, and how much I longed to copy it.

"Zerah, what will happen if I die a natural death, hah? Not from a bullet and not in battle? From sickness, for example?" Edek used to ask jokingly.

"Then you'll die twice," Zerah replied.

"Why?"

"First from the sickness, and then from sorrow over such an ordinary death."

Sometimes the jokes died out and were replaced by somber reflections. Such evenings were painful, and we would go to bed early.

I can still recall one such evening.

"Will the time ever come; will we ever get to Palestine? What do you think, will I ever live in a kibbutz?" Edek would inquire of the room.

"Why don't you ask whether you are going stay alive at all?"

"Isn't it the same?" Edek asked.

I don't know how we got to talking about the future. Not our people's future, but our own. We tried to speak quietly and objectively, as if we were talking not about ourselves, but about others, whose death was a natural and historical necessity.

"I don't care if they write an obituary or not; I don't care what future generations say about me."

"Don't talk foolishness. Everyone has an ambition to be considered a hero," Gedalyahu interrupted.

It was Gedalyahu's way to say what he thought. His honesty, and his ability to uncover his friend's secrets as well as his own, won him sincere friends and acquaintances even among the Communists. Gedalyahu was allowed to say everything, no one was ever insulted, neither his close friends nor our allies.

"And I tell you, Gedalyahu, for my part they can cut my body into little pieces and scatter them to the wind. I don't care; the important thing is to be here, to fight here to the last breath. After that, come what may," Zerah tried to convince, doubting and understanding Gedalyahu.

We did not talk much about death. It was something we understood, and knew as inevitable.

That restrained male friendship did not prevent silent concern for one another. That winter Gedalyahu had been ill with pneumonia. Then he coughed all summer. He used to hide his handkerchiefs so that they would not be seen, since his spittle was dark, between red and greyish-brown. We pleaded with him to go to the doctor but he vigorously refused. When we insisted he went about like a dark and angry shadow, but he did not go. Zerah decided to fool him. He called the doctor and made an appointment, and I took Gedalyahu, supposedly to a meeting with the communist representative. When he saw that it was the doctor's house he was hurt but he did agree to an examination, and to take the prescribed medicine. We never referred to this event again. Gedalyahu accepted the fact of friendship silently, but appreciatively.

The younger people among us found relief; first of all, in action, imagination, which carried them to the heights of heroism and self-sacrifice.

They taught themselves, steeled themselves. The mission aided them and their task spurred them on to be at once strong and humane. There was a seminar for movement activists in the ghetto, a seminar devoted to character building. We did not study how to educate our pupils, but how to educate ourselves. We wanted to revive old doctrines in the light of the new reality; to examine them and bring them up-to-date. There was the great danger that fundamental truths would devolve into the scrap heap of history. At that time we looked, first and foremost, toward the Soviet Union. We had to believe in this country to strengthen it, to rally the workers of the world around it in the war against fascism. We were commanded to fight nazism and its allies as a war of the Jewish masses. We also clung to the doctrines of Marx and Borochov and their new truths. We invited Sheina Levin to join us since she was concerned with problems of education in wartime. She began with the children, and we carried on with the masses.

Important inter-connected events occurred. Hitler's armies were nearing the gates of Palestine. Those were the days of el-Alamein. We suddenly seemed petrified. Hitler's African armies were approaching the borders of Palestine! The days were gloomy and sad. Edek no longer asked whether he would ever get to Palestine; we asked ourselves whether Rommel would succeed in crushing our last hope. For hours and days our hearts beat wildly. We read the newspapers nervously, and listened to the radio, our chests tight with pain and fear.

One certainty, however, comforted us: there there would be no Ponar, no Chelmno. The el-Alamein affair was short. We received the happy news that the British were attacking, and that Rommel had been repulsed. A few days later we were worried by a new rumor: *Akzias in the Warsaw ghetto! That live and fermenting ghetto, in limbo for two years, the center of Jewish life in Europe, with half a million Jews, was no longer secure. When the evil was unleashed we knew, from the experience of Lithuania and Bielorussia, that there would be no holding back the wave. It would grow, sweep away and destroy everything. When the Germans put their annihilation machine into operation it finished the job. We were very fearful, mostly for what might not happen. We were worried about the resistance, we prayed that our Warsaw comrades would take their revenge, we prayed for some strong blow that would come in time, and spill German blood.*

Warsaw, can I still see you through your fighting, stubborn Jews? Can I see you, your beggars clinging to life by their fingernails; your fighters and the members of your great underground? Will we no longer be able to read the "Kalendarz Rolniczy" or "Jutrznia" (Upward), the movement paper in 1941 which we would smuggle across borders in order to read the original and yet mature views of Yosef and Mordechai, of Josya and Shmuel? Was nothing to remain of your precious, fermenting wine, the wine of a youth movement maintaining its values as of old?

What was to happen to the half million Jews fighting for their existence? What was it the madwoman sang in the ghetto's tumultuous streets? What was it that crazy Rubinstein, that poet and perhaps prophet, said?

"I do not want to give up my food card! I do not want to die!", and he sang: "Alle gleich!" (All are equal in death). You are mistaken, Rubinstein, not all are equal in death. There is no equality in dying. That is why we worried, prayed for Nazi blood to be spilled in Zamenhof, Nalevki, Gensia and Muranowski streets. That, however, was only the beginning. The bloody end came later.

Meanwhile, the Germans were taking refugees to the ghetto primarily from the small towns in the Warsaw environs. For weeks and months they had been driven from place to place and finally were cast into the boiling caldron that was Warsaw. Now they were being taken out again. They lay in the streets, hungry and they were the first taken to annihilation.

The *aktzia* in Warsaw began on July 22. On July 27 Rostov and Novocherkesk fell; once again there was retreat on the battlefield and all comfort gone.

In Bialystok ghetto life proceeded as usual. Except for the expulsion of hundreds of 17 to 25 year-old Jewish girls, to the work camp at Volkovysk, nothing noteworthy occurred. The summer skies were unclouded. The girls' removal to the work camp did not shake the foundations of ghetto life. It was noon; the ghetto streets were closed, a curfew was declared. All girls of the above ages who did not have appropriate papers certifying that they were working for the Germans were taken from their homes or hiding places and sent to Volkovisk. That was not the worst of the camps; its ties with Bialystok were actually normal. Anyone with some family connection, or with influential contacts, was back in Bialystok in a few months. Some remained there until the annihilation activities began in all the provincial cities, including Volkovisk. We had our helpless ones of course, myself among them: I did not work in a factory, nor did I serve the Germans. I was one of the fortunate ones of the movement whose assignment was not in the regular workplaces of the ghetto inhabitants. I sat in my mother's home, and could not even cross the street to approach Barash and ask for some "shein". Movement in the streets was stopped, completely. Now Barash revealed his greatness. He had never asked why I was not working, and I had never asked him for a forged work card. I don't know how he heard that I was imprisoned at home. Within an hour after the curfew order, Engelman brought me a note from Barash, saying: *"Hiddishe ordenungsdienst; bitte nisht nemen froi Grossman zu kein andere Arbeit. Sie ist zu ferfiihgung fur des Presidium,"* ("Jewish Order Service: please do not take Miss Grossman for any other work. She is at the disposal of the Presidium.") signed, A. Barash. Once again we were surprised by Barash, and tried to fathom his personality. When the expulsion ended, the ghetto people sank into their illusory tranquility, suffering from hard labor and occupied in expanding production for their hangmen.

The problem of securing weapons became increasingly pressing. Our home production was primitive, and we very much needed firearms. There were some in the vicinity, among the Poles we innocently believed. We thought that the peasants were the only source of these. Who else could have hidden those that fell from the hands of the dead and wounded in the battles in which the Red Army battalions were encircled near Bialystok? Jews told me afterwards that they had found abandoned firearms; many Jews, however, were more afraid of guns than of the Germans, and considered the rifle their greatest enemy, liable to betray them during an examination or an attack. These Jews hurried to throw the rifles into the toilets, to break the stocks, and to destroy them. You had to know the Nazis well, to hate the enemy properly, to be able to love the rifle or the pistol and to appreciate their true value.

However, the first guns did come to the ghetto, and from German hands. It was reported that there were gun-dealers among the Germans. Our comrades did not have the good fortune at that time to meet either German Communists or Germans ready to sell firearms. Our young comrades, Sender and Israel, stole weapons, part by part, under Franek's tutelage. There was a fence on Chenstohova Street, and on the other side of it a courtyard that was half within the ghetto and half outside of it. If you watched for the moment when the sentry turned the corner, it was possible to throw a package in, and to jump in after it. A waiting comrade would seize the bundle and disappear through the neighboring courtyards, and you turned back to the other side. However, what was brought in nonchalantly in that way was meager, and with difficulty we obtained a rifle and two pistols during the whole summer of 1942. The same was true for the Communists. Our united front with them slowly strengthened, but the distrust didn't completely disappear. Leibush Mandelblit's place was taken by Yoshko Kawe, who was chosen as their representative in an organization we later called "Block A" (at the end of the summer and early fall, a "Block B" was organized with Dror and Hanoar Hatzioni). Mandelblit was a veteran member of the Communist Party and found it difficult to cooperate with people who were looking toward Palestine. He was a worker who had obtained his political and ideological education solely within the party. His horizons were too limited for change. We felt, in all our meetings, that he was making a great effort to overcome many psychological blocks in order to relate to us as people of his. For that reason, arms acquisition plans were not unified. However, we did make progress, especially in joint branches of work. The cells were uni-party, but the heads of the cells would meet to exchange experiences and arms. For instance, we had a rifle, and they had grenades. We exchanged weapons so that all the cell members could get to know all about them. Our commanders and theirs met to coordinate plans. There were also many activities we carried out jointly. There were frequent false alarms in the ghetto. Sometimes, a German would tell the Jew working near him that in the evening the Jews were going to be taken out of the ghetto. Sometimes there were rumors of *aktzias* without our knowing their source. In any case, there were many intimations, and not all were unfounded. It was possible for one German institution, the "Sicherheitsdienst", for example, to want to carry out a small *aktzia* and another group, such as the "Schutzpolitzei" or the civil administration, to oppose it. Our information services joined with the communist intelligence. Every bit of information that Gedalyahu brought from the police, or that I brought from Barash, was transmitted to them, and they did the same for us. They maintained contacts with their comrades outside the ghetto, who sometimes garnered some news. The mobilizations, in such cases, were united. We would meet in pre-planned positions. These mutual tests were always successful. It was from such combat activities that our solidarity grew.

Among German Soldiers

I received a postcard from Vilna. After the failures at the Malkinia border we tried to maintain our connections by mail. The mail could not, of course, take the place of direct meetings. Our ties with Warsaw were cut, and reports of *aktzias* recurred. A trip was not within the realm of possibility, and postal ties, too, were stopped. Our mail from Vilna was our only link to other areas. The siege was closing in on us. Our activities became limited to our own area, or perhaps were not limited but were approaching their peak and, therefore, every action had to be limited to its own site.

At that time we succeeded, for the last time, in breaking the siege. Through a postcard I was asked to come to Vilna immediately, at all costs. The wording of the message surprised me somehwat; our Vilna comrades knew what that kind of trip involved. We understood that the matter was of special importance and that I would have to take the risk. When the comrades saw the postcard they shook their heads, without anyone voicing an opinion. That was a sign that they were leaving it to my discretion. Edek was the only one who understood that a person should not be forced to rely upon himself for such a decision. In these cases it was easier to implement decisions than to make them.Until Grodno the checks were not too thorough. They were carried out completely only in the cars reserved for Poles. Travelling this road was easier than the one in the Warsaw area. Here, however, you needed a permit from the Bialystok "Politzei, " and permits were difficult to obtain and required a recommendation by a German employer. I decided to go into a German car and see what would happen. On the outside of the railway car a sign proclaimed: "Germans only!" The car had large, enclosed compartments, with benches along the wall. On both sides there were windows and one door at the side — the one and only exit. At the end of the car was a toilet. Within the compartments there were seven or eight German soldiers. They examined me from head to toe; I asked them with a laugh whether I could come in, and they too laughed. "Why not, Kleine?" (little one).

The game began. It was a fine day, a Polish fall day. The strong rays of the sun turned grey from time to time, with rainclouds in the sky, but no rain fell. The train moved. Before Grodno, the police did not visit us at any station. The soldiers were in a good mood; all were returning from leave but were not going to the front. They belonged to an echelon force, stationed in Lithuania. "We are all from Vienna, ha-ha-ha!" one laughed. What was he so happy about? Was it because he was Austrian and not a "boche?" Or because he was not going to the front? In any case I had managed to land in good company. They offered me cake which they had brought from home. I took it willingly, and thanked them. Suddenly, I told them: "You know, I am traveling without permit!"

"What do we care? We are not police, we are soldiers," one replied.

Still, my announcement left them ruffled. One pointed at the military coat hanging on a hook. "Maybe we'll hide you in that!" Another wanted to even outdo his comrade: "No, under the bench!," and they played with the ideas as though it was a game. But I really did look for some hole in which I could hide. The soldiers were in a good mood, and each of them tried to surpass his comrade in generosity and in his desire to help me. The trip to Grodno was only an hour and a half. When the train stopped in the Grodno station I still had no idea of what to do. The German shouts could already be heard in the Polish car:

"Raus! Raus! Ausweis! Ausweis!"

Perhaps they would not come into the German car. I couldn't cross myself as the Polish peasant women did before every examination. I couldn't even pray to God. I could only hold my breath, try to relax, and smile.

Thank goodness I was a girl. The soldiers crowded around me, came even a little too close, but this time I did not care. The main thing was that I should come through the check safely. The door opened, and closed again. When they saw the soldiers seated at the bench, they apparently thought they were playing some game.

When the train moved I was free again. I looked through the window, waiting until we reached the Marcinkance station. I was glad that the soldiers were going on, but I knew that the border check would be serious. They would enter every compartment, even in the German car. This was where my fate would be decided. The soldiers continued to make jokes and I smiled at all of them.

We reached the border. The platform was empty, except for the men in dark green uniforms and boots, German boots. Shiny, well-polished boots. I heard their echoing steps on the platform. They approached our car. The soldiers looked at me, slightly frightened. They apparently felt some loss of honor in the fact that eight knights, Austrian knights, could not protect a young, smiling, German-speaking Polish girl. Soon the door would open. I jumped into the bathroom. I had hardly closed the door when I heard the well-known shout in the compartment I had just left:

"Keine Zivilisten da?" ("Are there any civilians here?")

Silence. A good sign. I heard the German's steps in the compartment. He apparently was searching in all corners, among the bundles and under he benches.

The toilet door opened. He opened the door widely, and in so doing hid me completely behind it. The compartment door opened, and closed again. There was a moment of silence and then a burst of laughter, and a "hurrah".

I opened the door and sixteen hands tried to grab me. They surrounded me and laughed. They apparently liked the game. The trip from Vienna was a long and boring one, and they hadn't hoped for such amusement. And maybe, who knows — maybe these young Austrians also hated the German police? I enjoyed the cookies they gave me and was happy that the train was moving again. After crossing the border we would have to transfer to another train. I went out to the booth and bought a ticket, and when I came back I did not find the same passengers. The day was darkening, and my mind was at ease. Light was not an ally. I found a car crowded with soldiers and I pushed into a corner, near the window. I examined the place well. There were a lot of bundles on the shelf, with soldiers' packs and coats, short and long coats swinging in rhythm with the train's motion. During an examination I would squeeze in among the coats in the corner. The cars were not lit. The blackout was complete because of the danger of bombs. In any case, it was preferable to fail at a regular station than at the border, and I had already crossed the border safely. Here, too, a travel pass was required, but I had a Vilna identification card in my pocket, and if there was not a thorough Gestapo examination I could use the excuse that I was going home.

Most of the German soldiers were asleep. One, opposite me, still awake, did not stop talking, praising himself, and talking about beautiful Germany. I heard the story about beautiful Germany every time I found myself in the company of German travellers. It was apparently the only non-risky subject they could talk about. Or maybe they just didn't have anything else to say.

I recalled a story told me by Lonka. She had been riding on the train, and her neighbor was an officer, or under-officer. He did not talk about beautiful Germany, but all the way he spoke about himself, boasted and tried to make an impression. True, he had been handsome, tall and blond, with a nordic face and body — according to Hitler's "standards." His face was without any expression, without a spark of intelligence; but the lines were just right. In his desire to win Lonka's heart, the German told her that he was an important person. In his pocket he had a letter from the Third Reich Ministry of Health, suggesting 15 of Germany's beautiful young girls for him to fertilize. If he succeeded in fertilizing all of them he would receive 600 marks as wage and the contract would be renewed for a longer period, and for an additional number of women. When I heard that story every young German seemed to me a bull. I feared them, and mocked them in my heart.

Before we reached Vilna the permits of the civilians were examined a number of times. I squeezed into the darkness, covered myself with a long coat hanging over my head untill we arrived. I had not been in Vilna since July, more than three months. Maybe the procedures had been changed or the travel regulations. In the darkness I saw a Polish woman loaded with baskets get off the train and approach a Polish railroad worker. The worker took the baskets and they both turned aside, not toward the main exit.

"Sir, I want to leave the station and I have no permit; maybe you can help me? Of course I will thank fittingly . . ."

"Follow us."

I walked along, some distance behind them; after all, I could not trust these strangers. To the right of the passenger station there was a freight station, apparently where he worked. He led us through twisting side exits; we passed freight trains, crossed the tracks, and were breathing fresh air on a broad street on a Vilna fall night.

"Where are you going tonight," the Pole asked me. "It's curfew now."

I didn't know what to say.

"Come!" I followed him without additional questions. I had no choice. We crossed the quiet, dark street. A cold, pale autumn moon dimly lit our steps. We approached a barred door. He took a key out of his pocket, opened it and the three of us went up the steps to his clean and warm railway worker's flat. He lit a fire in the stove, and we all drank tea. He did not ask me anything. Maybe he thought I was a "shmuglarke" (smuggler). He made room for me on the floor, spread a mattress and added a blanket, and so I slept that night in the worker's home. I didn't find the Pole at home in the morning. His wife paid no attention to me, and busied herself with her household affairs. She did not even say good morning. I took out some tens of marks to pay her. She looked at me with expressionless eyes, and continued her work.

"Ai, panie, have you fallen out of the sky, or what? Go your way. Why are you making fun of us?" I wondered how they would have acted if they knew I was a Jew.

I thanked her, and left. I found myself opposite the railroad station near the home of the German, Schmidt, who had sacrificed his life for us. I went to seek some way to get into the ghetto, turning toward Vitka's apartment. In the courtyard of the Catholic nuns I looked for Mrs. Pardu, the former head of the charity restaurant on Zavalna Street, and Vitka's employer. The neighbors looked at me in surprise.

"They are no longer here," they said.

I went to Yadwiga. When her former landlady recognized me she gave me Yadwiga's new address. Yadwiga was living in a room in the home of some acquaintances. She made me welcome. I rested there, and washed. She was living on Makoba Street. Here I had met Rivka, before we separated. Rivka had gone to Bialystok, and I to my aryan room in this neighborhood, on Shenna Street.

Mission to Moscow

How much time had elapsed since then? One year and three months. How many rooms had I left since then? How many rooms, trains and names had changed? How many things had changed since that summer of 1941! And we too had apparently changed a great deal. We seemed to have grown older by decades; we had gained experience, became more serious, accumulated disappointments, became more determined, stubborn and patient.

Yadwiga's situation was difficult. Yesterday they arrested her landlord, and only Yadwiga and his wife remained in the apartment. The Gestapo might come at any moment to search, and her room was full of contraband. She had to clean everything out and move it somewhere else, but it seemed to her that they were watching whoever came or went. When she left they were liable to stop her and examine her bag.

"You've come at a good time!" Yadwiga packed and hid all the underground contraband, the forged papers and permits, addresses and letters, and a few pistol bullets. She was angry: "The truth is that my landlord dealt with the black market. He wanted to get rich during the war, and because of him the movement was liable to suffer." Yadwiga urged me to get out quickly. She had arranged to meet Vitka at noon at the green cafe on Mitzkevich Street. Perhaps she shouldn't go; they might follow her. "You go," she said.

I found Vitka, and she greeted me with her usual aggressive enthusiasm. I entered the ghetto with her. From the "Germans" Street an alley called Konska Street branched off, and it was there that the battalions entered the ghetto. Most of the work groups turned into Konska, and from there to the gate on Rudnicks Street. Vitka knew all the groups, their kolonenführers and the workers. She was used to going in and out of the ghetto, spending days in the city, running about, attending meetings, and returning toward evening. The patch was hidden in her pocket; her hands were fast and her feet light. Only her frizzy blond hair might arouse suspicion. Vitka didn't have my flaxen hair but she had boundless courage. She went ahead, and I followed. I looked about to see whether I was being followed, carefully entered a side court, and donned the patches Vitka always carried in her pocket. I never carried them. I always had yellow paper and scissors handy. During an examination they would not be as suspicious of prepared cloth patches. My warnings, however, were to no avail. Vitka did as she wanted. "They won't look; leave me alone." She became angry at what she considered my excessive caution. Vitka did not want to go into the courtyard, did not look to see whether she was being followed. She jumped into the line and pulled me after her, pinned the patch on her breast and marched along with the others. Vitka took the offensive, I exercised caution.

We came to the ghetto. Among our comrades there was a great to-do: a ray of light had come from the east. Hearts were filled with new hope, enthusiasm and energy. Contact had been established with the world that was fighting Nazism. From now on the antifascist struggle of the Jews in the ghetto would be part of the Soviet front.

I felt as if I had entered a new world. The few comrades who had been made privy to the secret considered it very important.

They had met a group of Soviet parachutists who had reached the Vilna region, and who were authorized by the Soviet authorities to organize the underground for armed resistance behind the German lines. Much will still be told of the heroism of the commissar-soldiers, sons of the Soviet people, who sacrificed their lives in battle against the enemy, far from their own country, villages and families, deep behind the lines. Contact with them meant that the siege had been broken. The meeting was encouragement and reinforcement for the isolated underground; cooperation meant integrating the ghetto battlefield into the long front, from the icy northern seas to Crimea and North Africa. It was not a matter of abstract moral value, of the height of human feeling and experience. It was the search for military-battle coordination, real aid in arms and means. The perceived integration of our fighters into this front was not an insignificant matter either. When our comrades met the parachutists in the Bialevaka region near Vilna, they soon found the organizational and ideological connection. The parachutists were authorized by the general partisan command in Moscow which recognized the P. P. S. as an integral part of the general Soviet partisan movement. During discussions with them the problem of the efficacy of the ghetto organization — that viewed the ghetto as its primary and main front — was raised.

When I heard of these discussions I recalled a similar one with the Polish Communists in Warsaw, the Jewish Communists in Bialystok, and with the Soviet espionage group which we had met through Sheina. There was the same lack of understanding, the same first questions about wasted fighting forces, the same inability to understand the events and processes taking place in ghettoes doomed to total annihilation. However, when the goal was a joint one, the methods also had to be coordinated.

During one of the meetings the parachutists suggested putting us in contact with Moscow. The proposal was so promising that enthusiasm overcame logic. Here I discovered the reason for the postcard I had received in Bialystok: "Come at all costs." When we began to discuss the details, the prospects did not appear so promising. Radio contact had been lost, either because of the station's failure, or because the code had been discovered. Our comrades assumed that they would be helped by regular air transportation (since the parachutists had come from Moscow by plane . . .); that there was a hidden airfield in the depths of the forest, where a wonderful steel bird landed, parachuted weapons, received information and picked up people. Only after some time did we understand that every underground, even the one backed by a tremendous socialist country, faces difficulties. We were fighting in terrible isolation, but they, too, these parachutists behind the enemy lines, were prepared at any moment to fight completely alone, only by their own wisdom and will. The beautiful dream of some speedy message to the world evaporated. It became clear that the way to Moscow was long, difficult and dangerous. It would take months of travel, if it could be done at all. According to the plan they proposed, we would have to get to the front in the vicinity of Wielike Luki, through Polock, across borders, forests and villages, on twisting, unpaved roads. The parachutists gave us the code words for the partisans in the Wielike Luki area who would help our emissaries get across the front. According to the parachutists' information, there was a break there in the front and it could be crossed. After learning about all of the difficulties of the plan, we decided, nonetheless, to carry it out.

The idea of seeking some support from the world from which we had been cut off and which our terrible cries did not reach was not limited to the Vilna fighting underground. In Warsaw, too, they had tried to send messengers to warn of the impending annihilation of the Polish Jews. This process had already engulfed Vilna, Kovno, Minsk and Kovel. It was spreading through central Poland, the tranquil General-Government, Lublin, and Warsaw, and the first reports about Treblinka were already coming in.

We said then: "They must start killing all the Germans living in the European countries, and in America; they must announce the total extinction of prisoners of war; threaten to do to them what the Germans were doing to us, if the Germans didn't stop the slaughter of the Jews." We naively thought, then, that England and America were not reacting to the annihilations, to Ponar, Chelmno, Belsetz, Sobibor and Treblinka because they were not known. Despite our great disappointment in the proposed plan, we decided to carry out the mission. What could we lose? If it succeeded the mission would be extremely valuable. If it didn't, well we were taking risks every day, every hour anyhow. The prospects for success were slight but what better possibilities did we have? We had to do the best we could, even if there was little hope of success. We also had to see to it that the mission did not harm our work in general. It was finally decided to send Tzesia Rosenberg, from our movement, and Sonia Madeiska, from the Communists. I was to return to Bialystok.

We two had to reach the front thousands of kilometers away but we did not have the first permit for the closest station, and without a permit you could not even get into the Vilna station only 200 meters from the ghetto. A permit had to be forged, but we did not know what it looked like. We had never seen one. I went to Yadwiga, but Yadwiga was unable to help.

There was a pretty young girl in the ghetto of whom it was said that she drank with the Germans, and that the Lithuanians in the civilian administration were her friends. She was no fool, and knew what was happening in the ghetto underground. She offered her services through an acquaintance who was linked to the underground. I don't know how she got to the F. P. O. and why they trusted her. I relied on Abba, investigated and decided that she could be trusted. I was to go out of the ghetto the next morning, together with Sonia, and go to the Lithuanian civil administration on Mickewicz Street. We were to ask for a certain Lithuanian, whose name I can't recall. I was to tell him a story about my mother who lived on the border, and from whom I had received a telegram stating that she was dying; to tell him that if I didn't receive a permit I would go to her without one. Sonia dressed up in her friend's coat, painted her lips, with the rouge emphasizing the gentle lines of her face. She was not a typical "shikse", as was said of her, but she did have bright eyes and a small nose, and the complexion of her oval face was white. Her hands moved gracefully, and her steps were small but energetic. Above all, she was brave, in a restrained way.

A sentry stood in front of the broad entrance to the Lithuanian civil administration building. I asked him, in German, for the Lithuanian. The sentry was Lithuanian, and since I spoke to him in German he did not ask for an entry pass to the building, which was barred to the public. Unfortunately, we did not find the man we were looking for (we supposedly had an appointment with him). He may have left deliberately, the meeting may not have been well prepared. The place had been an excellent restaurant, and we used to have dinner here with guests from afar, from Lemberg, or Kovel (while our friends went hungry for at least two days). The offical we did get to to see explained that the matter was not within his authority. He could, perhaps, give us a travel permit to some closer station, but not to Welika, which was considered to be across the border. Please go to the large building opposite, the Sicherheitsdienst offices.

"You are Volksdeutsche, aren't you?" he asked.

"If so, you can give us a permit to the border, can't you?" Sonia asked, smiling.

"If they give you a permit to cross the border, I will give you a permit to the border."

"How are you helping us, then?" He smiled and held out his cigarette case.

"But I'm forbidden, you understand,without their permit!" His "highness", however, did not permit himself to show weakness before another authority:

"I'll give it to you if they promise you a permit to cross the border. I will wait here for a phone call. Go, go, don't be afraid, say that I sent you. There is an old man there, called . . ."

We left him not knowing whether to do as her suggested. The Siecherheits Dieust was the abomination of the occupation regime; superior to the police, it was the Gestapo's real force, its implementing tool; it even supervised the Gestapo. We wrestled with the decision: to go, or give up. We went.

Here, too, we asked for someone by name. There was a telephone near the entrance. The German spoke to the officer for whom we had asked, and when we said that the Lithuanian official of the Civil Administration had sent us, we were permitted to enter.

The sentry looked at us searchingly, the officers going up and down the wide stairs smiled at us and when we asked directions pointed to a door down the corridor, to the left. We found the German there, and once again we told our story, from the beginning. We especially stressed my acquaintance with the Lithuanian and in the civil administration. I tried to speak of him as an acquaintance or friend.

"But what are you doing here? We don't issue such permits."

"Who does?"

"Perhaps the police." He was already trying to get rid of us.

But we sat down in the upholstered chairs, smoked cigarettes, and made no move to leave. When he saw that we were in no hurry he began to ask questions.

"I work in an office as a translator. I am Volksdeutsche. The civil administration knows us" I tried my luck again.

The ice thawed. The German laughed.

"We don't want two permits, only one; actually, we aren't asking you for it, if your office (with the stress on "office") doesn't issue them. I will be satisfied with the one from the civilian administration. I only want it extended to Vielike".

It was a good strategem. He went out for a moment, and then returned. He told us to bring the Lithuanian permit. Once again we left emptyhanded. The Lithuanian received us once more and made us feel welcome. He was sure that we had brought the transit permit. When we told him what had happened he thought about it and told one of the typists to type out the permit — one for travel through Lithuanian territory, to the border. We ran back to the SD. The sentry recognized us and let us in without any delay. Now we felt a little more comfortable in that terrible building. We met the stout officer on the stairs. He stood there, joking, and the passing officers looked at the three of us. And then once again we were in the small office with the upholstered chairs.

Again we were smiling, I winked at the fat man, and Sonia looked at me as if I was insane. He went to the adjoining room and returned this time and stamped the other side of the Lithuanian permit for one trip and that it was issued by the Sicherheitsdienst of the Vilna district. Above the stamp he put his signature, and beneath it a red stamp with the SD swastika.

We thanked him very politely, stayed a few moments, extended our hands graciously and left the splendid but terrible building. We were worried about the big stamp with so many words, which would be difficult to counterfeit. When we returned to the ghetto and told about our visit they looked at us as though we were insane.

"Did you ever see anybody go into the SD building of his own free will?"

Abba sat up nights drawing the big stamp with the gothic lettering. During the day he was busy with his regular chores, and at night he worked on the forgery, and produced a second permit for Tzesia, exactly like the original. It was hard to distinguish between the two.

Two days later we said goodbye to the girls. Our greatest hope was that they would get to Moscow.

Sheine Patt

I was leaving Vilna now for the last time, in a freight train, on a cold, cloudy fall day, without a permit.

The train was long, the cars loaded with vehicles and heavy weapons covered with cloth sheets; damaged equipment, apparently, being sent to garages in the rear. The back of every car was a "stork's nest" a shed and tower for the escorting guards. It crawled along, stopping at every station to let the express passenger trains, carrying military personnel and German civilians, pass. Among the freight cars there was one used for passengers, carrying a group of railway workers and two soldiers going on leave. On both sides of the car there were doors to the outside. The trip was an easy one, the compartment was spacious, and until the border they did not examine permits or tickets. It was a military freight train, and civilians were not permitted on it. The passenger car was swallowed up among the loaded freight cars and was not noticeable. At every station the train was moved to a siding, far from the center of the station. After I promised the engineer's assistant fifty marks, he showed me to the passenger car. The railway workers were not particularly surprised, and did not ask me how I had arrived there. Polish railway workers knew how to keep secrets. From time to time they too, apparently, smuggled something, or somebody. There was a solidarity of silence during the German occupation. The two German soldiers who were returning from the front did not know anything about civilian travel regulations; they were experts only at boasting. During the whole trip they talked only about themselves. They also did not seem to know too much about the front.

We approached the border. Again, the train stopped at a siding. Suddenly I heard the sound of hob nailed boots on the gravel. I knew an examination was going to take place. The door opened in the adjacent compartment, separated from ours only by a high bench. I heard the German's voice, as he was examining someone's papers, apparently a railway worker. I looked about for some way out. The only one was to jump out of the car and creep under the high railway wheels. The train had not stopped at a platform and so it would be easy to hide under it; it was high enough above the track. I tried to open the door opposite me but I couldn't. The minutes passed; they would soon be here. With a desperate move I pulled down the door window and jumped out. The stupid Germans just stared; the railway workers looked aside. As I jumped, I heard the door closing in the adjacent compartment. I crouched near the wheels, and from underneath the car I saw the well-known polished boots. One boot was already on the first step to my compartment. I crept away, toward the cars that I guessed had already been examined, and came out from behind the track. Soldiers guarding the machines waved to me; they did not know I had fled from the train. I walked around a bit outside, and then returned to the compartment. The soldiers there began to pester me: "Why did you run away, you didn't have a permit, did you?" I didn't know whether they had betrayed me or not.

Apparently I had not been betrayed, since I was not being sought.

"You don't need a permit on a freight train," I replied innocently.

"Then why did you run away?"

"Civilians are generally forbidden to ride on a freight train," I told them.

"Why are you travelling then?" one of them did not give up.

"Because I missed the regular train." Only a complete idiot would have accepted that kind of answer.

One of the railway workers smiled under his mustache. He evidently understood German and was smiling at the stupidity of Europe's "elite". The train moved on. Now I didn't care about the soldiers, the important thing was to cross the border. Finally, the border was behind us, slipping away toward Vilna.

The train reached Grodno late at night. Before Grodno it slowed down and stopped. That was a good time to get away. In any case the train was only going as far as Grodno and in that station they surely examined all arrivals. I reached Grodno late, on foot, tired and filthy. Here too it was forbidden to wander the streets at night, but there were ruined houses through which one could steal into the station and rest, squeeze into a corner and nap. Here, too, it was dangerous, but how could I stay out in the open the entire night? It was damp. I had not yet decided what to do when I saw a figure stealing from court to court. The woman was frightened when she noticed me, but when she saw that I was a woman too, she asked whom I was looking for. I said that I was waiting for the morning train and was looking for a night's lodging. She did not ask for my identification card, or name and address, but took me into her home, gave me a clean, warm bed and disappeared. In the darkness I saw a sewing machine and some unfinished dresses. She was a seamstress, by all appearances. Why hadn't she been afraid to take me in? I might steal something, or perhaps I was running away from the police, or maybe . . . I was a Jewess. I was freezing and worn out. In the unknown seamstress' home I washed, combed my hair and rested. I remembered that the train from Grodno to Bialystok left between six and seven in the morning, and so I rose before dawn. Once again I took money out of my purse and had to put it back; the woman had disappeared. Another in the long list of quiet and simple anonymous people who offered a helping hand without asking questions.

I pushed into the entrance of the Grodno station. Fortunately, a lot of people were travelling that day. I took out an old permit, one that had been stamped a long time ago in Macinkantze and Malkinia, and that was long outdated. It had betrayed Solomon, Lonka, Roshka, Sarah Tosya and Jacobowsky. I waved it above the heads of the passengers pushing through the exit and passed through with almost no examination. I already knew the German apparatus so famous for its order and supposedly so foolproof. I also knew it was only a legend. The railway police in the Grodno station did not necessarily know what the border police knew.

I arrived in Bialystok safely.

In a small meeting in which Sheine Patt-Levine participated, I reported on my trip. When I told them about Gens'* theories, the doctrines he was promulgating in the Vilna ghetto, vain ones, destined to destroy all desire for resistance, cultivating the illusion of autonomous Jewish life and the development of cultural and spiritual life as the panacea for all ills, a principal of passivity, the comrades decided that I should tell Barash about it.

A few days later I appeared before him. I told him about the theater in the Vilna ghetto, the concerts, the development of educational and cultural autonomy. Barash listened attentively without taking his eyes off me. He knew that we were not too sure of him. I drew a picture of Gens, explained his tenets and added: "He is cultivating passivity and submission and camouflages it as the spiritual resistance of "eternal Israel". He believes that he can outwit history." I sensed that Barash was becoming irritated so I stopped. He blurted, "Gens is an utter idiot!" Why, however was he so irritated? Did he see in Gens a caricature of himself? This time I had succeeded in my visit. Of course there were important differences between them, of nuance and perhaps even of principle. Gens was an enemy, a tool of the Gestapo; Barash was a loyal Jew innocently seeking to save Jews, even if only the fewest. They had no common denominator, neither in their lives nor in their charac-

* Jacob Gens was the head of the Vilna Judenrat.

ters, but only in the place reserved for them in the blood-stained history of Polish Jews.

I told Barash about the "action" in Oshmiana, the notorious *aktzia* in which the Jewish police of the Vilna ghetto, with the Stars of David on their hats and on the uniforms of the Lithuanian police, had themselves helped lead Jews to the slaughter. Barash became angry when I described the sad picture of the rows of policemen, armed with sticks, their clothes pressed, standing at the ghetto gate.[17] Weiss, the German commissar, took them by car to Svenchany in order to deceive the Jews. Jewish police do the work of the SS and SD. Barash became angry, and shouted "Cowards!"

Three months later Barash was to face the same problem in perhaps an "easier" form, one demanding less responsibility on his part and on the part of the institution he headed. Still, it was the very same problem and it required an answer different from the one Barash found! The problem was the partial annihilation of the ghetto, which he unwillingly helped carry out for the sake of the others, the large temporary remnant whose fate, too, was sealed, as was that of all the Jews in occupied Poland.

In Bialystok, too, communications had been established with an authorized Soviet group, representatives of the Soviet forces behind the enemy lines. It was similar in aims to our contacts in Vilna, but differed in detail.

The connections had been made by Sheine herself, wisely and patiently. Sheine would come to our house almost every day, if even for a few minutes. She always maintained contact, even when she was not required to do so.

"I've just come to take a look," her dark eyes smiled. She was much older than us. Her daughter was a member of our movement, had joined the Tel-Amal group while still a gymnasium student, and had remained during the occupation. She was three years younger than us. We, however, never thought about any difference in age between ourselves and Sheine, her mother, who when just talking, or in serious consultation was at once young and old. How well she knew how to rejoice with us and to become enthusiastic over every achievement; how serious and deliberate she became when we took up some complex and almost insoluble problem. Sheine was a pedagogue, and not only in the orphan asylum which she supervised in the ghetto. She had been a teacher all her adult life, but it had never interfered with her political work in the Left Poalei Zion.

When we learned, first generally and later in detail, of her activities in addition to her work in the asylum, we were not surprised. It seemed appropriate that Sheine would be involved in an anti-German espionage network! During the Soviet period, Sheine had worked as a professional in the central station for pedagogical and psychological assistance, headed by a Russian woman who was also a professional educator. When the Soviets retreated, the woman continued her activities and, since she knew Sheine, coopted her. The two women were not alone; they were linked to commando groups made up of separate links which maintained direct contact by radio, or through partisan groups in Balovesh, and through them with the partisan high command and the underground. In the course of time we learned that the command had been working all along with all its cells and departments. Sheine and her group were given specific commando and espionage tasks the limits of which were prescribed.

Sheine had been recruited into the group by her Soviet acquaintance as an individual, not as a representative of a movement, a party or the ghetto as a whole. Espionage is an individual activity without any connections to a mass movement, but Sheine saw it as an outlet, a broader road to the greater anti-Nazi front for the underground movement. She did her work successfully and completed various missions. Very slowly she attempted to cultivate some understanding for our cause. Sheine's acquaintance, who had headed the group, had sensed that she was being followed. This was at the end of the summer of 1942. She had therefore, transferred to Sheine everything that previously had been in her possession alone. Some days later she noticed Gestapo men approaching her house. She hurriedly began to burn the papers and documents and when they knocked at her door, and she saw through the window that there was a siege around her house, and the Gestapo car waiting for her in the street, she shot herself.

After that Sheine was in charge of a number of activities, such as searching the big building, the "Palace", the offices of the "Bialystok District" authorities. The sign on the entrance announced that it was a "Zivil-Verwaltung", but Sheine knew the truth about the building. We never learned the details of the searches, but Edek and I knew that sometimes a German in SS uniform would come and take her with him. In the morning we would find her in the orphan asylum, her face glowing and a youthful smile in her eyes. After a while she told us that they used to go into the Palace through a tunnel leading from its cellars to one of the courts on Aleya Street. In the Palace there was someone who gave them access to the most secret documents. That is how we knew, before Barash did, of the activities the Germans were going to carry out in the ghetto and that the ghetto was to be closed some days earlier. In that way we learned the details about traitors and informers, and about the ghetto Jews listed in the German files as candidates for informers and traitors. The main goal of the night searches was to uncover information that had come to the Germans about the partisan army, its activities, size, location and commanders. Since they knew what information the Germans had, it was easier to lead them astray.

Sheine did her work with a wonderful, youthful strength, whose source was hard to fathom. When she had important information for us, she would hurry to inform our people. Above all, she was concerned with her aim to establish contact between us and the group. Our personal connections with Sheine did not end, of course; what we needed was a link that would also be authorized and accepted by the high command; de jure recognition. Sheine worked methodically and patiently to that end. At first, they refused even to hear of such a liaison. "That is not within the realm of our activities and authorization," they argued. Sheine used to tell us about someone called Vania, a wonderful person, very human, a good-hearted, tolerant Bielorussian type, but very strict. Sheine did not give up until they finally agreed to accept a memorandum from us about our activities, and promised to transmit it to headquarters. Edek worked on the memorandum for days, to make it precise and understandable. After all, our problems were foreign to those people, and we could not, therefore, use allegorical language and vague terms.The memorandum embraced all of the underground's activities, its political character, its practical goals and the background of its growth. The report stressed in particular why we had decided to fight within the framework of the ghetto. When we transmitted it they found that it was not complete, and we were asked to add a detailed report on the movement that had established the underground. Once again we worked on the composition of the memorandum. We felt the greatness of our responsibility. We seemed to be making history. A memorandum about our movement, Hashomer Hatzair, to the Soviet High Command! We had to be careful not to inadvertently distort even one detail. For many years we in the movement had looked forward to establishing such contact. These were gala days in our ranks. Only a few knew about it, but the happy spirit also affected the cells. Our comrades understood that something important had happened.

About two weeks later the answer came. It was instructive and encouraging. The concluding lines were: "We believe that young people like yourselves, young people who are so capable of organizing and initiating activities and who are motivated by the importance of their mission, would do better if they joined the general fighting forces. You would undoubtedly contribute a great deal to the cause. However, since you have decided to organize the Jews of the ghetto for resistance, we can only congratulate you and promise you our support." It was signed by the high command of the Soviet partisan movement. An order also arrived awarding Sheine the Order of Lenin. In those days Edek went about exhilarated and Sheine once again urged her comrades to give us their aid.

It was not a simple problem: they helped as much as they could with secret information. They did not have any weapons in the city. The closest partisan unit with which they were in contact was in the Bialowiez forest, 80 kilometers from Bialystok. Two meetings between Edek and Vania brought us closer, and despite his practice of not intervening in "civilian affairs," as he called them, Vania decided, on this occasion, to allow himself to interrupt his own activities. Vania was enthusiastic about Edek, and Sheine returned from the meeting quite excited, laughing and beaming. It reminded me of Edek and Heniek. I knew that Vania and Heniek came from two different worlds. One was a product of the socialist system, the Komsomol or the Party; Heniek grew up in a neutral youth movement. The differences, however, did not lie only in their divergent political educations. Heniek was a young man who had worked all his life, a simple person with the ordinary man's common sense. His non-political education could not adversely influence his character, and most important — diminish his love for freedom and justice. Edek, the product of a socialist Hebrew youth movement, found the connecting thread between the two. I am sure that if Heniek had met Vania, with Edek present, the three would have found the common language of young people risking their lives because they thought it was their duty.

The Judenrat

While the espionage group was beginning to deal with the problem of weapons the first *action* took place in the ghetto. On November 1 the Bialystok ghetto had been closed. On November 2, no Jew left for work. Fear was rampant. A week earlier Sheine had told us of a program to remove 12,000 Jews from the ghetto. A rumor spread that only those working in the factories would remain. Barash's carriage rushed back and forth every day; there was a great deal of movement in the streets, and everybody looked for work within the ghetto. Jews who watched Barash's movements, noted how often he left the ghetto, guessed what Germans he was going to see, and what institutions — the Gestapo, the Wehrmacht, Kanaris[18] of the Gestapo, or Klein of the Ghettovervaltung.[19] The mood fluctuated between hope and despair, and back again. When the rumor spread that the Germans did really plan to reduce the number of Jews in the ghetto, but that they would not do it all at once, as they did in the provincial towns, or in Grodno, Jews in the ghetto breathed more freely, as though the danger had passed. Barash ran from one German institution to another, found the "good" Germans (those who took bribes), promised, proved, and brought investigating committees, one after the other, from every institution. People worked diligently, as if nothing was happening. When the committee left, Jews reassembled, and asked for news. The committees were as numerous as the German institutions behind the lines, and they were numerous because there was no lack of those who wanted to avoid going to the front, and still earn a "living." For the O.K.W., the "Ristungscommando,"[20] the Gestapo and the "Zivilvervaltung" and representatives of the concerns, the ghetto was a source of profit (free labor, free machinery); for others it was a source of enrichment (taking bribes), and for still others a singular opportunity to rise in rank. The last were the worst, and the most fanatic. Those who valued position more than money were incorrigible. Barash, however, worked hard, and the O.K. W. and the "Ristungscommando" were on our side. For now, they satisfied themselves with the total liquidation of all the provincial towns in the Bialystok district. From that day on there were long lines going from the towns to the concentration camps in the district, by wagon, train, and on foot. Concentration camps were scattered throughout the district:[21] in Wolkovisk, Kelbasin, near Grodno; in the "10th Polk" (division), near Bialystok. From here the Jews were carried in sealed freight cars to Treblinka. It was no longer a secret. There were stories of young men who jumped out of the windows and were killed; of a rabbi in a Polish town who called upon all the Jews to die martyrs, singing; of the Jews of Krinki who killed the guards and fled to the forest. Altogether 150,000 Jews from the district were then taken to their death. The November days in Bialystok that began with sighs of relief and relatively light decrees in due course brought the horror stories of survivors, some of whom had escaped from Treblinka; they were witnesses whose stories could not be doubted.

A tremor went through the ghetto: for the first time the 50,000 Jews there knew that the stories of the extermination were true. The ghetto was reduced in size to 25,000 square meters, and with the added refugees from the provinces, the crowding became even worse. But no one paid any attention to such a trifle. It had been the main issue once; now it was unimportant.[22]

Barash told us of his plan to transform the whole ghetto into a kind of work camp. Up to 25,000 Jews would work in the factories, and since the German registers only counted 35,000 Jews (after the liquidation in the provinces there were between 50-55,000 Jews in Bialystok), most of the ghetto would be working. The rest would be employed in various outside occupations. Exit permits from the ghetto should be limited, as well as the number of Jews working outside. Industry should be developed. "We will have to produce something from nothing," Barash concluded, "but we will do it. They still need us, and they have therefore promised not to take even one Jew out of the ghetto."

Edek and I listened to his words, stunned and depressed. When he saw that, Barash added: "Of course I am not infallible. I cannot keep on promising forever. For the time being, there are no grounds for fear. The main thing," he hesitated for a moment, "the main thing is not to accelerate the process, not to commit any provocations. To work, to work! When there is no longer any choice, I will inform you, and I will not hide anything. Now, Koenigsberg (the site of the supreme administration for the eastern occupied regions, in East Prussia) is also on our side. Be careful, be careful!"

We asked him for money. We promised to be cautious. But we needed money, now. Of what we should be careful, we did not discuss. We had a sort of gentlemen's agreement. When we raised the question of money, Barash was embarrassed. Giving money involved responsibility. It meant becoming a partner to something specific, and he didn't even know what that was. He replied in the negative, saying that there were many difficulties.

"You know that our treasurer, the 'finance minister' as we call him in the ghetto, Sobotnik, is a hard Jew and closes his ears to anything about your 'partishine'. In any event, he mustn't know anything about it. He and Goldberg, haven't learned a thing from reality. Perhaps I'll use some subterfuge. I'll ask for money for some other purpose, and give it to you. It is a delicate matter, and I don't want to get involved with Sobotnik."

We knew that the Judenrat coffers were full to overflowing; that Sobotnik was distributing gifts to his many friends. This observant Jew, who had been known before the war as a leading figure in the kehilla and considered a "fine Jew", was distributing precious stones, wines and public properties to his own people: friends, including girls. We knew that Barash, if he had wanted to, could have found money without recourse to Sobotnik. He alone negotiated with the Germans, and no one would dare look into his expenses.

We received a piddling sum from Barash. We knew that it was only because of his concern for his good reputation that he had done so, and also because of his desire to maintain a "relationship" with us.

We were not surprised, later when we heard Barash deliver a characteristic and unequivocal speech, early in the winter of 1942-43. Posters called on the Jews to gather for a public meeting in the Linat Zedek hall. This is approximately what he said:[23]

"Jews, it is only with difficulty that I have succeeded in saving the ghetto from the calamities that have befallen our fellow Jews in the neighboring towns. We were helped by our successful and productive work. With our own hands we created what we have. Look at the factories, at our orderly and organized lives. Everybody works and lives. People do not die of hunger among us, as they do in other places. By our own energy and initiative we have created something from nothing, and that has helped and will continue to help us in this difficult war period. There are, however, those among us who want to stop the work, to commit sabotage and to declare war against the Germans. They carry out propaganda within the factories, in the shops and on the street; spreading views different from ours. I hereby declare that these people are traitors and provocateurs. They do not belong in our midst. We will uproot them and we will say, 'Take your hands off the ghetto. If you want to fight the Germans do so anywhere you like, but not in the ghetto. Get out of there lest we all bear responsibility for your actions. We worry about the tens of thousands of ghetto inhabitants, and you — you want to be heroes? If you want to blow up bridges, cut telephone and telegraph lines, good, do what you think is right. But it is not our concern. Do not touch the factories that we established with the sweat of our brows, and in which all our hopes for salvation lie. The important thing is to be patient, and not to be tempted into committing provocation.'"

Barash finished his speech and left. He did not brook arguments or criticism. The resistance was growing; in the various factories, at the machines and during the rest periods, the workers looked for some justification of Barash's words and did not find any. Meanwhile, the expulsions continued during the hard winter months. Jews from the towns were driven into the camps. Around the stations, in the vicinity of the 10th Regiment camp, we could see the sad caravans we still remembered from Vilna. After weeks and months of camp life, if the inmate was still alive, and had the strength to escape, where could he go? Where was there a house that would accept him? During the fall rains and the winter cold, people rotted alive in the camps. The only road led to Treblinka.

That was what the workers were whispering about in the factories of the Bialystok ghetto, the working ghetto, that had been saved for an hour because it was productive. Illusions were toppling, the sources of hope were sealed. Barash went his way, and life continued on its own "normal" way. If you knew how to look, to see without being seen, you could find the notes, written in small letters, passed secretly beneath the machine, from one shivering swollen veined hand to another. Surreptitiously one looked, read what was written, and thought. There was information about Treblinka, testimonies in print, calling upon the readers not to believe in the Germans or the illusions of the Judenrat, but to remember who the enemy was, and to seek ways to harm him. The signatures on the appeals were strange, they were not from Bialystok or from the neighboring towns. The notes moved from hand to hand, seemingly haphazardly, as if they had, somehow, come from Warsaw and just appeared here. The truth was that they had been printed here, not far from the factory. We did not get too involved in mass action. That would be the climax on the decisive day of revolt. Meanwhile we took only deliberate and purposeful steps; to prepare the ground, to win support among trustworthy persons, who tomorrow, or the day after, would join us. For that reason we arranged to distribute the propaganda material so that it would seem to come into one's hands accidentally. You looked closely into the face of the person reading the paper, and watched his eyes. Only a few days ago he was a total stranger, but on the recommendation of his fellow-workers, someone would approach him and say, off-handedly:

"Look, this was given to me by a friend to read; he asked me not to show it to anybody. Read it, and give it back to me. No, not now! During the break." And then, without realizing it, he was given a lesson in underground tactics.

He might be inexperienced, and cause harm: "Do as I do. Go to the toilet. Read it there."

If you thought that he could help, that he would dare, you spoke to him more openly, and recruited him for the factory cell. These cells were constituted according to their functions. The fighting cells were the highest stage; propaganda cells were in the middle, and then there was the periphery composed of people who carried out special assignments out of the cells, but would also perform its general functions within. The purpose for creating these cells was: 1) to go beyond the framework of the existing movements, ours and the communists, and to extend our influence to a broader public; 2) to obtain support for our activities within the production system in order to damage German war production; 3) not to depend upon a spontaneous mass uprising when the time came for the decisive battle, but to prepare for that eventuality by organization; and 4) to carry out the plans with a minimum of risk.

The periphery cells worked without knowing that they belonged to an organized underground movement. Organization within the factories had been the most appropriate answer the high command had found after the alert that had been announced for all the fighting units on that black November night. The signal to relax in the ghetto had not meant that for us. Those who had taken position in the ghetto that dark night, in cellars and attics, could not just go home as if nothing had happened. Something shocking had taken place, and we had reached a new stage in our enslavement. Ghetto streets were bleaker; there were people there. The winter was cold, and wet. Snow turned to slush in the streets, and the dampness penetrated into our bones. Even the beggars looked for better locations.

"*Varft arein, die krom is offen fun acht bis nein!*" (Throw something in, the store is open from eight to nine . . .) The voice came from one of the courts, from under the staircase roof. It was hard to stand in the alternating snow and rain with your shoes in puddles. Even the cripple from the first world war, crawling on wheels instead of logs, was not to be seen in the misty street, somewhere between fall and winter.

Inside the houses the darkness seemed even deeper; the make-shift stoves emitted smoke and dust, and it was difficult to keep things clean. The Health Committees, examining the houses and courts in the name of the Judenrat, could not help very much. They were unable to supply dry wood and coal for the big stoves that once had provided a pleasant warmth. We didn't, however, look at the quiet streets, the poverty and darkness. We fled to the cells, and our eyes lit up. Here were entire factories employing thousands of workers. If you knew how to look, if you had the ability to distinguish items hidden from the Wehrmacht and SD committees, the Ristungscommando and the Zivilvervaltung, you could see wonderful things.

Barash once told me that the ghetto had received an order for 600 Soviet soldier and officer uniforms: hats, trousers and coats.[24] The order had been received from the SD with an accompanying note: "The uniforms do not, of course, have to be made of new materials. Used clothing can be found and repaired. We must not waste new material." Where were Jews supposed to find cloth for Soviet uniforms? They could not ask the SD. "Do it, do it! If you fill this order you will receive additional orders. We will increase your food rations. We rely upon Barash." Then, as usual, a friendly slap on the back. The rest was up to the Jews. Barash told me this in great secrecy, and then added:

"You can understand what purpose these uniforms will serve. I am only surprised that the Germans trust us."

"But they do not really trust us. They simply cannot conceive of Jews understanding so sophisticated a strategem. They do not believe that Jews can revolt and harm them. Either they judge us, as they were taught to in their academies for Jewish problems, to be persons without self respect, or they characterize us according to what they think are our characteristics. Maybe they believe that because they have imprisoned us in the ghetto, we will not break their laws or find a way out of slavery and inform those who should know of this ruse."

There was a large hat factory in the ghetto. Members of the organization working there were ordered to put a square piece of yellow cardboard under the cardboard visor in every Soviet cap. That was one sign. There were others, too, and there were little pieces of paper stating: "This man has betrayed his homeland!", and the like. We made these notes known to Sheina's and the communists' commando groups and also their Polish and Bielorussian comrades outside the ghetto, who were in contact with the partisans in Bialovich. The operation was listed in the "Palace" archives with a special notice aimed at sending infiltrators, Red Army deserters or other traitors from the neighborhood who had joined the Germans' services to the partisan concentrations in Bialowiez. They were supposed to join the partisan groups as escaped Soviet war prisoners, become part of the partisan life, rise to command positions, and maintain contact with the Gestapo or the SD. six hundred traitors — that was a large number. The operation did not have to be too expensive. If they were suspected and killed the SD would not be concerned.

The plan did not succeed. We organized a "hat operation": it was operation versus operation, and hundreds of traitors were caught. Perhaps in that way we helped to keep the partisan movement from disintegrating from within.

Other operations should also be credited to the factory workers. When Hitler's soldiers somewhere in the cold north refused to march forward "führ den Sieg," you should know that this was the contribution made by the workers of the shoe and boot factory in the Bialystok ghetto.[25] They produced fine, shining, polished shoes; wool-lined boots that everyone longed for in winter. Who would imagine that the soles of these strong, hobbed-nailed shoes would fall off? And who could guess that the padded boots would last for only one month before they fell apart in the snow? Skilled hands constructed them that way. They compounded a special glue that they poured into the canvas manufactured in the ghetto in the big factory on Yurovika Street. A month later, when the soldiers reached the front, and the officer wanted to warm his frozen feet at his post in a –60° frost, the warming canvas would disintegrate; that soldier and that officer would no longer want any part of this war, or believe in Germany's certain victory.

This was beautiful and modest work. Nobody knew about it, it was not publicized in the papers. The underground dug in like moles and scores of workers joined in the sabotage action. The ranks increased, and so did their activities. The leading, guiding, initiating hands were young and daring. Yentel, for example, was teaching members of the cells within the factories. Who would find any connection between the hats and boots operations and Yentel's quiet work at the knitting machine? Zerah became the unofficial unseen manager of the shoe factory in spite of the fact that he had never been a cobbler. The others, the veteran craftsmen, listened to Zerah's quiet voice, and understood the inferences. Alongside these young people were veteran revolutionaries, accustomed to prison. There was Lilka, Lilka Maleravich. She worked with Yentel. Together, they were responsible for underground activities in the knitting factory on the corners of the Kupiecka and Yurowiecka Streets, whose noise kept the street awake day and night. With Zerah you could find Daniel Moshkovich, the veteran shoemaker, most of whose life had been spent not at the cobbler's stool but behind Pilsudski's iron bars until he contracted tuberculosis. Daniel was slight, thin-faced, young and intelligent; one of the underground's leaders. He and Zerah were responsible for underground activities in the shoe factory on Rozhanka Street.

Mordechai Tenenbaum came to us at that time as the emissary of the Jewish Fighting Organization in Warsaw. He came to Bialystok to prepare the movement for armed resistance. He had stolen across the border, disguised as a Tartar, had been stopped, and came through safely. His coming presaged the formation of a united front of "Hechalutz" and all the left parties. "Hechalutz" was comprised mainly of members of Mordechai's movement, "Dror." Members of "Hanoar Hatzioni" could, like the other Zionist movements, join the front either as groups or as individuals, but they could not constitute the nucleus. Indeed, a short time later we were joined by a group from "Hanoar Hatzioni," and even a Revisionist group. The front as such emerged only after the unification of the Chalutz camp.

Once again Mordechai was busy day and night, struggled against the weakness of his own comrades, their illusion-brooding mistaken conceptions, fought compromise and hesitancy, denounced those sitting on the fence, evading the struggle and seeking momentary tranquility and comfort. In particular, he gathered the nucleus of movement members who were faithful to their pioneering role. He broke down all barriers. Mordechai was at once naive and intelligent. He would become enthusiastic over people when he saw in them a spark of determination and devotion; he believed in people's good will. Sometimes he believed too much, loosened the reins of discipline, and was burned as a result. In his feverish activity, driven by the realization that time was pressing, that the holocaust was coming closer, a desperation he had developed in Vilna, Grodno and Warsaw, he sometimes became a tyrant, imposing his authority over all those about him, over his kibbutz, Dror, his activist comrades, and his closest friends. When he succeeded in winning people over, in finding fighting comrades-in-arms, he would be all smiles, exude good will, and was happy when you came to his underground room. However, when he was disappointed in someone, when he discovered evasion, or met former members of his party who were complacent, believing that the evil would not touch them, Mordechai would unleash torrents of fire and brimstone. We knew Mordechai and loved him, for his frailties as well as his courage, his exaggerated faith in people who were not worthy of trust, his stormy spirit and sharp mind. In the winter of 1942-43, when Mordechai came to us, the pragmatic cooperation between our movements evolved into a militant and ideological partnership, and then we began to demand a united front of the Commando.

Here we came up against a stone wall. The Communists rejected any idea of unity. They used the old arguments, the ideological and practical excuse. Ideologically, they said, the new people were not capable of fighting an effective anti-fascist war "since they oppose the Soviet Union." From the practical standpoint, too, they were not worthy of unity. After all, they belonged to the reformist wing of socialism, the rightist Poalei Zion.

We told them that their mistake was linking a pioneering youth movement to worn-out concepts. This adoption of "accepted" ideas, taken from the past, depressed us and frustrated any possibility of struggle. It is difficult to debate when there is a lack of knowledge. The Communists knew something about Poalei Zion but did not grasp or understand the great difference, the changes in the Hechalutz youth movement and the changes wrought by time. How could we shake them free of their prejudices and inflexible positions? The time had come to close our ranks. Yesterday's allies moved apart, and tomorrow's drew closer. Only a fighting force, knowing what it was fighting for, could have drawn together the scattered groups of the Noar Hatzioni, the Bund, Poalei Zion, and even the Revisionists.

Our partnership with Dror was established immediately after Mordechai arrived. We elected a joint leadership and joint committees for military training, organization, production, armaments, finances, and political affairs to which I was delegated. After a time representatives of Hanoar Hatzioni and the Revisionists were included in the leadership. Their work was never really defined, their sessions lacked content or action. There were a number of reasons for this. First and most important, was its composition: the addition of the representatives of movements without any numerical or organizational force behind them. Mordechai often had to work to convince them that armed resistance within the ghetto was the proper way for pioneering movements. In this he was not always successful. The negotiations with Hanoar, Dror, and that part of the Bund that did not belong to Front "A" with us and the Communists, we assigned to Mordechai, since Front "A" was already organized. We attempted to convince Mordechai that there was another organized and partially armed force within the ghetto in addition to Hashomer Hatzair. We tried hard to convince him not to look upon the ghetto as a void, with the first signs of revolt coming only after his arrival. Mordechai did not want to hear anything about bringing in the Communists. He, too, had his prejudices about movements and parties.

Because of his great trust in people, he often suffered bitter disappointments, and he convinced himself that others were interested in only making speeches: "what I don't do myself will not be done." Mordechai's instability was becoming very disturbing. True, the times were mad, the responsibilities almost beyond a human's capacity to endure. For example, we faulted Mordechai's enthusiasm for the revisionists' childish behavior; they played conspiracy, boasting of their strength and their arms.

Mordechai related that he had arranged to meet someone on the corner of Biala Street. The sign was to be a short stick in the hand. At the corner Mordechai didn't find anyone holding a small stick, except for an old Jew. It was twilight and Mordechai looked in vain for some young person in the darkness. The old man, however, kept moving about and Mordechai understood that it was only a disguise and gave the slogan. The surmise proved correct, the meeting was held. We asked Mordechai why the other man had disguised himself from Mordechai. Mordechai shook his head and laughed. He had found the game interesting. We warned him that the game was only a cover for impotence and the lack of any desire to act. One day their representative brought an explosive. Mordechai rejoiced and said: "I told you, I told you they are good fellows!"

The time came to coordinate the cells. The list of section commanders had to be brought to the meeting of the military committee in order to prepare a gathering of all the commanders. The Revisionists put if off from one session to the next until Mordechai himself gave up, and got rid of them with a Russian curse.

The Noar Hatzioni affair was more serious, though less tiring. The Noar Hatzioni were a group of people who were good and loyal but lacking in organizational and ideological training. They used to meet and discuss Palestine, the commune, and even study the geography of Israel. At times I would come to their leader, Sonia's home. One of our comrades lived next door to her and we sometimes held hurried meetings there. Sonia would then stop me and demand my attention. She really wanted to know what was happening on the front and in the Jewish world.

"Chaika, what is there to do? You must be doing something and don't want us part of it."

Sonia's questions were completely positive. First we helped her to find work for her people in the Judenrat vegetable gardens; later we spoke to them and hinted of the only choice before us.

"But, how and with what do we start?" Sonia and her comrades would ask. We were always surprised by the small group's obedience and wondered at its helplessness. We, however, appreciated their honesty and innocence and especially their good intentions. Modechai decided to take them "in hand". They fulfilled all his instructions, brought a list when they were asked to do so and carried out their own census. But they never displayed any of their own initiative. They never promised anything, and never dressed themselves in a clothing other than their own like the Revisionists. Mordechai never concealed his repugnance at the passive obedience of the Hanoar Hatzioni, nor his enthusiasm for the military glamour of Betar, and his disappointments always cost him dearly.

A special case was that of the Bund and Poalei Zion parties. The bund members in Bialystok, except for those who had joined the "A" block, were like their comrades in Warsaw. The ties among them were weak, the fear great and their innate compromising nature consumed the rest of what was left of their workers' tradition.

"Is it worthwhile? Is it possible? Maybe it is better to save Jews and help them exist? Is it worthwhile, for one act of heroism, to endanger the whole ghetto?" These were the questions that they always asked in response to our demands.

Rubenstein of their members, who headed a Judenrat committee, would sometimes do a small service for some needy comrade, but never, under any circumstances, would he obligate himself. Here it was that the evasion was revealed. Chmelnik and his Poalei Zion comrades were like him. They were all like sons of one family while we, the members of hechalutz, Hashomer Hatzair and Dror, belonged to a different group. The only expression of their bad conscience was their strong desire to know what we were doing. When the ties with them were cut completely, they complained, were hurt, felt themselves discriminated against. When we used to tell Sheina about the meetings with the Bund and Poalei Zion representatives, she would smile and say:

"What do you want from Rubinstein, from that Jewish householder?" Rubinstein, incidentally, was Sheine's brother-in-law.

We asked Mordechai to leave them alone but he was looking for public support though we believed he was not looking in the proper place. The matter of our relationships with Barash too was painful and worrying, and here, too, the Communists rejoined:

"We told you they are Barash's accomplices and you trust them and even ask us to unite with them in a single front?"

We knew that the Communists were haunted by nightmares from the past, by treachery at home and suspicions of anyone who was not one of their own. The Judenrat was a bone of contention among us including Mordechai. Here we found ourselves caught between Mordechai's mistakes and the Communists' inflexibility. Mordechai knew what the Judenrat was like. He had seen it in other cities and had been one of the most consistent fighters against its illusions and contemptible service for the Germans. Like us, he too considered the Judenrat members to be traitors. Barash helped; he provided information, and even supplied money for the underground.

"You don't understand. He is serving us in everything. Why not use him?" Mordechai would argue.

We agreed that he should be utilized. Barash, however, was too clever just to serve, without any accountability. We feared that Mordechai, because of his excessive faith in people, might reveal things which should not be done to Barash in payment for "his great understanding" for our cause. We feared that if the day ever came when Barash had to choose between the fighting Jewish underground and the Germans, a choice aimed, of course, at saving Jews, he would choose the Germans and betray us.

"Mordechai, do you really believe that when the time comes Barash will come over to our camp, to this side of the barricades?"

"At the last moment, I believe, he will come over."

"And when is that last moment going to be; when the first Jews are taken or when they are annihilated, to the last of them and he is the last one left?"

We knew that Mordechai was troubled by the complex problem of collective responsibility: should we start when the first Jew was taken, or wait until it became evident that the Germans were liquidating the ghetto? That was a vital question for all of us. We decided that the decision of when to start should not be left to Barash and his Judenrat colleagues. When we took up arms we would also assume the responsibility for doing so. We warned against relying upon the Judenrat's weak reed. Their potentialities, money, shops, and storehouses had to be utilized, but they could not be asked to give more support than that. Not one superfluous word, not a hint of the underground's structure, real aims and activities, could be revealed to them. They would have to go their way, and we ours. We would not bring Barash over to our side. A man establishing and cultivating industries for the Germans and also endeavoring to maintain a high level of production, mediating between the Jews and the Nazis, who, instead of telling the Jews the truth was deceiving them and himself, would not suddenly become a fighter. He could help us for his own reasons and we would accept his help gladly, and use it as effectively as possible, but trust him? Never. He could help, but he could also betray.

Mordechai succeeded in obtaining from Barash more than I or any other comrade had. In the end, however, Mordechai was badly burned and the time came, much later, when Mordechai had to hide from the Jewish police sent by Barash. Meanwhile, good relations prevailed.

The second bloc came into being — Hashomer Hatzair, Dror, Hanoar Hatzioni, the Revisionists and part of the Bund. It was established parallel to our bloc "A" with the Communists. Groups of five with the commanders were set up, the battle sections with their commanders, active committees and leadership. There were many problems, however. Unity was weak, and cooperation in matters of armaments, money and organization was incomplete.

Edek's vital slogan that we repeated on going to bed late at night and on waking early in the morning, was: "The unification of the two blocs into one fighting front."

We searched for weapons; every movement separately, and all of us together. Mordechai met with his comrades, Reuven and Hershl, two strong and trustworthy fellows, and decided to manufacture grenades. They knew that we were already occupied in making some arms, but had not yet succeeded in making a real grenade. We agreed that Franck would coordinate his activity with that of the workers that Mordechai had recruited. Consultation certainly would not hurt, though each side would continue to work separately in the hope of finding the correct technical formula. Franek spent whole days with various experts in order to produce the most destructive grenade possible. The time for trials came. The first model seemed to be perfect but it was miserable. It consisted of a thick, round iron or tin box, seven to eight centimeters wide and ten to thirteen centimeters long, filled with dynamite and sharp pieces of metal and hermetically sealed. In order for the dynamite not to explode in our hands when it was ignited, we devised a fuse, one end of which led into the dynamite-filled box. By the time the grenade reached its destination the fuse would have burned and would then reach the dynamite and the grenade would explode. We sewed thin sacks, one-half centimeter wide made of special cloth and filled them with dynamite. The fuse was primitive and not uniform; in some places the fire would spread swiftly, and in others it took too long. The dynamite we found was damp, and of little value. We built an electric dryer, and were in constant fear of some sudden explosion.

This period of experimentation did not halt the search for arms, which came into our possession in very meager quantities. We looked for some large quantities of weapons which did not require an outlay of money, but the good will of the seller or mediator, so that we could arm thousands of people. This search for improved arms was beyond the capacities of Mordechai and Franek.

From the end of December, until the beginning of January, 1943, the district's communities were wiped out before our eyes. The last Jewish towns had died. The camps, too, were being liquidated. Very soon they would come to us, and we still had no weapons. If the end came tomorrow, you could not say, "too early!" but we would have to begin immediately. With what — a few pistols and a few rifles? Or maybe with the grenades that had still not been perfected? The Jews of Yashinovka, Krinki and Sokolki were fleeing to the forest and to the Bialystok ghetto, but most were sent directly to Treblinka. Carloads of rags, the clothes of the Jews being returned without their owners from Treblinka, were received in the "textile industry." Barash showed us patches and papers that had been found in the pockets. Yellow patches with the Star-of-David. From Krinki, Wasilkow, Bielsk or

Volkovisk? Who knew? All the yellow patches were the same, but the names of the slaughtered had been erased and very little remained in the few identification and work-cards. These documents were all that the 150,000 Jews of the Bialystok district had left. Barash was a decent man; he called us and showed it all to us. Was he, perhaps, acknowledging the justice of our views? He did not say anything, but went about silent and gloomy in those last days, and like him all of the ghetto, all those Jews still able to move about.

The Explosives Expert in the Lion's Den

We learned that our comrade Kuba was incarcerated in the Volkovisk concentration camp. He was a movement veteran, a member of Edek's kibbutz, Bamivhan. He was still in the camp and it was said that he had "golden hands," and most important, he was an explosives expert who would surely be able to find the proper formula for our grenade.

"We have to bring in Kuba at all costs, at all costs!"

One of our comrades worked for a money-hungry German who had a taxicab and was prepared to go to Volkovisk for 1,000 marks, and include passengers. Who they were didn't interest him. Zerah went; we managed to obtain the money to save Kuba and his girlfriend and to protect his "golden hands" so they could build a model grenade.

Zerah returned terribly depressed. The camp was securely closed. The man who had promised to bring Kuba out of the camp in return for payment, a Jew who still had a permit to move about in the city, had failed.

"I will go again, alone, without the taxi; we must get him out!" Zerach suddenly cried out.

"You won't go, I'll go."

Everybody looked at me in wonder. How? With what? It was impossible to spend any more money for that purpose.

"You'll see. I can try."

The next day I was equipped with three forged travel permits, signed by the "burgomeister" of a town near Grodno, a mayor who, perhaps, had never even existed. One was for me, and the other two were for Jan or Yakub Rogozinsky and his wife. From a Jew who had fled Volkovisk we got the address of a Polish woman who lived in a court where Jews were working in German garages. According to him, Jews came to her house and she helped them to purchase food.

It was winter again when I left the ghetto this time to travel to Volkovisk. In this direction workers rode to work in the mornings, in old creaking and rattling cars. That day it didn't take long. I arrived in Volkovisk before noon and went to look for the Polish woman's house. The streets of Volkovisk, a beautiful and busy town, were almost empty. Was it because of the cold, or out of fear? A golden-haired little girl showed me the street and the house, and ran away. I found the Polish woman, of whom I knew nothing. She was young, tall and plump, but well-shaped and seemed quite healthy. She had a beautiful face, bright eyes, braids around her head, and absolutely glowed. I found her in a little room, seated before a large mirror doing her beautiful nails. Who was she and what was she like? Her mother brought me into her room and remained in the doorway to hear what this strange woman sought from her daughter.

"I would like to speak to you alone," I turned to the daughter.

She motioned to her mother to leave, and she did so unwillingly. I introduced myself as a Pole from Bialystok seeking to help two Jews, friends from university days, and to take them out of the camp. "If you could at least help me contact Jews working in the city I would be very grateful."

"Who sent you to me?"

I mentioned the name of the Jew who had given me her address. She no longer hesitated.

"I would gladly do what you ask. But how? For two days now the Jews have not been taken out of the work camp. Two days ago it would have been easier. The Germans say that the Jews won't be allowed out of the camp any longer because they spread disease, germs, filth and typhus in the city. We know better: in another two or three days they are going to liquidate the camp. That is why it is tightly closed. Only two days ago you could find here, in this court, many Jews, under guard, of course. Still, it was possible to exchange words with them."

Once again she reflected: "But how is it possible to get them out? You know, if there had been some place of refuge many of them could have escaped before, but now even that is almost impossible. I'll ask and look around, maybe there is someone left in the city. But I'm not sure. The prospects are very poor."

She left, and returned in a few minutes.

"I've heard that not far from the city park, where they are removing the ruins of a building, a few Jews are still working. This is apparently their last day. Go there; maybe you'll learn something. I'll go out, too, to ask."

I listened to her gloomily. The camp's last days, I only had one more day. And if I did find those Jews: they also knew that it was their last day. Could I be helped by a Jew about to die and ask him to help another Jew in the same situation? Every drowning man looks for some miracle; what would I do if he agreed to help on the condition that I took him too? I could only take two. If I took more, all would be caught. Kuba, I had been told, had a gentile face. I would also have to smuggle his girl friend, Naomi. If this matter became known in the camp there would be a tumult, and there would most certainly be Jews who would threaten to inform if we didn't take them too.

I found the broad square surrounded by barbed wire where the Jews were. I gestured to one of the Jews. He looked about and when he saw the sentry moving away, came to me swiftly. I asked him if he could transmit a package to some Jew in the camp. Disappointed, he asked me: "To whom?"

I told him, and said: "Maybe you can tell him to get out of the camp tomorrow?"

"I'll tell him, but how will he get out? It is doubtful whether we will go out tomorrow.

"Hurry, Panie. It is forbidden to stand here. Tell me what you want, don't be afraid, a lot of Poles are trying to save Jews. I won't tell anyone." His eyes, however, were examining me suspiciously.

A second and a third came up. I moved away, gesturing to the first to wait. When I moved away the others went back to their work. I returned. "In any case, tell the man, Kuba Rogozinski, that he must try to get out tomorrow to work with you. If you can, help him. I have important news for him from his family in Bialystok."

"Good, I'll tell him, if I can.", the man replied gloomily. "I know him; he is a metal worker, right?"

"Right. So all the best. See you here tomorrow."

I left, with worry in my heart. "What have you arranged," I asked myself. "Nothing." Nothing had really been accomplished. I had done what I could only in order to satisfy my conscience, not to return to Bialystok empty-handed. Could I really trust that Jew? Maybe he would help Kuba get out, but he would surely demand "payment". And how was Kuba to get out of the camp?

Once again I dragged my feet through the alien streets. The afternoon hours were passing, soon it would be dark. Where was I to go? Unconsciously I moved away from the park along the street. I passed an army camp; there were fewer houses. I came to the end of the street. According to the Polish woman the concentration camp was a few hundred meters from the army camp. Was I going to the camp? My feet carried me further without my being aware of it. There was the barbed wire at a distance; heavens above, a double fence, no, a triple one. In all the camp corners there were high "stork's nests" with searchlights. Within the nests there were machine guns manned by Germans. At the entrance was a sentry, his leather boots in giant straw shoes so that his feet would not freeze. His rifle was slung on his back and he was marching back and forth between the wire fences at the entry. Not a soul was to be seen in the street. I was all alone in the camp. The sentry noticed me. I went up to him. Once again I spoke German.

"Sir, I have come to take the keys of our (emphasis on "ours") storehouses from the cursed Jew who worked there yesterday. He didn't come to work today. The devil knows what he and all these other parasites are doing. Why didn't he come? He didn't think it necessary to send me the keys."

The sentry gave me a courteous look when he heard my German. He was helpless, however; he had been stationed there to guard the entrance, and nothing more.

"The madame will forgive me; it is forbidden to enter."

"Who wants to go in? Who needs them? Please call that Jew to give me the keys. Do you want me to stop work because of him?"

"No, no! But what am I to do? I am forbidden to move from my place and there is no one I can send."

"What do you mean, no one? There are Jews moving around here, and there is a Jewish woman. Call her and order her to look for him in the camp."

I didn't wait for his answer and moved closer to the camp and gestured to the woman to come closer. The picture revealed to my eyes is difficult to describe. Concrete bunkers were scattered throughout the camp. In order to enter you had to bend over and go underground. Among the bunkers thin and silent human shadows were moving about. One shadow passed and fled, disappeared in the black mass of the bunkers. There was one bending over, attempting to light a fire at the bunker entrance, with the help of two stones. The wind was blowing, the wood was damp, and the black pot resting on stones fell. A second wraith appeared bringing two potatoes to cook. All of them seemed vague, old, worn out, dragging their feet with great difficulty.

The woman came up to me, a little scared. When she came close I saw that her face was quite young. I told her to immediately call Kuba Rogozinski. She laughed, "I know him, he is a relative of mine." I shouted at her loudly. The sentry smiled at me, but she understood; I hinted in a whisper that the matter was important. Once again I waited, the minutes passing slowly. Somebody might come up suddenly to find out what I was doing, and that would be the end.

Kuba appeared. He was not yet worn out like the other apparitions wandering about the camp. He was blond, a typical aryan, but very dirty.

The German guard was polite and did not listen to our conversation.

"The keys! The keys!" I shouted, and then whispered, "My name is Chaika, here are travel permits for the railway, for you and Naomi.

"Get out tomorrow morning. I will wait for you in the city." (I gave him the address of the Polish woman.) "I'll wait all day, in case something happens you have the permits. You can get to Bialystok with them."

"There is a Jewish watchmaker in the city. He works at . . . . If he wants to, he can get me out tomorrow. He will work another three or four days outside."

"Good, I'll talk to him right away. You contact him too. And now . . . Jew . . . "I shout and turn towards the sentry.

"You see, everything can be arranged. Thank you for your help, soldier."

I had barely finished talking when a loud voice shouted at me from about 40 or 50 steps away in the camp:

"Ein Moment, Fraulein," and facing me was a tall Jew, dressed in a short but warm coat, riding pants tucked into his high leather boots. His boots are shined, too, I thought. His hands were thrust into his coatpockets and he had a high fur hat on his head. He turned toward the sentry:

"Ist dieses Fraulein eine Polin oder eine Judin?"

The sentry was somewhat confused, rolled his eyes and did not know how to answer. He had not asked for my papers at all. I understood that this was the Jewish camp commander. I had heard many stories about him. He would not let a Jew escape. He would watch them lest they get out of the camp and disappear. He would demand ransom money or betray you to the Gestapo. He was like the "shmaleowniki" in Warsaw, and worse. I recognized him by the typical dress of the traitors, speculators, those who get rich from their brothers' tragedy. This was the new social class that had arisen during the occupation.

I decided to repeat the old game:

"Was will dieser Jude?" I asked the sentry. The Jew moved back. Now he spoke to me in Polish, good Polish, with pretended politeness:

"I thought you were looking for somebody. Maybe I can help you? Who are you looking for?" He winked at me: "Maybe you want to save somebody, I'll help you." Good that Kuba had disappeared. Good that the permits were in his hands. I was a Pole, and he hadn't seen me talking to Kuba.

"Thank you," I hissed slowly. "Thank you very much but I have no need for your very good services. Get out of here, and don't mix into affairs that are not your own." And finally, to make the impression stronger: "I don't need the help of a dirty Jew."

Now I had to hurry to the watchmaker. I found him and told him that I was a Pole who was seeking to get a Jew out of the camp. If he agreed, I would help him, too. The first condition was, however, that he get Kuba Rogozinski and his wife out.

He sat stooped over his bench repairing German watches. I took off my watch and showed it to him. He opened it, looked at it and listened to what I was saying.

"I'll get him out. I'll find some way. There are Germans here who are interested in me. They know that the camp's days are numbered and they want me to repair all the Gestapo officers watches before I die. This is an exceptional opportunity; I repair them for nothing. They will fill any request I make. I'll get them out. I don't ask anything from you; I only want you to take my daughter with you."

"I can't take your daughter. I don't have any permit now. I'll send it to you or bring it myself; maybe you have some acquaintance, some Polish woman through whom I can send it?"

"Good, I'll trust you. I'll run away, in any case, either I'll escape or I'll be caught. The only thing is my daughter; she is so young, and in Bialystok I have family who will take her in."

"Will you be able to hide them until I come for them tomorrow?"

"Yes, they will be able to wait here. How will the matter of my daughter be arranged?"

"Tomorrow I'll give you the address in Bialystok."

We separated with a handshake. He bent over his bench again and I went to the railway station to ask when the trains left for Bialystok. When I was told that they left at eleven in the morning and eight in the evening, I decided that we would leave in the evening. At eleven it would be more feasible but dangerous. Naomi's Jewish face might give her away, and they were both dirty and ragged. Better that we go at night. I returned to my Polish woman. I told her that I had succeeded in contacting Kuba and his wife and that their exit was assured.

"I am only looking for a hiding place for them until the evening. I don't want to travel with them during the day. We'll go by night train. Can you help me?"

"I think so; I'll tell you right away." She went out to the kitchen, whispered to her mother and returned.

"My mother will go out and ask; don't worry. But we have to find a place for you to spend the night. It's not good at our place; Germans are always moving about.

Her mother returned a little later and told us that I could stay with her neighbor. They would give me dinner there, and tomorrow I could bring the other two. I followed her. Evening had already come. It was about eight o'clock an hour before curfew, and the streets were already deserted. Except for the dull and distant echoes of the soldiers' and sentries' boots, there was not a sound to be heard. We sneaked into the second court on tiptoe. The narrow stairs creaked under foot. It wasn't safe for the neighbors to hear that some stranger was coming to lodge here.

Once again I was in a clean and warm apartment; one room divided into two by the country stove which radiated a pleasant warmth. Pieces of lard were frying in the pan spraying the hands of the landlady. She worked, and talked. She complained of the troubles of the times, of the Germans, and of the terrible things they were doing to the Jews.

"Panie, I used to move around with the Jews, trade with and help them in the best way I could. Recently, however, when the Jews of Volkovisk and the whole neighborhood were imprisoned in the cursed camp, the abominations have become worse each day. Jews I knew for many years, my neighbors, educated and intelligent Jews, Panie, came to me recently and asked for my help. I helped them as much as I could but when they left, Panie, they left the chair full of lice. That is what the Germans have done to human beings, who were once rich and intelligent. Now there are only 1500 or 1700 left, Panie. Once there were many, very many."

She talked and went on with her work, frying, cutting bread, pouring tea. Finally, she said:

"Panie, you can feel comfortable here. Don't be afraid. You are doing a great thing. May Jesus help you."

I looked around, seeking some hiding place in the apartment. I wondered where we would hide Kuba and Naomi tomorrow.

She understood what I was thinking.

"Everything will be alright. This apartment does not lack hiding places. Look . . ." and she pointed to a low door behind the stove. "That's where I keep wood, but there is enough room for them if someone comes knocking at the door. If only my husband doesn't come home until tomorrow evening. He is not a bad man at all but he is too afraid. In any case, he says, we are in danger all the time in these bad days and there is no need to take additional risks."

I tossed from side to side all night. The landlady noticed that I couldn't sleep and comforted me:

"Don't worry, everything will come out all right."

In the morning I went to the watchmaker. They had come! I brought them to my hostess, put them in her hands and went back to the watchmaker. I thanked him for keeping his promise and arranged to come back in two days to bring him the permit.

"No, you don't have to bother. I will send a friend of mine to you. I want you to give me an address in Bialystok where she can be brought and where they will tell her how to get into the ghetto. That's all. Maybe my friend will use the permit and take my daughter as her little girl," the watchmaker said, as if thinking to himself. Since yesterday he seemed to have grown older and his face had saddened. I gave him Olla's address without even asking her. I knew that I could trust Olla. I only asked the watchmaker to promise me that after sending his daughter, he would escape, himself. He nodded, thanked me for the address and added:

"If there are still people like you who are prepared to risk their life to save Jews, it is indeed worthwhile living in this world."

I did not tell him I was Jewish. Let him believe that such people did. After all it was true, I myself had found many. Yadwiga and Irena, Olla and Stefa in Bialystok, and this woman in Volkovisk, and those dozens of anonymous persons I did not know who extended me their aid. I left him and returned to my hostess. Naomi looked terrible; she had just recovered from typhus. She was withered, thin, her hair shorn completely, her nose too long because of her sunken cheeks, and her eyes . . . God in heaven, they were like two burning coals in her white face. How could they help recognizing that she was Jewish! And their clothes!

I helped them wash and straighten their clothing. They rested a little, ate to satiety for the first time after months of hunger. I asked them to try to avoid appearing sad on the way to the train and during the trip better that they just talk; their Polish was good. If they were heard speaking Polish without their faces, the faces of Jews coming out of the camp being seen, they just might make their way in safety.

We came to the train at night. There was light only in the station. I took their permits, and bought tickets for the three of us. The permits were stamped with the Volkovisk station stamp. I left them in the dark, outside, near the entrance, and when the train arrived pushed them ahead. We found places in the corner of a dark train. I told Naomi to lay her head on Kuba's knees and to sleep. Kuba could talk to me. He should hold his head up and not bend over. They examined our permits once and returned them without saying a word. Naomi napped; she was weak and moved only with difficulty.

We reached the Bialystok station at night. The station was lit and filled with people, some reclining, some playing cards, drinking muddy beer or dozing on the benches, on the floor or on their bundles. There was a bad odor in the stuffy air, caused by the body heat of the travellers. We found a corner. Once again Naomi lowered her head as if napping and Kuba sat and talked with me. Now we had to find a way to get them into the ghetto. I had yellow paper and scissors in my purse. We couldn't wait until evening when the Jews come back from work. There were examinations from time to time in the station, and most important - during the day it was difficult to hide a Jewish face. I had an address in the city, though that too involved great risks, both for the addressee whom we might still have to use, and for Kuba and Naomi. Finally, I found a way not using the street in daylight. At 4:30 in the morning a group of Jews left the ghetto to go by train to work in Starosheltze. The train left the Bialystok station at five. Five minutes after five we would have to leave the station; at that time it was still dark. I would lead them through Poleska Street, a side street, to the city limits, almost until Chista. There I would pin on their patches, and Kuba would lead a limping and groaning Naomi to the guard and say that one of the Starosheltze workers had fainted, and the commander — the kolonnenfuerer — had ordered him to take her back to the ghetto. The plan worked perfectly. Before we turned into Chista I pinned the patches on their clothing and said goodbye. I stood aside and watched them being swallowed up within the ghetto gate, Naomi limping, leaning on Kuba, and Kuba supporting her.

Olla's Home

I turned to the city, toward Olla's. Olla was a whole world unto herself; seemingly similar to all the others of tens of thousands of families living in the city. She, however, had a special importance for the underground.

Olla was one of my sister's Polish friends. During the Soviet days she had worked with her in the telegraph office, and when the Germans came she had helped my sister with food. She lived outside the city with her family, a veteran workers' family. Her father, a man of about 60 or 65, had been a railway worker, and had continued at his occupation during the invasion. Her mother, a short, plump Polish woman, was always busy with her household chores, the cooking, tending the pigs and the chickens. Olla's husband was young, a driver for the city mail. He, too, had continued his previous work. Olla stayed at home and took care of their little daughter.

My sister had introduced me to them and they invited me to visit them whenever I was in the city. I never took contraband goods from them to smuggle; I was never loaded with vegetables and bread, like the other Jews. They, however, never asked me my reasons for leaving the ghetto. In their home I could spend the extra hours instead of roaming the streets between leaving the ghetto and train time. In their home I could rest after wearing myself out running about the city. Here no one ever remarked that I was Jewish and had to be careful; they did not exaggerate in expressing their sympathy, nor in their generosity or caution. In short, I was a welcome guest in this home. I could sit in the garden near the house, warm myself on a bench and watch birds nesting in the trees, without anyone paying attention to me. The old lady would sometimes break into my silence and reflections with a natural and simple sentence:

"Halina, come and taste, see what good cakes I've baked!" She never exaggerated in offering food, as one might toward a hungry or poor person. Her chubby hands were always busy among the pots and only at rare intervals would she sit with the members of her family and indulge in the usual women's talk of neighbors in the laundry, of the very expensive lard, of some relative who was trading in the market, or of some woman it was wiser to avoid.

The old man would return from his work breathing heavily, dirty and tired. He would sit down on the bench in front of the house and take off his shoes. He did not speak much and only rarely did I see him angry. He would greet me with "How do you do, Pani Halina, what's new?" and never waited for my answer. When he was angry it was a sign that he was bitter about the Germans pushing him around, after his sixty years of life, and many years of service for the railroad. Olla's husband, Vladek, was a young man, not too heroic or strong looking. He was dark and had a short mustache and was the only one in the house with a short temper, quite excitable and easy to arouse. He was the only one who cursed the Germans out loud for their abominable actions.

However, he kept quiet when some stranger came to the door. Sometimes he would hint to me that he, too, had some "contacts." He was also the only one to intimate that he knew what I was doing, and why I was running about outside the ghetto. Olla would silence him immediately.

Olla was fair, blonde, and had a slight, typically aryan snub nose. She was the most important person in her family; quiet, deliberate and courageous. She was intelligent, and always scolded her mother or husband when they talked too much.

Olla's family happened to find an available apartment near the ghetto. From then on we breathed more easily. Their new quarters were at the end of Bialostochanska Street, which was half on the aryan side. Their room was the last one, nearest the wall. Only the partitions of the privies and the pens in the courtyard separated the aryan side from the other one in the ghetto. You only had to climb to the roof of the pen, hang on with your hands and push your feet onto the other side, then jump; three or four meters, and you were standing in an empty lot which was one of the ghetto courts. It once had once been a park.

The court in which Olla lived housed a lot of neighbors, people of all kinds. Most of them lived from smuggling into the ghetto. They smuggled butter, sugar, lard and milk through a hole that was not too apparent in one of the privy walls. After you pushed your goods through, you simply put the plank back into place. You went to the toilet purportedly for your private needs, and if it was arranged that someone would wait on the other side, everything worked out.

The people living in the court, however, were not fools. If strangers began to use the secret passages for smuggling prices would go down and the profits would drop. In addition, all their business could come to a swift end.

The cursed patrols moving within and about the court would notice the business and all inhabitants would be punished. For that reason, a stranger could not enter. The Jews, too, in the adjoining court, wanted a monopoly, but it was easier to come to terms with them. In addition, we had a policeman who would arrange to receive the people inside. I couldn't bring Kuba and Naomi into the ghetto this way because Naomi couldn't have jumped from that height, and I also had not arranged for Gedalyahu to wait at the appointed time, to help her down. I could not have known in advance when and how I would bring them. At first I was the only one to utilize Olla's address, the only one to visit her home and use the privy wall. In the course of time her home became a day refuge and a night entry into the ghetto for many of us. In the event of unexpected failure in other parts of the city, this apartment could always serve as a place of security.

One day I was asked to leave the ghetto in order to receive an automatic rifle (a Russian rifle, firing 10 shots in sequence). Our links with the outside had become closer at that time. At the end of autumn the partisan group that had begun to work within the city was caught. They were Polish Communists, and Soviet workers and civilians, who had been left in the city after the Russian evacuation and had organized to fight the invader.

For some time contacts with the first ones to organize outside the ghetto had been cut, but they were soon renewed. These were contacts, from before the war and they were not given any new underground information. The forces outside the ghetto were dispersed, and most were in hiding, but the search for real contacts did not stop. In the winter of 1942 Nita Cherniakowa, a Bielorussian woman Communist, had gone to establish contacts with the partisans in the Grodek area but had been caught.

However, even then not all contacts were lost. In the camp which housed an SS military unit, in what had been the home of the 42nd regiment of the Polish army, some Jews and Poles were working, among them Communists and two of our comrades. It was they who heard from a Polish comrade about the Russian automatic rifle. They found the weapon, examined it in the graveyard opposite, hid it and fixed a time for us to retrieve it. Our joint organization with the Communists assigned me to the mission.

I left the ghetto in the morning with the work battalion, dressed in work clothes. I had a bag in my hand and in it a big hat, like those worn by the German women. In one of the courts I took off the dirty cloak, put the hat on, and left the court looking as splendid as could be. I had to get to the site precisely by eleven and to wait at the side entrance to the Christian graveyard. After a few minutes two men appeared. I recognized one of them, as one of our comrades; the other one was a member of the Communist cell.

One man began to dig in the ground while the other prepared two straight boards, thick paper and strong, light cord. A quarter of an hour later I received the package; the rifle had been secreted between the two boards wrapped in rags, and everything had been packaged in attractive paper.

Now I had to carry it some distance through the city to the hole on Sienkevich Street, and from there to the ghetto. I had to pass the railroad station to get to the freight yard across the tracks and go along Washilkovska Street to 63. If nothing untoward happened and I succeeded in crossing the tracks I would reach no. 63 safely. The main thing was to get to the court of no. 63 safely. In the court of no. 61 there was the Beutenager, the spoils stores, housing weapons too. Some members of the organization were working in the Beutenager, and they had to divert the attention of the guards so they wouldn't look into the neighboring court, no. 63. In there was a tall tree whose branches made a kind of ladder. Behind the tree there was a fence of about three meters high; above it two rows of barbed wire and below, near the ground a loose board. You had to move that board, give the sign, and when it was acknowledged from within, hurry and push the package through. Trustworthy hands would take it, and leave swiftly. I had to climb the tree fast, crawl carefully through the barbed wire and jump into the ghetto. Here there were possibilities of being caught on both sides — on the German, and on the ghetto ones by the ghetto police

The package was swinging at my side. I didn't hurry. I had to get to no. 63 quietly; it wasn't feasible to pass the package through the hole in Olla's court, since Olla lived on the other end of the city, and to get there I would have to cross the center which was crowded with people.

I arrived at the court of number 63 Shenkevich Street, and it was empty. I went first into the privy. From there I surveyed the entire court. There was no one. It was five minutes before 12. They were supposed to wait for me until 12:30. Everything was in order. I crept under the tree, rapped on the board, but nobody answered. Something must have happened. They weren't waiting for me; a sign that I shouldn't enter. I left the court. A patrol was passing. They looked, but did not stop me. There was no choice; now I must cross the entire city right through the center, to get to Olla's. Better to try to cross with the package in my hand than to stand about in one place, especially near the ghetto, and wait for some sign of life from within.

Sienkewich Street is broad. German police headquarters was on the right, near the bridge and a little further on, in a big and splendid building, at No. 15, was the Gestapo building. The whole block was occupied by the Gestapo, up to the crossing to the parallel street, Zamenhof. That building had to be bypassed some hundreds of meters away. There were many policemen and detectives there and anybody who looked suspicious would be examined. From Senkevich Street I had to turn right, through Koschiuschko Street, to what was formerly Pilsudski Street. It was interminably long. Near the Russian Orthodox church a gendarme was surveying the passersby. The weather was fine today. Why wasn't it pouring? I hoped that he would tire of moving about and rest in one of the shops! The street was full of people. I met a gendarme and couldn't move to the other sidewalk. He was examining a woman's basket. Soon he would examine my package. I shook my package intentionally as if playing with it; fixed my hat and whistled. I whistled a German tune that the city inhabitants were accustomed to hear all day long, when German SS or army units passed in the streets. Be careful, don't overdo it, walk slowly, slowly; stand right at his side; look at the shop-window you have time.

I passed safely. From Pilsudski Street I had to cross to Poleska Street. Here it was possible to go through side streets, cross courts; there was less danger. I reached the entrance to Olla's house. It was a clear day and the neighbors were moving about the court, one going to the pen and another to the privy. Well, there was no getting away from the neighbors. The main object was not to meet a patrol. There was no one. I reached Olla's house in the afternoon. I put the package in the kitchen, between the table and the window, openly, and said hello.

Olla said:

"You won't be able to go over now; they are moving about here. Wait until dark and until all the smugglers and speculators have finished their work. You have time."

"I can't. I should have returned through another opening an hour ago, but I couldn't. My comrades in the ghetto will be worried about me."

"Foolish girl; better for them to worry about you until evening and see you safe than for you to be caught now," Olla said. "Come into the room, lie down and rest. Soon we are going to have dinner."

I stayed. The package remained in the kitchen, and I in the other room. If I took it with me I would arouse suspicion. But I couldn't rest. Olla quieted me.

"No one will take the package from there. Even if gendarmes come to look for "shmuggle" they won't look in the kitchen. Who keeps contraband openly? They will look in the rooms, in the closets, behind the beds."

When her father returned from work and went into the kitchen to wash, he noticed the package.

"What is that? Whose is it?"

"It's nothing; it's Halina's," Olla called from the other room. In the evening, when it became dark I started to go but they held me back: "Patience, wait a little longer; Jesus-Mary, why are you so nervous today? It's not like you."

I knew that the machine gun was endangering the whole family. I sensed that Olla and her husband were guessing something but didn't want to ask. They were also trying to prevent me from telling them. At 10 o'clock, after curfew began and when the court was dark and all the lights were extinguished, Vladek went out to scout the court. He entered the privy and knocked on the wall. He immediately returned to tell me that somebody was waiting for me on the other side but he didn't know who. Now I went into the privy and whispered, "Gedalyahu". Gedalyahu replied with restrained joy. They had apparently thought me lost. Vladek, however, still did not let me go. He climbed up on the roof of the pen and peered into the second court, close to the ghetto, by the factory. Never before had Vladek displayed such caution. After that he took his position at the court gate to see whether gendarmes were coming. I put the package into the hole in the privy wall. Anxious, nervous, trembling hands seized the weapon; grabbed my hand and pressed it in the dark. I climbed up on the roof of the pen, crossed the barbed wire on tip-toe, held on with two hands to the roof's edge and was hanging in midair. Gedalyahu's two hands seized my legs, pulled strongly but slowly, gently (so not in keeping with Gedalyahu's character). He put me down on the ground. The ghetto was already sleeping, and we two walked its streets; he the policeman with the machine gun under his arm, and I at his side. "How did you think of coming to Olla's at 10 o'clock at night? We arranged to meet in 63 Senkevich Street . . ."

"There was a failure there. The police surrounded the court and did not let anyone approach, not even me. We feared for you. Since you didn't come we decided to wait for you here. I have been waiting since nine, and I would have waited longer. But here you are safe and sound, and even with the gun."

We were living then on Bialostochanska Street. We had moved there because our old apartment on 6 New World Street was already too open. How can I describe the joy of our whole group, the trembling hands that freed the weapon of its string and paper and took hold of the cold steel and looked at it with shining eyes? Can I describe Gedalyahu's trembling with joy, with the delight of the future battle to which we would no longer go empty handed? I can still feel his trembling hands holding me and I will feel them forever.

Grodno's Time

From the very beginning of our activity in the Bialystok ghetto we had tried to organize combat cells in adjacent towns. We did not succeed, for a number of reasons. Our movement's units had disintegrated in the towns; movement life had died with the onset of the war. Those of our youth who had not gone to Vilna dispersed to the larger cities. Railway travel in the Bialystok area was barred to Jews, and even Poles needed a special permit to travel from one city to another. It was easier to sneak across the borders than to move from one town to the next. The number of people we had who were able to move on the roads was very limited. We did not have enough "aryans" even for the activities that were carried out; and we lacked the money to expand our influence and activities in the many Jewish towns in the Bialystok area.

The only place where we did lay a foundation was the relatively large Grodno ghetto.

Grodno was a Jewish metropolis, with masses of Jews maintaining their culture and tradition; pioneering youth and revolutionary movements, "Tarbut"* schools, a Hebrew high school, and a seminary for Hebrew teachers. Grodno at one time boasted of having one of the best of the Hashomer Hatzair branches. Generations of pioneers were educated there, moved by the stormy spirits of young people seeking more beautiful, more just and more honest lives.

Grodno is situated on a crossroads. The Berlin-Minsk-Moscow railway passes through it. For us too, Grodno was an important station, linking the three points of our organizational triangle: Vilna-Bialystok-Warsaw. For a long time the Jews in the Grodno ghetto had lived in relative tranquility. Except for the usual persecutions, beatings in the workplaces, and the actions of Grodno ghetto's two infamous hangmen, Gestapo-head Wiese and ghetto-head Streblov, nothing unusual happened to Jews under the Nazi regime. Frequent visits were made to this ghetto by special emissaries and

* Culture.

intermediaries. We knew that a younger generation was growing up in Grodno, the age of the members of the Tel-Amal group in Bialystok who had been 15-16 at the beginning of the war. We knew them from meetings, and from stories. Tosia, too, on returning from Vilna, had visited and been impressed by them. After starving Warsaw, and dying Vilna, she had found a little encouragement and light in Grodno. We knew that we had to help them.

It happened in the winter, at the end of 1942. The news was that the annihilation of the Jews of the provincial towns was decreasing. Grodno was one of the ghettoes that had been liquidated. The process had not been accelerated there, as it had been in the other towns.[26] It was a large and organized ghetto and had fought for its existence like a miniature Bialystok. There, too, attempts at increased production had been made, there too respectable and noteworthy persons stood at the head of the community. They, like many others, in their devotion and with good intentions, wavered between passive resistance and total surrender, and their end was like that of tens of thousands of Jews — Treblinka.

We sent Zerah, with instructions to help our young comrades carry out the ultimate action, armed revolt.

We accompanied him to the fence; Edek, Zerah and I walked along the ghetto streets in order to be together for as long as possible. Zerah and Edek went into the court. I stood watch outside. Zerah had not yet climbed up to the privy roof in Olla's courtyard when one of the court's Jewish tenants burst out, grabbed Zerah by the foot and pulled him down.

"I won't let you go over. Because of you they'll punish all of us. Let's get out of here!" A torrent of wagoner's curses fell on Zerah's and Edek's heads. He was a giant of a man. With his strong veined and muscled hands he grabbed the bag and began to hit about on all sides. Edek quickly grabbed him, twisted around and emerged safely. The Jew shouted and grew even angrier. When he couldn't hold on to Edek he began to curse even more, and completely lost control of himself. Edek called out to Zerah in Hebrew: "Climb up, I'll take care of him."

"But the bag."

"Climb up, I'll throw it to you."

The struggle continued another few minutes. When Zerah had climbed on to the roof, Edek seized the bag, pushed the giant to the ground with his foot, and before he could recover, Edek had thrown the bag onto the roof, jumped over the low fence separating the court from the street, and disappeared.

That was how Zerah left. I was upset, and told Edek that we should not have acted that way. The tumult could have aroused the ghetto police and the gendarmes outside.

Edek, however, still tense from his strange farewell to his comrade, concluded the affair by saying:

"Chaika, I didn't want to say it before, in Zerah's presence. Zerah was right, maybe we are already too late. Maybe this one day will be decisive."

This was not Zerah's first mission to Grodno. Earlier, in the fall of 1942, at the time of the first "actions," Zerah had put on the "aryan" hat, grown the trace of a Don Juan mustache, and gone to guide the Shomer groups who were maintaining themselves by their own strength, and that of their pre-war traditions and education. Twenty five thousand Jews had been concentrated in Grodno's two ghettoes. The tribulations and decrees that were the lot of all the Jewish communities in Poland had not, of course, passed by this ancient community. The Nazis' annihilation methods were similar everywhere, but there were variations. Only the goal was the same. That goal was the disintegration and degeneration of the organized Jewish community, its spiritual enslavement, and complete domination, culminating in betraying the trust of the governed masses. For that reason the Germans had barred the entry of Jewish intellectuals into the city, sent them off (some hundreds all told) in to forced labor from which they never returned. These were the well-known teachers of the gymnasium, engineers and doctors. Not all of them, however, were arrested. The Germans distinguished between intellectuals and those remaining alive were made governors or members of the Judenrat. Gymnasium and seminary teachers Braver, Belko, and Landeh were the Judenrat mainstays; they were good naive Jews, representatives of the liberal Jewish middle class. In other circumstances they could have served good causes, too. To the surprise of many, and perhaps to their own as well, they served the conquerors, and when their surprise grew stronger it was already too late, and there was no road back. Perhaps, too, they had chosen that path from the very beginning. The commander of the Jewish police in the Grodno ghetto, the former respectable Rubinchik businessman, or Srebrnik, head of the ghetto works department, a former factory owner — would they have conducted themselves differently in "ordinary times"?

"It is good that the Soviets have gone; otherwise I would have long since been buried in Siberia," Rubinchik would say publicly, and thus perhaps hint at hidden sympathy for the Germans who had "saved" him.

Indeed, these two continued, without any pangs of conscience, to help the Germans kill their brother Jews until their German employers grew tired of them, too, and liquidated them as well. The Germans knew the secret: government within the Jewish community should be entrusted to the best of the bourgeois circles, so that they would be accepted and repected by the Jews themselves. The Germans wanted to put the ghetto in the hands of unwitting traitors, Jews who were faithful and treacherous at one and the same time. It was said of Braver, "He is a good and fair Jew," but can a good Jew by his own hand give the Germans lists of Jews to be executed without the Jewish public's revulsion? Were those respectable traitors listening to the voices of their consciences? Had they become so foolish as not to sense what was going to happen? And perhaps they were just afraid of the enemy's power as well as of the hidden forces of the man who has determined to fight, against them too? There is no reason to be ashamed of that fear; it was nothing new. It is more surprising that there were those who did not succumb to it in those times of abomination. It was more difficult to live in those days than it was to die. It was easier to surrender than to live and fight against them.

Until November 1, 1942, the ghetto had been under the control of the Wehrmacht. The Jews worked in the army carpentry shops, making canvas, tanning (the "Niemen" factory) and shoemaking shops. The work did not always serve purely military purposes. How, for example, did the manufacture of women's clothes? This did not prevent the high German officers from ordering the mobilization of all forces for the war effort.

For a whole year the two Grodno ghettoes had lived in relative tranquility. Not for nothing had the Grodno Jews, after the Nazi occupation, asked for a ghetto. They had become weary and were stunned by the Nazi soldiers breaking into their homes, by the brutalities, the rape and robbery, and they longed to be separated, to be fenced in in order to be protected. This desire for a supposedly protective ghetto was short-sighted, but understandable. Most of all, the Jewish population was frightened by the fact that the Germans had ordered the organization of two separate ghettoes; one for the craftsmen (that was the elite ghetto, of course), and the other for all those who were not craftsmen, and did not have the money to buy the saving craftsmen's ticket.

On November 1, 1942 both ghettoes came into Gestapo hands, and both were closed. The liquidation of the second ghetto began. Few of the inhabitants of that ghetto were saved. The Judenrat had in its power the right to move some Jews to the first ghetto, and indeed, it did so. It was, however, impossible to move them all. Therefore, only those were moved who had some protector, some intermediary, and money. Did Braver pocket the money? That is of no importance. it was said that he made "contributions" and "bought off" the Germans. With the money he was able to find "good" Germans who promised to do their best to keep the remaining Jews alive. Weren't his actions therefore, justified? Was it not permissible to save Jews by money? The situation was complex and almost hopeless for someone who had entangled himself from the very beginning.

Zerah had come to Grodno for the first time when the ghetto had been closed and the expulsion from the second ghetto began. He had been preceded by Tosya and Edek. Tosya had come here on her return from Vilna with the message of Ponar. Edek had come with the news of the armed resistance. They found an organized youth movement, with all its groups working, holding meetings and discussions, dealing with mutual aid and maintaining its great educational achievements. They looked for new ways to maintain the movement since they knew that yesterday's activities would not do for tomorrow. A fighting underground movement does not, however, arise out of nothing. One step after the other, in internal debate and under the guidance of the leadership on the other side of the Vissula, the Narev and the Vilia, which did not always come in time or according to need, the youth of the Bitzaron group, the older members of the Carmel group and the members of the Ba-Sa'ar training kibbutz were organized into a fighting unit aware of its goals. I remember Yocheved Taub from the Warsaw vicinity, who had come to Grodno during the war; her thin face, slanting cheekbones, deep-set eyes and thick hair, tall and somewhat bowed from hunger. She had been put at the head of the Grodno underground young leadership. Eliyahu, "Gingi" as we called him; Zila Shachnes, at once delicate and daring in spirit (we will meet her again in Bialystok), Miriam Popko who looked for a way to get to the partisans, and Chaska. These comprised the leadership. There was merry and mischievous Chaska, with whom I would live and fight together after the liquidation of Bialystok's Jews. The Bnai Midbar children's groups were dispersed. There was no point in maintaining any organization contact with them. These little ones, who came knocking at the doors were sent away empty-handed; we couldn't maintain fighting units of 12-year olds. Some of them stubbornly accompanied the underground, were couriers, carried information and demanded to participate in more important activities. We organized mixed "fives" of members of Dror and Hashomer, made detailed plans of the ghetto and its environs, of the passages from one court to the next, of hidden openings to the aryan side. Zerah sat in the closed ghetto for two weeks, instructed the "five" commanders, planned points of attack, and organized the preparations of materials and weapons. The arms were not good or numerous; once again light bulbs filled with sulphuric acid, brass knuckles, sticks and other primitive materials that were easy to obtain and to pick up in the courts. Our joint organization with Dror numberd about 100 persons. Zerah and Yocheved looked for ways to establish a united front with other movements. Time was pressing, however. The

Sword of Damades was hanging over the ghetto, unendingly turning and reaping its bloody harvest.

Thousands of Jews in the ghetto were executed, and the day of judgment was coming for the first, supposedly productive, ghetto. Zerah sought some contact with the Communists, with the few remaining Bundists and the Revisionists, but found them all helpless. The Communists here were not a united and organized force. Some opted for resistance, while others considered it madness. They were not a unified party and worked separately, as individuals. The Revisionists promised to contact us but never arranged even one of the promised meetings. The attempts to establish a united front produced sad results. The only prospect lay in part with the Communists with whom Yocheved maintained contact. Meanwhile means and arms were lacking and the links Zerah labored to establish with the aryan side never materialized. Grodno was always a city of anti-Semites, and all the good elements among its population had fled with the Soviets, or were consumed by the ultra-nationalist and anti-Semitic virus. Zerah, therefore, attempted to obtain money through the "good Jews" in the Judenrat. We knew that the Judenrat, with Braver at its head, would oppose any armed resistance. They never even come up to Barash's level; or ever even conceived of whispering the things that Barash had told us: "Armed resistance — all right, but only as the very last resort. Meanwhile, not the slightest action, no weapons, no opening the door to the devil." That was what Barash argued. Braver, Belko and Landeh never dared to go even that far. They ferreted out information that the young people of the pioneering movements were organizing. The youth were very fine and pure, but also uwise, and rebellious. They warned Yocheved; they warned Zerah not to carry out any childish or hot-headed actions. They helped people, found them work, provided social aid, and were sympathetic toward the Hechalutz movement. Once again they proved that they were "decent Jews." And in their sympathetic attitudes toward the youth, they revealed the secret that they were working so hard to hide from the ghetto: The Judenrat had prepared a list of names of Jews who were destined to die within the next few days.

Zerah returned to Bialystok the first time with the shocking story that the place where those selected for death were to be concentrated was Kelbasin, a large camp about eight kilometers from Grodno. Here, too, the Jews from the nearby towns of Yeziory, Amdur, Indura, and others were brought. In all about 50,000 persons went through that camp. Here only death was the redeemer. Here, all those who did not find the strength to take their own lives hoped for a speedy death. For weeks they lay in the bunkers, suffering from hunger and sickness, swollen, covered with boils from head to foot.

They had to stand at attention every day before the camp commander, a German worthy only of the name of degenerate, the garbage of the human race, torturing the unfortunates for his own pleasure. It was said that he hated Jewish women in particular. He loved to beat them, and shoot them before the eyes of his German comrades, to smash their heads with his infamous cane and, above all, to choose the most pretty to serve him. When he was in good spirits and felt an "overpowering love" for his "sweetheart," he would invite his comrades, treat them to champagne and order her to show herself naked to the world's "Elect." He would boast of her beauty, show her to them all, fondle her and finally take out his pistol and shoot her in the head. That was the way he "loved" and killed. As the dead increased, from shooting or "morning exercise," hunger, disease or cold, the commander would order the men to bury them, to dig the graves and to sing the song he liked best, "Yidl mitn fidl." Thousand were buried daily, and thousands more were brought to the camp.

The Kalbasin Station is a small, quiet station a few kilometers from the camp. The laggards who weren't able to run from the station to the camp were killed on the spot, and the wagoners of the Grodno ghetto were mobilized daily to pick up the dead and wounded lying all along the torture road.

And the mobilization, the total mobilization for "the war." "All wheels must roll for victory," shouted the posters in giant type in the railroad station, the buses, the streets; and the wagon-drivers returned daily to the ghetto, filthy with their anonymous brothers' blood. There were busy days and some less so, but the flow of death never stopped. When the transports from outside stopped, Grodno itself began to supply the victims. The bloody road went from the ghetto gate at Zamkova Street through the city streets and the center. The long files kept coming, to the delight of the Germans and the traitors among the population, and to the sorrow of some of the Polish passersby. They walked the eight kilometers; advocate Gozhansky danced and beat a drum, danced and clanged the cymbals for the whole eight kilometers, to the accompaniment of Skivalsky, who had been the Wehrmacht translator, a music-lover and violinist. Dressed in clown's garb, they played, and behind them marched the long column of those sentenced to die. Whenever the dancing stopped and the violins were still, they were beaten and once again they would try to sing, play the fiddle, strike the cymbals and beat the drums. The gendarmes were in good spirits and laughed heartily.

The second ghetto was liquidated, and at the beginning of December the rumor spread that the first, productive, ghetto was doomed. Christmas was approaching, and as usual the Germans were busy with preparations. The army heads became concerned lest the Jews not manage to complete the gifts for their wives and lovers. Christmas eve and the gifts temporarily postponed the death of the 15,000 Jews in the Gordno ghetto. The liquidation was put off until after the holidays, but "small actions" continued nonetheless. Every Monday 2,000 Jews were deported. In three small actions 6,000 Jews went to Kelbasin, most of them poor, and without any support or protection within the ghetto. Once again the Judenrat prepared secret lists, and the Jewish police went from house to house to send the doomed to the big synagogue. These actions went off quietly, in exemplary order. Every transport also had some notables who had lost favor with the Judenrat, or just had no patrons. Our comrades discovered that these latter were to serve the masses of the poor as camouflage, since the ghetto did not know about the lists prepared by the decent Jews of the Judenrat. The latter, too, became less sensitive from day to day, and helplessly turned into Nazi servants. Workers in the factories were not taken in these actions. Lipshitz, formerly a wealthy businessman, headed all the factories. Entry into the factories was limited by protection and money. "Contributions" had been demanded again, and money was always necessary. Jews still believed that the ghetto would remain a work camp. The rule was: if you wanted to please the Nazi with gifts, work and good services, you also had to make contributions for his services, and if you made these donations you also had to include lists of brothers for execution; and when you prepared lists, of course you named those who could not pay ransom, and you also had to send the police to pull the doomed out of their hiding places and to bring them to the synagogue building — the first station on the way to Treblinka.

Zerah went to Grodno a second time. He arrived in Grodno two days before the big action.

The first to reach Bialystok were Chaska and Zila. From them we learned about the action to liquidate the ghetto. Zerah foresaw the ghetto's end and wanted first to establish an organizational link between the Grodno and Bialystok undergrounds. In a cadres meeting on the eve of Zerah's arrival the question had arisen whether it was not more worthwhile to move all the fighting forces to Bialystok, which was better organized for armed resistance. They had very few weapons and except for one pistol in the whole underground, they had only "cold" weapons. The majority voted to remain and to organize whatever resistance they could. Once again Zerah became busy, deciding on the positions and assigning tasks. It was decided to kill Streblow, the commander of the ghetto and the one carrying out the actions. Chaska and Zila demanded their rights: "If you have all decided to remain here, why are you sending us to Bialystok?" The debate went on until 12 o'clock at night; Zila and Chaska proved that their place was in Grodno and

Zerah tried to convince them that they had to be the couriers between Grodno and Bialystok and the aryan side. The first task given them was to carry to Bialystok the document laboratory for aryan papers and travel permits that had recently been improved by our comrade Dudik Rozovsky. "Even in these bloody acts of aktzias we must not lose our wits and allow precious underground material to be lost," Zerah said, attempting to convince Chaska and Zila that they had to go to Bialystok.

Chaska was a typical *shikse*, tall, blonde, with light, blue eyes. Though her Polish was not grammatical, she had good prospects of succeding. Zila, too, did not look typically Jewish. She had trouble with her Polish, but her deliberateness and wisdom would help her overcome that. That was Zerah's calculation. He wanted to send them to the aryan side to stay, but the two girls made a condition: "We'll go, if we are given the choice of remaining in the Bialystok ghetto or returning to Grodno, without remaining on the aryan side." Zerah did not reply, and sent them. Chaska and Zila came to us. The laboratory, with its jars, erasers, brushes, and chemical materials arrived safely. The two were searched at the Bialystok station for contraband, together with many other Polish women, but came through safely. In this first round, this initial direct encounter, Chaska emerged even better than we had hoped. Zila told the story. The condition Chaska had set with Zerah did not help her; she had succeeded, and would therefore have to continue. She would have to go out to the aryan side and manage there by herself. That was how Chaska came into the underground; we simply threw her into a strange world, without any money, any address or support, and told her: "Find your way!"

Then Yocheved came and brought us details about the ghetto at that time. The young comrades had decided that she must leave the ghetto and move to Bialystok. The young people wanted in that way to protect their spiritual mentor. They knew that her strength was not in weapons but in education and guidance, and that her tubercular body would not survive physical combat.

We understood the young people, but we did not understand Yocheved. We all believed that after having educated and led the youth of the Carmel and Bitzaron groups, the Grodno *ken's* adult and younger members, she should have remained with them to the end of the battle. Not with arms, but with guidance, she could have been of help to the underground in its test. What right did the young people have to decide her fate and actions? Was it not her task to guide them, and not the contrary? We listened to her story with concern. When Zerah had come to Grodno the activists had decided to send him back; he would still be needed in Bialystok. Zerah had not, however let them decide his fate. "Well, if he does not leave now he will do so on the eve of the action," they voted unanimously. Zerah had imposed his authority and had not allowed a debate over his personal plans. He was an official emissary and could allow them to participate in his conclusions only on local matters. Zerah did not return until the bloody affair was done.

On January 16 they began to take Jews away for execution. Srebrnik, head of the police, sent his men to look for hiding places, break down walls, search under the beds, in closets and crannies. Sometimes, when the Germans returned empty-handed, the Jewish police would send them back to look again in suspicious places. That was how Chaska's sister-in-law was killed when the Germans returned on the advice of the Jewish police. They returned, shot into the wall, and hit her in the head. She died silently, without revealing the whereabouts of other members of Chaska's family.

In the course of two days, January 18-19, 10,000 Jews were taken out of the ghetto in the big *aktzia*. Wiese and Streblov, the two Gestapo commanders, moved about the ghetto, machine guns in hand, shooting anyone they met. They were the angels of death and Srebrnik publicly announced that they knew about the young people preparing to fight, and were laughing at them. And Srebrnik added his own contemptible laugh to theirs. Still, Wiese and Streblov went about the ghetto accompanied by strong SS and Gestapo guards, with machine guns in readiness.

Many Jews fled the ghetto, but there were signs in big letters: "anyone catching a Jew must hand him over to the Gestapo; anyone not fulfilling this order will die, with his family, and have his property expropriated." These signs did not make too great an impression upon us; we knew them and their stereotyped language from other places, Warsaw and elsewhere. In Grodno, however, the Germans found a new strategem: why should they look for Jews outside the ghetto; better let the Judenrat look for the Jews within. The Gestapo threatened the Judenrat with a "contribution" demand if Jews were found outside the ghetto, and the Judenrat transferred the responsibility to the heads of households. These were obliged to inform the police of the disappearance of any Jew. The veteran administrator, Shpindler, and his second-in-command were hung from the railing of Eliyah Tankus' parents' house because of young and beautiful Prenski who was out of the ghetto without the old man reporting her disappearance in time. The bodies cooled and swung in broad daylight, in the cold and snow.

Between one *aktzia* and the next the terror increased, but the games with Jewish lives did not end. They seemed to enjoy shooting at the head of a little girl running across the street. At home they would amuse themselves by shooting at cups, furniture and toys. Whenever Wiese and Streblov came to the ghetto the number of victims increased. The gate itself was a hell. The approach to the gate was a narrow street closed on all sides, so that those entering could not escape or throw in their loads without being seen. The punishment for smuggling a small bottle of oil was 25 blows, and you had to drink the oil to the end. When you entered the gate through the narrow street you came into a snow-covered field. Streblov ordered the Judenrat to meet at three in the afternoon. He ordered everyone with a spoon in his hand to kneel down, and clear away the snow with their spoons. Streblov and his company watched, their hands deep in their pockets and cigarettes in their mouths. Braver, Belko, Landeh and all the rest scratched at the snow with their spoons and cleared it away.

Wiese was tall and thin, and when he beat someone he would stretch the gloves on his long hands, take a thin stick and strike, especially at the feet and head. Streblov, on the other hand, was handsome, young, light of movement and agile. He jumped easily in his shiny boots. He was an excellent marksman, killing with the first bullet. We will meet him again in Bialystok, on the train, and in the ghetto gate. Despite all our efforts we did not manage to kill him.

The Kelbasin camp had been liquidated even before the big *aktzia*. Now all went directly to Treblinka. The Kelbasin remnants were not considered worth a special transport and were moved into the ghetto. Chaska and Zila saw them taken to the synagogue, lying prone in the wagons, sick, covered with sores, some swollen and some only skin and bones. They were naked in the winter snow, barefoot, hungry, shouting and crying. Wiese kept them in the wagons in the street for a whole day before he put them into the synagogue. From there they were destined to be sent, together with the Grodno Jews, on their last journey.

In that period, from the 20th to 25th of January, 1943, we heard faint echoes of attempts at resistance within the ghetto, of victims and of shooting. Zerah had not yet come, there was no contact, and no one knew anything. We decided to send Zila back to Grodno to examine the situation, to see whether all had been killed, or whether anyone remained to be saved.

On January 25 Zila and Zerah returned, and after them some young members of the Bitzaron Group. Zila had extricated them with the aid of Eliyahu, who worked as an aryan in the municipal government press. I do not remember the details, but I do remember the shocking story of the revolt that failed. The *aktzia* had lasted from Monday to Wednesday. Almost everybody had been taken out of the ghetto, and only 4,000 remained, of them only 2,500 legally. The "legals" had been called by the Jewish policemen during the *aktzia* and removed to a special place in the ghetto. The rest were brought to the synagogue. Anyone resisting was taken by force. Many hid, and those who were not found remained, as "illegals."

Wiese and Streblov who walked about the ghetto during the aktzia shot into all the corners, court, windows; every crack. On Tuesday the underground decided to kill Streblov. Units of German soldiers came into the ghetto but did not break into the houses; that was done by the Jewish police. A face-to-face confrontation was out of the question; there were no arms and . . . no enemy. Streblov came into the ghetto from time to time. At night he would walk around with a searchlight and a machine gun slung from his shoulders, turning his searchlight on and shooting, without any specific target. Our couriers informed us of Streblov's habit of coming into the ghetto. Mottel Koppelman and Nachum Kravitz, two members of the Carmel group, waited for him at the gate, with brass knuckles and the one pistol. Streblov came closer. When they began to come out of the gate they were suddenly lit up by the searchlight, and before they managed to aim the pistol, shots were heard and the two fell, wallowing in their blood. They were killed, and with them, our only pistol was lost. The news of the failure swiftly spread throughout the ghetto and anybody who was able, wagon-drivers or just ordinary Jews who had some sort of weapon, tried to leave the ghetto at night to make their way to the partisans.

The revisionists did not come to the cell-meetings, and when Zerah demanded their weapons — since they did not intend to fight — they refused to give them up. The Communists, too, gave up the idea of open battle and decided to leave the ghetto, each man as best he could. The Dror unit and ours remained in their isolated positions, with the feeling of having failed. Zerah assembled the comrades and after a short discussion they decided to make one more effort. This time they decided to "be taken" to the synagogue, and from there to organize a mass flight. The action was organized by Shaike Matus, Gedalyahu Brovarsky and Miriam Pupko. When the crowding in the synagogue reached its peak, Shaike threw an iron bar at Wiese, who was seeking to make his way through the crowd. There was a tumult in the synagogue. There were high, narrow windows on both sides of the Ark. Shaike broke a window, and called to the Jews: "Escape!" The noise increased. From two other corners of the synagogue Gedalyahu and Miriam called to the Jews, "Kill him and escape!" All our comrades in the synagogue broke out, through the window or the door, but the mass did not move . . .

Then our comrades decided to go to the forest. Zerah helped them. Only the older ones, 18 member of the Carmel group, led by Eliyahu Tankus, without any contacts, any clear goal in mind, left to seek some new place to fight. They turned toward the Ogustow forests. On the way they spent one night at the peasant Jan's home, where Mottel Solnitzky's family was hiding, in the village of Koropchitze, 12 kilometers from Grodno on the Bialystok road. After some time we learned that they had bought two rifles from him, and hurried to leave the village. From the peasants, Jan learned that they had been caught on the way, while lying asleep under a haystack. A farmer had found them with the help of dogs and betrayed them to the Germans. When they woke they found the Germans all around them. They shot a few rounds with their scant weapons and the Germans killed them all. The only member of the group who continued to fight was Mottel, who had stayed one more day with his family at Jan's.

Zerah came to Bialystok with Lontchuk Pinchevsky, Dudik Rosenberg, Rachel Belitzka (Chaska's sister) and Meir. The latter had organized the daring break out of the locked ghetto. These members of the younger group became part of the fighting stream and individually filled special roles in the history of the young Shomer company. They dug the tunnel in Bialystok, broke through the barbed wire, prepared instruments with which to dig, cut the heavy barbed wire, uncovered hiding places and opening to the outside in order to smuggle arms and people. These were not the only young people we were to move to Bialystok. The others were to go gradually, in the course of the next few days, with the aid of forged certificates and permits from Druskieniki and Skidell. They came to fight and fall, all of them, like their comrades everywhere.

In Grodno 4,000 Jews remained. On February 13, 15 and 17, the last of the Jews were removed, each time 1,000, or 1,500, were taken. Only 500 Jews remained; the Germans intended to move them, with the "Niemen" factory, to Bialystok. Among those also taken were Braver, and then Belko. So ended the chapter of Grodno. By March, 1943, there were no more Jews in Grodno; Grodno, too, had become "Judenrein."[27]

Once Again: The Ghetto and the Forest

The noose was tightening around our necks.

We were an isolated Jewish island that had not yet been touched when all around annihilation was rampant. After the first *aktzia* in Warsaw, on June 22, 1942, the number of Jewish communities wiped off the face of Poland grew. The *aktzias* spread from place to place like a brush fire, and there was no one to put it out, only the faint glimmer of heroic resistance here and there in the towns of Polesie in Novogrodek, Niesviez, the news of which encouraged us. All about was the greyness of winter and melting snow. Our days, too, melted away and disappeared. In the Bialystok ghetto, the people of the underground were eager for action. We also had to prepare ourselves for the day that would announce the annihilation of the 50,000 Jews in the Bialystok ghetto.

In addition to the armament efforts we decided to prepare support positions outside the ghetto, first, to provide a refuge for anyone managing to get out. "Aryan" girls were supposed to occupy these positions and guide the refugees, and second, to prepare combat positions. The girls outside the ghetto were supposed to seek contacts with the fighting forces in the forest, in the city, and to maintain the existing links. When we sensed that the time for "aktzia" was coming close and that the ghetto would be closed at almost any time, we decided to accelerate the establishment of those positions. We also wanted to save individual escaping Jews. There were many refugees from Grodno and the towns nearer Bialystok. There were many young people who had managed to jump from the death cars, and members of the Grodno underground who had managed to get to Bialystok after all their positions in Grodno and the vicinity had been burned. We were able to enlist many of them in the Bialystok fighting movement, and many of them filled combat roles of the first rank.

I was asked to find an apartment outside the ghetto and to register as its legal aryan tenant. I was not to stay there permanently, but only to create the first link in the chain of positions. Later on I was supposed to register a second girl in my apartment, to maintain the position. We found it very difficult to find the position, examine it, and establish the legal conditions for an aryan existence. Our aryan papers were no longer valid in Bialystok. Two months earlier the police had announced the replacement of all former passports by German documents. It was not easy for "proper" citizens like us to replace our papers. We would have first to register in the labor office to obtain a work card, but that could mean being sent to forced labor in Germany. Moreover, all papers were to be deposited with the police, in exchange for a note testifying that the possessor had applied for registration. The German passport itself would be received only a month or two later. What would they do with the "original" papers in the meantime? Perhaps examine them administratively or chemically? When you came for the passport on the appointed date you might not come out alive. It was decided that I should be the first to register, and after the situation was clarified the other girls would apply, too.

It was in my search for a work card that I met Shade, who was the manager of a large textile plant, Textileindustrieaufbau Betrieb 4. A number of Jews, especially experts and department heads, were working in the factory, among them the Kiselstein family. The eldest daughter, Mina, a former teacher, worked as a servant in Shade's home. Mina was close to our circles though she did not belong to any cell. According to her, the actions of the fascists against the Jews were hateful to him and he was prepared to save Jews from death. At that time Shade was also the head of Bialystok's largest textile factory, Betrieb, near the ghetto. This factory stretched from Bialostochenska Street in the ghetto to the second street parallel to Yurovecka. It had three gates, on Bialostochanska, one on Yurovecka on the Jewish side, and another, also on Yurovecka but on the other, the aryan side of the ghetto's fence, barred by a big gate.

After a few days we received the answer: on Saturday, at five in the afternoon, after work, I could come, accompanied by Mina, into the factory area. The gatekeeper would receive advance notice and would allow us to pass through without any special permit. Shade would wait for us in his office. The answer did not please us at first; we wanted Mina herself to arrange the matter without my having to meet the German Shade, himself. Mina knew him well, and we did not. How could we put our trust in a German managing a big factory, who had, of course, been appointed by the authorities and, above all, was also a member of the Nazi party? We asked Sheina to use her channels to investigate Shade. Her reply was positive. True, he was a member of the Nazi Party, but there were no signs to indicate his ties to the Gestapo. They could find no fault with him. Our meeting was cursory, and cold. If I had known then how much Shade's name would, in the course of time, be linked to our underground, I might perhaps have been interested in a more serious talk with him.

Who could imagine that the robust German sitting in his chair with a fat cigar in his mouth, slightly bald, with watery eyes, would become an important link in the development of the fighting ant-ifascist committee of the whole Bialystok region? Who could know that under that typical German rigidity, under the cold mask and the swastika in his lapel, we would discover a courageous man who hated fascism? On that winter day of '42-'43, we hardly even said hello. He looked at me, stretched out his hand and asked me to be seated.

"Was wunschen Sie?" he asked, as if he had no idea what I wanted.

"I want you to give me a work card from your factory."

"Why do you want it? For that you have to work," pretending he did not understand or know what we were talking about.

"I don't want to work. If you want to give me a work card without my working, please; if not I will have to look for such a card somewhere else. I need the card in order to obtain a new German passport."

He became more polite. A stubborn smile hung on the corner of his mouth.

"Yes, yes, I understand. How will you manage outside? What about an apartment? And registration?"

"I am only asking you for the work card."

Mina knew that I was Jewish, and Shade knew it, too. Mina also knew that I was a member of the fighting underground, though she didn't know exactly what my position was. Perhaps she had told him something, perhaps not . . . In any case he acted as though he knew nothing. His face was blank, a cold mask.

"Good, I will send it with Mina. You will receive it on Monday."

"Thank you very much. Goodbye!"

"Goodbye and au revoir!" Not too courteously, without any emotion, as if he had not promised to do something exceptional, as if he had not promised to do something he was forbidden to do. He opened the door, called the gatekeeper and ordered him to allow us to pass through into the ghetto.

On Monday I received the card. Now I had to find an apartment. I found a room on 1 Charna Street. It was a large one, a little too big. It was cold and filled with useless furniture. The landlady was very anxious to know who I was, and where I had come from. I told her some story which I no longer remember. But I apparently made a good impression, especially after I told her that I worked in Betrieb 4, in the factory office. She rented me the room cheaply, apparently fearing that the Germans would appropriate it in any event.

That night I slept in that big cold room on Charna Street. Once again a new apartment, strange and cold. The house was clean and neat, slightly old-fashioned. The windows faced north, to the narrow Charna alley, and east to a closed porch with broken, colored panes. I lay sleepless all night, planning how to turn this place, open to all the winds of the world, into a tightly closed underground flat. Tomorrow I would receive the registration stamp on my old Vilna passport. I would go into the ghetto and bring Fania, Lipkes, the first Grodno girl, to stay in my room. How was I going to introduce her to the landlady? Maybe she would not want a second tenant. And how was I going to explain the fact that it was not I who was staying in the room, but another girl? After all, I couldn't tell her that my real home was in the ghetto, among the Jews, my comrades.

In the morning I received the registration stamp. I walked about the city, visited Stefa (no mail had come, of course). I decided not to visit Olla this time; that address should be left alone for a while. When it became dark I went to Yurovecka Street. I decided this time to try a new entry. When I had visited Shade in his office I had seen that Poles were walking about the area freely; Poles were working there. In my pocket I had the work card from Betrieb 4. Would the gatekeeper notice, in the dusk, that it was a card from 4 and not from 1? In any case, Shade was the temporary plant manager, and some connection could be found. I would therefore walk along the railroad tracks from Stefa Shenkevich's house on Shenkevich Street; after bypassing some alleys bordering on the ghetto to the north I would come to Yurovecka Street. Here there were no residences, and no civilians. There was only one house, the home of the manager whom Shade was now replacing. There was a second court, also tightly fenced in with barbed wire, and ditches. That was the factory. The gate was still open, workers were leaving and a second shift was coming in. Directly opposite was a fence about three meters high also with barbed wire on top, that crossed the road. That was the ghetto boundary. The gatekeeper didn't ask many questions, and allowed people to go through. The factory area was very large. There had previously been a number of textile plants there, and the Russians had consolidated them after nationalization and had established the first "combinat."

The Germans were benefiting from that change, and their slaves were producing a lot of cloth and wool for the conquerers of Europe. The Bialka River flowed through the court, Bialystok's smelly river, carrying all the city's sewage. Crossing the river at the right place, you were in a part of the court that reached the ghetto fence. The court was a maze; however, it had to be tried; I would have to look around the site. It could be a good way out of the ghetto, and a good way in. In any case it was a path that had not yet been used much.

When I very slowly climbed down the twisted fence on Yurovecka Street it was already completely dark. At that time the streets became more crowded. I moved towards Kupiecke Street with my head swimming. Dim figures moved in the dark, rubbing against each other in the bone chilling dampness. Tomorrow I would leave the ghetto again, in order to return to it from the other, living, breathing, expansive world. There I would have to stand in line for registration. I would hand over papers, and who knew what they would do with them. There, in 1 Charna Street, in the desolate cold room I would meet tomorrow with Fania and give her the room, and leave to her the registration and the struggle for "aryanism," and the assignment she would have to carry out.

Meanwhile the search for organized partisan groups continued. Front A, we and the Communists, saw one possibility for partisan action in joing existing groups in the forest. We did not imagine that with our meager forces and few weapons, and lacking any contact or support in the neighboring villages, we would be able to work independently as combat units. We thought that the Communists were better able to establish contact. We did not know then that the underground could not rely upon the heritage of the past alone. That referred to an underground working under unprecedented circumstances. It was not for lack of desire that our Communist comrades did not find the organized partisan movement. Yoshko Kawe and Marek Buch ran about a great deal outside the ghetto to meetings and in searches, consulted with worker comrades, with Vladek Niesmalek and Lorek. They finally did find scattered partisan groups, working without any connection or any definite political line. We found that the law was: first work alone, then you will find partners.

Why were we afraid of the open space? Why did we believe that proximity to the city safeguarded our existence and our capacity for combat activity? Why did we not understand that the city was a very apparent trap for any partisan group, that it was only distance and space that could give us freedom of action, while the city tied our hands? Why didn't we look for a way out in the forest rather than near the ghetto and the district capital city? Did we lack courage? On the contrary, if daring meant self-sacrifice, we had that, both our couriers and those comrades who were given the task of seeking a way to the partisans. We were all burdened with the diaspora mentality of an urban people feeling itself alone and abandoned in the forests and villages. Buying our bread in a store we forgot that the source of the bread was the soil far from the bustling city.

We saw separation from the city as separation from the source of bread and supplies. And arms? The same held true. Afterwards, didn't we find weapons in the villages, in the forests that hid the spoils of fighting armies? Only after bitter experience, after spilling the blood of many young people, did we learn the basics of strategy and tactics for anyone fighting the war of the few and weak against the many and strong.

In those days, however, instead of sending our emissaries into the depths of the woods, to the Bialovez region famous for its impenetrable forests, we sent them to look in nearer places, and sparser forests, 20 kilometers away, at most. The Communists who were our partners in the ghetto were divided on tactics. Judita Novogrodska, one of the Communist leaders, organized a group of comsomol youth and made contact with ordinary Jews who singly wanted to escape from the ghetto, and sent them all to the forest. She and her group maintained two principles: first, there was no possibility of fighting in the ghetto. It was equivalent to suicide; second, any Jew who wanted to go to the forest should be taken, without being examined too closely.

There were some who, in the course of time, formed groups of Jews who hid without having any combat role in the forest; there were others who simply became bandits.

The first of Judita's groups had left the ghetto back in December of 1942. Most of its members were refugees from the neighboring towns, especially from Krinki. Two weeks later they returned to the ghetto, after having confronted German units a number of times, fought difficult battles and lost six of their people.

At the beginning of January we sent a first group to the forest. The questions that were the bone of contention between those Communists who worked with us and Judita's group were not discussed among us. On the question of combat aim there were no differences between us. That was the first principle, the ideological ABC of our partisan activity from its very inception in the winter of 1943, until its last day in August of 1944. Even in the most difficult days, we did not abandon the principle of combat. The differences between ourselves and the Communists, however, widened when we began to put the partisan idea into practice.

The question at issue was the ghetto's priority in determining the underground's combat and ideological programs. The problem was not only theoretical. Its roots were also ideological, but its expression was erratic. Its roots lay in the different attitudes of the Communists and ourselves toward the Jewish people as a nation. For us the people was our origin, our being, and our very essence. We argued that the weapons that had already arrived in the ghetto were sacred for the war there. They were prepared to supply the groups going to the forests with the best of the arms that had been obtained so laboriously and smuggled into the ghetto.

We argued that arms for the partisans had to be obtained separately from the weapons in the ghetto stores; they believed the opposite. We decided to divide our manpower, to send good fighters to the forest but to calculate carefully so that the partisan activity did not harm the ghetto's fighting capacity. They sent their best fighters in to the forest. What is more, if they had enough weapons they would have sent most of their able bodied people to bear arms without considering the needs of the ghetto.

"There will always be Jews in the ghetto," they argued, "and when the time comes they will fight." We rejected that somewhat mechanistic view of the ghetto revolt. We knew that there would be no armed resistance if it were not headed by the most courageous of us. We did not develop any ideology of dying; of the desperate and demonstrative suicide of a small elite group in the ghetto, but of a national war in the streets. Since we were fighing for our national existence in the broadest sense of that term, we organized the contact positions outside the ghetto and sent our first emissaries to establish a base for the absorption of thousands of forest fighters.

The first group of seven included two of our comrades, Elyahu Varat (Alyosha) and Yaakov. The Communists among the other five included Rywa Voyskovska and Marek Buch. Their road was difficult. They had to find their way without knowing the terrain and without any contact in the nearby villages. Because of that, we had to provide them with all their needs. I can still see Yaakov coming to the ghetto to shoulder ten kilograms of food, in his wet clothing and bare feet. Immediately upon their exit they met patrols. They were too close to the city, not far removed from the army camps and police stations, and above all, too close to the ghetto, their only source of supplies. Their attempts to cross the forest failed more than once, but their spirits did not flag. They tried a second and a third time.

They had to learn the topography of the area without a map. Their first times with the partisans were also treacherous. Everybody hiding in the forest was called a "partisan!" True partisan fighting meant organization, discipline, planning, and first and foremost, an overall combat goal. The first groups that our comrades met pretended to be partisans, but they had nothing and no one to back them up. We concluded agreements with persons who could only speak for themselves. They were scattered groups of individuals who had fled from prisoner of war camps, escaped criminals and refugees from persecution who were united only by flight, and were not yet bound by a common purpose. They, too, fought for their lives. They too battled the Germans; our comrades seized every opportunity, looked for authoritative persons in every group, and only after some time had passed and after bitter disappointments, anti-Semitism, and dubious arms deals, did they learn from their mistakes.

There was no alternative but to keep trying. There were some who at that time did find in the forest people with political and fighting consciousness and people who, like us, were seeking partners and allies, but a center was lacking, and a partisan organization. The nearest center was far away, some tens and hundreds of kilometers, and at that time neither we nor the groups of non-Jewish fighters and non-combatants had found it.

We took upon ourselves a great deal of responsibility, in that period, for non-Jewish groups. I still recall how Gedalyahu "confiscated" a motorcycle hidden in a cellar, seizing it in the name of the Judenrat and the Jewish police — he had a police cap for that purpose. The motorcycle did not serve its owner, in any case, and would have either fallen into the hands of the Germans, or rusted in the cellar. We needed it to maintain our contacts with the non-Jewish groups.

Strangely enough in their negotiations with us these latter made very concrete demands, but we fulfilled obligations. We also provided for them merely suppliers, instead of equal partners. There was also the disappointing realization that the ghetto was forced to pay such an exorbitant price for an imagined link with the partisans. We were burned more than once and suffered grievously. Slowly, however, a road was being paved. Through trial and error, vain hope and mistaken trust, in the course of setbacks, we learned to differentiate, to look more closely, to find honest partners for our battle and our ultimate goals. There were many groups that were organized privately in the ghetto. There were also many speculators and arms dealers. Commerce in arms flourished. One man sold another man's weapon, which was still in the hands of a third man. It was hard to get to the source, to the real owner. Prices rose. As the number of refugees from the neighboring towns increased, so did the rumors of an impending aktzia. In the Bialystok ghetto, the only one still left, prices went up, and middle men increased. Our group in the forest was almost without weapons, while the arms in the ghetto were also in short supply and were mostly home-made and antiquated.

It was then that "Operation Gedalyahu" was brought off. With the cooperation of the Communists we searched for an arms dealer. It took a few days before we found a source. Gedalyahu took Avramel with him, both of them wearing police caps. Other comrades remained outside to guard against a surprise. Gedalyahu awakened the householder and said:

"The police know that you have arms. Do you know what is in store for you? You, and with you all the ghetto, will be held responsible for the weapons. We will all pay with our lives. We have received an order from Barash to confiscate your weapons and to destroy them."

"I don't have any weapons."

"Do you want me to arrest you and hand you over to the Germans?"

The Jew was frightened. He took the weapons out and handed them to Gedalyahu, and said nothing. We kept quiet, too, and the weapons remained in our hands. They consisted of a few guns that needed thorough repair and cleaning, and could serve only us. For the Jew, the guns were business, for us they were weapons needed.

Our position on the question of the forest had been formulated early, in the winter of 1941/2. After vigorous debate we had decided on the priority of the ghetto in our war. The argument was costly, and led to insults and aggravated relations with many of the younger comrades, who thought they could save their lives in various ways since they were young and quick. They still tied their fate to that of the ghetto as a whole. Were we right? The evidence will be found in the armed resistance in the ghettoes which these agile young people headed, organized and carried out. The revolt in the ghetto itself justified our determination.

Back in those days, however, in January and February of 1943, and later, too, the argument raged in all parts of the underground and was contested after every test, both when we succeeded and even when we failed.

Every day the Revisionists came with new ideas. One day they leaned toward the ghetto, another — toward the forest. After a time Mordechai too learned not to take their declarations too seriously, and firmly demanded of them that they help in bringing weapons, working in the shops, and in finding sources for obtaining explosives. More serious were the meetings with the Noar Hatzioni and the internal discussions among the members of Dror. Mordechai's views, however, were solid. He shared the desires of his comrades who sought to preserve the movement's nucleus even after the catastrophe. In Mordechai, who had come to us from Warsaw, we found a comrade and a partner in ideology and goals. He guided his Dror comrades and was a source of strength for us.

Mordechai did not know how to conceal his suffering. In his room on Yurovecka Street we sensed the deep sorrow he felt for the young people who had no prospect other than honorable death. To his last day he shared his comrades pain in not being alive to enjoy the new life that would come after they all died. Above all, however, he was firm in recognizing our justification for fighting. I can still hear those fragments that he read us from his diary. He also brought the minutes of a meeting of his Kibbutz Dror, in the Bialystok ghetto. "Our people must complete their duty in the ghetto, but they don't necessarily have to be killed. On the contrary, they have to have a positive goal. After fulfilling your role in the ghetto and surviving, get away to the forest, and continue to exact vengeance."

Once again I moved from my apartment on the aryan side. I had decided to move in order to change my registration in the Commisariat.

I found a place at 17 Vesola Street. It was not a real street, but a path at the city limits looking south, toward the forest. The room was comfortable and adequate. The landlord and his family lived in a second room, next to mine, with a country-style kitchen along side. The apartment had two entrances, one through the kitchen and another through our room. Two German women, or volksdeutsche, had lived there before us, and the landlord was happy to rent it before the German authorities expropriated it. It was a real find: a room with a separate entrance from the staircase. Ours were simple people who hardly knew how to read or write. He was a grave-digger in the German cemetary, and she a country woman, the mother of two children, who spent all of her time in the kitchen. They had, however, an "intelligent" name, Slovacky, like the great Polish poet.

First, we worked on our room. We bought an old bed in the market. We hung a curtain and arranged all the colorful articles that Sheine had placed in Hanka's bag. Hanka bought an icon of the Holy Mother in the market for a few pennies, and hung it over the bed. She ran about the room, met the landlady, and introduced herself as my cousin. We decided that the next day Hanka would go to look for work, before she went to register at the Politzeipresidium, and before she went to the work office.

I began to care for Sarah Deweltoff. Haska had found employment with a childless German family, the Luchterhand's and had also found a temporary apartment, but Sarah had not yet taken the first steps. She still had neither an apartment nor work. Bronka was working in the home of two German railway workers. She had been here for some time*; her room on Varshavska Street was not fit for the underground since it served the landlady as a passage to her own room. Her landlady, too, was not a proper partner. Young and elegant, she lived luxuriously because of a German Gestapo officer called Willi, a young and handsome fellow. He spent long hours in the house, day and night. The apartment was therefore at once both secure and dangerous. Bronka had accustomed herself, somehow, to her landlady's way of life. After all, she was not a Gestapo agent but only a fancy prostitute

* Her aryan name was Yadwiga Skidell. She is now in Israel.

who wanted to live comfortably even during the enemy occupation of her country. She understood nothing about the underground. Willi, however, was experienced, and we had to be wary of him.

I could come at anytime to Bronka's home; I was also at ease in her place of employment. The Germans knew me and more than once helped me move about. We had made these strange acquaintanceships through Tamar and Lanka.* They knew how to find Poles and even Germans who would help them without their knowing who they were helping. Bronka cleaned the two tiny rooms. She worked little, and exploited the stupidity of her employers, both of them "zugsfuerer (railway workers)." One, Grimm, short and stout, who knew nothing but his home, his family and his many children somewhere in the German provinces. He treated Bronka in a fatherly fashion, worried about her livelihood and agreed to all of the sometimes cheeky requests of his serving girl. He did not like Hitler, the Gestapo or the war. He would talk about the Jewish transports he had encountered in his travels, about human suffering, his heart melting with a fat man's good nature. Bronka did not attempt to get him to join the opposition to Hitler; she knew her master's soul, and that the likes of him could serve the underground unknowingly, doing what he did out of his good nature. He would stop short of revolt for fear of punishment, and of his hatred of spilling blood, even that of criminals.

The second, Kaldenbach, was a different sort. He was even more stupid, degenerate, and rotten like many of his brethren, at once sly and ignorant. He would send packages to his family, and bring home doubtful women whose filth Bronka had to clean the next morning. The two men were equal, however, in their respectful attitudes toward Bronka. When Bronka asked for anything they never said no.

Their apartment was opposite the station, in a house off to one side. In the first floor were two semi-military rooms. Below, on the ground level, was a small kitchen used by a number of transportation officers. Bronka asked for work for one of her friends there. They found a job for Sarah. The work was easy, and most important — it supported her. We were very concerned about Sarah. She was not meant for such times, with her gentleness, her psychological restraints, her silence and her quiet and reflective manner.

"Sarah, this is a time for force, for elbows," the comrades would reproach her, but Sarah did not change her ways, nor stop reflecting, her wide blue eyes becoming even wider and her steps even more deliberate. She never

* Tamar, Mordechai Tenenbaum's friend, and Lanka Kozibrodske; both fell during underground activities.

opened her heart to us. On those long winter nights, when she came to us from her labors in the little railway officers' restaurant, Sarah was as deep in her thoughts as always.

In the feverish bleak winter evenings when Hanka could not restrain her sighs for the ghetto, comrades, her imprisoned family, her little sister — whom she did not know if she would ever see again — Sarah was quiet, looking out at the black street through the only window. We were glad that we had found her "good" work where nobody would bother her. There, while peeling potatoes, she could reflect as much as she liked.

We all looked for an apartment for her. I was free and worked only on this job of settling the girls. I was in a great hurry to return to the ghetto but matters here were taking up too much of my time. We did succeed in finding an apartment for Hanka, we had found work for Sarah, and not the worst kind of work at that. Hanka had also found employment. Willi, the Gestapo man, told us that the Gestapo department on Ogrodova Street needed a servant.

The next day we sent Hanka there. Hanka told them that she had been sent from the work office; she was accepted at once and the next day came with a work card in her pocket signed by the municipal Gestapo department. The work took only four or five hours; she would wash the floors of the men's rooms, and go home. We were glad because we thought that in the course of time she might also gain some benefit from her employment in the lion's den. She might even hear something of importance, and if she were energetic enough, might also become acquainted with one or two members of the Gestapo. Hanka, too, was glad of such success, after only her first step! The underground sometimes labored days and even months to establish contacts with workers and servants in such institutions, and not always successfully. She, on the other hand, had found the place immediately. Now she could apply for registration to obtain a German passport. The registration went off successfully, and after a week or two she was supposed to receive an invitation from the work office to register her place of employment.

Hanka was not afraid of the Gestapo men. At first they tried to frighten her, and joked: "Do you realize where you are working and what can happen to you if you don't do well?"

Hanka would smile and not reply. After a few days they left her alone.

It was Wednesday, my third day outside the ghetto. That evening I would go to Olla, and when it got dark I would go into the privy in the courtyard. At eight-thirty I would talk to Edek through the cracked privy wall.

The meeting took place on time. I passed on a letter from Hanka to her mother, and a short written report on our work. Edek told me that there was tension in the ghetto. It was said that within a few days there would be an *aktzia*.

"Hurry and get Sarah settled. Find her an apartment, and come again tomorrow at the same time."

The discussion this time was short. For the first time I noticed some nevousness in Edek. His voice quivered a little, his words seemed to hiss through his mouth unnaturally. His speech had always been fluent and measured.

"Edek, maybe it isn't worthwhile for me to continue outside. Maybe Sarah can manage without me?"

"No, no, they must be settled very carefully. They will all be needed. Don't leave them too early. Who knows how long they will have to live alone, afterwards."

A noise reached me from the court. Preparations were apparently being made for some smugglng. Or perhaps a patrol had arrived. I had to finish talking.

Edek pushed a small paper-wrapped package into my hands.

"Keep this at Hanka's. We may need it later. Goodbye." (It was a small sum of money in dollars.)

The next day was February 4, 1943. I found an apartment for Sarah, a wonderful place completely isolated, in the attic. It was a big room. Two small windows looked out on a side alley leading to the forest. The stove was in the middle of the room and behind it there was a niche in the wall, deep and dark, a good hiding place. Here, it seemed, we could live for years without anybody noticing. We had been looking for a long time for this kind of apartment, without landlord or neighbor. The landlord living below didn't bargain, and agreed to accept any price, just not to have the apartment empty.

Sarah's room was very close to ours. It was on the second path off the main road leading to the vacation spot in the nearby forest. The pathway was dark and winding, unpaved, and our feet would sink in the clinging mud. It was a typical suburban road, neglected and poor. From here I would go to Sarah's at the restaurant near the railroad station. It was a long way, and that evening I still had to return to Olla's and meet Edek.

Toward dark I returned home. Hanka was already waiting for me. It appeared that something had happened . . . Another girl had come from Grodno and had to be settled on the aryan side. I announced that it was not my job. The girls were angry, complained that I was hard-hearted and without any human feelings. I was tired and worn out, and could not convince them that I was in the right, that there were no private arrangements in the underground. The girl's situation was difficult, but she insisted on remaining on the aryan side.

"I am not opposed to her being settled but I cannot take care of it. When all of you are as responsible for the cause as I am, you will understand that I was right." I was silent and immediately regretted my words. Little Rivkele's childish blue eyes stared at me in surprise:

"How can you talk that way?" and in her heart she certainly must have felt, "What pretensions of importance!" I was very sorry for what I had said. I knew that it was my duty to explain, to clarify and to convince. Was it really possible, however, to explain a doctrine that could only be learned in battle and through suffering? That evening there was tension. We were afraid of what was likely to take place that night in the ghetto. Haska tried to support me, and said that she would make arrangements for the new girl, and would try to find work for her and a room. She had heard of a German family that was looking for a girl servant.

Once again I walked the muddy streets and alleys. It was dark, and sleet melted in my collar. My shoes filled with water and chilled my bones.

"What would Edek say?"

Once again we met in the dark near the privy.

"Chaika, they closed the ghetto today. It is almost certain that there will be an *akztia* tonight. We still don't know the details. Gedalyahu is trying to find out."[28]

"I'm coming in."

"You mustn't." His voice shook again. "We have decided that you must stay there. Maybe there will be a need to organize something. Sheine and I have still not decided upon it, but we are thinking about the comrades. We can't leave it to the inexperienced Hanka. The matter is too serious."

"Edek, I am coming in!"

"Don't be insane! Stay calm (his own voice was quivering). Don't be nervous. See you again, Chaika, see you again! I have to run. No matter, it will still be good! See you again!"

The next day it also snowed and rained. Mud stuck to one's shoes and the cold penetrated to one's bones. The street was empty. Only the increased movement of the gendarmes presaged evil. I wandered around the ghetto walls, back and forth. Not one Jew could be seen, not one work brigade. Deathly silence prevailed. I turned my steps towards Olla. Along the whole length of Poleska Street, every ten or twenty meters, stood gendarmes. Some of them looked angry; one was merrily singing a jingle, another winked, apparently out of boredom.

"Yes Halinka, they evidently began an *aktzia* tonight." It was with these words that Olla's mother received me.

At night there was shooting! The bloody game had begun. Members of the household seemed to guess what I was thinking and warned me: "Don't consider going in. They're watching this court very carefully. They are in the nearby houses, here opposite, in that neighbor's, do you see? They are watching from the windows. They have no wish to stand outside in the cursed wet."

Once again I went out into the street. I still had to take care of a number of things in Sarah's apartment. I had to find a white washer, and an electrician. My feet were heavy.

Sarah's apartment needed repairs. Maybe we would really have to shelter fighting comrades there until we could get them out to the forest. In my imagination I already saw them coming, appearing one by one out of the cold winter night. Yes, they would surely come. I must hurry to prepare them a proper shelter, so that they would feel warm.

Sarah's room was readied after a fashion. During the day I roamed the streets, and in the evening I visited Olla. One morning I found my sister there. She had fled the ghetto at night. She sat for hours in the privy, and when she heard the gendarmes' hob-nailed boots moving away a moment from the gate she knocked at her friend's door. She did not have too much to tell. The aktzia had begun early Friday morning. Since then, some thousands had been taken out of the ghetto. Jews were hiding. She left the ghetto on the second night of the aktzia. How many had been taken she did not know. Meanwhile, the ghetto was dead, silent and waiting. I could not even ask for details. I couldn't speak. How strange this meeting was, how unnatural and unreal. Olla apparently thought that I was not very happy at my sister's coming, since I was not emotional enough.

"If you can't settle her in the city we will help her. She won't get lost. We have acquaintances . . ." I thanked them, and asked my sister to dress quickly. We left the house, and at the gate found a gendarme who looked us over from head to foot, wavering between suspicion and certainty. He evidently decided that we were not Jews and allowed us to pass. He had apparently been deceived by my sister's height, her painted lips and her hair, set high over her brow. Her face was not characteristically aryan at all, but Germans could not distinguish too well. A Pole would certainly have recognized her Jewishness.

That very day my sister found employment with a German family in the SS Werkcentrale in Haska's neighborhood. We could not give her any help; she would have to make do as best she could to obtain a German passport and find a place to live, which she did, in the same German family's kitchen. She told them stories of her estate that had been destroyed in the war. We made jokes about it: only Germans believed everything. She also went alone to obtain the passport. One of the clerks recognized her as being Jewish; she escaped, and returned to a different desk, and succeeded. Now we had another person in our family. Sarah Shevahovich, too, had found employment. The aryan colony on Parkova Street, in the center of the SS, with its shops, offices, families, apartments and gardens, was growing.

Silence prevailed in this street whose houses were clean and whose courtyards were orderly on rainy days as well as on sunny ones. Snow melted in the gardens. Here Jews, too, worked tending the gardens and in the make-believe shops that helped keep the sons of German nobles and gentlemen away from the front. For some days, however, they were not to be seen (my sister Miriam's landlady said that "there were decent Jews" among them). It was already Tuesday. Wednesday passed without any news from the ghetto. That evening, too, shooting was heard. Our nights were sleepless. Sheine's emissaries did not appear. Living on the aryan side did not seem to have any point. The young girls asked a lot of questions, and only with difficulty did I convince them that in activities such as ours, results were not to be measured by ordinary criteria. Sometimes large actions were carried out swiftly, and sometimes small ones required patience and persistence.

"Try not to forget the main thing for which we are here. It is not to sweep the SS barns, Hanka, or to wash their dirty dishes, nor even clean the house of the Nazi doctor, the specialist on the forms of Jewish bodies, Rivkele. There is a time for everything, and the day will come when we will give them their just desserts. We shall attack them not at the time they want or in the place they wish, but when it is best for us and in the place we want."

It is hard to believe that I said those things then, and it seems to me now that for the most part I used to satisfy myself with some short, nervous, and firm remarks. I think that in those days I lacked an understanding of how to deal with the girls who were younger, weaker and less experienced than I was.

"You know my corner in the apartment, facing the Jewish cemetery on Zabia Street. Yesterday, I stood for a long time at the window and looked into the night. Something pulled me outside. Actually for many days I had thought about it, and planned the idea. I decided to crawl under the barbed wire and go into the ghetto, no matter what."

"Haska, who gave you permission? Why haven't you spoken to me of your plans?" I blurted out, but Haska smiled at me. I did not understand whether it was a smile of guilt, or of revolt.

"I put on my coat, put on my muffler and said that I would soon return. I went out into the court. It was empty, dark and silent. I went close to the barbed wire and tried to bend over . . ."

"What, did you go in?" they all shouted out with eyes sparkling.

"No, I didn't go in. Let me tell the story. Someone grabbed my hand and pressed it so hard I thought it would break. I looked up, a gendarme! I threw him the muffler to hold, pulled down my panties before his eyes and passed water . . . He was boiling mad: 'What are you doing here, Jew?' Then he was silent, the muffler in his hand and my kneeling there convinced him apparently that I was not a Jew but had come to pee.

'Mach mal raus!' he shouted. I, of course, grabbed the muffler and returned home. I did not succeed in getting into the ghetto."

They were all silent. The story was amusing, but the question "What about the ghetto?" gave us no rest.

Another day passed and I was roaming the streets again, from Vesola to Shenkevich, from Shenkevich to the length of Pilsudski Street, and from there, beyond the station. Maybe I would go to Bronka, or to Sarah. On the street I saw a familiar figure, and stopped. I crossed the street:

"What, Hazek?" Yes, he had escaped from a transport and was wandering through the streets. It was Wednesday or Thursday, I do not remember. I took him to my room. He did not say much. Hiding in the ghetto, he had been caught, escaped once more and was caught again, and now he had fled again without knowing where to go. Hazkel Zabludovsky was one of our veteran comrades. His task in the ghetto, in addition to the regular Jewish occupations in the factory, had been to gather news from the radio and to disseminate it. If you wanted to hear the news, to know where the front was, who was on the offensive, how many German and Soviet divisions were being deployed, you turned to Hazkel. He knew about every small stream, every occupied village, every innovation in military strategy. He listened to Moscow radio, to London, and to Berlin. There was no one to equal him in the ghetto.

I spread a blanket on the floor near the stove and told him to lie down. It was forbidden to stand since everything taking place in the room could be seen from outside, through the window. I brought shaving materials, a dish of water and a bundle of German newspapers I had bought at the nearby kiosk.

"Yesterday I heard that some group had resisted, but I didn't manage to make contact with any of the comrades. When I came out of my hiding place I was caught." Hazek reported.

The next day, before morning, we moved Hazek to Sarah's room. He was joined by Chaim from Grodno, a Dror member and one of the resistance activists there. He was one of the comrades who had been sent to join the police, and was then withdrawn. He had come to Bialystok with our address. Until the situation in the ghetto was clarified they would both remain in Sarah's room. Sarah closed her apartment from the outside upon leaving for work. It seemed as if no living soul could find that isolated attic.

That day Hanka was going to the "Arbeitsamt." It was Friday. She had received a request, as usual, from the labor office, to come to register before receiving her passport. There was no fear; she had a Gestapo work card. I was afraid, however, that Hanka would not restrain herself and would do something mad. For days now she had not stopped talking about her family in the ghetto. Her little sister's name never left her lips. She did not cease sighing and disturbing her comrades. I once impatiently blurted out: "Hanka, be brave, try to control your suffering a little." She was insulted, and remained silent. Her very silence led me to suspect that she might be planning something. I considered myself responsible for her. In the morning I spoke with her gently, I even tried to fondle the dark brown hair falling in waves over her back. It seemed to me that Hanka understood.

"I'm only going to the labor office. I'll come back early from work," she promised.

Evening came, however, and night fell, and Hanka did not return. Sarah remained in my room to sleep since she had given the bed in her room to the boys. She did not come. We were sure that she had gone into the ghetto, and in the city there were rumors that a Jew had already been seen coming out. Our landlord, the grave-digger, told us in great secrecy that with his own hands he had buried five Germans who had been killed by Jews.

"The Jews are fighting. What do you think, is it possible?"

"The devil knows," I said, and escaped from the kitchen to tell the girls the news. Night fell. There was no Hanka. We couldn't sleep. Toward morning there was a faint knocking at the door. Believing it was Hanka we jumped from our beds in our nightgowns. A fellow we did not recognize came in. In a whisper he told us he had been sent from the ghetto. He was one of our comrades from Grodno. He had gone into the ghetto one day before the *aktzia*. He had been sent by Zerah. The *aktzia* had ended yesterday afternoon. Today was Saturday. He handed me a note. I didn't care to open it. I asked questions, wondering about his evasive looks. "I don't know very much," he stammered. "Read it, Zerah writes everything."

"Why had Zerah written and not Edek?" Silence.

The note was in front of me.

"Chaika, the *aktzia* has ended. Our comrades tried to resist. Here is a list:

Yoshko, Yisrolik, Zivia, Roshka, Yentel, Sender . . ." It was a long list, 19 names, with Edek's at the end.

"Don't come in today. I will send some one to you. The ghetto is still closed. Au revoir! Zerah."

The room disappeared, wrapped in a dark black veil. I only saw the dear young precious people with whom I had worked. They had fought and were no more. Edek was at the head of the line smiling. Until evening I walked the streets and Hanka had not returned. Edek was no more. To my question whether Hanka was in the ghetto I received no answer. "Edek is no more," I repeated in my mind. I did not realize that I was crying.

Good that the streets are empty. Can an underground person weep for the world to see? When did I last weep? What's the matter with you, what are you crying about? Didn't you know that that was the way it was going to be? Five Germans buried by my neighbor Slowacki? Five criminals on the one hand, and on the other thousands of Jews, and nineteen courageous fighters. Evening came. Suddenly I determined to disobey Zerah's instructions. I would go into the ghetto.

I hurried to Olla's house. Without going in, I climbed swiftly to the roof of the pen and the privy and hurriedly, without looking around, stretched myself along the wall and jumped into the empty ghetto court. Night had fallen. There was a deathly quiet in the ghetto but the sounds of crying seemed to hang in the air. I ran to our room on Bialostachanska Street. The door was open, the room empty. The beds were unmade. Here people had slept in their clothes, not lain down but fallen from exhaustion. The neighbors' room was also quiet. Once again someone was weeping. From far away came a sudden wild cry.

That was the way the ghetto received me in its desolation. I escaped from the empty room on tiptoe, from the dead room, and the empty court. I felt as if I were walking on a grave. All the ghetto was a graveyard, and I was not sure that I was not treading on the blood seeping through the melting snow, washed away no more to be seen.

I stopped before the door of the "communa"* twice. Innumerable times I put my hand on the latch; I tried to push, and stopped. I was not brave enought to look upon the comrades' faces and to read in them what had happened. I saw them later, pale, their eyes deep-set and burning, lips closed tightly, silent. That was how I saw Zerah. His bright eyes seemed to be covered by a deep fog. Hanka wasn't in the ghetto, neither in the "communa" on Kupiecka Street nor in her mother's Kupiecka Street home. The ghetto was

* Communal living quarters of the movement people.

bereaved, and so was the Shomer community. The dead were gathered in piles; shot in the court, killed in their hiding places, suicides by hanging and poison; the victims of passive and active resistance.

They made fiery speeches before their death, proudly spitting into the faces of the murderers. Piles and piles, a thousand rebelling Jews, gathered up and buried in a single grave in the cemetery on Zabia Street. The wagons loaded with the dead rumbled all day through the bloody streets in the same direction — towards Zabia. All the victims had not yet been found; they were still looking in the cellars and attics, still finding children who had been strangled when they cried in the hiding places; their mothers' own hands stopping their cries in their throats. People were running through the hiding places, searching for traces of relatives and friends who had disappeared. There were stories of many whose families had been butchered and who had gone out of their minds, of cases of hysteria and madness, of shouting despair.

There had been one thousand victims in the ghetto during that week, and about 12,000 had been sent to Treblinka. On Yuroviecka Street those sentenced to death were gathered, by the hundreds and thousands. Here one woman teacher had spewed all her hatred at the Germans and spit into their faces. Here national pride had flowered in all its impotence. Here for the first time in the history of the ghettoes there had been the passive resistence of a people without arms. On Fabrychna Street the Germans had caught mad Feingold. He did not want to go with them. They beat him and tied him, while he laughed loudly, until he choked. The Germans wondered at their victim's insane laughter. At the end, in order not to leave his last crazy laugh unexplained, he told them: "Ha, ha, ha! You can take me, but Stalingrad — that's something else! Ha, ha, ha!"

Hundreds had not allowed themselves to be taken like sheep to the slaughter. Our terrible prayer at the beginning of the *aktzia* in Vilna, in 1941, was fulfilled: the *aktzia* prayer that the masses would not die in their hiding places but in the streets of the cities; the prayer that the blood of our Jewish brothers would flow in the open streets and not in far away Ponar. Impotently, we had prayed for passive resistance, only that the masses not be murdered in silent acceptance of the fates.

That was what had happend in the Bialystok ghetto. One thousand Jews did not allow themselves to fall into the murderers' hands alive! The prayer had been answered and the news of masses of Jews rebelling, spread throughout the world. Moscow radio told the world of the Bialystok Jews who had revolted against their Nazi-enslavers, and had decided not to be taken alive to Treblinka.

Here, in this house, in the little room on Febrychna Street, our aged teacher Frania Horowitz had fought against the Nazis and managed to swallow poison so that she would not fall into their foul hands. In this court at Kupiecka Street, Yitzhak Melamed hanged for 48 hours. A simple Jew, a craftsman; in his time he had fled burning Slonim. His family had long since been murdered by the Nazis, and here he had decided to repay them as best he could. He had poured sulphuric acid in the eyes of the SS man who came to take him to Treblinka. The German was blinded, and the comrade who came to his aid lost his mind and shot wildly without any target. The band of murderers panicked, and one of them was killed. One blind and one dead — that was the sum total of Yitzhak Melamed's rebellion. He was lost in the maze of attics, and disappeared. Some distance from there, on neighboring Shlachecka Street 120 people from Melamed's court were shot because they refused to disclose where their heroic neighbor was. Shot one after the other, the women, the elderly and the children.

A little distance from there a family poured boiling water on the approaching Nazis. They, too, were shot, the popular revolt was put down, but the honor of "Europe's elect" had been seriously damaged. The Germans lost only a few men, but were greatly shamed. The legend of the "heroic" murderers of women and children was blood stained and false. Melamed, however, was not at peace, because the Germans threatened to destroy the whole ghetto if he did not give himself up. The Germans could not find him, and no traitor could be found to betray him. He, however, came out of hiding and freely surrendered to the *aktzia* command.

"I don't regret it," Melamed began to tell them, and continued to talk. He spoke at length. They beat him, but he continued to talk. "You will pay for your actions." All the Gestapo men came to look at the strange sight of the hanging of the Jew who "hat Wiederstand geliefert" (had shown resistance).

The official quota imposed upon the Judenrat for the ransom for the remaining 45,000 was 6,300 souls who were not working in the factories. The Judenrat was ordered to prepare the list. It was prepared and Barash himself rode in his carriage early that bloody morning to Polna Street where the aktzia was due to begin. The Jews hid, between the double walls, in the hidden attics and secret cellars. No one wanted to be one of the 6,300 sacrifices. The Jewish police who were sent for the first time to find their way through the maze of hiding places, more than once reaped their reward for their service to the enemy.

Actually, the Bialystok Jewish police were not very outstanding in its service during the *aktzia*. It tried to evade, not to look too carefully, or not at all. The people's anger, however, was directed first of all toward them. The

Germans had grown wiser. After having received such a surprising reception from Melamed and others, they became very careful, preferring victims that cost nothing. They sent Jewish policemen armed with axes and iron bars to break into apartments, and more than once a vengeful axe fell upon the heads of the invaders themselves.[29]

Two days before February 5, when the *aktzia* began, Barash had known what was coming but kept it secret "so as not to cause panic." The information spread, however, and on Thursday, February 4, masses ran about the streets looking for places of refuge. Barash tried to find his good Germans, contacted Klein and the "Wirtschaftsabteilung — ghetto Verwaltung," Pehse of the Ristungscommando. The latter promised that only 6,300 Jews would be taken. The ghetto would not be liquidated. They came once again, examined it and deliberated and then decided: "This ghetto cannot be liquidated. We will not sabotage our war effort. Only those who aren't working will go." Implementation, however, was in SS Obersturmskuehrer Friedl's hands, and he and Klein were sworn enemies, with Barash trying to mediate.

The *aktzia* did not come to an end on Tuesday when the quota was completed. The Jews were still hiding, and the SS was afraid, and did not come into the ghetto except during the day. They had a full day's work, from early morning to late evening. After that they looted the abandoned property of the hiding Jews. Drunk with blood and wine, they left the ghetto. Darkness filled the streets, and that was treacherous. The action continued beyond the quota of 6,300 victims, and Barash was still waiting. This was the time for Kanaris, responsible for all the region, to bring the order to terminate the *aktzia,* and he was taking his time. The numbers of those taken for execution were growing. Every day they were taken from the concentration point on Yurovecka Street through Fabrychna to a side station. There they were loaded on freight trains and beaten. The weak were killed, as were the elderly and the sick. The rest were locked in, and the train moved west, to Treblinka. Kanaris was still delaying and Barash was afraid of two things: the Germans who were not keeping their promises, and of the youth who were rebelling and preparing to strike back.

Something else happened during the *aktzia.* There were traitors willing to frustrate the people's will to revolt. The Germans' passed the word that "anyone revealing a place where Jews were hiding would live." Some few elderly Jews came out of the transport, old people who still wanted to live even at the expense of tens and maybe hundreds of young Jews. These received certificates stating that "this Jew has aided the German authorities in evacuating the Jews from Bialystok." That man's sleeve showed the shameful ribbon announcing, "Judenverrater." One traitor exposed 200 Jews, young and old, women and children, and the Germans laughed; they had succeeded, they had found a way. From now on they would not be afraid, they would walk about securely. Our people's righteous anger, the anger of the tortured masses, would conquer them, and give them their just reward, wipe out the shame of treason at home, and with the blood of the traitors wash away the stain of shame! Where was the organized resistance?

Midnight. It was dark in the room on 15 Bialostochanska Street. Edek's bed was still empty as it had been; no one dared touch it. Zerah sat opposite me. His head was bent a little and he spoke in a low voice that quivered from time to time. Gedalyahu was stretched out in his clothing on the second bed, staring at the ceiling. Zerah said:

"Mordechai had been in close touch with Barash, and in the meetings of the B Front it was decided to wait a few more days. If the *aktzia* does include only 6,300 persons, it is necessary in order to avoid a clash to put off the day of revolt. Meanwhile, we would entrench ourselves. Edek argued that the Germans could not be trusted. They had promised not to touch the factories and on the second day of the action they had taken all the "Mechanische Tischlerei." What justification is there to sacrifice 6,300 victims as ransom for the 45,000 who would supposedly remain alive? In the end they, too, would be killed. The debates wavered between a decision to begin the revolt with the first Jew to fall, or to wait for the 6,301st. Edek left the meeting with the sad conclusion that our comrades of the B Front, with Mordechai at their head, were not prepared to act. Mordechai put his trust in Barash, and his comrades were speaking of rescue activities. They had an excellent hiding place, large enought to hold all of their people.

"Our own debate was also bitter. Edek's vigorous position won out: to take to our positions and to prepare with the meager arms in our possession. Only Gedalyahu and I knew what was in Edek's heart. He felt responsible for the comrades' lives and deaths. We deliberated: if we remained in our positions would the resistance be effective enough? Would we be able to strike at the Germans sufficiently to justify the speedier death of the fighers? Perhaps we should take the road of rescue? No, this was our last opportunity to raise the banner of revolt. Otherwise, we would die with the entire ghetto, disillusioned and impotent, mute and humiliated, with the stain of enslavement covering our graves in the furnaces and concentration camps.

"We supported Edek. Like him, we declared that any plan based on assumptions other than the fact of total annihilation were incorrect and misleading. We insisted in our previous decision: to open the armed resistance the moment the first Jew was taken out to be executed. Our plan was not an offensive one. We knew that only an offense could promise some small victory, but was there any room to talk of victory? We did not have sufficient weapons for that purpose. Cold arms, the acid-filled bulbs, the iron rods, the axes — these were not weapons for effective attack. What use was there in the single pistol and the single rifle in our possession? The supply of grenades, too, were few. They were old, hidden in the ground, would certainly be wet and would probably not explode.

"Front A, we and the Communists, remained in our places ready to attack the Germans when they came. Edek commanded the area beyond Yuroviecka Street. I remained in the other part of the ghetto. There was a house on Smolna Street with an attic and a basement. That was Edek's position, together with eight of our best comrades and ten of the Communists. Among them was Eli Goldberg, their theoretician, Shaike, and Rivka: all had determined to resist as best they could to the very end. A second group on Fabrychna Street included the girls of the Tel Amal commanded by Franck. The positions were not at all entrenched but were well hidden. In any case we hoped to surprise the approaching Germans.

"We maintained contact with Edek and Franck at all time. Gedalyahu moved about the streets in his police hat, and was our courier. The bundists who belonged to the A Front mysteriously disappeared. Gedalyahu did not, of course, take part in the aktzia as a policeman, but his services for us were very important. More than once he was apprehended by the Germans without a permit to be on the street, and was arrested. The Germans took away his hat, beat him, and wanted to shoot him. Gedalyahu, however, miraculously escaped and continued his activities. Through him we were told by Mordechai to join them in the factories. He had organized food supplies for all those who had found refuge there. Perhaps he wanted to justify his decision to place his people first in their hiding places, and later in the factory. Perhaps it was because of his troubled conscience and his desire to help Jews, that he sought by these actions to make up for the lack of resistance on his part. Mordechai believed that the time had not yet come.

"One day, it was Tuesday, the Germans attacked Franck's position. The resistance did not last long and ended, victims on either side. The position opened the Germans' eyes. They did not have to grope in the dark but opened fire before they approached the house, unlike their usual practice in other places. It was treason; someone had apparently told the Germans that there were young people there planning to resist. The attack was organized and except for their proud conduct and some wounded murderers, those caught could do nothing. With their hands raised they were led to the concentration point on Yuroviecka Street. That same day a group of Communists, among them Lolek Mintz, was taken to Ciepla Street. Their resistance had also been futile. Their arms consisted of sulphuric acid and axes. Like our comrades, they too succeeded in hitting the Germans and wounding them. Two of the resisters were shot on the spot, and the others were taken to the concentration point. On that very same day Communist Frieda Feld, who had served as a contact between us, and her comrade, Bluma, threw two grenades from their window to the street. One did not explode, and the other caused no serious damage to the German patrols. They were both shot on the spot. We had many losses that day, but the Germans were frightened. The ghetto dug deeper into the underground. Jews no longer allowed themselves to be caught without resisting the Germans, by spitting in their faces, by fiery speeches, with axes and fingernails. The group of fighters grew that day on Yuroviecka Street, where those sentenced to death were being assembled. Gedalyahu ran to the Judenrat to demand that they take the fighers out of the transport.

"It was known that Barash had freed many Jews from the transport, mainly relatives of Judenrat members and other important Jews and family members. Barash received Gedalyahu with surprise: 'What do you want, 24 'Scheins' (passes)? For whom are you speaking?'

'For every member of Hashomer Hatzair in the transport to Treblinka.' Gedalyahu also asked for the Communists.

'And why didn't you go to the factories? You wanted to resist?'

'Let us say that is so; let's stop the argument for now. Time is pressing. In a little while they will be put into the cars.'

'But I don't know you. How do I know that you represent Hashomer Hatzair? Where is Grossman? Let her come here and I will give them to her.'

'She is not in the ghetto now.'

'I don't know you. Excuse me, I don't have time. Anyway, I think you are too late; they are already leaving the ghetto.'

"The argument ended. Barash looked at his watch and Gedalyahu thought that Barash wanted to get rid of the rebellious young people. He had demanded of these 'dynamic' youths that they give up their hasty actions. There was a troubling suspicion that Barash was involved in their capture. They were, of course, taken out of the ghetto and Gedalyahu could not even see them when they left on their journey.

"Yentel returned from the transport, wounded. He told us that the comrade had decided to jump from the car. Shlomo Yudovich also came back. He too had jumped from the train. A debate started in the death car: the men insisted that the girls jump first. The patrols might notice, and all would be stopped. In any case, the first had the best prospects of saving themselves, and would undoubtedly divert the attention of the Germans. The girls argued: you jump first, you are more needed by the resistance units that will certainly continue after our death. In the end, they all jumped; only Yentel and Shlomo arrived. The train travelled fast and left the jumpers kilometers away from each other. Yentel saw her friend Rosshe fall under the car and have both her feet cut off. She had seen Zivia Kruglak, wounded by a round of shots, fall nearby, to lie in her blood. She fell after they did and was thrown unconscious, far away. Shlomo also said that he too had lost consciousness. Before him Yisrolik and Sender had jumped. He had seen them from afar whole and well. After that, he remembered, Yisrolik had carried him on his shoulders, took care of him, and laid him down in a grove. He had been happy that they were in one piece and safe. They had returned to the place where they had jumped in order to extend aid to one of the comrades who had been hurt. He had awaited them in the forest, but they had not returned. He got to his feet, wandered reeling through the forest to look for them. He hadn't found them. He had thought they might have gone to the ghetto. But they did not arrive. They had been safe and he was wounded, but they had not returned and he had. All had jumped, but only two returned to the ghetto.

Wednesday was not better. Edek's position was discovered. He used the pistol, and the men attacked the SS with their bare hands, but here, too, there had been traitors. Their position had been known to the Germans in advance. Since Edek had been deprived of the element of surprise, he also did not have the freedom to move as he liked. That day the rumor spread throughout the ghetto: someone was organizing resistance. It was not just a spontaneous mass outburst, there was a guiding hand. They saw the group in the transport. Gedalyahu pushed himself close and tried to speak to them, to encourage them. The Germans shoved him away. He managed to hear Edek's last remark:

"We shall still give them their just desserts. Carry on." His last words continued to reverberate: "We shall still give them their just desserts . . . carry on . . ." Their hands were raised. The Germans searched in their pockets and their clothing and waited. Edek stood at the head of the group, his face burning and his eyes feverish.

We never saw him again, not Edek nor any of his comrades in the fighting group. The transport left the ghetto, and from afar we could still see blows being rained on their heads and the fighers responding proudly. They were hurt, but hit back, bit, and dug their nails into the SS men's flesh. That day, too, Barash refused to help, refused to give the "Scheins", and would not intervene. Even the fact that his friend Edek was in the group did not move him. Likewise, Mordechai's late intervention did not influence him. Maybe he was afraid to help the rebels; perhaps it was just his suppressed desire to get rid of them. Was he a Jewish Pontius Pilate in a ghetto of tens of thousands of crucified? Was he to blame because the Germans had dragged them away?

That was the way Edek went, the first commander, and the first organizer. Some echoes reached us from afar. Jews who had been in the same car, and were later saved, told of the brave commander and comrade who had decided, together with his fellows, not to jump from the car. They only helped others to do this, and when those in the car were taken out, near Treblinka, half-fainting and without any will to live, on the edge of the furnaces, Edek and his comrades organized a rebellion so that Jews did not enter willingly. Edek and his friends were killed on the threshold of the furnaces, but they never went in. They encouraged Jews to flee, and were shot . . . That is what they said.

It is 1949, and the grass is green at the door of my new home. The sprinkler is spraying golden drops, and the wind is blowing from the blue sea beyond my window scattering the water on the flowering garden. What a dream of serenity! That peacefulness wraps our whole being and compels us to relax, to forget and perhaps only in a peaceful spirit to remember "those days", perhaps in twilight, reflections to be stopped by the fresh voices of children playing, to remember the past, "those days."

No, I cannot. I tremble remembering the past. The forgotten things stir in me and do not give me rest despite the green lawn and the sprinkler's golden drops. It was not right for us to remember "those days" that that revolt of free people broke out, not for the sake of complacent sighs that those young spirits evoked in the struggle for progress and against evil. On that Sunday, February 25, 1943, the air was cold and damp. We wanted so much to break the siege of bondage, to break through to great things, to a great revenge that would shake the foundations of the conquerors' world. Outside, however, the evening was gray and the horizon was swallowed up in the winter dampness. Step by step the difficulties and sacrifices piled up. Step by step our hearts forged the ability to hold firm; to hold firm against sorrow at the loss of a comrade dearer than all, and who you would never see again. Hold fast against depression and the feeling of impotence against a victorious enemy strong against the desire to break down the limits of reality, action, discipline and the yoke of patience.

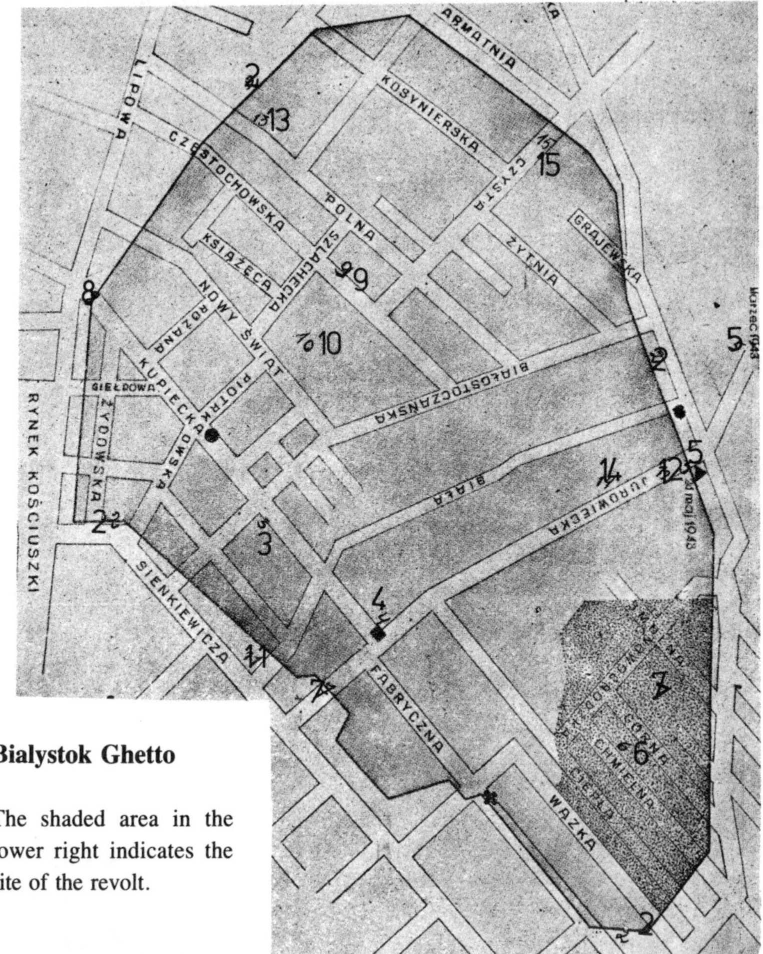

Bialystok Ghetto

The shaded area in the lower right indicates the site of the revolt.

1. The site of the uprising.
2. The Ghetto borders.
3. The Judenrat building.
4. The Wall of the 71.
5. Sites of battles with Germans during the exit of armed groups from the Ghetto.
6. The bunker on Chmielna Street.
7. The main Ghetto entrance.
8. The Ghetto entrance on Kupiecka Street that was eventually closed by the Germans.
9. The commune of Hashomer Hatzair.
10. The vegetable garden of the Judenrat where hand grenades were tested.
11. The Gestapo building.
12. The gate through which Jews were taken to Polska at the time of the revolt, on August 16, 1943. From there they were taken to the death trains.
13. The apartment in which the last staff meeting was held.
14. The area of Textile Factory #1.
15. The side gate to the Ghetto that was closed by the Germans.

Jews were forced to build the Ghetto walls.

Inspection at the Ghetto entrance.

The well serving as entry
to the bunker on Chmielna Street

Bekanntmachung

1. Jede Person ist verpflichtet, Juden anzuhalten und der nächsten Polizeidienststelle bezw. dem Amtskommissar zuzuführen.
2. Es ist jeder verpflichtet, das in seinem Besitz befindliche jüdische Vermögen sofort bei dem zuständigen Bürgermeister oder Amtskommissar bezw. dem Stadtkommissar in Bialystok anzumelden.
3. Es ist verboten:
   a) Ghettos, Judenwohnungen bezw. Grundstücke unbefugt zu betreten,
   b) jüdische Vermögensteile sich anzueignen, beiseite zu schaffen oder dritten Personen dazu Beihilfe zu leisten.
4. Wer dieser Anordnung zuwiderhandelt, hat schwere Bestrafung zu erwarten.

Der Oberpräsident
Zivilverwaltung
für den Bezirk Bialystok

OGŁOSZENIE

1. Każda osoba jest zobowiązana zatrzymywać Żydów i doprowadzać ich do najbliższego posterunku policji lub do amtskomisarza.
2. Każdy jest zobowiązany znajdujące się w jego posiadaniu mienie żydowskie natychmiast zameldować miejscowemu burmistrzowi lub amtskomisarzowi względnie Komisarzowi miasta Białegostoku.
3. Jest wzbronione:
   a) zwiedzać osobom nieuprawnionym getta, mieszkania lub posesje żydowskie,
   b) przywłaszczać mienie żydowskie, roznosić je, lub pomagać w tym osobom trzecim.
4. Kto przeciwdziała temu rozporządzeniu, będzie surowo ukarany.

NADPREZYDENT

АБВЕСТКА

1. Кожныя асоба забавязана затрымліваць жыдоў і даставяць іх у найбліжэйшы урад паліцыі або да амтскамісара.
2. Кожны забавязаны знаходзячуюся ў яго ўладаньні жыдоўскую маемасьць зараз-жа заявіць мясцоваму бурмістру ці амтскамісару або гарадзкому камісару ў Беластоку.
3. Забаронена:
   а) [illegible]
   б) [illegible]
4. Хто супроцьдзее гэтаму распараджэньню, будзе цяжка пакараны.

НАДПРЭЗЫДЭНТ

Announcement of rules pertaining to the Jews of Bialystok, issued by the president of the Civil Administration, printed in German, Polish and Russian.

№ aktu 14356/36 **RZECZPOSPOLITA POLSKA**

Rok 1936

Wolne od opłaty stemplowej na podstawie art. 160 punkt 1, w związku z art. 142 punkt 6 Ustawy z dnia 1 lipca 1926 r. (Dz. U. R. P. № 98 poz. 570) jako wydane w sprawach

Świadectwo urodzenia

WYDANE NA ZASADZIE KSIĄG METRYCZNYCH.

Zaświadcza się, iż Woronowicz Halina

urodziła się w Warszawie przy ulicy ... pod № 37 dnia dwudziestego listopada tysiąc dziewięćset dziewiętnastego 1919 roku

z ojca Mieczysława

z matki Józefy z Janowskich

Zgodność powyższego świadectwa z oryginałem stwierdzam.

Warszawa, dnia 7-go sierpnia 1936 r.

Urzędnik Stanu Cywilnego

Chaika Grossman's false aryan birth certificate, written by the hand of Mordecai Tenenbaum.

Name Woronowicz
geborene
Vorname Halina
Geburtstag 20. 11. 1919
Geburtsort Warschau
Wohnort Bk, Schwarzegasse 4
Kreis Bialystok
Beruf Textilarbeiterin
Volkstumszugeh. polnisch
Glaubensbek. röm. kath.
Staatsangeh. am 1.9.39 polnisch
Personenbeschreibung:
Grösse 153
Gestalt mittel
Gesicht länglichrund
Haar hellblond
Augen braun
Besondere Kennzeichen keine

IW1840

Linker Zeigefinger Rechter Zeigefinger

Woronowicz Halina
Unterschrift des Ausweisinhabers

Bialystok den 5. 1. 1943

Polizeipräsident
Der Bürgermeister
Amtskommissar

Dienststempel

Unterschrift des ausfertigenden Beamten

Chaika's false identification papers, under the name of Halina Woronowicz.

Mordecai Tenenbaum, leader of the Bialystok Ghetto revolt.

Zerah Silberberg

Edek Boraks, the first leader of the Bialystok Ghetto fighting organization.

Tamar Schneiderman

Lisa Chapnick

Daniel Moscovitz

Ronia Venitzka

Rivkele Madeiska

Joseph Kaplan

Tosia Altman

Lonka Kozibrodska

Frumka Plotnicka

Marek Birck

Yandzia Liboch

Maryla Rozyska, with her young daughter, after the war

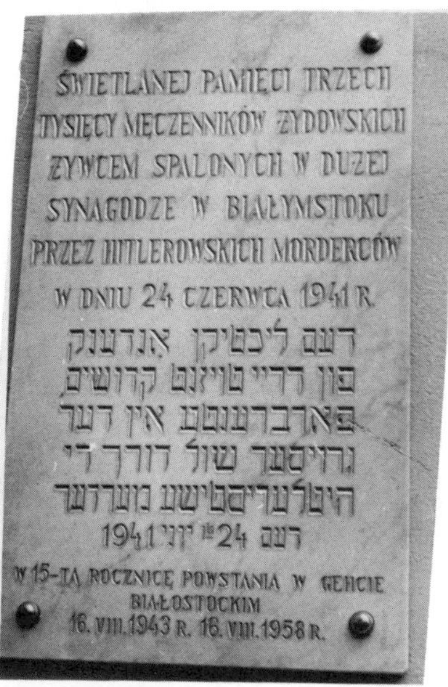

The monument to the 3,000 Jews who were burned alive in the city synagogue in Bialystok in 1941.

Lisa Chapnick, Hassia Vilitzka, Anya Rud

Hassia Vilitzka

Otto Busse (Pictured in 1963)

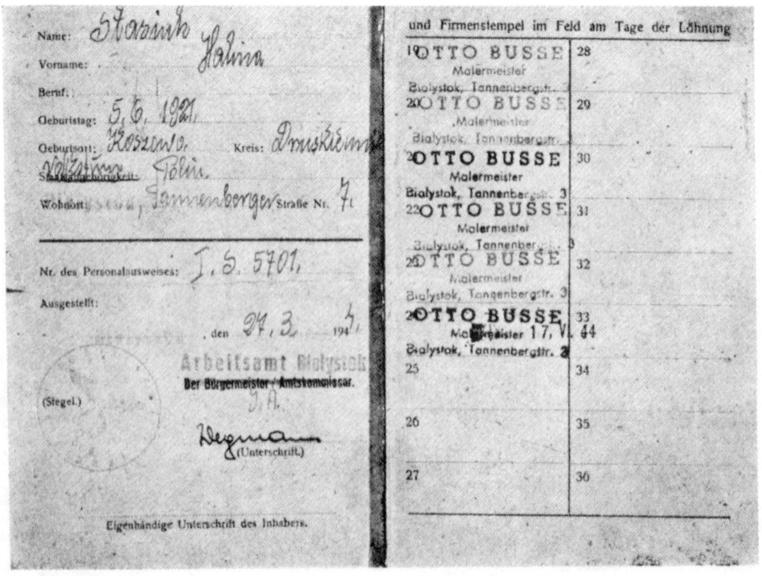

Name: Stasiuk Halina
Vorname: Halina
Beruf:
Geburtstag: 5.6.1921.
Geburtsort: Koszewo. Kreis: Druskienniki
Volkstum: Polin
Wohnort: ..., Tannenberger Straße Nr. 7
Nr. des Personalausweises: I. S. 5701.
Ausgestellt:
, den 27.3.194
Arbeitsamt Bialystok
Der Bürgermeister / Amtskommissar.
I.A.
(Siegel.)
Wegmann (Unterschrift.)
Eigenhändige Unterschrift des Inhabers.

und Firmenstempel im Feld am Tage der Löhnung

19 OTTO BUSSE Malermeister Bialystok, Tannenbergstr. 3	28
20 OTTO BUSSE Malermeister Bialystok, Tannenbergstr. 3	29
21 OTTO BUSSE Malermeister Bialystok, Tannenbergstr. 3	30
22 OTTO BUSSE Malermeister Bialystok, Tannenbergstr. 3	31
23 OTTO BUSSE Malermeister Bialystok, Tannenbergstr. 3	32
24 OTTO BUSSE Malermeister 17. VI. 44 Bialystok, Tannenbergstr. 3	33
25	34
26	35
27	36

Chasia Bielicka's work card in the name of Halina Stasiuk, supplied to her by Otto Busse.

The mausoleum in honor of the martyrs
of Bialystok in the city cemetery.

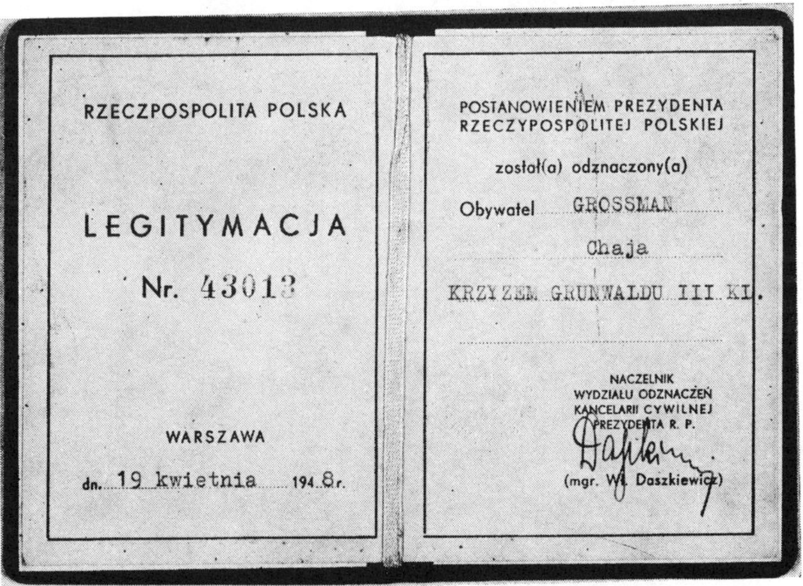

RZECZPOSPOLITA POLSKA

LEGITYMACJA

Nr. 43013

WARSZAWA

dn. 19 kwietnia 1948 r.

POSTANOWIENIEM PREZYDENTA
RZECZYPOSPOLITEJ POLSKIEJ

został(a) odznaczony(a)

Obywatel GROSSMAN
Chaja

KRZYZEM GRUNWALDU III KL.

NACZELNIK
WYDZIAŁU ODZNACZEŃ
KANCELARII CYWILNEJ
PREZYDENTA R. P.

(mgr. Wł. Daszkiewicz)

Certificate of Honor, the Grunwald Cross, given to
Chaika Grossman after the war by the Polish government.

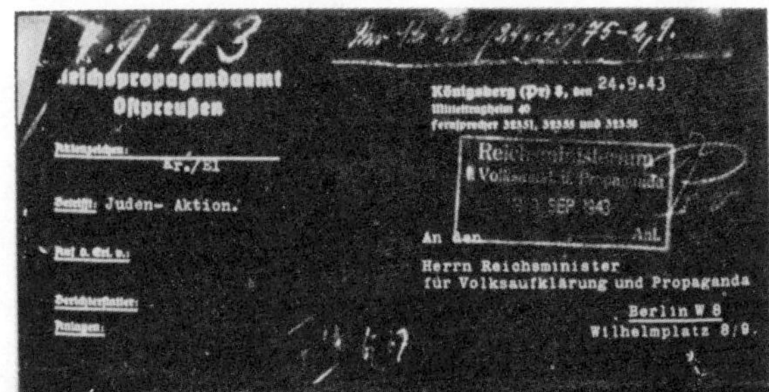

…9.43

Reichspropagandaamt
Ostpreußen

Aktenzeichen: Kr./El

Betrifft: Juden- Aktion.

Ruf u. Ort. v.:

Berichterstatter:

Anlagen:

Königsberg (Pr) 8, den 24.9.43
Mitteltragheim 40
Fernsprecher 38351, 38355 und 38356

An den
Herrn Reichsminister
für Volksaufklärung und Propaganda
Berlin W 8
Wilhelmplatz 8/9.

Auf Befehl des Reichsführers-SS und Chef der Polizei, Himmler begann unter Leitung des Gruppenführers-SS L u k o t s c h n i k am 16. August 1943 in den frühen Vormittagsstunden die Räumungsaktion des Bialstoker Ghettos, das etwa noch 3o ooo Juden beherbergte. Der Einsatz kam so unerwartet und plötzlich, daß gegen sonstige Gepflogenheiten die Juden diesmal überrascht wurden. Zur Absperrung des Ghettos wurden in der Nacht zum 16. August 43 Kräfte eines Polizei-Regiments, das auf dem Transport nach hier am Abend des vorhergehenden Tages eingetroffen war, eingesetzt, die auch in den darauffolgenden Tagen die Durchkämmung des Ghettos ausführten. In der Nacht zum 17.8.43 wurden von den Juden die ersten Brände angelegt, die von der dortigen städt. Feuerwehr und und herbeigeholten Bezirksfeuerwehr gelöscht werden konnte. Es konnte festgestellt werden, daß sich ca. 3 ooo Juden in Kanalisationsröhren, Kellern, ja sogar in schon vorher angelegten Bunkern versteckt hielten und ganz erheblichen Widerstand leisteten. An einer Stelle war sogar ein Bunker 6 m unter der Erde von einer Judengruppe angelegt. Diese bewaffneten Juden haben während der gesamten Aktion immer wieder versucht nachts aus dem Ghetto auszubrechen und die Absperrungskette zu überrumpeln. Bis auf ganz vereinzelte Durchbrüche sind aber diese Versuche immer abgeschlagen. Im großen ganzen waren die widerstandleistenden Juden reichlich mit Lebensmitteln und Waffen versorgt. Neben Handgranaten, Gewehren usw. konnte auch ein Teil automatischer Waffen, sowohl sowjetischen als auch deutschen Ursprungs festgestellt werden. Im Verlauf der Gesamtaktion flackerten immer wieder Brände von neuem auf, die zum Teil Panik unter den Juden in den ersten Tagen verursachen sollten, später aber zum Teil die deutsche Wirtschaft und hier vor allem die Kriegswirtschaft, schädigen sollten. Durch

Durch Einsatz der Feuerwehr konnten größere Schäden an Gebäuden verhindert werden. Auf dem Abtransport sind ca. 2oo Juden ausgebrochen. Der größte Teil von diesen ist erschossen, der Rest bis auf 3 Mann gefaßt worden. Die Aktion stellte einwandfrei fest, daß das dortigen Ghetto lebhafte Verbindung mit Warschau aufrecht erhielt. Funkanlagen sind nicht gefunden worden, dafür aber eine Anzahl Rundfunkgeräte. Der bewaffnette Widerstand hatte auf deutscher Seite 9 Verwundete, darunter 2 Offiziere.
Der Bezirk ist damit judenfrei, bis auf einige Plünderer und vereinzelte Judengruppen bei Banden, die aber größtenteils sich aus jenen Juden zusammensetzen, die in der Februar-Aktion aus dem Ghetto ausgebrochen waren. Am 8. September 1943 war die Räumung des Ghettos abgeschlossen und zur weiteren Verwaltung der Treuhand, Bialystok übergeben worden.
Die entstandenen Schäden sind mit dem Abschluß der Polizei-Aktion als erheblich zu betrachten. Die Sabotage der Juden hat in einem Großteil der Betriebe derartige Verwüstungen angerichtet, daß beispielsweise in dem Krankenhaus so gut wie alles erneuert werden muß.

In Vertretung:

The German report on the Bialystok uprising.

A German Document on the Revolt in the Bialystok Ghetto

The following document (copied from "Yediot Yad Va'shem", December 31, 1963) is the only official German document on the Bialystok ghetto revolt. It was written by the Koenigsberg branch of Dr. Goebbel's Propaganda Office in Berlin, on September 24, 1943.

The document reached the Propaganda Office in Berlin, as we can see from the stamp, on September 26, and was stamped to be filed as just another paper. It was discovered by the historian Yosef Wolf, and a photostat was sent to "Yad Va'shem".

Reich Propaganda Office
East Prussia
(stamped) Reich Office for
Information and Propaganda
September 26, 1943

Koenigsberg, September 24, 1943

Re: Jewish Operation

To Sir
Reich Minister for Information and Propaganda
Williamsplatz 8/8, Berlin

In accordance with the order of SS Reichsfuehrer and Head of Police, Himmler, there began, in the early morning of August 16, 1943, the operation of clearing the Bialystok ghetto that still contained 30,000 Jews, directed by Gruppenfuehrer Lokocnik.[1] The operation was so unexpected and sudden that, in contrast to the general rule, the Jews were surprised. The ghetto was cut off by 43[2] persons of the police regiment who had arrived the previous evening and who also served during the following days in searching the ghetto. On the night before August 17, 1943, the first fires set by Jews broke out and were extinguished by the local firemen and regional firemen who were called in. It may be determined that about five thousand Jews hid in the sewage pipes,[3] cellars and also in previously erected bunkers, and they put up considerable resistance. In one place a group of Jews had built a bunker eight meters beneath the ground. These armed Jews attempted again and again in the course of this operation to break through the encircling chain during the night and to escape from the ghetto. Except for some isolated breakthroughs, these attempts were repulsed every time. In general, these rebellious Jews were equipped with a great deal of food, arms, hand grenades, rifles, etc. It may also be affirmed that there was a certain amount of automatic arms of Russian and German origin. During the course of the general operation, fires broke out from time to time. These were intended, in the first days, to create panic among the Jews, but afterwards were intended to cause damage to the German economy and especially to the war economy. With the aid of the firemen it was possible to prevent great damage to the buildings. At the time of the transport, about 200 Jews fled; most were shot, the rest — except for three, were captured. The operation clearly showed that there was a live link between this ghetto and Warsaw. Transmission equipment was not found but a number of radios were. The armed resistance resulted in the wounding of nine Germans on their side, among them were two officers.[4]

The region is now free of Jews, except for a number of hoodlums and isolated groups of Jews among the bandits.[5] The latter are mostly the same ones who fled the ghetto during the February *aktzia*. On September 8 the clearing of the ghetto was completed, and it was transferred for further management to the "Treuhand"[6] in Bialystok.

With the cmpletion of the police action we must estimate the damage caused as quite considerable. The Jews' sabotage was responsible for extensive damage to most of the plants. The hospital too will have to be completely reequipped.

Notes

1. Intention is to Globotznik, of course.
2. Here there is certainly a mistake; the real number was in three figures at least.
3. Jews could not hide in the sewage, since Bialystok's sewage system was not adaptable for it.

4. If the report admits that two officers were wounded, the real number of losses was undoubtedly much higher.

5. The German term for the partisans.

6. The guardianship authority.

(Notes according to N. Blumenthal's explanations of the document in "Yediot Yad Va'shem," above cit.)

The Girl from Grodno

Hanka was not in the ghetto.

At six in the evening I leaped into Olla's court and without delay ran to look for Hanka.

The city streets were empty and dark. Dim lights could be seen in the houses. The anti-aircraft blackout intensified the darkness and the silence.

Pilsudski Street was deserted and quiet. Only the sound of hob-nailed patrols who were marching at the other end of the street could be heard. Where was I to look for Hanka? For safety's sake, or out of reluctance to return to the desolate cold walls of our shared room, I turned toward Sarah Dobeltoff's. Here were the dark stairs leading to the attic. They creaked under my feet. The door was locked from the outside. It was half-past six. Could Sarah not have returned yet from work? She knew that two men were sitting in her room and waiting for her to bring them a little food, and some news. Maybe they had already heard that the aktzia had ended and they could return to the ghetto? Zerah had warned us not to dare try to enter, since the ghetto was still under siege. He had ordered us to wait until the crowds of guards left and I had passed the warning on to Sarah. Why had she let them leave so soon? Maybe something had happened here, too? Perhaps that had something to do with Hanka's disappearance.

I stood by the locked door wondering, and decided to wait a little while longer. The minutes passed slowly. In the staircase the darkness was spread like a black veil. Finally, I went down the stairs carefully and decided to go to 17 Vesola Street. When I was half-way down the landlord's door opened suddenly and a broad ray of light focussed on me.

It was the landlord. He stood in the doorway, tall and erect, with angry eyes.

"I . . .I've come to visit your new tenant."

"Oh, it's you? Please, come in and we'll tell you where she is."

His voice became even angrier and harder. Now I no longer had any way to retreat. In the kitchen sat the entire family; a woman, an older son and I do not remember how many children.

"Wait here. I'll get dressed and we'll go to the Commissariat," the landlord said. My heart beat loudly. Sarah had been caught, the men were probably no longer in this world.

I turned toward the people in the house. They looked away and said nothing. Neither "murder" nor pity. They had apparently decided to do this without any delay.

"Panowie," I turned to them, "maybe you'll tell me what happened here. After all I am not a stranger to you and you cannot, as Poles and cultured people, act in this way. You are not Germans."

The bombshell hit the mark. They all became excited.

"What, Germans? What kind of Germans are we? But we don't want our children to die because of you. Do you think you are more precious to us than our own children? That one opposite you was beaten today by the gendarmes and they will keep on beating him, maybe to death, if we allow you to go out of here freely."

I grasped their words only later from the fragments of threats they made when I began to preach to them about patriotism. What had happened was the following:

Sarah had gone to work in the morning, as usual, and had locked the door. In the afternoon a Polish woman, apparently a collaborator, came in the company of a German officer and said she was looking for an apartment. The landlord replied that all the rooms were taken. "Taken does not bother me," she replied, "you'll find one for me," and began to look into all the rooms. When she came to Sarah's and found it locked from the outside she did not hesitate and in a loud voice, leaning on the half-drunk officer, she examined the lock. The officer helped her. They pulled at it but it did not help. The German asked for a wrench. The door was opened and two men were there. They could not believe their eyes. The German, who was drunk, did not understand very much and asked for their papers. Chaim, who had come from Grodno, showed them and the officer was satisfied, but the Polish woman began to laugh:

"What are you asking for? Don't you see they are Jews?"

"How do you know they are?" The German asked, surprised at his mistress' knowledge.

"Look at their faces. And, why are they sitting here locked in from the outside?"

The German became even more confused and instead of arresting them began to shout; perhaps he was frightened by the Jews. In any event there was confusion; the two men seized the opportunity, broke the window and jumped into the alley. One succeeded in escaping but the second was caught. All the neighbors, both children and adults, ran after them.

"One of them was fast, and escaped. One was caught and taken to the gendarmerie." Afterwards the gendarmes told the landlord that if the Gestapo learned that someone came to visit the tenant and he, the landlord, had not given her into their hands, he and all his household would be punished. They beat the landlord's elder son until he bled, kicked him with their hob nailed boots and tortured him because he and all in the street had not succeeded in capturing the second Jew. The whole family's end would be bitter if they didn't turn in anybody who visited the room in the attic.

Which of the two had been caught and who had escaped, I do not know. Was it Chaim or Hazek?

My brain kept insisting: don't give in! Try every possibility. Sarah had come home from work and they had "welcomed" her. They put the lockback in place — a trap for those coming after her. Now I was here, I after Sarah, Sarah after Chaim or Hazek, and before them — Hanka, and before that — Edek at the head of the line.

The landlord was holding on to my hand. Did he sense that I had the desire and strength to resist? to fight back?

"So, you have all decided to turn me over to the Gestapo?"

There was a sudden silence in the kitchen. The woman motioned to her husband to come closer. He, however, understood her intention and once again shouted.

"Woman, is this one whom you don't even know more precious than your son. Your children and your husband? We are not to blame that she decided to put herself in this dirty business! All the neighbors have already seen her and what will you do if the whore opposite betrays us? No, it is impossible! Do you want me to rot in prison or give up my soul in torture because of her, because of the devil knows who she is? Maybe she too is Jewish? No! Hurry and come with me. I am going to take you there."

I decided to go with him if only to get out of the suffocating kitchen. We went out. A wave of cool wetness touched my cheek. My mind became absolutely alert. I must not give in. The movement needed me, our ranks were growing thinner. I did not want to die. And he was holding my hand tightly. We turned right at the first corner. The darkness was oppressive. I walked quietly and submissively. At the corner I attempted to free my hand but he dug his fingernails into my flesh. Suddenly I fell upon him and began to bite his hand. He cried out in pain but did not let go.

"Let go of me, you bastard!"

"No, I won't let go, I am afraid of the Germans."

"Nobody is going to know; tell your family that you turned me in to the gendarmerie. Nothing will happen to you and your conscience will be clear in not having served the Gestapo."

"No, I am afraid it will become known."

I realized that I would not be able to convince him. He was terrified. His like could not be convinced. Most of the citizens of the country were, like him, slaves of the Nazis, slaves out of fear. I took a few more steps, and suddenly pulled my hand out of his. It hurt very much. I hadn't managed to run more than a few steps before he caught me and began to pull me back.

"No, you are not going to get away, psiakrev! See how strong she is! I am not going to be endangered because of you, I won't be able to pull you to the commissariat," he muttered into his mustache and actually pulled me back. I found myself once again in the kitchen "among" the family. All the doors were locked and the landlord watched me so that I would not move from the chair. It was eight o'clock, or even perhaps later, when the door of the kitchen was opened by two gendarmes. The landlord was terrified. The strong peasant, tall and stout, with the bristling mustache, did not have the strength to bring me to the nearby commissariat and had sent someone to call them. Now the gendarmes were in front of him. In their green uniforms, armed and healthy, they burst into the apartment and filled the little kitchen with their shouting.

"Papers!"

My papers were in order; a German passport in the name of Voronovich Halina. I had only recently received them from the police presidium. My work card was also completely valid; I had received that from Shade. The gendarmes did not know what to do; according to my papers I was a pure Pole. I also had a new passport.

"How did you get here? What is your business with the Jew? You are apparently also Jewish," one of them said. He was taller than his comrade, and younger. He had an amused expression, seemed pleased with himself, and was quite courteous.

"I do not understand, please translate for me."

The Poles attempted to explain what he had said. The German did not believe at first that I did not understand his language and tried to trap me with a German question. I determined, however, to be careful.

"I do not understand. Please translate."

The gendarmes became irritated.

"Who of you can explain it to her in Polish? Who knows German?" One boy, about sixteen years old, stood up. When the gendarme finished his question I turned to him. He mixed up the gendarme's words and I replied in accordance with his mistakes, of course. The gendarmes were angy.

"What, where I am working? Here, it is written here. I have a work card."

"But I asked you where you live!" the gendarme shouted. The lad blushed in his efforts to understand and I managed, in the meantime, to absorb every question, to consider it and find excuses.

"What is your business with the Jew if you are not one of them?"

"First of all, I didn't know that she is Jewish. I have known her a long time. To the best of my knowledge she is Polish."

"But answer, what do you have to do with her?"

"I wanted to sell her furniture for her new room. I have used furniture."

"Where do you live?"

I tried not to reply to that question though they asked me three times. I blamed it on the translator, after all I did not understand German. In the end they tired of the game, looked at my papers again and found the permit given to me by the housing office to live in a special room on 17 Vesola Street. The permit was made out expressly for two persons.

"Who is the other one who lives with you? The permit is made out for two."

"Don't put me on! I am tired of this game, you fresh bastard! Come, let us go to your house, to 17 Vesola Street. Come, Hans, let's go. You can see that we can't get anything out of her."

Once again we were plodding through the muddy puddles. Water seeped into my summer shoes. The torn rubbers did not help. We crossed empty fields. The water became deeper. Despite their high boots they crossed, and did not take their eyes off me. One was on my right and one on the left. There was no escape. I could not escape. There were only a few isolated houses here, no streets or courts. They were watching. If I couldn't do it by force I would try cunning.

"Jesus, Mary! How wet my feet are," I began in an ingratiating voice. Except for the Jesus, Mary, they apparently did not understand anything. They, however, understood the soft sounds of a woman looking for comfort. I showed them my wet feet. The younger one, with the green cold eyes came closer to me and his hand pressed on mine a little less tightly.

"Do you hear, Hans, she says her feet are wet, ha ha ha! Did you hear her say Jesus, Mary, ha ha ha!"

I also tried to laugh. By the time we reached Vesola Street I had regained control over my nerves and movements.

Hanka was not at home. The window was dark. The young gendarme grew more enthusiastic, laughed loudly at every Polish expression I used.

He even tried to spice his own remarks with Polish words. The second one looked at him suspiciously and reminded him that they had to search my room. The key to my room was with the landlord. That was bad. Otherwise, they might have been satisfied with visiting my room, but if they found the key with the landlord they might question him. There was no choice. The landlady gave them the key and they searched in my empty bed, the drawers and table, everywhere. The handkerchiefs and sheets were carefully examined. They were looking for Jewish monograms. They looked at the icon over the bed and shook their heads. The papers and money in the room were hidden under the wallpaper.

"To whom does that man's hat belong?" He pointed to one hanging on the wall. It was Hazek's.

"My boy-friend, " I replied and succeeded. I winked at the younger one and he took the hint.

His comrade, however, did not give up. Where was my roommate? A list of tenants was posted in the staircase. It stated that Halina Voronovich and Anna Kovalska lived in this room.

"Where is she?"

"I don't know; maybe at her boy-friend's."

"How: it is five after nine," he pointed to his watch. "From nine on, it is forbidden to be in the street."

"She is there," I said motioning with my head and hands, "at her boy-friend's." In order to explain that she slept there I inclined my head and closed my eyes. The younger gendarme tended to believe me, but his partner did not give up. They entered the landlady's kitchen. He turned white and the landlady shivered. She told them that the other tenant had been gone from the house for two days now and they didn't know where she was. In the other room, there was another girl who was waiting for Halina Voronovich since noon. According to her, she was a cousin.

The gendarmes didn't understand a word she said but I had learned from them that Hanka was not there and that someone was waiting for me in the landlady's other room, someone who had come to me. In a moment the gendarmes would discover this and still another one would fall into their net. I tried to divert the younger gendarme's attention. I laughed out loud, leaned against the younger man and attempted to draw him into my room. He followed me, but the landlady did not stop and pointed to the next dark room, explaining over and over again. The gendarmes lost their patience. One of them went to the place that was shown to him and I was left in the kitchen with the landlady and the young gendarme. From behind the half-open wall I heard:

"Du, eine Judin, nein?" and a slap echoed in the kitchen.

"Her papers are forged, the stamp is forged, I recognize them as papersfrom 'Druskeniky'".

"I am Jewish."

Again a slap, and then a blow. The sound of someone falling and then quiet. Now he was dragging her on the floor. In the kitchen opening near the bit stove stood a young woman, actually a girl, blond hair and black eyes.It was Hancia Yezerska of the Grodno Hashomer Hatzair. We had not managed to inform her that the address was not safe. She saw me in the kitchen corner but did not look at me and tried not to see me.

"I came in to rest a bit," she said in broken but understandable German.

Chana said that she had come to Mrs. Slovatzki's by accident, and she wanted to rest from her long journey.

"Tomorrow, why do you ask? Tomorrow you will do to me what you are doing to all the Jews. Kill me and have done with it."

The gendarmes were astonished. The elder began to mutter:

"But if you weren't what you are, they wouldn't be killing you."

"Oh, yes, of course," she said sarcastically, "the Jews wanted this war, the Jews are the source of all the tragedy in the world, aren't they?" Chana continued angrily. She straightened and lifted her head. In vain did I hint to her from behind their backs to be still; in vain I tried to turn her mind to the main thing: never to burn the bridge to life, or to give in to the enemy's pressure too fast. She was spewing hatred.

"Yes, I am Jewish and I hate you! Ich hasse euch!"

A large blob of spittle left its mark on the gendarme's green uniform. The Germans stopped for a moment, shocked.

"Intelligentes Madchen," one of them attempted to joke. His joke did not, however, relate to the situation. The second took handcuffs from his pocket and locked Chana's soft thin wrists. The gendarmes ordered the landlord and me to dress and we were between them with handcuffed Chana in front of us. On the threshold we met the neighbor who lived opposite to us, whom we had never known and who had always watched Sarah when she left our room.

"I wanted to tell you," he turned to the gendarmes and spoke in Polish, "that the other tenant in this room," he pointed at my room, "is in prison now for two days as a Jew." I stood still. Hanka in prison! In another few hours perhaps we would meet there, with Sarah, with Hanka, with Chana, with . . . whoever else was on the list.

It was very late, we were the only ones in the street. The landlord marched at my side, down and silent. Chana walked in front of me. Her hands were manacled, her head erect, with her wild hair blowing in the winter wind. Chana paid no attention to me. She did not want to disclose even a hint of connection between us.

"Chana, if we are going to make a last attempt, we must make it here, on the way to the police station. Chana, find the strength for a last try, the minutes are passing, and we are coming closer."

Chana didn't listen and continued walking, erect. Only her gleaming blond head shook slightly in a sign of refusal. I hardly heard her whisper:

"They don't know anything about you. You try. Don't meddle in my affairs. I have finished."

I moved closer once again to the younger gendarme.

"Jesus-Mary, where are you taking us in this cursed darkness? It's wet. Look at my shoes, they are full of water. In the end I'll catch a cold." I lifted one leg almost up to his nose.

I cannot remember all the foolish things I said. I spiced my words with coarse German ones, laughed a lot and told him to send the "Jiduvka" to hell. Why was he dragging her around with him? In any case they would kill all of them in their cursed ghetto. Why was he bothering with her instead of me? He could bring her to the ghetto gates and there they would do what they liked with her, and I would meet him whenever he wanted. I laughed again and he willingly responded to my invitation. Today he would send the "Judin" to the ghetto. He would only register her with the police. That was what they did mostly with Jewesses caught in the street. And me . . , he wanted to see me tomorrow at five o'clock.

I didn't worry about the landlord. In any event he would tell them the truth, that Chana had come to me and introduced herself as my cousin. The stupid gendarme was lying. He didn't know anything. If he didn't free us before we got to the commissariat this last game would not help. There would only remain the bitter memory of my clownish-tragic laughter, and his stupid response. Only his ghoulish face would be remembered along with his nauseating obscenities.

Once again I spoke about the stinking girl whose place was in the ghetto and not among decent people. If he didn't send her off right away I wouldn't come tomorrow. Jesus-Mary! They had forbidden us to hurt people even if they were your enemy. I didn't want to be sullied by her blood. Let others do that work. I laughed again and leaned against him; how didn't the fool sense that my Polish was no longer pure but contained a lot of German expressions? How could he not understand the game? The road, however, was getting shorter and the gendarme hesitated and looked at his comrade. The latter pulled him by the sleeve:

"Come, what do you still want to do this evening? I'm in a hurry to go to sleep. Let's hand her over and be finished with it."

The police station was in front of us. We went through the wide corridors and entered a spacious room. Two desks were in the two corners. At one sat a stout officer in uniform. Our gendarme stood erect and informed the officer: "This is a Polish woman, Chief, whom we found in a Jewess' home. This is the landlord, also a Pole, in whose house we found this Jewess" (pointing to Chana).

"She is a fresh Jewess and hates the Germans."

"Come here," the chief said to me. Once again the gendarme intervened:

"She doesn't understand German."

The chief, however, did not yield. "Come here, what is your name?"

"I do not understand," I said in Polish almost mechanically.

"Call for a translator," he ordered. After a minute a Pole was before me and translating every word.

"Your name. Family name, the names of your parents, your place of employment, where do you live?"

I replied to the questions one after the other.

"Papers."

I held out my papers.

"Everything is in order," the chief declared.

"But what does she have to do with the Jews?" he turned to the gendarme. The latter replied:

"She does some business, or something, I don't know."

"Let her go but she will have to be watched," the chief ordered.

"What did he say?" I asked the translator.

"He says you can go home."

Where was I to go? They would come back for me again as soon as they questioned the landlord. It wasn't important; I would go there; there was no point in standing here like a fool.

And then once again I was outside. I walked as if intoxicated, weaving on my tired wet feet, groping in the dark, falling and getting up again. Only with great difficulty did I get to my room. I had to do a thorough housecleaning before they came to look for me a second time. I had to remove the documents, money, and anything else that could lead the Germans to our comrades in the ghetto or to the other girls on the aryan side. It was already midnight when I reached my room. I silently opened the door so that the landlady wouldn't hear. Suddenly I couldn't hold back any longer. Something impelled me to knock at the neighbor's door. My nerves were at the breaking point. I could no longer control my movements or mind. I knocked at the door of the hostile and treacherous prison guard.

"Who is there at such a late hour?"

"Excuse me, sir, but perhaps you can give me details about my friend's arrest? Maybe you can help me?"

"*Paszol Zydowka*, run away fast or your fate will be like that of your imprisoned friend. Such nerve!"

The door was slammed.

There were still a few hours until dawn and the end of curfew. What would I do in my room? I certainly wouldn't be able to sleep. I extinguished the light and sat near the table, dressed in my coat, the packed bag in my hand, ready to leap from the room the moment I heard a suspicious noise from the end of the street. If they didn't come to take me by dawn, it was that the investigation of the landlord was not over, and that Chana hadn't revealed anything. Chana had the same papers as Hanka, forged from the same town near Grodno. Maybe it was those documents that had trapped her? First, I would have to inform Grodno not to use papers from Druskieniky and Skiddell any more, and not to come to Vesola Street. Second, I had to warn Haska; perhaps, she should change her apartment. Haska's papers had long since been filed away and it was doubtful whether anybody would look at them again. If she moved to a new apartment she would no longer be in danger. It would be better for her to change her address to a different commissariat. I had to save the other girls. But what about those who had already been caught? Should I return to the ghetto? Was there really no way out? Would tricks really no longer help? To run away? Or perhaps I should go to meet the gendarme? But what could he do? The game was dangerous. I was not deterred by the moral consideration, though the business nauseated me. What was this danger, however, in comparison with the other ones facing the movement and the underground? Could I take the risk when the prospects for success were so slight? The hours crept by slowly; it was still a long time till dawn. My head dropped tiredly to the table. The landlord had not yet returned. In another hour or two the night would be over. There was still time to weigh all the possibilities. She certainly would not reveal anything. Was it worth going tomorrow to the meeting with the gendarme — if I didn't fall into their hands before then? Would I be able to sit and wait in this room until five in the afternoon? By that time wouldn't they have discovered the connection between the prisoners and myself? Chana had the same papers as Hanka, forged from the same town near Grodno. Maybe it was those documents that had trapped her? But Haska, too, had had the same, and she already had a genuine German passport. What if they later learned about the forged papers? They had her papers; they were in their hands, they would arrest her too. Who else had such papers? Sarah Debelteff? No, she had Vilna papers that had not yet been discovered. Sarah, too, is in their hands, and they found you knocking at her door. All the threads lead to you. The proof is there. And still, perhaps I should try one more game?

As soon as the first weak ray of light appeared I went out. I moved about the streets for a while and then went to Haska. Haska didn't show any signs of concern for herself. Her papers had long since been filed, she would look for a new apartment immediately. She thought, however, of Sarah who still had no German passport, and only two days before had handed over the passport she had received in Skiddell to the police registration office. It was Sarah's idea to waive the passport and return to the ghetto. Then I told Haska of my hesitations over whether or not to return to 17 Vesola Street at five o'clock to try the game with the gendarme. Haska became very angry. Yesterday's mischievous girl suddenly became adult and strong.

"Shame on you Chaika! I didn't know you could be so careless. You who are always preaching to us about our inability to distinguish between necessary risks that hold some prospect of success and superfluous ones which serve no purpose! I cannot believe that the symbol of deliberateness and intelligence would want to commit that kind of foolishness! You know very well how little the gendarme can do. He is only a small cog without any initiative. What is more, all those who have fallen into their hands, Hanka, Sarah, the fellow and Chana, are all linked to you. If I could give you instructions I would forbid you to return to Vesola Street and order you not to move around the city. This very day you must get into the ghetto and hide until the danger is over. Chaika, you are not going to leave. I will keep you here until evening and then accompany you to Olla's house. I no longer trust you. Not you, nor the theories you taught us. Your experience, and intelligence are also suspect. I do not trust your inflexible willpower, either. You are as full of emotion and impulse as I. Why did you go back to Vesola Street last night? You could have hidden anywhere else, even in a privy, or gone to Bronka's, or come to me. It's not enough for you that some miracle saved you yesterday, you also went to question that traitor, the prison guard, about Hanka. He had already informed on you, as you said, though the gendarmes didn't understand him. Were you looking for some connection to Hanka through him? Ask any one of the girls, they will all say what I have. These inexperienced ones are as wise as you are, and they will face the test just as well."

I stood before Haska like a school child in front of an experienced teacher.

Her strength and judgment, her strong intelligence surprised me. I quietly said goodbye and left. I visited my sister. Here I learned that the man imprisoned was Chaim and the one who got away — Hazek. My sister had brought him to a Polish friend, Stefa, whose address supplied us with a mailbox and a source of information for a long time. I visited Bronka and Rivkele. Both listened to my story, and both agreed with Haska. For the first time I wanted to hear the opinion of other people and of those younger than I. For the first time, too, I was looking for support from the girls. I thanked them from the depths of my heart for having helped me make up my mind. I had suddenly discovered the true worth of those I had thought to be careless young girls. Now there was a high and strong wall, of fighting girls, on the aryan side.

Rivkele was not known at 17 Vesola Street. Today, after work, she would innocently walk past the street without entering the court, and try to see whether there were guards near the place. Rivkele returned in the evening with specific information: a man in civilian clothing was moving about the house. He had also tried to "accompany" Rivkele a little way but when he saw that she was only passing through the street, he left her. Rivkele had also seen a light in our room, a sign that they were waiting for me there.

That evening I went into the ghetto. A few days later, despite our explicit instructions to Grodno, some more comrades came to Vesola Street. Two more girls and a man were arrested. Perhaps the instructions had not arrived before they had left. Sarah Shevehovich was also arrested. She had not obeyed orders to leave the aryan side, and her papers had betrayed her. The laboratory we had worked so hard to transfer to Bialystok could no longer help. Two young girls who came from Grodno registered in the work office and were sent to a transition camp for Polish youth assigned to work in Germany. Bronka established contact with them and provided help and food. The next day one of the Polish women in the camp told her that they had been taken out of the shower by two gendarmes. The situation was clear. The investigation was continuing. The last girl to come from Grodno was caught and put into the ghetto. They were apparently searching for the source of the documents, the threads leading to the underground in the Bialystok ghetto. They allowed her to move about for two days and then arrested her again. We grasped the strategy and exercised caution.

Now the tragic and heroic epic of our group in the prison began, seventeen persons, all young and stubborn, proud and close-mouthed. Only echoes reached us after unending efforts to establish contact with them. For days and weeks we looked for a way to reach them, days and weeks of groping and searching until their voices seemed to reach us from beyond the prison walls, from beyond life.

It was the beginning of spring. Passover, too, was approaching. The better for Stalingrad was already history. The victorious Soviet march through Nazi Germany "lebensraum" began. Every morning brought new tidings of German armies being cut off, of new defeats.

Spring 1943 was marked by the barren struggle of young Jews locked in the ghetto and in prisons behind enemy lines. How much hope that spring brought us in the days of the Stalingrad victory; how hard it was for us to die thousands of kilometers away from that Stalingrad! Great Stalingrad, redemption, was far, hopelessly far away.

After returning to the ghetto I stayed for two days in one of our secret apartments. All contact seemed to me strange and superfluous. I was all pain, weeping. Any talk about those in prison was like salt in my wounds. I was filled with unrest, and pangs of conscience. Perhaps I had not tried hard or had not been sufficiently careful? Maybe we had used the forged papers too often? I took almost all of the blame, for the most part unjustly. My comrades looked at me and said nothing. I was grateful to Zerah for his wonderful silence, his efforts to guide my mind to practical matters. Any day now February's bloody slaughter might be resumed, and the underground needed organization. The ranks had been thinned, and at the fringes of the camp there were the rumblings of the revisionist ideas which inevitably follow defeat. And the imprisoned continued to suffer behind the walls.

"Chaika, we cannot leave them to their fate; we won't count the costs. I am sure of their courage, even without our help. I doubt whether we will be able to save anyone but it is our duty to do what we can to ease their isolation." Zerah was right.

The fraternity of fighters compelled us to seek some path to them.

Hanka's mother, our Sheine, did not find the strength to bear her terrible tragedy. Her eyes sank deeper in their sockets, her cheeks sagged, her back bent. I hurried out of my hiding place. The time had not yet come to settle accounts and admit our mistakes. It was impossible to stay imprisoned and leave Zerah and Gedalyahu alone.

Sheine did not respond to her Soviet group's call to continue her activities. "Until I do everything in my power for Hanka I will not be able to live and work," she told them. At first they took her situation into consideration, but ultimately went back to their tasks. They too tried to help, but could not. They were not happy with Sheine's activities nor with ours to contact dubious persons, agents and quasi-agents, extortionists and would be extortionists, suspicious mediators of all kinds, to save only one spark from the conflagration in the city prison. Sheine, however, was not to be deterred, nor were we. We knew that underground logic dictated that we not deal with prisoners. We must not disclose the connections between them and us and the centers of our operation. The Gestapo was looking for that link and we were liable to give it to them, and for what? For the fraternity of fighters, something that could not be defined? Despite all this, we continued to work contrary to all logic. We found a Jewish wagoner who drove to the prison every day and then returned to the ghetto. We found Jews who were working in the prison courtyard. We contacted the notorious Judovsky, who openly served the Gestapo. Through the wagoner and the workers we transmitted a note and received an answer. In that way we learned who the prisoners were, what they were being questioned about, whether they were being tortured, and how we could help them. Our written contacts with the prison continued. We attempted to adopt a matter-of-fact approach in our letters and to encourage them.

The comrades' replies were also factual. Yes, they were being beaten and tortured. Not one of the seventeen had revealed anything. They met often during the walking hour, in the prison courtyard. The investigation had one purpose: to find out who had prepared the papers; what organization was behind them, who the leaders were among those imprisoned in the ghetto. Other questions, mostly asked of Hanka and Chana, were: who was Halina Voronovich, Hanka's roommate at 17 Vesola Street? What was her real name and where did she live? Because she refused to answer the question Hanka received extra beatings and there were days when she couldn't go out to walk because she couldn't stand on her feet.

Jewish workers who returned to the ghetto daily from their work in the prison, and one speculator, who had in some miraculous way been freed from this, told about the "prisoners' queen," a young, beautiful girl they had seen walking in the prison courtyard during the exercise hour, thin and drawn, with marks of the beatings, and wounds on her face and hands. Her feet were bare and her clothing torn, she walked erect, and all the young prisoners considered her a symbol of suffering and heroism. They told us that sometimes the sound of sad singing would drift over the prison walls; the "queen of the prisoners" was singing, and encouraging her comrades to hold out and keep their mouths shut. Sarah, too, once wrote about Hanka.

Also in prison, Sarah Dobetloff was deep in her own thought. She wrote about Hanka and the other girls, how they had withstood the test of torture; but about herself she neglected to write. As if she were not there among the imprisoned and the tortured.

Hanka had been arrested in the work office. The clerks were about to register her when a German official approached and accidentally glanced at her papers, although she was not the only one in the queue. He took her out of the line, and detained her until the gendarmes came. She was not told anything, not even the charge against her. She had been brought to the "Criminal-Polizei" and from there, on the same day, to the prison. For a number of days she had not been questioned and meanwhile she learned that many comrades had been caught, like her, because of the papers made in Druskeniki.

We determined to get anyone we could out of prison. First, Hanka. Why? Here, too, there was a reckoning; we had at all costs to get Sheine and her mother back to work. The contact with the Soviets was very important. Sheine was completely shattered and did not have the strength to carry out that task. Because of her, the Soviets trusted us. We contacted Judkovsky the traitor. We knew that he was afraid of the underground and would not want to disobey. He agreed to get Hanka out so that he would have that in his favor on the day of judgment.

The game was dangerous, but we attempted to take every precaution so that he would not learn any details about the life underground. Judovsky demanded money, not for himself but for the prison commander. We found the money. Luckily it was not a very large sum. A few days later we learned that Hanka's case was already in the hands of the Gestapo commander, Dibos, and that the prison commander couldn't help. We got the finest present we could from Barash: a gold watch with artistic inlay.

For days we looked for some opening, some contact with Dibos. Barash was also enlisted to work for Hanka, so that she would not be executed but instead be returned to the ghetto police as a Jew who had tried to leave the ghetto with forged papers. Judkovsky demanded that in Hanka's pending questioning by Dibos himself (he did not deal with routine investigations) she answer two questions: her real name and my real name, and her connection with me.

In our view, these two questions were not too dangerous. The first, in any case, was of no value since the Gestapo knew that Hanka was Jewish. Sheine was not deterred by the fear of danger to her family if Hanka revealed her origin, and as for myself, we decided that I would disappear for a time, change my name or move for a while to a neighboring town as a Pole. One thing, however, she must not reveal, was my role in the work. We decided unanimously to ask Hanka to reply to the two queries, and since I was involved, I would write the letter myself. Hanka knew my handwriting and would have to obey my instructions.

Tensely, we waited for the outcome. Two days after she received the letter Hanka was called for the final questioning. Everything worked according to plan. Dibos conducted the investigation and without beating her this time or threatening her commanded her to answer the two questions and she would be freed and returned to the ghetto.

Hanka refused. Dibos was astonished. His agent, Judovsky had promised that she would co-operate this time, that Dibos would receive a splendid watch and in exchange the cursed Jew would be returned to the ghetto. They probably thought she would reveal something about the underground after she returned to the ghetto; she certainly would renew her connections. And Judkovsky could be depended upon. Hanka, however, stood erect, with her lips closed. Dibos repeated his questions, again and again and Hanka still remained silent. Then Dibos ordered her taken to the torture chamber. She was thrown into her cell unconscious and was no longer called for questioning. The gold watch was returned to us. Judkovsky informed us that he would no longer deal with the likes of these, over whom even the underground had no control. "I wash my hands of the business," he said through a messenger.

Hanka tightened her lips. Sheine's eyes gleamed when she spoke of it. There was a tragic look in her face. Hanka had not trusted the Gestapo. She had not believed them even when she received her comrades' instructions. Her commanders had made a mistake; they had not been strong enough, but it was Hanka who was being tested and not they. She did not have to obey childish orders. And she did not. Was she right?

The answer was in Sheine's pain filled eyes, shining with pride. The answer was in her unending whisper: "She did not talk . . . she did not talk . . ."

In the spring of 1943, when the snow had completely melted and there were puddles of water and mud everywhere, all seventeen were executed. In a hole near Novosolky, nine kilometers from the city, a place of pine forests and vacation resorts, they were all shot. We did not know the time of their death. One day the package we had sent to them was returned. The address written on it no longer existed. After a time we learned that they had been shot and then buried in a common grave. Their great secret of the Jewish underground in the ghetto, were buried with them. They revealed nothing to the Gestapo not a name, not an address, nothing at all.

Jan

That spring was strange; it seemed to be hiding all the human suffering and heroism from the pale sun only to reveal them again suddenly. It was in Warsaw that the depths of suffering and the heights of heroism were revealed in all their searing light.

We had waited for news from Warsaw for a long time and there had been no word. On one of those spring days I went as usual to the prison. This was when we still hoped to rescue our comrades from the claws of the Gestapo. I thought that perhaps I might see the prisoners through the high, barred window.

Hundreds of women and children were knocking at the prison gates. Poles of all strata, all desperately trying to hand over packages, looking at the dim shadows in the little windows. I mixed with the crowd and attempted to hear something about the transports that had been taken out of the prison. I heard that the day before yesterday a transport with 200 persons had left, but they had all been men. Women were running and weeping. They still did not know if their husbands, brothers or fathers had been among those selected for execution. For an hour or two I stood in the muttering crowd until the police dispersed us.

I moved about the streets idly, without any goal. I went to visit Stefa. A postcard had been received from Yadwiga, in Vilna, but the address was strange. It was from Grodno, a Polish family on a Polish street. The card said: "I have received a letter from Irena: 'Yosef had died after a short and painful illness. His family is no longer at the old apartment. You need not write to them any longer. Yosef was fully conscious to the end, and acted like one who knew the nature and seriousness of his illness. We are proud of him. Yadwiga.'"

I recall that this was in March. It was hot and cold, intermittently. The strange news from Yadwiga about Yosef and his comrades shocked us. Vague information about the fighting in the Warsaw ghetto had reached us a few weeks earlier. Until the beginning of the aktzia in our city we wrote often to the addresses we had but none of our letters were answered. And then, suddenly, this news. We decided that I should go to Grodno, to the address on Yadwiga's card. Since the great failure on the aryan side, only a few weeks had elapsed and it was apparent that the investigations were not over. There was no alternative, however. The information was important, and the trip to Grodno was necessary. We decided that I should take this opportunity to visit Jan in Korupchice near Grodno. We had heard about him from Yocheved, and it was worth asking him about the possibilities of buying weapons.

In order to travel to Grodno, a permit from the "Polizeipresidium" was required. For every passport there was a file in the Polizeipresidium, and I could not be sure that if I went in I would come out safely. However, I decided to take my place in the long queue in the Polizeipresidium building and to try to learn the procedures.

This time the queue was not long, and moved rapidly. I decided that when my turn came I would watch carefully; if the clerk took out my file I would get away. It was difficult to assume that my file was clean; there must surely be some suspicious entry in it. Still, I recalled dozens of cases where someone had been under suspicion in one institution while in a second one his file had been clean. I would, then, approach the window, hand over my papers, and look into the clerk's face when he took out the file. I would try to read his face; if he found something wrong there, his facial reaction would surely show it. My turn came. The clerk studied the application, asked for my identification card and the purpose of my trip.

"To visit my family. I have received a two-day vacation from my work, and the third day will be Sunday; altogether three days."

The clerk hesitated. He could be Polish or German, he spoke both languages. His Polish was fluent but he had a foreign accent. He arose, went to the long tables where the boxes holding the files stood erect and threatening, like armed soldiers. He found my file, and returned to the window, his eyes lowered to the paper. I received a permit to travel to Grodno and back.

The control at the railway was very strict. In addition to the transit policeman that day two Gestapo officers were also watching. One of them, whose uniform was pressed and shining, looked at the permits, especially at the passports. Not all the travellers had German passports; he examined their documents with scrupulous care. My papers were in order of course. After he left the car one of the travellers whispered into my ear:

"Streblov. He is looking for Jews. For a long time now he has been appearing suddenly at the trains on the Grodno-Bialystok line and examining papers."

I shivered — Streblov, and I hadn't known. He was looking for forged papers from Druskieniky and Skiddel. My name hadn't told him anything. That was system for you, their wonderful organization!

I arrived at Grodno toward evening and went to acquaintances of Yadwiga, through side streets filled with gardens and trees. I passed a monastery with a church at its side, standing on a hill overlooking the whole neighborhood, with the Niemen river below. It was a grand view. Spring had burst with full force into this beautiful city, and I was going to look for traces of the dead.

The house was intimate, one-storied, within a garden, its windows glittering in the rays of the setting sun.

The lady of the home, a pleasant young woman, led me into a room with colorful upholstered cushions. I told her the purpose of my coming and asked her when Yadwiga had been there last, and whether she knew where I might find her.

"She was here a few days ago and returned to Vilna. She stayed with us, but I cannot tell you very much about her. Perhaps my husband knows more than I do. He will return from the city shortly. I know that she contacted someone by the name of Skovronsky. He, too, occasionally comes here. For some days, however, he has not visited us; I think my husband knows where he is."

I decided to wait for the landlord.

The landlady, a seamstress, returned to her work without asking me who I was. She courteously invited me to stay in her house as long as I was in Grodno.

"When my husband returns we shall have supper. This room is at your disposal. You can lie down, wash, rest."

I learned a lot from her husband. Yadwiga had stayed there, and it seemed to him that her single task had been to warn a number of people to move from their apartments and not to write to Warsaw. He had heard of failures in Warsaw, of someone called Yurek who had fallen into the hands of the Gestapo with arms and archives, including addresses from Grodno, Vilna and Bialystok. That is why Irena had not wanted to write those addresses. She had informed Yadwiga and Yadwiga had crossed the border somehow. She had not been able to get to Bialystok and had therefore had to inform the people there in writing. He had also heard of Yosef, who had recently been killed by the Gestapo. He had been arrested and executed as the leader of the underground in the Warsaw ghetto. Irena had written with admiration about him and his heroic death. Yadwiga had contacted Skovronsky here; he worked in a printshop and I might still find him. He could certainly give me more details. Tomorrow I could visit him.

In the end he added, reflectively: "All Yadwiga's information, however, is out of date. She received it from Irena a long time ago. By the time she succeeded in crossing the border and getting here we had later news. There was a revolt in the Warsaw ghetto that broke out in January; many Germans apparently were killed. In the end they were deterred and stopped the aktzia."

The landlord's story revealed many details. Yurek, that was Aryeh Vilner — had been discovered by the Gestapo, and Yosef, Yosef Kaplan — had been arrested and executed. That was certainly not everything that had happened in Warsaw. There were rumors of an armed revolt. That proved that not all the arsenals had been discovered; that Yosef's work was being continued. Who were the fighters, the commanders? Who was still alive and who had died?

The next day I went to look for Elyahu Skovronsky. In the printshop they told me that he had gone to work in Germany. He had apparently decided, for lack of choice and without any possibility of remaining here, to try his luck as a Pole in Germany.

I turned my steps to where the ghetto had once been. The streets were open and desolate, signs of the destruction were everywhere. A shutter was open to the spring wind, swinging back and forth, creaking. Through the window I could see a table, chairs, beds, and most of all, torn pillows, white feathers. Have you ever seen the white snow in the Jewish homes, the whiteness of the feathers? They were outside too, the air was filled with them.

The paving stones were dry; there was no sign of mud. The spring sun and the winds had dried them. All the doors were wide open. You entered a house and found only traces of life. The whiteness of almost empty flats. Where had the closets and dishes gone, the clothing, shoes, the shawls with which Jewish grandmothers used to wrap themselves on Sabbath eves after lighting the candles? There were only tatters of rags and floors with torn-up boards.

I went out into the street. A peasant wagon was passing, the frightened peasant looking about, searching for some piece of furniture or clothing, easy loot. Leaving the alleys you came to the busy city, golden on the Nieman's banks, wagons loaded with the remainders of a life that had ended; closets and bundles, beds and chairs, and, on top of these miserable goods, sat a grey peasant in his coarse coat, shaking with the wagon and pulling on the reins . . . No. . . .

Was this to be the memorial of Polish Jewry? The peasant bouncing on the wagon loaded with Jewish goods? The memorial to three and a half million Jews in Poland?

Warsaw, and the inspired legacy it left its Jews: revolt and war, armed battle for the honor of Israel. That revolt would live forever. The shaky furniture would disappear without leaving a trace . . . Warsaw, Oh Warsaw!

Warsaw was our flag and our victory. Rebellious Jewish Warsaw was our pillar of fire. When the ghetto went up in flames that April when we heard over the underground radio of the rebel commander's last call, his final announcement that the Warsaw ghetto was dying in battle, we knew that it was not the call of the dying but of heroes whose spirit would live forever. Our hearts tightened and we were proud. We knew that our fate would be like theirs. Our end would be the beginning of renewed life, the lives of free men growing out of our graves.

That day I went to Jan's. He did not recognize me but after I introduced myself as the comrade of the people in the Grodno ghetto he welcomed me. His house stood alone at the edge of the village, on a hill overlooking the Grodno-Bialystok road. On the other side of the road, opposite Jan's house, was a deserted flour mill, which belonged to him. The mill did not operate, but Jan was not concerned. He made a living. His house was a typical country one. In the courtyard pigs and domestic fowl of all kinds burrowed and filled the air with their noises and odors. Jan lived there with his wife. They had not been blessed with children, but he was a wealthy farmer. His wealth did not come only from the soil; he was also a good businessman. His closet was loaded with goods. His wife would return from the city dressed like a city woman in fancy dresses. Watches, gold rings and precious stones were hidden in her linens.

I came to know them later when I began to feel at home in their dwelling, the most involved underground position I knew. In this house the Jewish underground benefitted from the earthiness, courage, crudeness and cunning of the Polish peasant. He exuded an air of wealth but he had remained a peasant at heart. It was difficult for me to understand his wife's concern about the pigs and the cows and the extent of their stinginess in preparing their primitive meals. She loved wealth, and accumulated gold coins, and could buy anything she wanted even in wartime, yet they lived like peasants. The chase after wealth had not damaged Jan's moral character. He was young, likable and brave. In return for his courage and the risks he took, he demanded payment, but he could also act without it. He helped devotedly, and was not deterred even from the difficult tasks of hiding Jews.

After spending that day with them, eating and sleeping in their house, I saw that they were attracted to me, charmed by my aryan appearance, by my conduct and by my daring to come from the Bialystok ghetto to ask about lost comrades. Jan's tongue was loosed and he opened his heart. Jan had loved our comrades, who used to come to him from the Grodno ghetto, loved Mottel, who used to buy arms from him (he did not say "buy" but "take"), and all the company that stayed in his house on their way, and who were later annihilated in a short battle. Jan was able to rise to loyal friendship with peasant simplicity. He revealed to me that on his farm there were 15 Jews in hiding, in the attic of the abandoned flour-mill, among them Mottel and his sister.

When it got dark and a cold, wet wind began to blow, he was sure that neighbors would no longer come to visit and to drink his home-made beer. His wife filled a big pot with potatoes and two loaves of bread from the oven and set out for the mill. I followed her. Jews were lying on piles of straw in the loft. The cracks in the walls were wide and the wind blew through them. It was very cold in the loft. The Jews were crowded on the straw, half-asleep. At the sight of my face they stopped talking. When I started to talk in Yiddish their fears increased. "Another one?" The more people hidden in the loft the greater the danger.

I quieted them and told them that I was from Bialystok. I had come to visit and to ask what help they needed. Mottel recognized me at once and whispered to me not to reveal my name. In the semi-darkness I made out his figure, somewhat too big for his age. He looked tall and strong in the cold, desolate mill, lit only by pale starlight coming through the many cracks in the walls. His hair was black and his brow was framed in curls. A lot of questions were asked about the front, the Bialystok ghetto, the gentiles and the Jews, and especially the question I heard from thousands of Jews everywhere:

"What is the end going to be? Can we hold out until salvation comes?" And there was always one pessimist or realist (anyone foreboding evil was considered a realist) who said: "By the time we find any relief we will all have given up our souls."

I told them about various things; about 350,000 Germans who had been cut off and destroyed on the Stalingrad front; about Soviet cities that were being liberated by the Soviet army. I told them about Voronezh, Kursk, Rostov and Sumy, of Nazism's numbered days, about the partisans burning bridges and sabotaging German transports to the front. I spoke at great length, in whispered enthusiasm. I told them more than I knew. I didn't care whether everything was true. I didn't care if I was exaggerating; I wanted to encourage them and myself to believe that it was worthwhile fighting for life, hanging on to it by one's fingernails, as it were. And finally, I said:

"To have any chance at all, you must yourselves use weapons."

Silence fell in the flour-mill. I wrapped myself in my coat and motioned to Mottel to come down the ladder with me; I wanted to speak with him alone.

The Jews sat in their places. One of them peered once again through the window looking out on the road, where military units passed; automobiles moved eastward, police and punitary units went to near villages that had not yet filled their quotas of meat, milk, lard and eggs. They had to be careful that no car stopped in front of Jan's house.

From Mottel I learned that Jan had arms, especially, a machine gun on a stand, that he did not want to sell and which he was keeping for himself. Perhaps I could get it from him. In any case, smaller arms could certainly be received from him for money, but not just ordinary money. He wanted foreign currency or valuable cloth, for a suit, furs and the like. Mottel wanted to go to Bialystok; why was he hiding when his comrades were preparing to "do something?" I agreed with him, but how was he to get to the city with his typically Jewish face?

"If you don't help me, I'll come by foot, at night."

I promised to clarify the matter of his coming; perhaps some way would be found to bring him. I asked him to see that Jan would not sell arms to anybody else and to examine his own possibilities. Jan could not be relied upon. Neither his promises to provide nor his declarations that he did not have any arms were completely true. Mottel accepted the task willingly.

"At least there will be some point to my sitting here," he said.

Jan promised to see whether his "friends" had anything to sell. I knew that first of all he would have to examine himself. After all, he did not know very much about me. He couldn't reveal to me, after a first meeting, that there were arms hidden in his house. First he would pretend that he had "none of his own," in order to enhance his security and perhaps also to raise the price. He was cunning, and I had to act as if I trusted him; in any case I must not spoil everything at our first meeting.

We parted as friends. He accompanied me on the 12 kilometer journey to the railroad station. He knew all the side paths, and he did not take me along the main road. We arranged that I would return a week later, and that until then he would gather all the necessary information about arms that could be bought through his mediation.

Before we separated, we drank a few glasses of home-made vodka at his brother Michael's house, near the station. Michael wondered about our business, and when the brothers were made cheerful by the drinks, they exchanged hints. I found, however, that their normal relations were not too friendly or sincere.

Michael said: "You understand, you have already begun to do business with Jan and I don't want to interfere. . . I don't want Jan to know that you can buy from me, too. When you come back, you will pass my house. Come in to see me first. Then you will go to Jan's who will not know that you first visited me."

One thing became evident: I had to keep my eyes open. Both brothers wanted to make profit, and neither wanted to reveal to the other how much he was making. I left them and returned to Bialystok.

In the ghetto, life once again became routine. In all the region only Jewish Bialystok remained. There were no longer any Jews in Grodno nor in Krinky nor in Vashilkov, Bielska, Volkovisk, nor anywhere else. The concentration camps, too, had been liquidated. The remaining Jews of Grodno, together with the Niemen factory and Grodno's Jewish police head, Srebrnik, were brought to Bialystok — 500 Jews all told. Remnants came from the towns, people who had fled in time, a Rabbi from one town and some young people from another. The number of Jews in the ghetto grew a little, and this addition apparently filled some of the space left after the killing of 12,000 victims of the first Bialystok aktzia. Once again Jews went to work every day at dawn and wearily returned at dark. Once again there were the long lines along the sidewalks on the aryan side, coming back with hidden milk and lard, alcohol and beer. Spring smiled at us, but we were imprisoned. The Spring of 1943 was beautiful.

At the Yurovieck gate hundreds of Jews milled about, coming home from work in the evening. Every one wanted to be the first to pass the examination, which had become more strict of late. As if there were not enough Gestapo men already, a new tyrant appeared. Once again the infamous name, the Grodno-ite, Streblov. In Grodno there was no longer any work for him; there were no more Jews there. What was he to do, then? By day he roamed the trains on the Grodno-Bialystok line and looked for Jews who had escaped the Grodno inferno, Jews who had dared to remain alive. In the afternoons he came through the ghetto gate in a storm. He came suddenly, and the persecutions began. Streblov had his own style; he distributed his blows in his own way. For a bottle of milk hidden under one's clothing, so many blows; for a bottle of oil, 25, and you had to drink the oil there and then. You also had to drink alcohol, and beer. A Jew caught that way was immediately brought to the hospital. Streblov would come into the ghetto generally on horseback. Sometimes he would order Barash's driver, nodding as usual in his carriage near the Judenrat building, to drive off somewhere. He was the first of the Gestapo men who dared to take away Barash's single symbol of power, his carriage. Streblov would run amok in the ghetto for a few days and then disappear, as suddenly as he had come.

Not satisfied with power and giving orders, he loved the implementation, offering the sacrifices. Young and brutal, Streblov was a child of the "New Germany." Only his family name aroused a suspicion of Russian origin. We determined to get rid of him once and for all. Since my path in any case led me to Grodno, and it was clear that I would have to visit that city more than once in business connected with arms acquisition, I was asked to look around to see what the possibilities were. Implementation, itself, was given to Pinchevsky. Lonchik, we thought, looked less like a Jew than any of the other young people who had come from Grodno. It was clear that we could not deny the Grodno-ites the privilege of repairing their debt to Streblov. We made Jan's house our first place of refuge. It was far from the house to the city, but a safer place could not be found. It was decided that I would leave Lonchik in Jan's house and return to the city that same day, to find a more appropriate shelter closer to the city, and begin to scout Streblov's court. We knew that it was not a job for one or two days and I therefore had to find Lonchik a place to stay for a week or two. It was to help him at first. After he learned something of the practices of the aryan underground he would complete the task himself.

Lonchik's first steps were a difficult test, and who knows what his end would have been if I had not been close by. He was young and straightforwardly courageous. He did not understand that circuitous paths can sometimes lead directly to a great goal. It was his test of fire, and he emerged from it after a few days, a different Lonchik, a new man, with new understanding. His large eyes, always wondering at the chaos of the mad, harsh world, were covered with a thin veil and had narrowed, with wrinkles appearing at their edges. The new Lonchik wrestled with heart and mind to understand the nature of this strange world, to wonder less and persist more.

We left for Grodno on a splendid spring day. I started toward morning with the work brigade, and at the first corner slipped away. At Haska's I changed clothes, put on my sister's big "German" hat, and at eight o'clock went to meet Lonchik. I tried to make his exit easier. He went out with the group of wagoners who left every morning for the freight station, to unload goods from the railcars and carry them to the German storehouses. According to agreement, the Jew responsible for the workers was supposed to look aside and allow Lonchik to get away from the station. When I approached the station I saw Lonchik moving about among the cars. The area was open for passersby; only one side, from which we had come, was closed by barbed wire.

I motioned to him to get away. We had agreed that we would meet at the first corner away from the station, toward Wasilkova, the main street. Haska and I walked along the barbed wire fence and waited until Lonchik managed to take off the yellow patch and get away beyond the cars. But he did not see the proper moment to get away. The matter was very simple: the cars were open on both sides; he could have gone in on one side, taken off the yellow patches and come out a pure aryan on the other. But we couldn't help him with our advice. Suddenly he disappeared, and showed up again without the patches. I left Haska and went to the meeting place.

We made our way safely. I had a travel permit, the old one, on which I had changed the dates. Lomchik did not have a permit, but he was dressed like a young boy. He had the kind of hat that Polish peasant boys wore, and sport trousers tucked into country boots. Before the examination I sat him next to me, supposedly in my care.

"Who is this?" the policeman asked.

"I've taken him to the doctor; he is my cousin from the village," I replied in German. Why not speak German? Here they wouldn't think me Jewish. Neither my looks nor my papers would arouse that suspicion. So that they would not look into my big bag, it was better to speak German. These were only railway police, not the Gestapo. In my elegant bag there was a pistol wrapped in a silk kerchief.

The voyage to Grodno and the exit at the station before Grodno passed safely. It was already noon when we set out on the road leading to Jan's. I didn't want to use the path Jan had shown me because I thought that during the day it was more dangerous than the road. Only suspicious persons went by side road, and it seemed to me that on the main thoroughfare no one would suspect us. We walked along slowly, enjoying the sun and the wind moving the branches of the many trees growing on both sides of the road. We were not alone. Peasant men and women, from the neighboring villages were returning from the city with their empty baskets. Inhabitants of Grodno suburbs were running about on the village side streets branching off from the road to the city. There was movement, and we felt as though we were on a vacation hike, as in preoccupation days on these trips, with the broad fields around us. When we came closer to the village we were sorry that the twelve kilometers were passed, that the spring sun had grown cooler and had begun to set, that the cool, soothing breeze had grown stronger and was whipping my broad-brimmed hat.

We were close to Jan's house; another two, behind them an empty space, and then the hill with the house that was our destination. Suddenly, without our having noticed at all, a German in civilian clothes was in front of us, bobbing a little and calling to his Polish friends from the nearby house.

"Look, look! A little Jew! Come, come, little birds! Did you think you would go by here without my noticing you?"

Some Poles dressed in the uniforms of urban electrical workers or supervisers of public works on the roads came out of the house. Only now I noticed that nearby they were repairing the road. The German foreman and his Polish workers were standing in front of us.

"A Jew, you're a Jew," the German chattered over Lonchik's head. A crowd left their work and came to see the sight. Children stopped playing and crowded around Lonchik. I stood at his side and did not let go.

"You, who are you?" the German shouted at me. "If you are watching him so closely you are apparently also a Jew. You probably were hiding, and now you decided to run away to Bialystok. We know your faces. Every day they come by here. They are trying to escape the German authorities."

There was a tumult all around us. I tried to stand in the middle of the road and prove that I was not Jewish, and that the boy, too, was not.

"How do you know we are Jewish? Who are you? You aren't a policeman."

"Keep quiet, you fresh Jew! Police, police . . . I too am the police, I'll prove that you are Jews. Show me your papers . . ."

"I won't show you any papers. Call a car and come with us to the police in Grodno. There everything will become clear, and there they will find out what kind of policeman you are."

"People, did you ever see so much Jewish nerve? I'm a German and if I like, we will decide their fate right away, and here."

He drew his pistol, but his hands were shaking a little and his feet were wobbly. His tongue, too, got mixed up. He was speaking Polish like a German. Suddenly he turned to me and said in German:

"You understand, little Jew, don't you? You all understand German."

"I do not understand."

"Good, if you say you aren't Jewish we will examine the boy. You know how to examine. If he is Jewish it is a sign that you are Jewish too." I decided, finally, to show my papers. The situation was really serious and it was necessary to immediately adopt any measure possible.

Meanwhile we had both been brought into the house of the village head. I remember a spacious room, larger than the other peasant homes I had seen. The wooden floor was clean, recently washed, and there was a very large stove. Parallel to the stove was a large closet. The closet and the stove formed two ends of the wall. Between them there was a rolled up curtain behind which could be seen a small, narrow room. The room we were in was so large and crowded that I felt as if I had been brought into a courtroom, with the audience as judges. Everyone in the audience held my fate in his hands, and his mood might change if I could find the proper strategem.

I held out my papers. No one wanted to look at them. The German threw them on the table, stood in a corner and shouted;

"Let's get to work! Let's examine him, the little Jew."

He was apparently more interested in the game of examination than in the reason for it.

Some of the peasants tried to use some common sense: "Maybe we'll look at their papers, and if we find that they are really 'ours' we'll let them go free?"

Their voices, however, were drowned by the noise in the room. I looked at Lonchik and he looked at me. The crowd was wild and looking for a sensation, the voices of sanity were drowned out by the brutal cries. I sought some trick, something to say that would feel like cold water in their faces. I tried to appeal to their logic, to threaten them and give us the hope that perhaps we might escape from our predicament. The German, however, dominated the crowd and his half-drunken workers followed him.

"No, we'll examine the boy!"

Nothing had helped, neither my good papers nor my aryan looks nor my somewhat insolent talk. The German and his helpers dragged Lomchik in to the small room behind the curtain. In a moment the bloody game would begin. Everybody was eager to know what was happening. The door suddenly burst open and Jan broke into the room. Everybody turned toward him. Those behind the curtain also lifted it up a little in order to see what was going on in the house, who it was that suddenly began to speak so loudly and convincingly: "Halina, what have they made you — a Jew? Ha ha ha! People, have you gone mad?" Jan embraced me and laughed. I understood that the "examination" in the other room had not yet been finished. They had stopped their work and dragged Lonchik, buttoning his clothes, into the large room.

"So, tell me, who tried to tell such lies about Halina? Let him be brave enough to tell me. Oh, you," he turned to the astounded German. "Come, let's go, what are you afraid of? You'll see who Halina is." He hinted to the German: "Come, and you'll find out; you know me, don't you?"

The room was silent. After the first amazement some of the people began to leave. One of them said:

"I told you that we should examine her papers first."

The German slapped Jan on his shoulder:

"Why didn't she say she was going to see you. I would not have acted that way with her. I would have shown her the way."

Now we were all going together to Jan's house. How had Jan learned of the business, and why had he dared to take such risks for our sakes? Was he afraid that I might mention his name, lead to a search of the mill where the Jews were hiding? Or maybe it was just courage? One way or another I will always remember Jan for that day. How much intelligence and cunning he showed that evening! No one noticed how a bottle of beer appeared on the table, and on the stove in the small kitchen there was the sound of bacon and eggs frying.

Evening came with the shadows of the German, Jan, Lonchik, and my own, moving on the wall. I gestured to Jan to get Lonchik out of the house without the German noticing. I would make sure that he did not sense anything and would not leave in order to tell the police to come and conduct a search. We had to "hold on" to the German.

Lonchik disappeared. Jan went to help him. The German was opposite me, with his shadow, the shadow of a drunkard following him on the wall. The sooty oil lamp gave a dull light. The beer on the table had a nauseating odor. I thought I would choke. The German was thin, his skin smooth and wet, sweating from drunkenness and lust. He did not stop belching, and reeked with the stench of beer. In a moment he would throw up and be sober again. I poured more beer for him and drank with him again, and he watched that I did not pour any of mine under the table. He did not trust me so he poured: "Drink, Halina, drink."

His hands weaved in the air, groping blindly. I found some old, sentimental record. Long live the phonograph! In a hoarse tone it played some romantic songs and we danced, the drunkard and I. It was hot and suffocating in the house, the light poured rays of filth on the ceiling, the walls, the beds in the corners, on the table with the leavings of the bacon and omelets. This night, I thought, would never end. Once again I poured for the German frog, he drank, and so did I. He was stunned when the cold dawn broke. We lay him down in the kitchen in Jan's mother's bed. He slept, snored and muttered fragments of unintelligible words.

The village slowly awoke. A cock crowed, a cow lowed, a door creaked. A bucket was lowered down the well. Jan's household also woke. The first one was his wife, who went out barefoot in the cold spring morning to feed the animals. Jan got up after her. He, too, drank a lot the night before, but his mind was clear. He knew what had happened yesterday. He patted me on the back and said:

"Don't worry, everything will come out all right. I fooled him yesterday, but watch out for him today."

"Where is the boy?" I asked him.

"Out of danger. First I took him to the woods. I was afraid they might make a search. At night, when you were taking care of the bastard, I put him into the mill. Too bad, a young lad, and it's cold at night in the woods. You know how I found you had fallen into a trap? A neighbor came to tell me. He is one of the decent people in the village. Truthfully, however," he whispered into my ear, "I am afraid to keep the Jews in the mill. Good that the matter ended as it did, but some old chatterbox is liable to talk about yesterday's tumult and then they will begin to investigate and ask questions."

Jan's wife brought me water in a pan. I washed, ate breakfast and waited. The shining spring day was in all its full glory when the German awakened. First he did not know where he was. Slowly his memory returned, and a little, weak frightened man appeared. Now he no longer shouted arrogantly: "I am a German!" He looked at me with his small, scared mousey eyes, and began to talk. I listened attentively.

He was a German who lived in Gdansk. That was where his knowledge of Polish came from. He had been a tailor, a simple craftsman earning his livelihood with difficulty. Now, too, his life was hard. He had run a cigarette stand. He was married and had children. He was ill, his strength had dwindled from bearing the family burden for so many years. Now he had been mobilized to supervise Polish workers. The power in his hands was a problem at times; everybody was afraid of him. He was a party member, lived in the city in a nice room, and he sent his salary home. From the Poles he received bacon, eggs, and beer, but he was afraid. He was always a little man and now he was big and important, and that was why he was afraid, of his German masters and his Polish workers. They were saying: "Hitler kaput." What, then, would his end be? Who would worry about him in time of trouble?

I heard the confession of the little frightened soul. How strange that it was to me that he poured out his heart! When the effects of the beer wore off the weakness came. Yesterday's power and domination had vanished and his real fears were disclosed. His emotions had apparently grown so strong that he could no longer help pouring out his heart to someone. I will not deny that his words pleased me, so much so that I invited him to accompany me to the railroad station, since I would have to return the very same day. Jan introduced me to him now as his relative, and invited him to visit once in a while to sip a little "bitters."

In order to let the scandal settle we decided that I would leave the same day. Lomchik would remain in his hiding place until the affair in the village was forgotten. On my next visit I would receive arms. Jan promised a larger quantity of grenades, and a rifle this time. I bargained on the price but Jan promised that we would come to terms:

"First see the goods," he said.

The German accompanied me to the station on his bicycle, in order to remove any suspicions that I was Jewish. Proof — the German himself was accompanying me and exchanging friendly talk. The trip along the road crossing the village was successful. I felt the curious glances of the peasants, heard their whispers behind my back, and knew that I could return to this village; the bridges had not been destroyed.

When I returned to Bialystok and entered our room on 15 Bialostochanska Street, I felt an overwhelming weariness. It seemed to me that my nerves were breaking after the tensions of the past 24 hours. The Vesola Street affair had only just ended, not even a month had passed. And now there had been another failure, and another resurrection, not by using a magic wand or by a wave of the hand, but with great trouble and pain. This time, if I hadn't succeeded, it would have meant the end of 15 Jewish souls, in addition to Lonchik, Jan and his wife, and me.

I locked myself in my room with my nightmares for two days. I could see the dirty lamp, the German's reeling shadow, and hear the worn out songs on the phonograph. I could still smell the nauseating beer, and there was a bitter taste in my mouth. It was all suffocating, even the confession of the frightened little German, dirtied by the blood of his victims. When would this game of hide-and-seek with the enemy end? Was this the part I was to play in our drama until the Gestapo caught me? Was that my only destiny?

Once again Zerah appeared and did away with the pain by berating me gently for my dark thoughts. Zerah also understood what I didn't say. There was no alternative. We had to overcome. The arms were ready for shipment and Lonchik was waiting to carry out his mission. Mottel, too, was waiting for us to get him out of there.

Two days later Lonchik arrived in Bialystok alone. In the village there had been tension. Even previously the villagers had whispered that Jan was doing business with Jews, and after the affair with Lonchik, the danger to the hidden Jews increased. It was hard for Lonchik to stay with them since they complained that he was bringing catastrophe upon them. Since he had no other hiding place he had no alternative but to return to Bialystok. It was a miracle that he arrived safely. He had ridden the train without a permit, under the eyes of the Gestapo and Streblov, its agent, watching the passengers day and night, but he had found a way. He had gone to the Todorkov Station, between Grodno and Kuznica, a small, almost unpopulated station. When the train slowed down a little he had jumped on it and hid, and before it arrived in Bialystok he had leaped off again. Mottel couldn't come that way because he looked too Jewish, and even aryan papers would not help him. We decided to look for some way to reach Jan in order to get Mottel and the arms Jan had promised us.

It was then that we found the German, Kudlashek. What his job was I do not know. It was not a very important one, but he did have a car at his disposal. Kudlashek did not know very much about politics and the underground. He related to Jews as he did to non-Jews, to the extent that he could do good business with them and keep from being swindled by them. We had found the link to him through one of the Communist members of the underground who worked in the textile factory.

I was sent to him as a Pole, an acquaintance of the Communist, who wanted to do business with him. At the first meeting we discovered that he was about to go to Grodno and was prepared to serve me for a small payment if I was going there. I arranged to meet him on Sunday near his office. We were intrigued by the idea of carrying arms in a German car. I didn't speak to him about Mottel for fear that he might refuse to take me as well if I told him in advance that I intended to bring a Jew in his car. Better add to the price at the last moment than to frighten him.

It was a fine Sunday in Spring. We left columns of dust behind us on the road. Kudlashek drove and I sat, in all my finery, at his side. Once we were stopped near a German police station, but the examination was cursory. They looked at the driver's licence and didn't even ask anything. Kudlashek and I were so absorbed in our discussion that the Gemans couldn't imagine that a Jew was sitting in the "Textile Industry" Center's German automobile.

What did we talk about? About matters so banal that it is even difficult to remember them. About the weather and the fine scenery, the spring, and clothing. Kudlashek's face was broad and pleasant. He was wide-shouldered, held the wheel firmly with his big hands. He seemed unpolished, and apparently I made an "excellent" impression upon him, a female speculator doing well in wartime, too, with both Jews and Germans.

We reached Jan in the afternoon. The village was quiet, as it was on every Sunday noon. The car was parked some dozens of meters from the village. No one was to be seen. Jan's house was the last one coming from Grodno, and the first going towards Bialystok. I asked him to wait until I told him my program. Jan was very happy that I came, but my own pleasure was spoiled: I would be able to receive the arms only in another day or two. What was I going to do?

"Wait."

"But the car won't wait for me! How am I going to lose this opportunity, send the car back empty and then have to smuggle the arms on the train."

"It is Sunday and I cannot help you. They promised to give me the arms tomorrow. Maybe you can send Mottel," Jan said. "In that way you will utilize the automobile and we'll find a way to send the arms."

I informed Kudlashek that I would remain in the village for a day or two with my relatives, and if he wanted company on his return trip he could take one of my acquaintances in the village with him.

"No matter. I am going to Grodno now, and I may find out there that I will have to come back here tomorrow, or the day after. In an hour I will know. Your acquaintance can get ready. When I return I will call for him."

Now we had to wait for Kudlashek's return and prepare Mottel for the trip, not a simple matter. How was Mottel to come out of his hiding place in broad daylight? Here again one of Jan's strategems came to our aid. He went to the mill, took off his Sunday clothes and Mottel put them on. His face hidden by Jan's large country hat, he went to the farmer's house. Jan's wife brought the clothes back to the mill, and Jan also came out. We decided to send Mottel's sister, who was blonde and did not look Jewish, by train. Jan took it upon himself to bring her to Bialystok. He would drink with the village head and get a recommendation to the nearby police station from him, in order to obtain a travel permit for his "cousin." Since Jan had promised, I was sure that he would do his part. He might disappoint us in matters of arms, but not where lives were concerned. Jan kept his promise, and a few days later brought the girl to Bialystok. Kudlashek, too, did not fail us. He returned in two hours with the joyful news that he would return the day after tomorrow. His mood was good; the trip to Grodno had apparently been worthwhile.

"Be ready on Tuesday. When I go there I will let you know. You will have another hour or two to finish your business. So, where's your 'cavalier'?"

"Of course," I replied, "we'll come to terms when you come the second time, right? I am prepared to pay right away what is coming to you. Will you agree that on Tuesday I can take some 'goods' with me? You probably have problems with your budget."

Kudlashek agreed, of course, that I prepare some goods. I put the 100 marks agreed upon in his hand and he rode off.

The Jews hiding in the mill were breathing easier. Kachik had gone, Mottel had gone, and the girl would also in a few days. The fewer the people, the less the danger. Summer was coming and they were preparing to go to the nearby woods and take shelter in a hidden bunker for the summer. Jan would bring them food. They did not want to go to Bialystok and had determined to wait out the war in hiding. The cup would ultimately be drunk in Bialystok, too. They were not as fast nor as daring as young people. They also did not want to join the fighters, for which reason Mottel and his sister had returned to Bialystok. I warned them to prepare arms for themselves, especially if they intended to carry out their plan to hide in the nearby woods.

I was going to stay in Jan's house for two days, and I decided to utilize the time and get to Grodno, to look at Streblov's house. It was difficult to accept the idea that because of our failure on that cursed day we would have to give up the whole plan. I also decided to visit Michael, Jan's brother, though he seemed to be less decent, both more talkative and more arrogant. The two were competing with each other. I could be the third, and benefit from it. In searching for arms we were prepared for any route as long as the arms reached faithful hands in the ghetto.

Once again I wandered for hours along Grodno's streets. I don't know why Grodno seemed to be so festive, a discordant festivity, arousing opposition and revolt.

The side street, 11 November Street, named after the 1830 Polish revolt against Tzarism, was so tranquil and clean that it was hard to believe that Streblov, the dregs of the human race, lived there.

The houses were spaced far apart, surrounded by trees and gardens. Somewhere a dog barked, a child cried. The silence was so deep that I heard the echoes of my own footsteps. I turned away from the street and continued along the nearby railway track. However, I returned; I could not take my eyes off the last house with only one sentry standing at the door. From outside nothing could be seen but the trees beginning to bloom and the low, painted fence. The windows were open and the sound of a radio came from within. Here they shot Jews, here they tortured and the battle was still going on.

I saw that the sentry was watching me, since this was the second or third time that I had passed him, and I decided to get away. It was enough for a first visit. This was the street, this the house and near the house, the railroad tracks. Two alleys turned right off the street. Where did they go — to the city or outside? In a little while it would be dark and it was a long way to Michael's. I had to cross the whole city, and the big Niemen River bridge. I passed the beautiful city park. People were strolling, mothers pushing baby carriages. The river was blue against the city, sparkling in the last rays of the sun like a ribbon in a girl's golden hair. This time I did not cross the Niemen by way of the big bridge, where papers were usually checked; I didn't have a travel permit from Bialystok to Grodno and my papers were registered in

Bialystok. The second bridge was a low, wooden one. It shook with every step as if it was about to collapse. I was dizzy looking at the deep water close to my feet. By this bridge I came to one of Grodno's poorer, dirtier suburbs. Here the inhabitants sat in front of their homes and chatted with their neighbors. The narrow streets twisted, with a swampy field behind them. There was a passage to the road through this field. When you came to it you could see from afar a broad area strewn with bunkers. That was the Kielbasin camp. The bunkers were dark, like the vague bodies of beasts of prey.

I arrived at Michael's in the evening. Michael's was also an impoverished village house. Many children, all about the same age, played between one's legs. The woman lying in the bed, recovering from pneumonia, was thin and weak. Only Michael was moving about the low house like a stranger. His tall figure and his robust body seemed out of place. His appearance did not match the poverty in every corner. Michael was eager for liquor, that became evident at once. Without asking me he put a bottle of "limber" on the table, rolled up his sleeves and began to fry flour pancakes in lard. I had no intention of enjoying myself in his company, but he did not yield.

"I have something for you," he hinted, "but we can't talk when we're dry, you understand . . ." *Nie posmarujesz nie pojedziesz.**

I decided to hear what he had to say. While he was busy with the frying I went in to see his wife. A woman is always more intelligent, especially a woman suffering from poverty and her husband's drunkenness.

She poured her bitter heart out to me. He tortured her. For a year they had been living together without his agreeing to marry her. She had been a poor girl, had worked hard in a restaurant kitchen. When she gave him a child he took her to his home but refused to wed. Now the fifth child had come and she was no longer young; she was ill and feared that he might send her away.

"Yes, yes, he can do many things. He can also earn money and maintain his home. He can also help you. I don't know what you want; he didn't tell me; Jan told me something. But he's a drunkard. Be careful of him, Halinka, don't give him money before he hands over the goods. I see you are a good and gentle city girl, be careful of him." In the end she whispered into my ear:

"He sometimes reads the underground papers. I saw with my own eyes. Once he even showed them to me, when he felt good toward me. A paper printed on very thin stock." Her last words were said with a little price.

In the meantime Michael had finished frying the pancakes. In the adjoining room I sat down to eat and drink with him. He drank a great deal, and poured some for me. He was drunk but sly, very careful to see to it that my

* Without grease the wheels won't move.

cup was not empty and that I did not avoid drinking. The liquid seared my mouth and stomach. I ate the hot, fluffy pancakes with a good appetite. The discussion that began with ordinary talk soon turned to weighty matters. His heart softened with the alcohol, he took a thin sheet out of his pocket, laid it in front of me and said:

"Look, Panna Halina, look and see that I'm not just someone from the market. See how much trust they have in me."

Michael did not come to his brother's heels. I trusted Jan because in Jan the good intentions, comradeship and hatred for the Germans were dominant. Michael's character and moral nature wer revealed in his chattering, his drunkenness, his arrogance and most of all his habits.

It was late when I left for Jan's, taking a side road that shortened the distance by four or five kilometers. There was still an hour to curfew. Nevertheless, I had decided not to stay over in Michael's home. He had promised that he would prepare a lot of grenades for tomorrow. How many — he did not know; perhaps twenty. I promised to give him the money after he provided the grenades.

"What, you don't trust me?" He was insulted. I, insisted, however: I would pay only after I had inspected the goods. I knew how to distinguish between old, wet grenades and good ones. And he had better not forget the detonators. I left and hurried to Jan's. The next day Jan brought the rifle, a not very modern French, but with ammunition. It was dirty, apparently it had just been taken out of the ground, and it was rusty, too. No matter, in Kuba's "factory" they would clean and polish it and it would shine once again. I determined to go to Michael's that very same day, to examine the grenades. Instead of the 20 he had promised I found 15, of which only 10 were worth buying. Michael once again tried to get me to drink with him so that he could make me take all the goods. This time, however, I was forceful, and told him that if he sold rotten goods to an organization fighting the Germans he would be punished severely.

"I don't know whether your friends who gave you the underground paper will apply the punishment; perhaps they are your good friends and will therefore take pity on you; but I will submit a report to my commander, and I would not like to say something bad about you. Better for you to keep your good name, and you will eventually win your reward in free Poland."

My words influenced him very little. For a moment he was deep in thought but apparently remembered that the organization in whose name I was speaking was a Jewish organization, and who knew whether any of them would remain alive. I was about to leave with empty hands when he changed his mind and agreed that I take only the ten I had chosen, together with two other, cheaper ones. These were egg-shaped hand grenades of Polish manufacture. I finally agreed, and the shipment was prepared. I packed them in a bag and promised to come with a car the next day to take them. It was not worth the risk of carrying the package to Jan's house. I determined to examine the contents a second time tomorrow, to make sure Michael had not changed the grenades. I gave him half the money — better to be on the safe side.

The next day before noon Kudlashek arrived. I was happy to hear that he and my acquaintance Mottel had reached the city safely on Sunday. I rode in his car to the path leading from the road to Michael's house and we arranged to meet there again at two in the afternoon. In Michael's house I examined the grenades again and wrapped them in my pajamas, and again in a towel, so they wouldn't rattle. I separated the detonators and packed my bag. On top, I put my toilet articles. I paid Michael the sum agreed upon and asked him to prepare something more if he had the opportunity.

Kudlashek arrived on time. The car came just as I reached the road. Everything went off in order. We stopped near Jan's house. I left the bag in the car, of course, not to arouse suspicion. I was afraid, however, that Kudlashek would think of looking in it, so I sent Jan to invite him in for a refreshment. My package was ready, well-wrapped in rags; Kudlashek also received a similar bundle. (We tried to make them look alike) with bacon and a bottle of beer. We hid them in the back of the car; in front — the bag of grenades. There was no point in telling Kudlashek that there was contraband in the bag, too.

On the way, Kudlashek tried to get me to tell him in what I was dealing.

"You're not going to tell me that for a few kilograms of bacon it was worth your while to travel so far and waste so much money on a car. That kind of merchandise can be obtained in the villages nearer Bialystok, and when there is no choice, can be brought on the train. Many are doing it. You must be dealing in precious stones and foreign currency with that peasant, ha! Tell me the truth!"

"Ha, ha, ha, what gave you that idea? Dealing in precious stones.!"

"Why not? Let's go into partnership and I will carry you as much as you like free of charge."

"I will think about it, maybe it is worth while entering into a partnership; you will provide the car and I . . . my connections and sources . . . ha, ha, ha . . ."

I laughed at him and his lack of imagination. The bag lay on the car floor, near the back seat, and the packages were in the back, under the spare tire. If only no search were made . . .

We arrived in Bialystok safely.

"Where shall I take you? Where do you live?"

I could not tell him that I lived in the ghetto, and I wouldn't stop near Olla's with the package. I must not reveal the address. There was no alternative, I would have to carry them through the city streets in the evening. It was good that the sun was about to set. I asked him to let me off at the end of Saint Rocha Street, not far from the iron bridge over the railroad tracks. Haska lived at the other end of the street. We agreed that I would telephone him at his office when I needed him. I wrote his number in my notebook; I had paid him along the way. I took the package and waited for him to drive away. As soon as his car disappeared I turned to Haska's. She had only recently moved in here, in a room in the home of a not-very large Polish family. The unfortunate thing was the proximity of the city court, where there were always neighbors, hanging laundry or just sitting on their doorsteps. They could always see you passing. There was no choice, however; the goods were too precious to be carried about the city streets. I had to wait until dark. Half an hour before curfew I would go to Olla's.

I found Haska at home. That allowed me to avoid the landlady. I was known here as Haska's wealthy cousin from Grodno who had come to visit and care for "Helenka." Haska was very happy that I had come, especially with my packages. Her eyes gleamed. The time had come to use her room on the aryan side. She was very enthusiastic about the trip to Grodno with a German.

"But I don't understand why you don't send me. After all, that is why I am sitting here." Immediately afterwards her mood changed, she remembered that she had been "arranged", not, like me, a free agent. Since that was so every day she had to perform her distasteful work in the home of the cursed Luchterhand family, brutal, anti-Semitic Nazis. She hated them so that she could kill them with her own hands. Suddenly Haska was silent. She realized that this was not the time to talk about her situation. The weapons were lying in her house and on that very day had to be moved to the ghetto.

When we went out, it was already dark. The distance to Olla's house was short. We tried to walk slowly, as if strolling for our pleasure. Haska talked loudly and laughed all the way. Even I found it difficult to recognize the artificiality of her laughter. When we went past the church Haska crossed herself with a seriousness that seemed to me to be a little exaggerated. From afar I noticed two gendarmes. I held the bag, Haska the package. However, we reached Olla's court safely. When we made the last turn into Bialostoehanska Street, where Olla lived and where the high fence was waiting for me, I noticed a patrol coming out of Olla's court directly toward us.

So long as they did not notice us we could continue directly along Poleska Street, but Haska grabbed my bag, and with a mischievous laugh ran ahead and whispered to me:

"Run after me and grab the bag."

Haska reached the entry and jumped in on one foot, laughing loudly, with the bag and package in her hands. The gendarmes looked at her and they too burst into laughter at the sight of the playful blond girl. The court was empty. When we came into Olla's house they could not understand how we had avoided being stopped by the patrol. They had been there that very minute, and all the smugglers had run away and hidden. Haska returned home; there were only a few minutes to curfew.

After curfew I climbed to the roof and jumped into the court beyond the separation between the ghetto and the city. Olla passed the bag and the package to me through the hole in the wall. I blessed Haska in my heart for her courage and fast thinking. I had seen the look of happiness in her face at having been able to deceive the gendarmes and smuggle the arms into Olla's house under their very noses. That expression in her blue eyes left me with a wonderful feeling that seemed to spread all through my body.

Less than a week after my return from Grodno with the goods, Mottel informed me that his sister had arrived in Bialystok with Jan's aid. She had ridden in a wagon part of the way and had walked the rest. Her feet were swollen and painful and she was unable to move.

Two days after I left Jan's house, the whole company had left the mill for the nearby woods. Jan and his wife provided them with food. Only Mottel's sister would come to the village in the evening. She was young, and Jan and his wife treated her specially, took care that she could wash, and sleep well in a bed. One evening returning from her visit to the village, she found the camp was gone. The bodies of the members of her family and her friends lay shot and torn nearby. One hanged from a tree. The bunker had been blown up by hand grenades. She returned to the village and there learned the details of what happened from peasants of the nearby town. A shepherd had noticed the Jews and had told in the village. In the village there had been a traitor who informed the police, who then came immediately. The Jews had attempted to defend themselves, but they had all been killed. The Germans ordered the villagers to bury the dead. The scene was so frightful that the Germans had had to force the men to bury the almost naked bodies. Everything in the bunker had been stolen. Mottel's sister returned to the village frightened and shocked, and Jan determined to move her at once to Bialystok. Since he still did not have a travel permit and time was pressing, and he feared a search in his house, he decided to leave at night, on foot. Part of the way they rode in peasants' wagons but most of the distance they covered on foot. Jan did not come into the ghetto; he returned to his village and informed us that we would have to wait until the matter was forgotten before it would be possible to visit him.

After some time we resumed our visits. Everything was back to normal. We sent one of the girls from the aryan side, Haska or Rivkele, to ask about "new goods." Jan promised to prepare another shipment, and once again we faced the problem of how to move the wares to Bialystok. Mottel gave us no rest. He would go, no matter what! If we did not send him, he would go anyhow. Perhaps something had remained after his parents' murder, perhaps arms? They did have two pistols. And, he just had to visit the place where his relatives and friends had fought against the Nazis.

We yielded to his exhortations. Mottel could not forgive himself for having come from Jan with empty hands, for not having brought any weapon, not even the pistol he had left there. Once again I went to Kudlashek. The central office of Bialystok's textile industry was close to Haska's and Liza's places of employment (the latter had come from Grodno and arranged herself on the aryan side. She was connected with Comsomol circles and had been Haska's schoolmate). A short distance from the textile office was a splendid red building displaying two statues. That was Becker's valve factory. Here the workers had once gone on a hunger strike. Here masses had at one time crowded around the building to offer their aid, food and drink, to workers on a sit-down strike. Here there had once been a clash with the Polish police.

Today the street was quiet. The scattered houses looked like small white boxes in a sea of green. Here only Germans lived. From the street's other end and beyond stretched the famous Bialystok forest, and further beyond the houses was the avenue of the city park.

It was difficult to meet Haska at this hour, when she was working in the SS officers' kitchen. I couldn't signal to her through the window that I would return in an hour, or that I would come to her house. On the other hand, I could go to my sister, who worked opposite and whose German employers liked her. For them I was my sister's friend, rich, of course, the owner of an estate. Anyone who they thought was wealthy was sure of a respectful attitude on their part. They hoped for gifts from the village, were eager for butter, cream, poultry. Prices in the black market were too high, and they were also afraid to go there. They were stingy and avaricious. Sometime, when I came there from "home," I would bring something I had bought previously on the black market. The deal was worth our while. Here I could spend some hours without being noticed. It was worth sacrificing a chicken for an hour of rest.

Kudlashek's office was nearby. There was a telephone in the control shed in front of the building, and it was a simple matter to contact him. We would meet and set the time for the next trip. He did not object to my acquaintance accompanying him again; on the contrary, he did not care. He was prepared to spend some hours in Grodno and to take the traveller from Jan's house when he returned. The deal was made. On the same day, Monday or Tuesday, I was to bring them together near the railway freight station. The meeting place was to be near the exit to the Grodno road and close to where the Jewish wagoners, with whom Mottel was to leave the ghetto, worked. The plan was a good one. I returned to the ghetto in a good mood. If nothing extraordinary occurred Mottel would get to Jan without trouble.

A few days remained until the set date. Our chief concern was money. Our treasury was empty, and Jan demanded foreign currency. Arms were within our grasp and we even had a German automobile, but we were being stymied for lack of means. What funds we received from Barash were ridiculous in view of our extensive need. Jan seemed to us to be a sure source of arms, but an expensive one, that might be closed for lack of wherewithall. I remember the sad faces of our young comrades when we told them that we had a source of arms but no money. On the morrow money began to flow in. "My parents don't need this money for their living," they said.

Other materials were received. Cloth for a man's suit, gold rings, old earrings and some precious stones. Everything was valuable.

When the day came Mottel wrapped himself in the cloth, (Jan would gladly take cloth instead of money), took the foreign currency and left the ghetto with a group of transport workers. The road was safe, we thought. That day Gedalyahu accompanied the wagons as the one responsible for order in the name of the Jewish police. I too left the ghetto to participate in the meeting behind the last barrier. We waited in vain for Mottel. Many Jews were moving about without interference or examination near the storehouses; Mottel did not come. I tried to stop one of the Jews to ask him if something had happened that day. He looked at me and actually spat. It was a Jewish wagoner with his own special style:

"It happened, it happened . . . the devil take them and their fathers' fathers! Such a young boy! Tfu . . . he didn't know what to do and was caught."

It was clear. I felt suffocated. Mottel, the money and the arms . . . And Kudlashek was waiting not far from here. We could not afford to lose him. Perhaps I would go myself, but I didn't have a penny. Who knew how

Mottel would handle himself in the police station. Perhaps they would examine him, torture him. he was a stubborn boy, but who knows?

I found Kudlashek waiting in his car. I acted as if nothing had happened; we would still need him, and I had to have some excuse for Mottel's absence. Kudlashek, however, received me with a smile:

"Actually, I only came to tell you that I can't go today. I have to put the car in the garage for at least two days. You won't be angry, hah? We'll still go, don't be sorry. Are you losing a lot of money because of me?"

I pretended that the delay bothered me, and we arranged that I would contact him by telephone at the beginning of the next week. That day I returned to the ghetto. Gedalyahu immediately ran to the work place to ask about Mottel. One of the wagoners, a sworn friend of Gedalyahu, reported:

"He came to the place, and I wanted to watch over him. I told him that I had heard from you that he had to get away at a certain time and that I would show him how. There was still a lot of time, and he had to act as if he was working in order not to attract the attention of the supervisors and gendarmes. But he was impatient. One of the gendarmes noticed him moving about idly and called him. He apparently did not reply properly, or maybe the gendarme just did not like his face. He began to beat him. Suddenly someone noticed that there was something hidden underneath his clothing. They searched him and found a large piece of cloth underneath his clothes. They immediately took him to the Criminal Police. Who knows if he'll come out of there alive?"

That was the way Mottel left us. From the prison we received information from him that they only found the cloth on him; he had managed to tear up the money and throw it away. The Nazis couldn't charge him with any crime except smuggling cloth. However, since he was young, they tortured him to get him to disclose who his comrades were. He ignored them. They knew nothing about him. He was determined not to remain alive in their hands. "I will try to escape; don't worry about me, take care of my sister."

We hoped that Mottel would succeed in fleeing, but he did not return.

Still, we continued to travel to Jan to buy weapons from him. Our mood improved with the procurement of every additional weapon.

We regretted that our plan to liquidate Streblov could not be implemented. Streblov suddenly disappeared from sight, from Grodno and from Bialystok. It was said that the Bialystok Gestapo had not liked his moving into their realm and interfering with their plans. It was rumored that he had been called to Koenigsberg, or that he had been called to Berlin. In any case none of the rumors was certain, and they added nothing to the plan which we should have carried out.

On Pain and Action

All this time the ghetto underground was still struggling to determine its right path. Revisionist ideas had begun to creep in. After the many failures and sacrifices, there were those from our own camp who began to insist that we change the principles guiding us. And these demands did not come only from uninfluential comrades. One of the complainers was Yandzia.

Yandzia had been taken to a transport, with employees of the factory where he worked. He had been caught in the "Mechanische Tischlerei." One day, before our failures on the aryan side, Rivkele came running with the news that a peasant from Ygnatki, a vacation resort not far from Bialystok, had arrived with a note from Yandzia. He was lying wounded in the peasant's barn, and asked for help. The aktzia in the ghetto was in full force and there was no way to bring Yandzia into the city. We had no safe address, and there were no prospects of finding a doctor who would keep the secret.

The next day, after work, Rivkele went to visit Yandzia. At that time she was living in the attic of the SS doctor in whose home she worked as a servant. Night after night she disappeared from the doctor's house and went to visit Yandzia, even though she was unable to help him. The action was raging in the ghetto, and he lay on a pile of manure, his hand shattered by a dum-dum bullet that had wounded him when he jumped from the train. Yandzia had no alternative but to remain in the barn a few more days. We could not give him any medical aid beyond sterilizing the wound, changing the bandages, and giving him injections against infection. Rivkele demanded that I use the funds I had to save him; I knew that the money would not help him and I insisted that we would need it for other purposes. That was the first clash between the demands of our activities and the efforts to save individual comrades. That dispute was enought to make the wounded man in the barn grow bitter and argue against our strategy.

But it had not begun there. Yandzia later returned to the ghetto and received proper treatment. The beginnings developed very much earlier, in those first meetings in which the decision on the revolt had been made, at the meeting in 6 New World Street. Now the commune was living on

Chenstohovska Street, in a large and comfortable flat. Since that first meeting of the activists in New World Street a whole year had elapsed. Then, too, we had fought against weakness, lack of faith, the alien ideologies urging that we abandon the ghetto, save ouselves, and join the partisans.

The whispering had stopped, the doubters kept to themselves. They seemed to be moving on tiptoe in order not to interfere with the accelerated pace of preparations, the ripening will to fight.

Now, after having survived a difficult test, we faced one even more so; one that would almost certainly be our last. The movement had barely recovered from the blows it had received, and there were comrades who wanted to apply the brakes. They picked at the wounds, looked for sins and sinners, guilt and the guilty. Wherever there was weakness, revisionism also reared its head. Weakness sought justification on ideological grounds, the general good, and concern for the masses.

It was late night. We locked the doors, blacked-out the windows and held a meeting. The tension in the room heightened. The rebels demanded that we stop preparations for a revolt in the ghetto and begin large scale actions to save our comrades: "To maintain the movement, guard the remnants of Jews for tomorrow, for the new day to come, for renewed aliya to Palestine. It would be better to seek ways for aliya and to save people. The most effective way to fight the Germans is to go to the forests. We must stop playing these childish games, the heroism that does not befit public individuals responsible for the fate of the movement and our people. Edek and his comrades' heroic stand gave us nothing, and only cost the loss of the best of our men." That is what the critics argued.

My impatience grew, and I poured out words of fire. Were my charges justified? Surely not. I had known Yandzia a long time as a loyal member of the movement. As a good friend. I knew his deep love for the Jewish masses, his people, for Jewish culture and national revival. I knew his wonderful gentleness, his personal grace, his great intellectual power. Why, then, did I say such things? After all, there were many who agreed with him, even among those who took an active part, sacrificed and fulfilled the orders of the underground. Could I indict them all for treason?

And still, how important was a man's will, how important was his love for the masses, his great concern for the Judaism that was being wiped from the face of the earth without any resistance? What was important was action, what good were the results that would be achieved.

Now the debate became heated and it is doubtful whether the comrades said what they really thought. I had apparently imagined their self-respect; I had gone too far. Perhaps with the enemy at the gates it was not the time for us to take stock. In any case, Zerah and Gedalyau understood the importance of the time better than I. Zerah explained, and argued that there was no other way, that still more failure would occur, that there was no way other than that of complete dedication, that Edek had been right when he had not abandoned his position. Otherwise we would have emerged from the aktzia with the sign of shame emblazoned on our foreheads; we would have demoralized the active ranks, and undermined the trust in us as leaders of a fighting movement. Time and again Zerah spoke. He never tired. Gedalyahu, too, revealed more than normal patience. He did not curse in Russian, as he usually did, at the sight of other comrades' weakness. He did not spit to emphasize his contempt and anger.

The tone changed and instead of ideological attacks, personal charges were leveled; "Chaika, you were responsible (not you alone, but in the main) for the failures on the aryan side. You weren't careful enough about the girls. You should not have sent them out with those papers. You should have better safeguarded their existence with money. They were left alone to their fate. And here, in the ghetto, Chaika should have been with us during the action."

The other comrades were quiet.

My wounded self-esteem needed an answer. I had not asked for a reward for my activity. I had wished only that they respect my efforts. I had always sensed my comrades' sincere concern whenever tired and worn out I returned to the ghetto. Now I really rebelled. I suddenly forgot about the comrades' concern, and felt only the charges being levelled against me. They were totally unjustified, but I had to bite my lips and repress my feelings of personal insult. I recovered. You must not deviate from your proper path, not allow yourself to stoop to petty arguments. Zerah was right; we must not allow the debate to become personal. We must stress the ideological tension concept of the discussion, make it a lodestone for the depressed and the disappointed. From that heated discussion the validity of armed revolt, of the fighting underground leading the way, emerged triumphantly.

I announced that I was prepared to carry out my former duties without acting as the formal head of the movement. This statement fell like a thunderbolt. I would not be telling the truth if I suggest that I made it with an easy heart. I was very much hurt by the terrible injustice of it all and especially by the general silence, and the absence of any general protest that greeted my announcement.

Great events were about to take place in our lives. We were swiftly moving closer to a united anti-fascist front. A number of comrades were removed from all activity, and finally their membership in the movement was also cancelled.

It was morning when we returned to our room in Bialostockanska Street. We still had two hours before our fateful meeting with the Communists.

I stated that I was going to speak for a quarter of an hour on the signicance of the liquidation of the Comintern. My comrades turned to me in surprise.

"I want to convince them that the conclusion every Communist must draw from the Comintern's liquidation must be the establishment of a united front with all existing antifascist forces."

Gedalyahu left for the work he hated. Zerah and I remained in the room. Precisely at eight o'clock Yoshka Kava and Daniel Moshkovich appeared. Daniel's appearance was a surprise, since he had not previously come to political negotiations. Daniel had been especially attached to Edek. We knew his views concerning the anti-fascist united front. We realized that his views were not like Yoshka's. Daniel was more flexible than his comrade. His opinions were not shaped by prejudice; he was more open to the sounds of the new times. Daniel was an activist, but not one of those who formulated the party's political direction. That was why we were so surprised that he attended. The only item on the agenda was the united front.

I had to speak shortly about my attitude toward the matter of the Comintern's dissolution. I spoke for only a quarter of an hour, and my conclusion was that the Comintern had been disbanded, first of all, in order to further the union of the anti-fascist forces throughout the world, especially among the peoples of occupied Europe. The union of anti-fascist forces had to embrace the broadest strata of peoples; the underground had to emerge as a popular national movement. Mass anti-fascist fronts had to be organized. War against fascism was both a social and national war of liberation. All people would have to unify their forces and struggle according to its specific circumstances *in keeping with the composition of its social forces.* The war against the Germans had to be transformed into a struggle for the most vital interests and needs of all of the people. The dismantling of the Comintern freed the hands of the Communist Parties and workers' movements in all countries to develop their own initiatives and their own internal forces to the maximum.

These conclusions were to be prepared by a committee which would publish them in the underground within the next two days for consideration by the cells. The resolutions pertaining to us were also presented clearly. For them to be adapted to our ghetto situation we had first and foremost to achieve the broad anti-fascist front while, of course, carefully guarding our comrades as a fighting force. Second, it provided an ideological explanation for a fighting Jewish organization taking the ghetto as its prime battle front and the Jewish masses as the broad national base, situated in special circumstances and obligating special forms of battle.

Third, we decided that all our practical decisions would be effective to the extent that they would fit in with the general struggle against Nazism in the country and among the people at large, and with the struggle of the forces for progress and socialism in the world as a whole.

Fourth, we decided that the Jewish underground combatting the Nazis, in all its circles and groups, looked upon the battle raging to the east, from Stalingrad to the Arctic Ocean, as our front; the underground's activities were the struggle behind the enemy lines in that battle.

That was the first time that we had ever achieved joint political formulas. It was a gala day in our lives. We saw the dream that we had carried with us from the very first days of the underground being fulfilled. On that day the united front for which we had fought, and which had been the goal of our work since coming from Vilna, began to grow. From that day onward the ghetto and the Jewish masses would be the most advanced front of our war, a bridgehead to living and dying as free men and women and socialists. On that front we would fight for the survival of a suffering people.

Do you remember Kuba, that tall blond, somewhat chubby and deliberate lad? He had been smuggled out of Volkovisk, the action and now he was running the Judenrat laboratories, the shops that repair delicate parts of tools that the ghetto had never seen. There was a night shift whose workers were all underground members, with Kuba its foreman. They repaired the damaged parts of the broken weapons that had been stolen, bought or found, specialized in preparing the metal for our hand-grenades.

We thought that Kuba would work with Franek, but Franek fell in the first aktzia and Kuba was then in the hospital, ill with typhus. He had recovered, and now he was spending his days studying sheets of paper, drawing, planning, calculating, always quiet. He persisted at his work night and day.

One morning, when we came to the commune, Kuba received us with a rare smile. His usually bowed head was raised and he was standing a little more erect. His eyes were alive and sparkling — not the Kuba of yesterday! He pulled us into the adjoining room and showed us:

"This is the detonator! I made it out of a rifle bullet. Any bullet can supply a grenade detonator. Look, it's set in a little and it sets off the explosive. And if one bullet isn't enough, we'll use two bullets. God in Heaven, where was I all the time? Why didn't I think of this before?"

Kuba was ecstatic! His face was flushed.

"You'll see, maybe tomorrow we'll be able to make the final test!"

Kuba was happy, and we were happy with him. The work, however, was not easy and bullets, too, were precious. Of course a rifle bullet was not as valuable as a grenade. Barash was afraid to give us the workshop for the night. The work had to be done in almost total darkness, and in complete silence.

The last trial revealed that the bullet detonator did indeed ignite, but either too far, and the grenade exploded weakly, or not far enough, and the grenade did not explode at all. We could not rely upon tests alone; they were quite expensive. The furnaces had all previously been exploded and our houses, and those of the Dror comrades, were being watched. Every trial, even if it did not succeed, made a suspicious noise. There had already been incidents when the grenades had exploded too soon, and only a miracle prevented the people who threw them into the furnaces from getting hurt. Nor could we afford to waste the precious material lost in these tests.

Kuba and the Communist engineer, Kovadlo, did not give up. He was sure that the last and successful trial was ahead of him.

Now, everything was ready. The grenades lay before us, not one but two. Both were to be tested that night, one by one, for the greater security. The metal gleamed; the incisions were of equal width and equal length, as exact as the machines producing precise parts for German arms could make them. The metal was rounded, as in the German grenade. It was thicker and a little larger. A round, shiny wooden handle protruded from it. It was easy to hold. On the handle was a needle, attached to a spring which was held by a ring. When you freed the safety latch the ring would fall, the spring would stretch and the liberated needle would hit the detonator; this in turn, would ignite the explosives, and the grenade would explode.

We knew we had to be careful not to disclose our arms to the enemy too early. The Warsaw ghetto had resisted, and they would therefore watch Bialystok very carefully. Once, they came to the aktzias as if they were going to a party; those times had passed. Now they were afraid, and very cautious. We had to be careful. The whole underground had been waiting for these grenades for months. They were our great hope.

That night no one slept. We could not even close our eyes until we knew the results. We all wanted to watch, but only Kuba and Gedalyahu would go. That night Gedalyahu was in charge of the section between New World and Polna Streets, with the big park in the middle. Gedalyahu himself would try the grenade. Gedalyahu the policeman, in his policeman's hat, would bring Kuba, under his protection, to the park late at night, during the ghetto curfew. There was a real danger that the explosion might be heard, but it would be difficult to tell where it came from. The park was big and the echo could be deceiving. In any case, there was no alternative. The grenades were waiting for the fighters and the fighters for the grenades.

The night was starry but with no moon. We lay in our beds in the dark waiting for the results. The explosions came, one, and then another, far off and dull, but strong, very strong. Once again the ghetto was still. No one had awakened, no one suspected. A few minutes later Gedalyahu appeared. Quietly, on tiptoe, he stole into the room and fell on the bed. We didn't see his face but we could almost envision his smile and the gleam in his eye.

Gedalyahu turned on his flashlight and a dull light fell on a bleeding finger of one hand.

"What happened?" I whispered, in fright.

"Foolishness. I was hurt a little, I held the grenade in my hand too long. But I did manage to throw it and it exploded wonderfully."

"What about the fragments?

"I'll go to gather them with the use of the flashlight. I'll wait a little until it's quiet. In an hour I have to appear at the police to report the end of my shift. Maybe I'll still be able to gather the pieces and hide them. I'll bring you a fragment. The rest we'll have to collect early tomorrow morning before the workers come to prepare the vegetable garden. Our workers must come to work before all the others. Zerah, you arrange it."

"How is it that you didn't do it before?"

"I didn't want to reveal anything prior to the test. Get Avremel and Lonchik."

That same night Gedalyahu brought us a fragment. The ghetto slept as it did on all nights, and in our room the joy was great.

The next day there were whispers in the ghetto that Soviet planes had come during the night and dropped bombs on nearby army concentrations. Others said that the Germans were conducting maneuvers. Some even had seen with their "own eyes" the destroyed Gestapo building as they marched past outside the ghetto. "Partisans apparently attacked the German guards at night and blew up the building." Those were the whispers, and everybody believed them.

Those were days of hope and good news: while the aktzia raged in the ghetto and the Nazis were "defeating" Bialystok's 12,000 Jews, they lost Kursk, Krasnodar, Voroshilovgrad, Bielograd and more. While the Bialystok Jews were gathering their dead and the ghetto was becoming a graveyard, the Soviets took Rostov-on-the-Don. Then Somy and Rezhev and Viazma were liberated. Do you know where Viazma is? The Jews in the ghetto knew, and they were calculating their race against time.

In April we learned that the Soviet army had intensified its mass air attacks against enemy concentrations. The Soviet bombings were coming closer every day. We heard that 500 planes had bombed Oriol. We marvelled: 500 planes at one time! The news spread quickly and strengthened our resolve to fight against time. We might still manage! Kiev was in flames from the bombings, as was Polotzk, Briansk, Smolensk. How far is it to Smolensk? In any case Smolensk is much closer than Stalingrad. The tovarischis were not wasting bombs, not uselessly risking their planes and pilots. If they had decided to bomb it was a good sign for us and bad for the Germans. Jews spoke of it in the factories, whispered about it in the street, passed it on. Jews scratched their heads and deliberated: "Look at the Soviets, see how much they suffered, how many were killed, how many defeats and they still did not yield. Now they are winning. What wonders can happen! You can rely upon the Soviets."

April passed and May came, with its high hopes. It was Spring again, and then Summer — the Summer of 1943. February's blood was washed away in the spring rains and the sun dried the puddles. Thé ghetto was quiet. Every day workers went to their shops and factories; every day Jews went out humbly to serve the Germans.

Hatred burned in the depths, embers in the ashes. It flourished and ripened in the secrecy of cellars and in the dark nights. It was the first of May. Tens of thousands of factory workers struck that day, secretly joining the ranks of the millions who had chosen that day as the day of freedom and justice for the working man and that day every Jew working in a German factory considered himself a fighter. The resistance to fascism spoke out wordlessly from every stationary machine, from every corner of the silent, sun drenched factory halls. That day people spoke in whispers, quietly, as if inspired. Workers who had not been organized into underground cells, people who had not been recruited for the struggle, Jews who had no weapons in their hands and had not been privileged to take part in the organization of the Jewish resistance, they too expressed solidarity with the fighters. They would not sew clothes for German soldiers in Waxman's factory that day, they did not work at the lathes and carpentry tools of "Stephan's" factory. No chemical production, no leather products, no textiles. It was May First. The ghetto was on strike. Festively, the workers came to the factories, and if they could not celebrate the day like free men they would observe it by sitting at their motionless machines. The foremen shut their eyes. They pretended not to notice that the machines had stopped, that today there were no goods to be shipped. They only pleaded with the workers to be careful, to post guards to see whether a German control was approaching, and if so - to start the machines at once. There was a new spirit in this submissive ghetto.

Our cells in the factories did not number in the thousands. We were satisfied with hundreds, and it was the influence of these, their latent but felt presence, that gave the Jewish masses the courage and the strength to celebrate May First of 1943.

May First, 1943. It followed Gedalyahu and Kuba's successful efforts at night in the park on behalf of the Jewish underground.

Then came other important events, presaging evil.

It was a summer afternoon and people with their burdens were streaming, as usual, out of the ghetto through the gate on Chista Street. For us it was an ordinary work day. Kuba and his assistants were busy preparing for their night's work in the shop, Zerah was occupied with organization affairs, making plans for meetings of the cells in the section under his command. Gedalyahu was running about the ghetto looking for arms, and I was busy with the negotiations between the groups.

Suddenly there was a tremendous explosion. It was so violent that houses on the other side of the ghetto shook.

The police began to run in the direction of the explosion, to Polna Street. Thousands of people ran into the street, seeking to find out what had happened. In less than a quarter of an hour the police began to block off all thoroughfares leading to Polna. When we all met in Chensohonska we were shaken. We gathered as quickly as we could.

The commune was close to Chista Street, and we were sure that the explosion had occurred at our place. However, nothing happened there, no explosion, and the police were not surrounding the house. Instead, a whole house on neighboring Chista Street had been destroyed. It was a wooden one; at the bottom there had been a bakery, and on another floor above, were two small, poor flats. Now nothing remained but one wall, dangling in the air, and the remains of a white stove gleaming in the sun.

The police blocked the approach to the house and dispersed the crowd. Firemen arrived. It was said that people were buried under the ruins. An hour later Gedalyahu informed us that a young man belonging to Judita's group had lived there. He and his comrade were shortly to leave for the forest, and they had dismantled two grenades. They had apparently wanted to practice the hand movements and one grenade had exploded. The second was detonated immediately afterwards.

Both men were blown to bits.

Dibos and Klein were said to be in the ghetto already, and the Gestapo was called in to investigate. The whole ghetto was waiting for the verdict. Some Jews were venting their wrath on the crazy young people who would bring catastrophe upon all with their stupid games with arms. Some had already gathered their children and hurried to their hiding places. There were also Jews who were deeply worried by what would happen if the young people were caught. Some mourned the two young victims who had wanted to kill Germans, and had killed themselves instead.

Barash was seen leaving the ghetto, then returning. He was very busy, apparently trying to smooth matters over. Once again he would use the Judenrat purse to try to save the ghetto from collective punishment.

The underground cells were put on alert, waiting tensely for new instructions. The arms stores were examined once again and concealed even more. It was assumed that searches would be made. Some comrade thought that the explosion would hasten liquidation of the ghetto, others felt that before the general liquidation the Germans would want to do away with the armed resistance. All the assumptions were reasonable; the weapons had to be kept well-hidden, but still easily available in time of need.

Once again I was asked to meet Barash. It was two days after the explosion; Barash certainly knew something. I visited his home and he agreed to meet me that very evening. I realized that he placed great importance on this meeting. I suspected that he would question me about the explosion. He would certainly want to know who and which organization had been responsible for it.

I found him and his wife tranquil as usual. She now had grey streaks in her hair, a sign that she was not really so calm. I was surprised to hear the words she whispered into my ear when Barash left the room:

"Maybe you can help me? I want aryan papers and some address outside the ghetto, so that I can flee with my son in the event of liquidation. I cannot help Barash any longer. He is going to believe until the end that it is possible to save the ghetto by negotiating with the Germans."

Barash returned, and the discussion stopped. The situation must be bad, I said to myself. Barash had apparently not convinced the Germans. He had not succeeded in buying new promises about the ghetto's continued existence after the explosion.

Barash, too, surprised me:

"Well, the danger has passed. I've succeeded. I convinced them that a grenade the Soviets had left behind and with which children were playing had exploded. I convinced them that two Soviet officers had formerly lived in the room where the explosion took place and what they left behind had led to the death of two children. I smoothed out the whole affair. Of course, I had to pay. I already knew when and how I can "give," and they like money. Even the best of them. Klein, too, took a bribe this time. I am sure you will not tell anybody, not even your best friends. You cannot imagine troubles you caused me. But what am I going to do with you? I have to take care of you. Your youth — the best we have."

Barash really believed that he had successfully explained away the matter with his naive story, and that there would not be an *aktzia*.

Only a few days passed before we were faced with another difficult trial. One morning of that same month of May we were informed that a gendarme had been killed on duty near the Juroviecka Street gate. Street movement was stopped for many hours during the day. Again there were investigating committees, and Jewish eyes followed Barash's carriage flying toward the fence on Yuroviecka Street, and back. The underground cells were mobilized and put on a state of emergency. Gedalyahu and I ran around for hours, trying to find out what had happened that night. We had a terrible feeling that we had lost command over what was being done in the ghetto. We had no control over underground forces that found arms, and acted independently causing great damage. Anarchy seemed to be negating all our plans and efforts.

The secret of the attack near the gate was revealed that afternoon. The Communists reported that a group of 16 of Judita's people had decided to leave the ghetto for the forest. They met a patrol, a short struggle ensued and one of the gendarmes was killed. The group had been compelled to return to the ghetto.

That very day we decided, together with the Communists, that they had to bring Yudita and her group back into the ranks of the organization, within the framework of the A Front.

Meanwhile, the tension in the ghetto remained high. Mordechai reported that Barash was seething with rage, but was trying to smooth the matter over. He was using his old reliable methods.

In the morning I visited him. This time the meeting was in his office. His mood was good, he even joked and tried to appease me since out last meeting was quite disappointing.

"Yes, yes, I know, it's not you but the Communists. And why shouldn't you cooperate with them? Hah? It would be good if one of them came to me, of course together with you or Mordechai. Why are our forces so divided? Why don't you organize so that you can control all of the groups? If you and Mordechai represented all of them I would be more relaxed. You are more responsible. In general, I believe that it would be worthwhile to bring the Communists into your work; they do have good people."

Barash's insistence that we cooperate with the Communists did not surprise me. He had hinted previously, but I pretended not to understand. I was pleased that Barash did not know the true situation, that his knowledge of our organization was so vague. From his questions and ignorance about the Communists he sometimes seemed to me to be pretending only in order to find out more.

The matter was clear this time, and Barash seemed to be interested in contacts with the Communists. I replied that I did not know whether it was the Communists who had committed the act. After all, it was well known that there were armed groups among the refugees from the neighboring villages and we did not know what they were really doing. Barash, however, held to his own view: he insisted that he knew for a fact that last night the Communists had wanted to leave the ghetto and go to the partisans.

Barash went on to say that this time, too, he had succeeded in convincing the Germans that it was not Jews who killed the German. He had produced "facts" that the man had been killed by an armed group of Poles who had sought to enter the ghetto to carry out a robbery. When the Germans appeared they were shot at. What these "facts" were I did not want to know. I knew "facts" that rang with the sound of money, the one language that the "best" of Barash's Germans understood.

The days passed with a series of wracking events. One day something in Vysoki Stochek, a Bialystok suburb, the Germans caught two Jewish men and brought them to the ghetto gate on Chista Street, where they were searched. Arms were found on one of them. When his comrade saw this he drew his own gun and shot the German, and then committed suicide. The first exploited the confusion and tried to escape, but was caught with arms in his possession.[30]

After a time it was learned that the two men were from Grodno. No one knew their names. They had apparently hidden in the neighborhood of Grodno for a long time, and were determined to get to Bialystok with their arms. The survivor was shot and both bodies were brought for Jewish burial in the ghetto graveyard. Wall announcements declared that two unknowns had been shot near the gate while trying to smuggle weapons into the ghetto.

Someone spoke a few small words: "They fell in defense of Israel's honor." The funeral ceremony was not public, but many Jews assembled in the cemetery to honor the unknown heroes. They did not die anonymously and abandoned.

The Germans concluded from all this that there were arms in the ghetto. They knew and kept silent, and life moved on as usual. No special punishments were imposed. One day the Germans began to repair and straighten the fence.[31] The Jews looked upon this as a good omen, a sign that the ghetto would live for a long time. Otherwise,what point was there in repairing its borders? According to the new plans the ghetto was supposed to take the shape of a square. A German standing at one corner would then be able to see the whole length of the area, to the next corner.

They could repair the borders and the fence today; if an order came tomorrow to annihilate the ghetto, it would be done. Order had to be maintained even on the ghetto's last day. Such a task was the responsibiliy of the local authorities, the SS, the police, and the regional "Zivilvervaltung." They would have to report to their superiors. They were required to detail all their activities in order to justify being in the rear, demonstrating their obedience to their superiors and their devotion to the war effort. Thus a single soldier could guard the old winding fence between the ghetto, and the aryan side could be freed for the front. As for the Jews, order would also be established among them and then would no longer be able to smuggle all kinds of contraband.

The streets hummed with activity as usual. It was a summer afternoon, on Fabryehna Street, known for its hospital. People came and went; there was a lot of movement.

It was one o'clock. The two Yudkovsky brothers and Zviklish, the ghetto informers and Gestapo lackeys arrived at the hospital entrance. Perhaps one of their friends was a patient in the hospital.

They had been watched for days. For days the rope had been tightening around their necks, until they were caught in our trap. They could no longer escape. Natek Goldstein was dressed in the overalls and hat of the city electricity workers; blond, fair, he looked like a handsome Pole. He fired and after him two others, Marck and Marylka, of the Communists "aryan" group, shot and ran. Yudkovsky fell on the spot, and Zviklish tried to get away. He ran zig zagging like an expert. However, he too was hit and fell. One of the Yudkovsky brothers was badly wounded, and lay on the sidewalk. The other had fled, and was apparently hiding. The streets suddenly became still, as if the entire ghetto were holding its breath. The "aryan" in the electric and railroad workers uniforms disappeared. It was said that the Polish underground had decided to take its revenge on the traitors and Gestapo lackeys, since it was well known that more than one Pole had been betrayed by them to the Gestapo. "They were Poles," Jews said, and the rumor took wing: Poles had killed Zviklish and badly wounded one Yudkovsky, while the second had managed to escape and was in hiding. Together with the concern, there was some joy and satisfaction.

The Jews learned from experience. One German had been killed near the Juroviecka gate, another one near the gate on Chista street; arms had exploded in the ghetto, and not a single Jew had been executed in return. Would there, then, be punishment for the death of two Jewish traitors? Jews were hanged in the ghetto and their bodies had swung over the slimy Bialka River for half of a kilogram of seeds they had taken from the oil factory. Now, after the events on Juroviecka and Chista Streets, where Germans had been killed, nothing had happened! Not a single Jew had been harmed. Well, in any case we were lost, let us at least live without traitors and bastards.

Yudkovsky's body was put into the ghetto prison; the wounded Yudkovsky was brought to lie there, in what the Jews called "Sing Sing." That is what Barash had decided, apparently in order to protect him. The second Yudkovsky came of his own free will; he had not found a hiding place in the ghetto. He was frightened, and imagined that in every house, even in those of his most loyal henchmen, an avenging man was waiting.

We decided to leave the wounded Yudkovsky to die alone. Gedalyahu was told to convince the second, healthy Yudkovsky, to go for a doctor in the middle of the night. It was dark and the avengers waited along the road. Would Gedalyahu succeed in getting Yudkovsky to go out, or would he be afraid and refuse to leave?

Gedalyahu, however, found a strategem. That night he was not working in the ghetto prison. He was well known to the police. Many of them, especially the younger men, had learned to listen to him and to obey his orders without hesitation, though he was not an officer. There was no written order anywhere stating that the healthy Yudkovsky was to be sent for a doctor from the "Linat Zedek" hospital, but it was still carried out. A few minutes after twelve, as agreed, Yudkovsky left the prison and began to make his way toward Roshanska Street. He crept alongside the houses and watched all sides. He walked in the shadow of buildings, jumped from one court to the next, and waited. He clung to the wall, and then he would take a few steps . . . He wanted to see but remain unseen. Now he had come halfway safely. So far, no one had been waiting in dark for him. He began to walk with greater confidence. Suddenly he was pulled into a court, and blows were rained upon him from all sides. He fell, and the attackers disappeared. He tried to arise but he was in great pain. Perhaps he could get to "Linat Zedek" and get help there? Once more he began to walk, drunkenly. Once again he was pulled into a court and there were more blows. This time someone stuck a knife in his back. They were quiet, there was no need to waste words. He only tried to escape. When he reached "Linat Zedek" they called the police from the nearby Kommisariat. Gedalyahu was among them. Yudkovsky looked at the policemen, sure they would help him; after all it was their job to maintain order in the ghetto. The police too had always been his partners. This time everything had changed. They looked at him, but nobody came to his assistance or even offered him a cup of water. No one called the commander, the Judenrat officers, or the Gestapo. They did not call the doctor. Where were all the "Linat Zedek" doctors? The policemen stood around him staring, and asked: "Who did that to you?" and "Why?", while he was on the verge of losing consciousness. He had been stabbed in the back a number of times and no one knew whether the knife hadn't been rusty. He was wavering between life and death and there was no one to help him. And he was returned to "Sing Sing." He and his brother were turned over to the Gestapo.

A few days later both were shot. The Gestapo didn't want to care for their wounds; apparently it wasn't worth their while. Thus the last of the traitors were liquidated.

"We need arms," called the commanders of the underground. "Give us arms," echoed the fighters in the cells. Weapons were demanded by the ghetto inhabitants, both the youth and the adults who sensed the approaching storm. They were also demanded by the refugees from the smaller towns who had found temporary refuge in Bialystok. The crowds in the streets returning tired and loaded down toward evening from their work outside the ghetto all sought weapons.

Do you remember the court of 63 Shenkevich Street? The court bordering the ghetto? Do you remember the wonderful tree whose branches were the ladder for daring arms smugglers? Beneath the trap was a hidden passage, nearby, number 61, also bordered on the ghetto. The Germans had begun to align the borders but they moved slowly; they were in no hurry. The work had to last a long time for those sons of SS and Gestapo notables, and they therefore had not yet reached these courts. In the court of Number 61 there was an interesting German institution, the Beutelager, a storehouse for loot, where some Jews, mainly machinists, worked. They helped the Germans polish and repair the accumulated objects and prepared them for use. Weapon parts lay all about. The work was not very intensive; the Germans in charge here, too, had a lot of time. Good weapons were lying about, unused. But exemplary order reigned there. Every weapon had its tag on which was written in black and white: taken as spoils on . . . in the battle over . . . village. Of greatest interest were the new inscriptions, not from 1941 but from 1943. These weapons had been taken in battle with partisans in the environs of Bialovez near some village or other, or the environs of Augustov, in the spring months of 1943.

Our plan was both daring and simple: expropriation! Nahum was asked to prepare the operation. He made molds for the keys, cast them in the ghetto, in our shops, and went at night with a group of five persons through the fence into the court of Shenkevich Street. The storehouses were guarded, of course, but anyone who knew the way also knew how to get around the guards. Nahum Abecvich was not a member of a fighting cell, but he served the underground. It was he who led the group that night. It was a mixed one. We sent Avremele, Gedalyahu, and Ruvchik of Dror, who also had a police hat, to aid the operation and secure the ghetto rear.

It was a quiet, hot moonless night. Streets were still. Only in the underground rooms in the ghetto were there some people impatiently waiting.

They returned, according to plan. Twenty-three "pieces" of long weapons (rifles, etc.) were brought into the ghetto.

It was then, at a modest celebration in honor of the occasion, that I came to know Marylka. We had met many times, sometimes in the ghetto, sometimes outside, in the company of my Communist acquaintances.She had a gentle, young face and acted like a veteran Polish working woman. But she was not Polish, she was slightly stooped, her long hands keeping with her short height moved nervously. Her face was child-like with bright eyes, smooth, white and soft skin. And her short hair, cut straight all around, was the color of flax. Gay and joking, laughing in a loud voice, she spoke Polish accented with Lodz Yiddish. The plaything of all the comrades, the object of their special affection, she was the chief courier between the partisans and the group in the city. All along Marylka would walk tens of kilometers at night, along secret paths, to contact our group and to seek new contacts with non-Jewish underground partisan groups. I also learned that she was smuggling arms into the ghetto. Daniel introduced her to me as a colleague by profession.

We became friends. We rarely met in the ghetto. Marylka's tasks were limited to the aryan side and the forests, while I was busy inside the ghetto. Nonetheless, our friendship ripened. We met later in circumstances neither of us had foreseen.

After that shipment there were others, smaller, but sometimes more important. At the end of Ogrodova Street, bordering on Shenkevich was a building that belonged to the Gestapo. Nahum was transferred to work there, to repair locks and the like. We decided that he and another comrade would take a machine gun out at night. Nahum made one condition: he would hand the machine gun over to the organization, but he must get it back to use at the beginning of the aktzia. We agreed.

The path was not smooth this time. They had to sneak out of the ghetto not to a neighboring court, but to one some distance from the fence. The building was nearby, but it was necessary to cross Ogrodova Street where German institutions were located. Twice the two had to retreat; the third time they succeeded in getting behind the building, and through the back entrance whose keys Nahum had, to remove the weapon.

That was one of our most daring "expropriations."

The number of weapons in the ghetto grew. Kuba complained that he could not handle all the material he was given to repair. He lacked expert assistants. Young Meir Lach, who worked with Kuba day and night, could not make up for the lack, and Franek, who could have been his chief assistant, was no more. We decided to increase Kuba's workers. Meanwhile many guns waited to be repaired.

The Judenrat shops were not the only ones utilized by the underground. The clothes stores were also at our disposal. The groups going to the forest wore out their clothes quickly, the shoes fell from their feet and the wetness soaked into their bones. The lack of necessary tools and medicines was also very troublesome. We could not demand that they manage as best they could by themselves. The villages were strange, their weapons were meager and their experience inadequate. Despite all our opposition to making the ghetto the main supplier of weapons and other needs, we had to take care of the groups.

Then the Judenrat storehouse was opened wide to us. That didn't happen by itself; the storehouse manager opened it. She was a short, black-haired, and very energetic woman, with wise, black eyes. She had been a Hebrew teacher in the Tarbut school and Sheine knew her. Apparently they found themselves to be sisters in outlook, although different in habit and social origin. Sheine introduced her to us. She did not belong to the ranks of the fighters but she too fought, the unknown mother caring for all the Jewish partisans whom we sent from the ghetto to find their way to the underground in the forests.

Mordechai — Last Days

The united front in the ghetto began to take shape. We continued to look for areas of joint action, with new problems arising from time to time. First we found it difficult to come to an agreement on the functions and the scope of joint activities. There were differences of opinion between Mordechai and the Communist leaders. The latter envisioned the joint organization acting only within the ghetto, while the aryan side and the forest would remain separate fields of activity. Even more than Mordechai, we disagreed with that approach. We believed that it diminished the capacity of the united fighting front to act, and clipped the wings of our fighting organization. In particular, we saw that our Communist comrades had not yet completely liberated themselve from old concepts.

We saw no reason, for example, for Dror members not to be part of the partisan groups sent to the forest in order to strengthen our fighting capacity there. We considered it very dangerous for every party to send its own groups to find their own way; we felt it divided our forces, and could attract the attention of the enemy. Planning would avert superfluous searches and unnecessary battles. The character and nature of the fighting organization, and its very definition of itself as an inseparable section of the Soviet front against fascism and Nazi Germany, were unquestioned. Even the non-socialist groups adhering to the B Front, like the Noar Hatzioni and even the few Bund members, did not oppose that reasoning.

I remember Mordechai then. He agreed to the separation of institutions and authority within the united front over our vigorous protests. Mordechai was in a great hurry, as if he already felt the end approaching. We wondered about him; Mordechai who was usually obdurate only when he suspected that someone wanted to damage his honor, or the honor of his movement and the cause he represented, now yielded on so important a matter of principle. The Communists, stubborn stand aroused the suspicion that they had not shaken off their distrust of other movements, and their preference for the forest as the battle front left a feeling of bitterness.

Mordechai, however, had only one argument: "I don't care about the forest; the main objective is that we succeed in uniting within the ghetto." I still remember the lesson he taught, his single slogan: "After fulfilling our duty in the ghetto, if we remain alive, we must go to the forest to continue with our vengeance." Positions in the forest were important, then, and they necessarily had to be made ready and strengthened. Mordechai knew that we had to send people to reinforce those positions so that they would be able to absorb those remaining alive "after fulfilling their duty in the ghetto."

What had happened to him to make him change his mind? I saw him in those days, going about in his high boots, dressed in a black "stalinist" suit, his trousers tucked into his boots and a pistol in his pocket. There was a different fire in his eyes. His enthusiasm was different, and so was his attentiveness. His eyes were black in a different way, too. What had happened? Warsaw! That was the answer. Warsaw was calling to him, the Warsaw that was no longer was calling from every corner, from every crack in the wall, and every stone in the street. The Warsaw revolt had brought an end to everything, to all his comrades, his movement, his sweetheart, everything that was precious to him. And the Warsaw revolt called out for one in Bialystok. "No matter what happens, we must first of all make sure of the revolt in the ghetto," was what Mordechai thought, and the reason he agreed to the limited program proposed by the Communists.

I remember our last meeting with the Communists. It was a beautiful summer day, before noon. In the morning rain had fallen and afterward the sun shone. The side street was removed from the tumult of daily life; it was an alley with a dirt path instead of pavement, and some scattered wooden houses on either side.

I can also recall the street named Zytnia. We had set a new address for our meeting; we thought that we were being followed. True, there were no longer any Nazi agents in the ghetto, but we thought that the Germans might have succeeded in recruiting new ones among the allies of the deceased traitors, the Yudkovsky brothers and Zviklish.

We met, and attempted to achieve a final formulation of the political and organizational program for the Jewish anti-fascist organization in the Bialystok ghetto. Sitting with us were Daniel, Kuba Yakobovica, and Yoska. They were the new heads. Daniel attempted to draw a preliminary and temporary map of the scope of the joint activities that would deal only with the ghetto, and might be expanded in the course of time to include the forest. Yoshko was opposed. We told them in Mordechai's name that he had not seen this problem as a reason to hold up the establishment of the united front. We told them that Mordechai agreed to any ideas that would provide a practical basis for the establishment of an anti-fascist front for the armed defense of the ghetto at the time of its liquidation. That statement was readily adopted. More difficult was the battle over the front's organizational form and and the composition of its staff. The Communists insisted that they deserved 50 percent representation in all bodies! The general staff and the various committees would be formed. Our view was that these groups should be set up on the basis of the equality of the two fronts. Since Front B was composed of more groups than Front A, the deciding principle must not be the number of members in each group which, in any case could not be verified now, but equality. We did not come to an agreement at this session, but decided to call for a meeting of all the groups in both fronts in order to sum up and clarify the principles behind the formation of the united front.

The general meeting of the representatives of all constituents was held a few days later with the participation of Dror. The speeches that day were not important; what was important, however, was the festive atmosphere prevailing around the set tables, covered with white tablecloths (or perhaps sheets). We had a cold sweet drink that was sold in the summer at every ghetto kiosk. A barrier had been removed. The ice melted. This time we did not cut the meeting short, and we did not limit the speeches. No agenda had been prepared in advance.

Mordechai in his role as host was gentle, smiling and extremely courteous. He was speaking for all of us, speaking of our fondest aspiration. ". . .That we have come to this time," all our eyes made the blessing, as did the pressed hands, the talk.

It was a great hour of inspiration in those dark days.

At the end of the meeting the Communist representative arose and announced that from that day onward he was also representing all other groups that had left the Communist organization. That was important news for us all. Unity was complete, then. The meeting ended and we separated, each to perform his own work.

Those were also great days. The Soviet offensive on the Oriol front was making great progress. For two years there had been war between the Soviet Union and Germany. Now, after two years of fighting, of defeat and retreat, the Soviet army was returning as the conquerer, moving forward triumphantly. How could our hearts not sing with joy?

And then, suddenly, other surprising news. The birds sang it, children played it as a game. In the past, ghetto children had acted the role of Melamed who had been hung after the first aktzia for pouring sulphuric acid on the Germans; now they were playing Mussolini. They organized demonstrations in the ghetto's crowded and filthy courtyard and shouted: "Down with Mussolini, down with the Germans, down with fascism!" They knew exactly why they were doing it; that was what Italians were shouting in northern Italy. Mussolini had disappeared, fled. Who could believe it? Mussolini had fled!

There were many more meetings, and more negotiations. In the end the committees were elected and went into action: financial, arms, and political committees. The command staff was formed. Zerah and I were elected by our comrades: Zerah for military planning and I for general affairs.Kuba opted for the arms committee. The Communists sent their key people. Daniel was chosen for the military planning committee and Zerah was very happy with his selection. Zerah then commanded a sector in the ghetto; from now on he would command the sector as a whole, not only Hashomer Hatzair and the Communists. Daniel was to be deputy commander, Mordechai's second in charge. Mordechai was the commander.

The Communists delayed a long time before agreeing but finally did and the institutions, the staffs and the commands slowly fused. The cells remained as they had been, but were put under their sector's joint command. There were three sectors, two in the urban part of the ghetto, west of Yuroviecka, one east of that street, in the ghetto's suburban section.

Zerach commanded the sector including Bialostochanska, Polna, Chenstohoska to Novy-Swiat. Daniel commanded the second one, south of Novy-Swiat, and Ruvchik from Dror commanded the third sector. During these last days a joint training course was conducted for the cell commanders in Mordechai's apartment, which stood alone at the edge of the ghetto.

The house had moved from the ghetto to the aryan sector after the border rectification, and except for Mordechai, who had to leave it in a few days, no one remained there. We utilized the empty house to teach the use of all kinds of weapons; street fighting, in accordance with plans that had already been worked out by the staff, and sharpshooting. Someone discovered a wonderful way to dull the noise of shooting. We shot into sandbags, without live bullets. Only a distant, dull sound reached the outside.

At the end of the course Mordechai found a deserted room at the other end of the ghetto, on Polna Street. Mordechai hastened to leave his former room for another reason as well: there was a rumor in the ghetto that two sacks of sugar had been stolen from the Judenrat storehouse at 6 New World Street. The Judenrat was looking for the thieves, and Gedalyahu and Ruvchik brought the information that Barash had ordered the police to arrest Mordechai Tenenbaum. Barash thought that it was he who had organized the theft from the storehouse for the benefit of the underground, and he would have to be punished. Ruvchik said that Barash also intended to hand him over to the Germans. Mordechai had recently demanded that Barash hand over the Judenrat treasury to the underground. Barash had not said yes or no, and now this had happened. Mordechai hid for a few days until he found a new underground room in another section of the ghetto. Our relationship with Barash deteriorated, however, and almost all our contacts with him were cut off. Now it had become patently clear: every time Barash had to choose between the underground, of which he called himself a friend, and his filthy service to the Germans, he chose the Germans.

The sacks had been stolen by the Revisionists for the general staff fund. It was found, however, that instead of sugar, they had stolen two sacks of salt. The storehouse managers were sure that sugar had been stolen, because who would be supid enough to steal salt? That was the reason for all the tumult. When the truth was discovered, the storm settled and Mordechai once again appeared in the ghetto streets. His connection with Barash, however, was not renewed.

During these last days of the ghetto something else occurred to shock us. We had divided our forces earlier at the beginning of summer, immediately after the first *aktzia*. Every position was precious and there was not one we wanted to or could abandon. Our ranks had thinned, through sacrifice and failure. We had, therefore, decided to divide our forces in the most rational way possible. We also decided to divide the leadership. The principle was that the cells would remain in the ghetto to fight; we would send to the forest only one more group, of five to seven persons, headed by Gedalyahu. Only when the united front was finally established and we received a few arms did we decide to implement the decision and send Gedalyahu and his group to the forest.

We equipped them as best we could. We stinted on arms, and equipped only some of them. The accepted principle was one-third with arms. That one-third itself would try to obtain additional arms in the course of its activities.

They made their way successfully; the contact found them at the agreed upon place. However, when they reached the camp they were ordered to leave. They would not be received without guns. Gedalyahu tried to resist, but he also knew how to obey. He returned, and determined not to go again. He too believed that arms should not be taken out of the ghetto. Those going to the forest had to receive some aid from the ghetto — and that was one gun for every three men.

Gedalyahu was angry: "Listen," he warned us, "even now they are not relating seriously to the revolt in the ghetto. Even now they look upon the war in the ghetto as some secondary action to be implemented from lack of choice." Perhaps Gedalyahu was right, and perhaps he exaggerated. In any case he remained with us, he and his group, among them Lonchik. We demanded clarification from the Communists, but the storm broke.

Those Who Left and Those Who Rebelled

It was August 15, 1943, on a fine summer evening. We had gathered for a staff meeting in Mordechai's deserted room on Polna Street. The meeting lasted longer than usual and ended after midnight. We had no permits to move at night and were compelled to steal through the courtyards, pressing close to the walls of the quiet houses. It had been the first full staff meeting. We had finished the distribution of assignments. The mood at the meeting had been practical, and matter-of-fact. When we reached our room on Bialostochanska Street it was quite late. The room was empty. We had not yet fallen asleep when Gedalyahu came into the room. It was about two o'clock in the morning.

"Get dressed. An SS unit has come in through the Yuroviecka gate and set sentries near the factory."

"What does it mean?"

"Don't ask questions. We have to dress and alarm the organization. I'm going to tell Mordechai."

The ghetto had been tranquil lately. Life had been normal. Not only that but new orders had recently arrived for the factories, from Koenigsberg and far-off Berlin. How happy the ghetto had been lately over the many Soviet victories, and Mussolini's downfall. And now, suddenly — an aktzia.

Our plan to meet the Germans before they managed to spread throughout the ghetto, to attack them immediately on their entrance into the ghetto, was no longer possible. They came into the ghetto suddenly, at night. In a few minutes the staff, the cells, and their commanders were all alerted. In a hurried meeting in the street we decided, first, to send the cells to their regular positions according to the original plan. The general plan had to be changed. The main points of attack, which had been set near the gates in order not to allow the Germans to enter the ghetto, had now lost much of their value. All the plans based on attacks from the houses near the gates, by grenade and a rain of fire, had to be altered. The initiative had been taken from us suddenly. Still, we decided to hold on to and entrench the existing positions. The first order, therefore, was to hold on to all the positions, and from them to attack the Germans as soon as they came close. Sentries were set and lines of contact established with the sector commanders. We sent people out to knock on doors and shutters to arouse the Jews:

"Germans in the ghetto! If they call on you to appear, don't go."

Actually, we still did not know anything. Until we were sure the ghetto was being liquidated, we must not leave the underground, or call loudly for resistance.

Modechai walked at my side, quietly, thoughtful. The minutes passed, and the ghetto awoke. A door creaked open; Jews, what has happened? And when the man received his answer the door closed. Fear quieted the Jews, fear walked with them, silently, knocking on doors and windows. Relatives and friends ran to each other's homes to rouse the sleeping. Our comrades were everywhere, in every courtyard. Mordechai looked all over, meeting the people and encouraging them. I saw the faces of our young comrades that night, the movements of their hands, the way they walked, and I saw their eyes, Avremele's and Yentel's, Sonka's and Lonchik's, gleaming in the night.

It was four in the morning. The sun's rays had not yet appeared when the posters went up on the ghetto walls: all the Jews of the ghetto, without exception, were ordered to appear at nine in the morning with small hand packages, on Yuroviecka Street. From there all the ghetto residents, as well as the shops and factories, would be moved to Lublin. It was signed by the commander of the SS and the police, Dibos.

Now everything was clear. The liquidation had come. The morning was pale and cold, under the clear blue skies. Streets filled with Jews, crowding around the posters. They read them once, again, and then dispersed, frightened. There was no time for questions or for explanations; the posters spoke for themselves. Jews read them and turned away quietly, each to his home. There was no shouting; no hysteria. They groped in the morning light as if they were lost in the dark. They were not yet really awake, the cobwebs of sleep and tranquility were not yet gone. There was no wailing or weeping, only quiet tension during the slow moving hours.

We gathered at the position on Piotrokovska Street. Mordechai was there, too. He suggested dividing the members of the staff on both sides of Yuroviecka Street, the place the Germans had designated for the transport.

"Those street may be cut off, and therefore it may be better for us to divide the staff," he argued. His proposal seemed logical, and we agreed. We decided to distribute the arms now in the stores. Those on the other side of

Yuroviecka we supplied to the fighting units in their positions and the weapons in this sector, among the cells and positions situated on this side of Yuroviecka Street. The difficulty in moving arms at this time through the ghetto was taken into consideration.

In addition, arms had already been distributed to the sectors according to the composition of the fighting forces and their numbers. Mordechai had left Piotrokovska Street and established his position on 13 Ciepla Street. We remained on Piotrokovska Street. Couriers between the two sections of the staff were chosen. The apartment on Piotrokovska Street had emptied and its occupants had all gone into hiding.

This was both a battle station and a command post for the whole sector. I can still see Gedalyahu and Zerah, Yoshko and Leibush; I remember the young people, Meir and Avremele. Every last one came to receive instructions and then returned to their positions. Most of all I remember Kuba: Kuba had not changed; he was quiet, as usual, slow and thoughtful. Only his expression had changed. He had always been friendly and easy going; now he was raging. He was angry about arms rolling about at his feet which were of no use. He had not yet managed to repair them all for combat use. There was a rifle without a safety-catch, a sub-machine gun that was capable of shooting bullets at the enemy, but it was useless, scrap iron. Kuba sat angrily at his bench and attempted to rehabilitate at least one more rifle and perhaps one more machine gun. Time was pressing: at nine exactly, the battle would commence. People were waiting for guns. The positions were anxious for ammunition. Time passed. Couriers came and went. There were too few of the promised "long" guns. People took pistols, but wanted better offensive weapons. They were not satisfied with guns for self-defense only. Kuba was angry as his hands manipulated the iron, his fingers shaking slightly. He sat at his bench working, with Meir helping him. The guns were finally distributed and still Kuba labored.

Suddenly Haska appeared. Yesterday she had come for a visit; yesterday had been Saturday, and Haska had come to help relax the tension. Gedalyahu ordered her to leave the ghetto immediately. Perhaps all the exits had not yet been sealed; before morning she could still get out. Haska refused.

"Haska, what will happen if some people come out of the slaughter alive and there is no one to receive them, to lend a helping hand outside the ghetto? We have a group in the forest, somebody will have to be the liaison between them and us, if we hold out. Haska, you must go, there is no choice."

We convinced her that she must leave and said goodbye to her quickly.

Haska left and we did not know if we would ever see her again. She headed for Bialostochanska Street, toward Olla's court. She walked, looking back, then moving forward, and turning her face toward us.

"Haska, hurry, it's morning!"

Haska walked, her bag swinging behind her. She rose on Gedalyahu's back and climbed onto the privy in Olla's yard. We stopped for a few minutes, listening. In the courtyard adjoining the ghetto there was silence. No shots broke the quiet, no movement was heard. Haska apparently had crossed safely.

The Piotrokovska apartment was in disarray. Clothes stores which we had managed to transfer to the forest were opened. Comrades were dressing, preparing. Who cared about woolen socks, about whole shoes; the main objective was that it be possible for us to move. There was no hysteria, not a single sign of confusion.

Leibush Mandelblit, a staff Communist member, leaned against the wall. He was running a high fever; he couldn't speak — an ulcerated throat. His eyes burned. He too was determined to fight, together with his comrades. A boy of about 12 or 13 was standing next to him; he had taken the boy along with him.

Our Avremele was there, as were Lonchik and Meir and Yentel who had returned wounded from the death car after the first aktzia. After that she had guided the cells and taught them how to use arms. She had excelled in the general course; the adults nodded their heads at her in amazement, wondering where that young girl obtained that facility and knowledge about the use of death tools. Pleasant and talented, gentle, the best of the gymnasium students, she was examining her weapon and looking at her shoes to see if they were strong enough. She had been wounded but her wounds had healed. She had leaped from the death car, fallen and rose again. The rest were there, too, the members of the Tel-Amal group, all in position; commanders, teachers, couriers, taking their places, coming back, and running to their officers.

I was the only one who did not prepare for tomorrow. I did not examine my shoes, did not turn over the store's goods thrown on the beds. I didn't go to say goodbye to my mother. I didn't go to her house to change my clothing. I just looked about at the tumult and the preparations and wondered. For years I had steeled them, these young people, had molded their characters, and gradually taught them the logic of action. Now they were passing before me, going to their decisive test, and perhaps travelling their last road.

Gedalyahu was there. He was joking. It was not "gallows" humor this time. He was joking heartily, because tomorrow he would no longer have to go to work in the despicable ghetto police contingent. He was a free man now. He too was preparing for battle, turning over the pile of stockings that Sonka had brought a few minutes ago from her father's little "factory", looking for some pair that fit. At daylight Gedalyahu, turned toward me. What eyes, God in Heaven! I had never seen them as they really were. I don't know why but it seemed to me that Gedalyahu was going to express his feelings of first love. It was ridiculous for me, I felt, to allow so strange a thought to enter my mind at such a time. Gedalyahu called me aside:

"A few minutes ago I spoke to Zerah, the other members of the general staff, and with our leadership. You must leave the ghetto immediately. Maybe it can still be done. After all, Haska managed to get out. There is no point in your remaining here."

"I don't understand. Do you want to send me away now? Can't I fight like all the comrades?"

"I didn't want to insult you, to question your honor. On the contrary; don't be angry, I'll explain it to you." Gedalyahu stopped in the middle, looked at the piece of black bread in his hand, and was embarrassed. "You understand, somebody is bound to come out alive from this business. I told Haska that we must organize the aid outside of the ghetto. We can logically assume that some of us will survive; nu — how am I going to tell you this? The world will still exist, there will still be Jews and the movement . . ." Gedalyahu couldn't help himself; he spit through his front teeth as usual. "In short, we think that you are the one to come out of this safely and relish the victory."

Gedalyahu stopped. I felt as if the world were sinking beneath my feet. My head swam. I wanted to fall on Gedalyahu and kiss him, to embrace him for his great soul, his precious character, the gentleness, wrapped in seeming vulgarity. How tall Gedalyahu had become! Suddenly he was concerned about history, about the world that would prevail after us!

"I won't go!"

After that we never spoke about the matter again. I met him a few more times, drifting from place to place, touring the positions. I heard the sound of his laughter, and I saw him shouting near the gate. Most of all, I remember the sound of the Russian curses he spit through his teeth. They were just ordinary curses, but they were directed at what he hated, with all his heart and soul. He hated traitors, the weak, and most all — he despised the enemy.

I met Zerah in the court on Chenstohovska Street, at the gate. Zerah wore his short jacket open to the breeze. He had on high boots. His face had thinned and had become even more handsome. His blue eyes were sunk beneath his dark brows. His wide shoulders were conspicuous in contrast to his sunken face. We met at the gate; each of us wanted to say something, but our voices were silent.

"You . . . you . . ." Zerah mumbled like a little boy, "are you going out?"

"No."

The discussion ended. I felt his warm hand in mine. It was a last handshake. We separated hastily and went our separate ways.

"Control yourself! Run, run away fast from Zorah, your dear comrade, the way you fled more than once from your own feelings and emotions. Life must be fastened tightly like a belt about one's hopes. We must not be emotional. Oh, life, do you know the taste of a last hurried farewell before death? Have you seen the morning sun rise early during such a parting? Have you felt the courageous and loving hand clasp expressing its love for you and people because they are people — our people — because they are our suffering people, whose freedom was so brutally stolen, all this expressed by the loving pressure of a hand? Can one ever forget a hand clasp like that? Will we not feel it for eternity? For love of life they died, and with their last handshake gave their love to the world. Zerah, the most wonderful of men, handsome Zerah, loving, obdurate, gentle and hard, stubborn in both his love and his hatred. That is how I will remember you, Zerah; that is how I will remember you in the open gate of the courtyard on Chenstohovska Street."

Our positions were not very well hidden. We did not intend to hide. We planned to fall upon the SS soldiers coming to pull their victims out by force. The Germans would scatter, after nine o'clock, when the concentration site on Yuroviecka Street was not full. We would defend the hiding Jews, and in that way they too would join the fighters. It was clear to us that the Jews would not go to Yuroviecka Street. In the first action no one had wanted to surrender willingly. Every house would be turned into a fortress. The positions had been stationed in high, strong-walled houses. They would not easily be taken. The one on Chenstohovska Street was on the third floor, that on Piotrikovska was also on the top floor. As they would approach the house salvos of bullets and grenades would greet them. The plan was simple. Fighters were standing at the gates too. True, the first groups of the SS had entered the ghetto earlier, at two in the morning, without our knowledge. They had established stations near the factories, which prevented us from sabotaging the factories. We knew, however, that we could outwit the guards scattered throughout the ghetto.

The positions were ready, and so were the armed fighters. In the empty rooms, abandoned by their tenants, scattered articles were lying about as if after a catastrophe. From these objects, and from the furniture, we would make barricades from behind which we would shoot. The morale in the positions was excellent. It was seven in the morning. Four hours had elapsed since the posters had appeared; all the ghetto knew what was in store. Germans were not to be seen there, except for those guarding the factories and the Judenrat building. There were still two hours ahead of us. From the staff position on Piotrikovska Street couriers were sent to the ghetto streets to determine what Jews intended to do. Two comrades were sent to Polna Street, where the fire-fighting station was situated. They would order the firemen to go home, and not to dare extinguish any fires in the factories. Parts would be taken out of their trucks, so they would not be able to move them. And, finally, gasoline had to be brought from the station.

Not half an hour had passed when the couriers returned with terrible news: masses were streaming to Yuroviecka with all their belongings. Unbelievable! What had happened? Were they going willingly? It was still only 7:30 ; why were they in such a hurry to die? Shameful news came from the firemen: they did not even want to hear about leaving their station and abandoning it to the crazy young people. They would not sabotage their machines, and would not supply any gasoline. We had been disappointed by the firemen, by the men who were not afraid to climb steep walls, who could make fun of everything. They were afraid of the Germans. We would have to include their station in the sabotage that would begin precisely at nine o'clock.

The situation in the streets was even worse. It was eight o'clock. Our couriers were scattered throughout the ghetto, holding meetings in the larger courts, explaining and persuading: "Jews, don't go willingly. This is not an evacuation to Lublin. The Germans are lying as usual. Going out of the ghetto means dying in the gas chambers. Don't go! Hide, then fight with anything you can find!" Comrades ran after the groups of Jews but the wave was streaming, flowing seemingly without end. Jews loaded down with featherbeds, pillows, dressed in winter coats, one dragging a warm fur (now he would no longer fear; he had dragged it through all the hells of the searches and now it was hard for him to leave it). Children crying, getting lost in the confusion and again finding their parents. A child's carriage, its wheels sagging under the weight of the load piled upon it, and a child rocking on top. Save Jewish property! The family marched in the sun, it was easier to die one among many than to struggle and suffer alone. Apparently a swift death was easier than a prolonged torture. Perhaps we had not fully understood the agony of parents looking at their famished children. What use was there in living such a life?

Perhaps it was because of all this that the masses were streaming that morning to their deaths.

In vain our comrades stood at the corners, in vain they closed the three bridges over the Bialka in a futile attempt to turn them back to their homes. They would not listen; they closed their ears to our appeals. The situation was critical. It was eight o'clock. The staff assembled once again in Piotrokovska. It was clear now that we would remain isolated islands in the desolate ghetto. We had no masses behind us. The Germans in the ghetto were nowhere to be seen. They would take out the transport and we would remain, small groups of fighters bent on suicide. We had been deprived of the public purpose of our struggle. The Germans, prepared by the experience of Warsaw, had hit the mark in their planning. They were succeeding in emptying the urban part of the ghetto, where it was possible to conduct street-warfare, where every house could be turned into a bastion. The Jews were being concentrated on and east of Yuroviecka Street. On the suburban side were gardens, empty fields and wooden houses that could serve neither as positions nor as shelter.

The situation was desperate and we had to decide immediately. To stay with our old plan meant giving up the very point of our struggle: to leave those who had been cut off from the fighters and to remain a group committing suicide to maintain its honor.

If we were to change the plan, there was only one way to do it — to go with the masses to the concentration point and arouse them to revolt. That meant giving up the city walls and narrowing the possibilities of street-fighting; our forces were not sufficient for open, hand to hand combat. Or perhaps — a short battle would enhance the prospects of drawing in all the people? We knew that the new plan was devised more in anger and in a spirit of revolt than on any well thought out strategy. Giving up the original plan meant that we would not direct the activities, and that we would not attack. There were serious considerations and time was running out. It was already a quarter past eight. The choice was difficult.

I suggested that we adopt the new plan. No one was opposed. My proposal was accepted because there was no time left and also perhaps, because no one had the strength to argue. Zerah and Yoshko took it upon themselves to implement it. We still had 35 minutes. What justification could be found for any plan except defending the masses and saving them, organizing and leading them to liberation — and to death with honor?

During those 35 minutes all the positions across Yuroviecka Street were rushed to the other side, where our people were, to the gardens and suburbs. A second, smaller part of the underground concentrated around Mordechai and Daniel. We had to transfer the weapons we did not want to reveal, before we opened fire. Our fighters began to mingle with the people, loaded down, like them, with bundles, feather-beds, pillows and blankets, and in them, the hidden arms — rifles and pistols, grenades and ammunition. Zila, from Grodno, carried a tremendous bundle on her back. She crossed the small bridge where there were great crowds. Everybody wanted to be first. She too pushed ahead, hurried. The arms had to arrive in time. It was a few minutes before nine. The streets were empty. The last of the Jews were hurrying, running, perspiring, carrying their bundles and their children. They didn't want to be late. They didn't want to be beaten.

The streets were deserted. Some houses had their doors locked from the outside; some Jews apparently wanted to secure the property they had left behind. A beggar had always sat in that corner and, opposite, a woman used to lean against the wall, her hand out, wailing. She wanted charity. She did not plead, she only wailed quietly, her head wrapped in rags, pressed against the wall. Her permanent spot was near the Judenrat building, and the Jewish police regularly drove her away. Now there were no police there, and no wailing beggar woman. The place was empty.

I looked for the last time at the main street and fled back to Bialostochanska. Our positions were being dismantled, one at a time. Now I only had to hurry to the bridge leading from Bialostochanska through the garbage dumps to Yuroviecka. I was the last one I think. My hands were empty. I had no bundles, not even stockings to cover my bare feet, only worn shoes that I had put on yesterday evening. It seemed to me that I was bringing up the rear of a bloody parade with the ghetto street remaining behind desolated.

All the fighters had already crossed the bridge. Only some small groups of twos and threes, remained, One was going to the Judenrat (where it seemed that the liquidation staff, headed by Friedl, was located). Another was headed for the factories on Roshanska Street where boots for Nazi soldiers were sewn, with tens of thousands still in the warehouses, and still another to the textile factories on Polna Street and the fire-fighting station there. The rest of the factories were on the other side of the ghetto, where the crowds were streaming. When there was firing on Fabryehna and Ciepla Streets they were to carry out their sabotage. They were armed mainly with grenades and pistols. They were to approach from the area, throw their grenades at the guards and destroy the machines.

We knew the factory plan well; it was easy to damage the flammable materials to be found in all the factories, the fuel stores and the warehouses. These groups, ten persons in all, consisted mostly of young girls from all the movements. They were all young, and they all fell in battle. Jews had worked for the benefit of the Nazi front for a long time, and were forced to help join a victory of the enemy of the human race for far too long. Today the factories were still. Today the fire consuming the installations and goods would prevail!

Ruvchik was sent to head and assist all the groups dispatched by the staff to Mordechai's place, on Ciepla Street. His special task was to direct the activity against the Judenrat building. We wanted to blow up the German command post there.

When Ruvchik crossed the border of the abandoned ghetto, Yuroviecka Street was already filled with Jews. A dense file of SS soldiers appeared along Yuroviecka Street. The way back to the urban part of the ghetto was already closed.

Ruvchik just managed to get by, and disappeared. We did not see him again. We concluded that he met his end from the sounds of the explosions, and the flames rising in that part of the ghetto.

Meanwhile, we had all assembled on 13 Ciepla Street. Here the tenants still remained, looking at us at once fearfully and confidently. The entrance to Mordechai's room led through the kitchen. The tenants had determined not to leave their apartment. They saw young people coming and going, with the weapons discernible under their clothing. They could see the sentries near the room, and had apparently decided that it was worth while staying with these people. When you left the apartment you found yourself in a suburban courtyard behind the house, from which you could get to Novogrodska and Hmielna Streets, where there were scattered houses separated by small lots and gardens. On the other side of Novogrodska was the attractive building where Barash and Rabbi Rosman lived. Behind the building were the large, spacious Judenrat vegetable gardens, with a barn and a tall haystack in the middle. On the right was the high ghetto wall and along the wall the small dirt streets of Gorna and Smolna.

I pushed into the crowd, making my way through Ciepla Street. What was I thinking about at that time? I don't know. I only know that I hurried a great deal, since the last minutes were nearing. Suddenly I saw my mother in the crowd. I wanted to slip by without stopping. I was afraid of the meeting, afraid to see her in the transport. I feared to see her wrinkled face, prematurely old, her grey hair. I was afraid to see her alone. I moved back, cowardly, as if fleeing from a battlefield, but she caught sight of me.

"Chaikele, where are you going?"

I kept still, kissed her on her dry lips, and fled. I never saw her again . . .

When I reached Ciepla the crowding was eased. In the triangle between

Ciepla, Novogrodska and Smolna our comrades of the fighting organization were stirring. Many moved back and forth, the guns obvious under their coats.

They discussed the plan: to break through the fence and to clear a path for the crowd behind us. In the ghetto itself no Germans were to be seen, except for those standing along the length of the far side of Juroviecka Street, looking toward the ghetto. We tried to estimate the size of their forces but could not get a clear picture. We decided to open the attack without considering the enemy's strength. There was no alternative; it was the only strategy. We knew that we would be the first to fall; that the vanguard, the attackers, would be under heavy fire and perhaps only a few would break through. The masses were behind us; if the barricade was broken they would flee by the thousands. More than 20,000 Jews were at the concentration site. Dozens would fall, hundreds might succeed; if hundreds fell, thousands might win. We would be the bridge to life for these people. We would make a way for the mass with our guns. Behind the fence was a broad suburb with twisting paths; from there the way was open to the forest.

Two fighters, one of them the Communist Zalman, who had been in a partisan group and had returned to the ghetto, would hide until dark (they were forbidden to enter the battle) and would come out of the ghetto at night to call their group to aid and assemble all those who had fled. Anyone leaving the ghetto alive had his place among the partisans. The staff as a whole voted in favor of the plan. Weapons were distributed, a hundred rifles, in addition to the pistols and grenades. There were many fighters; more than two hundred remained unarmed, or only had hand weapons, for self-defence. There was one old machine gun, and it was given to Nahum Abelevich, as we had promised.

He left the room, his face shining. The few automatic guns were distributed. Most of the girls remained unarmed, but they had a different task. The sabotage and incendiary groups were comprised mostly of girls. Others were couriers, and some were nurses. They had small arms. We would have to liquidate the guards and the patrols. Here the girls rebelled and refused to relinquish their roles. The staff, too, did not yield; they were to start the fighting: that was a fast decision. Only Mordechai and Daniel would remain in the room. A chain of runners was set up and the sectors along the fence divided. The division was not difficult; it was done according to cells and sectors. I found myself in the sector which included the Smolna front.

We parted from Mordechai certain that we would see each other again but we never did. Mordechai surprised me in these last moments. His room was orderly, the beds were made, there was a colorful cloth on the table. From a closet against the wall Mordechai took the arms that had been brought from this sector's stores. His hair was combed, he wore a grey suit, his collar buttoned, and his boots polished. He sat at the table, listening to the runners' reports. He listened without responding, did not curse; not once did I hear his favorite "holeira". He heard each one to the end, and briefly gave his order:

"Don't shoot at the Germans along Yuroviecka Street. If they try to enter our area, and the war sectors, don't let them. Shoot."

"Try to look over the roofs of the houses toward the fence. Impossible? Then creep close to the fence and look through a hole. Do this slowly without making a sound."

Was this Mordechai, the nervous, dynamic, quick-responding Mordechai, so easily enthused? True, his eyes burned, but his movements were deliberate and his answers were direct and clear. Was this the Mordechai whose imagination often ran away with him, whose enthusiasm so often deprived him of his equanimity? This surely was a new Mordechai. This was a commander who knew why he was doing his job.

When I informed him that the members of the staff of the other sector had all decided to go into battle, he replied:

"Right, very right. I was going to suggest that to them, but it was hard. Nu, good luck."

He no longer looked at us. Mordechai, who, whenever a comrade left on a dangerous mission grew emotional and followed him with ardent glances, Mordechai who was so enthusiastic about people; there was no memory of that Mordechai today. There was only the reality, of the liquidation of the remainder of Polish Jewry, of the last ghetto, apparently, and the fact of the approaching battle.

Daniel was quiet as usual. He, too, did not become emotional, and gave his advice deliberately and logically. Mordechai gave orders while looking at Daniel. I saw their glances meeting, and their lips moving in agreement. Daniel was pale and his cheeks were sunken. His face was pleasant even though tuberculosis had wasted it. From Cartus-Bereza, the infamous concentration camp of semi-fascist Poland, he had come with his tuberculosis to the command table in the ghetto.

This is the last picture, engraved in my memory, of the staff-room of the revolt in the Bialystok ghetto: the small room on 13 Ciepla Street, Mordechai and Daniel at the table covered with a colored cloth, the map of the ghetto spread out before them, the closet open wide, with arms inside. The two men had only known each other for a few weeks. I stood by the table for a long moment and looked out of the low window. The sun shone through the window. It was hot in the room.

"Didn't we decide that you would leave the ghetto this morning?" Daniel didn't raise his eyes from the table. He asked in a whisper, as if seeking not to break the last shared silence.

"I decided not to go. You can't force me, can you?"

Daniel was silent. I quietly opened the door and left. From behind I could feel their eyes on my back. It seemed to me that it was getting warmer. I unbuttoned my coat and turned toward the position; it was after nine. It would start very soon.

We found a house on Smolna Street, wooden one-story, with an attic, standing at the edge of the Judenrat's big garden. In front, it faced the fence. The house was empty, belongings were scattered on the unmade beds and on the large family table. There were pillows and featherbeds, blankets, and on the table the dishes from yesterday's meal. The tenants had apparently gone to the transport. Zerah commanded this sector.

Nothing. He caught a glimpse of the railway embankment. No military movement was visible; the embankment hid what was going on behind it. Ten o'clock approached. Suddenly a pillar of fire shot up to the sky, not far from us. That was the signal. We set fire to the haystack, to inform every sector, all positions and sabotage groups scattered through the ghetto. [According to plan, the action was to be concentrated, and sudden.] Immediately afterward we heard explosions from the other side of the ghetto, and columns of fire rose in the distance. We knew that the girls had completed their mission. Where Ruvchik was and what happened at Judenrat we did not know. Fabryehna Street was in flames, and the explosions continued. The canvas factory was burning. Another blast, and the barn was demolished. From the Novogrodska sector shouts of "hurrah" were heard, with distant echoes. "Hurrah," we all answered. We were breaking out. The fence was in front of us. We shot, and advanced. First there was silence. They weren't shooting back. Where was the enemy? Where was he hiding? We were at the fence, trying to surmount it.

"Ach, Gott," we heard a cry right near us. Here they were, hiding along the fence. We heard shooting. They were falling and groaning, not attacking us. They were frightened. "Hu . . . raaa . . ." the whole world shook, moved and we were reeling with the power of the guns roaring all along the fence. Suddenly we were under fire. One man lay in his blood. The house went up in flames; the adjoining houses were also burning like matchboxes.

The house was no longer a shelter, we had to retreat. We abandoned it and reached the broad parks on Novogrodska Street. In the other sectors, too, our comrades were retreating. Fire was consuming the houses, and we were standing in the open field where the enemy could easily see us. It would be a face-to-face battle.

Now they were shooting from the embankment. They, too, had retreated firing with heavy weapons. A machine gun began its rat-a-tat of death. Those behind the fence, who had shouted "Ah, Gott!" were using rifles, a sign that they were prepared and were ready for the revolt. Only guards armed with rifles stood along the fence. The machine gun rattled over our heads. We repeatedly attacked, and retreated.

I remember that I shot, fell, arose and ran to the fence, and then retreated with the others. I hit the barbed wire and my feet bled. I was filthy, covered with mud and soot. I shouted "hurrah" with the rest and clung to the ground with the others when the German fire grew heavier. I heard the wounded groaning, and saw a comrade fall near me. His shout was cut off. I can still see Zerah's coat flapping in the wind; still see Gedalyahu, the air still trembles from his swift movements, his blind running at the head of the attacking unit.

"Hey, chevra, hurrah, forward," his excited voice still reverberates. Avremele, Yentel, and Sonka and all the young people who ran with us and fell, got up again and though wounded, stormed ahead, Lonchik and Meir and all the rest . . .

There was sick Leibush, Chaia, the veteran Communist whose hair had turned grey in the struggle, Lilka, swift of movement despite her age, Lilka Malerevich — the last words she said as she stood to my left and ran after me, to advance and to fall, to cling to the ground and again get up and run toward the enemy, still ring in my ears: "Forward, forward, we have nothing to lose," shouting to me, to the comrades, to the wounded, and perhaps also to the comrade who had fallen to my right.

There was a field ahead of us, strewn with bodies. The battle was growing more fierce. The day, too, was getting hotter. The shooting became more intense; a heavy machine gun thundered in the air, silencing the voices of revenge. The garden, Novogrouska and Smolna Streets were strewn with dead bodies. All along the fence they lay. The sun was already high in the sky, the sound of shooting from the ghetto became fainter. There was no ammunition, no heavy machine guns. The gate on Fabrychna Street, closed and unused, was suddenly opened, and a heavy tank crawled towards Ciepla Street. It stopped suddenly; it was apparently hit by a Molotov Cocktail. There were more tanks in front of us.

People from the crowd began to join us. Ordinary people who had not been organized into cells, one woman I recognized. All kinds of derogatory things had been said about her, now she was shouting to the crowd: "Come on, what are you waiting for?" She ran past me, followed by policemen. I recognized them, Gedalyahu's colleagues, the best of them. They had always obeyed him and he had been helped by them. Factory workers, their faces furrowed with wrinkles, their clothes tattered; not many joined us, only a few dozen, but it was encouraging. Once again we attempted to break through the German's armed chain. Perhaps a way could be opened for the masses lying on their bundles in nearby Yuroviecka Street.

A plane droned overhead. It flew low, made a number of turns and disappeared. It came back, strafing us in the fields and the streets. The Germans at the embankment did not shoot even once at the masses nearby. Was it a trick? Certainly. Two columns of SS drew near, one after the other, carefully, stealthily, one from Ciepla, the other from the corner of Ciepla and Yuroviecka. Two columns, with their automatic weapons. Until now Germans had not been seen in the area of the fighting ghetto. The tanks had not succeeded. Now they sent in SS infantry. We shot at them, but the battlefield was narrowing. Many of them fell, but the column was long; they moved ahead and fired, came closer and kept firing. They came toward me from the direction of Yuroviecka-Smolna, closing the route between the masses and us. They surrounded us with blasts of fire. The SS ordered the people to lie down. We heard the commands coming from Yuroviecka Street.

"Liegen! Don't raise your heads! We will shoot all resisters, be careful."

They meant to isolate us from the crowds. They were protecting them from the bullets, and were aiming at the reckless rebels.

"Hey, braves, attack once more!"

We were isolated. Our ammunition was gone, there were many victims. The large groups would no longer come after us; we would not be able to draw them to the forests to join the struggle for freedom for the Jew. We had killed Germans, had fought, had become a bridge of bodies, but the masses would not break out. The Germans had used heavy arms for the revolt. The people would not dare break through after us. They were too weak.

The columns came closer and the encirclement was almost complete. Then the order came to try to break through the approaching columns and join the groups on Gorna Street. Our single machine gunner was ordered to cover the retreat. I moved, and reached the house. Behind me I heard shooting. I pressed against the wall and felt a wave of hot air, and then heard a whistle. Plaster fell at my feet. A bullet hit the wall just a few centimeters away from me.

The house was built of stone and brick, a strong building. Its other side faced Yuroviecka Street. The pistol in my hand was no longer of any use; my grenades and ammunition had run out. I had my worn coat on my back and my summer shoes on my feet. Feet and face were dirty with blood and mud, my mouth burned and my heart beat strongly. Behind me were the battlefield, the Germans and the comrades, many of whom apparently would also break through the encirclement. Before - the frightened people lying on their bundles on Yuroviecka Street. Now Ciepla, too, was closed off by the second column. There was no longer any passage to Gorna. In the distance, isolated shooting could still be heard from the sides of the battlefield, Smolna and Ciepla. Our comrades whose shooting it was not difficult to distinguish, had evidently not managed to break out of the trap, and were firing their last bullets at the enemy. I tried to steal into Ciepla Street, to get to Gorna but did not succeed. I had lost my group, my comrades, and before me was only the transport. It was already between three and four in the afternoon. I stood in the crowd searching for comrades; perhaps someone else had also come here instead of getting to Gorna Street. It was hard to search; people stood and sat huddled together. Faint echoes of isolated shooting still reached my ears, but it was clear: the battle was over.

Do not weep over the graves of heroes; do not weep and do not feel pity. It is not pity you are asked to give the world but deeds that will free mankind from the nightmare of oppression and enslavement.[32]

Look. Here is the grave. Here the last of the rebels were buried. They were seventy-one in number. Here they were shot, and here they fell, proud and with honor. Here, in this rubbish heap, they were buried. Look at the remains of their faces, at their fingers, that have not yet decayed. No, no, don't cry! Look at the clenched fists; they do not arouse pity. Death with a clenched fist, with your last few bullets in your pocket, is not so tragic. In the pockets of their coats, eaten by the vermin, you will find the last bullets they left for themselves. That was a sign they were not so wretched in their dying.

In 1948 the bodies of the rebels were taken out of the rubbish heap and buried in the graveyard on Zabie Street, the ghetto cemetery. On the 16th of August, 1948, on the fifth anniversary of the revolt, a monument was set up over the grave of the last 71 rebels, the last among the fighters, the last to fall. They held out for a whole week against the automatic fire of the Germans, covering every bit of ground in the ghetto. For a whole week they battled under the ground, and fought on. Today you can visit their grave and see the monument standing proudly. Five years after they fell, their remains were taken out of the grave underneath the garbage heap, the remains of their clothing and bodies. The sight of the torn, and vermin-eaten limbs brought to Jewish burial was frightful. But no one wept over their grave. Readers, do not weep either! But do not close your hearts and your ears. Listen to the voices rising from the grave. See and remember, but don't weep . . .

I was in the transport, it suddenly occurred to me. Was I going to go with the transport? In all my activity in the underground I had fought against going there like sheep to the slaughter . . . Every day and night. I told myself and others: "Don't allow them to take us!" I searched among the crowd. Except for the black, slowly moving mass, I saw nothing. on Yuroviecka Street, the bright sun was beating down on the black mass.

PART II

We Seek Our Brothers

Opposite me, a group of SS men blocked the way to the deserted part of the ghetto; behind them, to the right, was the big textile plant: "The First Combinat." From the factory there was a path leading to the Aryan side, the free city — and the forest. Where were the comrades, where were the remnants of the fighters? Was I to attempt to flee alone? I felt like one great wound. My whole being was weary, needing rest. Rest at the time meant giving up everything — life, and the last battle; I had taught my movement youngsters that the "madness of the brave" moves the world forward, and I had no strength.

Suddenly Kustin appeared. He was one of the Bund activists in the city and a member of the fighting organization staff. Apparently, he had also escaped the encirclement. He had seen about ten people whom the Germans had captured and led away. They had not succeeded in breaking out. The command had ordered all to break out of the trap and out of the ghetto at all costs. Some who still had ammunition fled. Most had gone down into the bunker, hoping to escape at the appropriate opportunity. He had seen them all, but had not been able to get to them. He had lain in the burned out barn with the Germans literally running over his head. Now he was here. He, too, had tried to get to Gorna and Hmielna where the bunker was, and to which the comrades had been told to go. Like me, he had tried and had not succeeded. The entire area from Ciepla to Smolna was closed.

"Kustin come, let's escape. There's nothing to lose," I said, though we were in the middle of the transport and all exits were closed.

"Come Kustin, let's find some way to the forest."

He stood still, thinking. He would not go; it was madness; there was no way out.

I pressed his hand and attempted to get closer to the factory watchman's shed. There was noise all around us. Some young men, who noticed my movements, made way for me, whispering. They would follow me if I succeeded. Kustin had remained in his place, clinging to the burning earth. The crowd started to move. The gate on Yuroviecka Street, near us, began to turn on its hinges. That gate had always been locked, never in use. Through it, it was possible to get to Polska Street, to a suburb called Balostochek. Behind that were fields and forests. Behind the gate there was a railway line and a railway siding. The gate creaked; it was hard to open. The crowd pushed together, against it, but it opened only slowly. The crowd moved backward and forward, like waves on a beach.

I was already at the factory gate. Opposite me was an armed German, his legs apart and his weapon at the ready. Apparently I was pushed and pulled by the sleeve of my coat. I did not see anything. I pressed against the high factory fence; there was a roaring in my head, my feet and legs were taut; one more step and I would be in the shed. An old Pole with a big mustache stood in front of me:

"How did you get in? They are watching me on all sides."

"Don't ask; just let me pass!"

"But . . ."

Before he could finish what he wanted to say I was already past the little gate and into the factory area. I found a handkerchief in my pocket. I wiped my feet and my face, without thinking, like an experienced underground person. A ray of light struck my eyes and almost blinded me. Here there were no crowds, no black mass moving back and forth. It was suddenly silent; a silence ringing in my ears and pounding in my temples. An intoxicating silence.

I had to choose a path, but my mind was blank. I knew the factory area and my feet led me intuitively. Not far away was a small bridge over the Bialka River. Across the span was the aryan side. The bridge, however, seemed to have disappeared. How far it was to the bridge, that once had been so close? Suddenly an armed German was in front of me.

"Who are you?"

Without thinking, I began to search through my pockets. I had thrown away my elegant purse, with all my papers, before the battle. Suddenly, I couldn't believe it — there was a paper in my pocket about which I hadn't known. When I had last left the ghetto a few days ago I had put the document in my coat pocket, since I was carrying some eggs in the bag. I intended to show the Germans at the gate, to prove I was a food smuggler, so they would merely take the eggs. In another place I was smuggling other "goods" — pistol bullets that comrades had stolen from the Germans.

The paper was a work card for the "Textile Industry," actually for "Combinat 4," but that did not make it invalid, apparently, for the German. It seems I gave the impression of a Polish factory worker. I wore a summer dress, and old coat, my bare feet in sandals, and I was dirty.

I was permitted to pass. Germans stopped me every few steps. The chain was apparently tightening. I routinely held out my card and moved slowly ahead. I was at the bridge; the factory was humming. They were working there that day as if nothing had happened, without the Jews who hadn't come to work. There were a few more buildings in front of me, and at every building SS guards were checking papers. I could have gone around them, but it was not worthwhile. The second gate, on the aryan side, was not far away. It was better to take the risk at the gate, than to go through the barbed wire from the side. They were probably watching more carefully there. The SS man at the gate was not sure my paper was valid. He looked at it, then nodded his head in agreement. I was at the gate. Here again there was a shed, with a Polish watchman. It was his task to check the workers going in and out. The watchman stopped me.

"Where are you going? Impossible to leave the factory in the middle of work." I shoved him aside without speaking. He retreated, but attempted to resist.

"Quiet, fool," I whispered to him. He kept quiet; and evidently undersood that something was different here.

Now I was on the aryan side of Yuroviecka Street. What a strange world, quiet and shining. A group of Germans was standing on the corner. They were talking in loud voices, about what had happened. Jews fought back, but now everything was quiet again. Opposite was the railway embankment. Heavy machine guns were being moved some other place. They had apparently finished their task. All along the embankment were soldiers; a real front. All along Poleska Street was a line of cars, unending movement, soldiers coming and going. A new flow of reserves kept coming continually, even though the battle was over. How still the street was. Of what were they still afraid? I was the only civilian on the whole street.

They did not examine my papers; they were soldiers, not policemen. I felt their glances from behind. I had no arms; I had given my pistol to Kustin. He had lost his own and perhaps would try to break out at night, with the aid of the pistol. My bullets had run out but maybe he would find some with one of the comrades. Unarmed, I was walking in the lion's den. I walked slowly, the sun beating down on my head, accompanied by the glances of the armed German soldiers. They had put down the revolt and I, a member of the command staff was walking among them. What had I done? Why had I left? The world was empty here; there was nothing left but the lone battle and the lone war, without the masses for whom we had fought. I was followed by the young faces and the enthusiastic, stubborn, believing eyes of Avremel,

Yentel, Lonchik and Roschka, Meir and Sonka, who had fought and were no more.

Near the Cathedral of Saint Roch was a small, empty lot. Half-naked German soldiers were washing themselves, talking in loud voices, whistling and attending to their needs. A steamy mobile kitchen emitted a strange odor. My lips were parched and my head throbbed. I could still hear the shooting despite the quiet. My mind, nerves and limbs were now slowly absorbing everything that had happened. The army filling the city beat at my mind; perhaps now it was possible to understand what had taken place in the ghetto. A strange, terrible knowledge. We had faced all those who had been mobilized and brought from afar to fight against the ghetto rebels.

On the corner of Pilsudsky and Saint Roch Streets a shoe-shine boy was sitting on a little stool. I extended my foot. All I had were a few pennies. I had not yet eaten that day. It was most important that I wear shiny shoes . . . Shiny shoes for the bloody festival. Who would now say that I was a rebel and had come from the ghetto? In the nearby court there was a water tap at the gate. I wet my handkerchief and wiped away the traces of blood that had dried on my foot. Now my feet were clean. I still had to comb my hair. Haska lived nearby. I wondered if she had managed to get over in the morning without any trouble. I would visit her. An interesting call, hah! The landlady would be happy to see me, the rich cousin from Grodno. The wealthy were always welcomed guests. Perhaps she would play the gramophone for me, and find the record with the tango about the two lovers, or about the one who waited, and waited . . . I was neat, I was going to my aryan friends, to Haska. Toward life, or away? Where would I find the strength to overcome my despair? How was I to start all over again?

Haska was at home. She had arrived safely that morning and was waiting for somebody to come to her. She had hoped that, at the least, I would come; why, I do not know. She was afraid to leave her room lest anyone who did come would be left outside. She wanted to hear all the details of the battle. She had heard the shooting and the explosions, seen the fires rising out of the ghetto, and the armed SS units moving about the city.

Haska was blaming herself. Only yesterday before coming into the ghetto, she had seen the motorized units in the city but had not thought to say anything about them in the ghetto. She did not think that there was any connection between their arrival and the plan to liquidate the ghetto.

"If only they knew yesterday, if they only knew," Haska kept saying, as if to herself. I knew that the matter was not important. Even if we had known we could not have changed any of our plans. But I couldn't talk. I asked Haska to leave me in peace, since I did not have the strength to say anything.

Haska was embarrassed. She fell silent. The landlady came into the room and wanted to express her happiness at my coming. Strangely, she did not notice anything different about me. She saw nothing, not in my clothing nor in my conduct, not even in my face. Soon she would play some sentimental song on the gramophone, and she would sing. Haska told the landlady that I had come to live with her, and to help her. Haska looked happy, and so was the landlady, who was called Misya.

"Well have fun, Halinka!" She was looking for entertainment, the company of young girls, merry friends, so that everything would be *klawo* (very nice).

It was between five and six when we left the house and went to look for the other "aryan" girls. We all sat on one of the stones that remained among the ruins in Legionova Street. The girls crowded around and listened to my story. The sun was already at the edge of the sky, red and round. They sat bent forward and listened. I did not see their eyes nor their faces. They were all there, Haska and Bronka and Rivkele, Liza Chapnik, and Ruth, whose aryan name was Anya, her sister-in-law. My sister had also come. We sat still, without uttering a sound. I looked into their faces, sought encouragement and support, some agreement from them that we had done all that we could have done, that what had happened was what we had all foreseen, that there really was no alternative, and that anyone who had come out or would survive the revolt would start anew and continue the war. They were still and lowered their eyes.

The red sun set. The transport was already moving toward Bialostochek. Where were our comrades? No one had arrived yet. Perhaps they would come; certainly they would come! We would go to look for them in the neighborhood of the ghetto. We decided then to break through, no matter what! Many certainly would come, and we would have to watch for them so they should not fall into the treacherous sea. I waited for one of them to recover and order us to do something. But they all remained quiet, and it seemed to me as if the whole world was standing at attention. In the center of the dead square there was one yard in which there was a whole house. It was apparently a Polish courtyard, and therefore had been left untouched. Children were playing there.

"Look, there are Jewish women sitting," the children began to shout, looking away from their game. They brought us back to reality. What had the little ones found Jewish in us? Was it the way we were sitting, the bent backs, the lowered heads? They couldn't see our faces. We got up and left, each going her own way. From now on we would scout around the ghetto neighborhood all day long. That was our first practical activity. All of them had to continue working and maintaining the underground apartments. We would look for any remnants and after that — our road led to the forest.

Why hadn't I thought of finding out where to look for our partisan group? It was moving about all the time and only the regular couriers knew where it was. Why hadn't I asked? Simply because I had not believed that I alone would need that address. The cells had been given explicit information; perhaps those who came would know. In any case we would do what we could, take them first into our apartments outside the ghetto. If only I could meet Marylka now; she sometimes moved about the city. I did not know her address but if only I could run into her accidentally in the street! We would have to look by ourselves. It would not be easy, of course, but in the meantime, all day from dawn to curfew, we had to search in the ghetto neighborhood for anyone who might have succeeded in getting through.

It was evening and in the empty streets it was still hot. We didn't dare go home where at that time no doubt the gramophone was being played. Little Vladek was at play, the grandmother was cursing and our landlady was looking for merry company. Haska and I walked the streets to put off the time when we would have to go "home." Unconsciously we turned our steps toward the ghetto; it was dark, and giant shadows crossed the road. Every figure looked like a wandering Jew searching for a place in which to hide.

We walked along the sides of the emptying streets, by the shadowy houses. Everything was grey. There was the dark bridge on Shenkevich Street and beyond it once again isolated, shadowy, slowly moving figures. There was the court at the corner of Yuroviecka Street bordering on the ghetto. Mordechai had once lived on the other side of the fence. In front of the gate was a large "billboard" column. Suddenly something moved in front of us. We were frightened and moved back. It was only a large piece of paper, a torn poster on the column, waving in the wind.

I was angry: "Where are your nerves, Haska?" And I, hadn't I been frightened, too? I vented my anger on Haska and she kept still, lowering her head. Stunned and silent we went around the ghetto. German patrols were moving about near the fence, near the gates on Yuroviecka and Fabrychna Streets. It was quiet, the whole world seemed dead. The sentries marched slowly back and forth. From within, not a sound could be heard, not a murmur of any movement. Smoke was rising here and there, turning black in the greyness, spiraling upward and disappearing. The German factories were still burning. The revolt had died, the fires had burned out, with only the smoke left in the summer air.

On Poleska and Smolna Streets there were very many sentries, but the army had disappeared. On these streets the fences were destroyed. In one place there was a big hole in the wall; in another twisted barbed wire loosely lay on the ground, amid bent and broken boards. That had been the ghetto wall. Here they had attempted to break through.

In the twisting streets were the suburban courtyards. Piles of rubbish, green gardens, it was impossible to stay there for any length of time. The sentries stared at you, watched your every movement. The fearful inhabitants had locked themselves in their houses. We stole through the yards and the streets, hiding from the sentries' eyes. We knew that we looked suspicious to them, but it was not easy for us to go away. Perhaps someone was hiding here, maybe someone had broken out and was wounded and waiting for help.

We entered one yard where a Polish woman was drawing water from the well. She asked us whom we were looking for. Haska immediately made up some name. No, she did not know where that person lived, but she told us about Jews who had tried, opposite here, to jump across and flee from the ghetto. There, where the wall was broken, only an hour or two ago. Most had been caught, one was wounded but succeeded in escaping.

"Look, Pani, there, behind that pit, he got away. But many were killed. They were all taken away immediately. Only one is still there, not far away, behind our house, in the nearby street. And you know, our 'bastards' have already managed to steal his shoes."

"What do you mean? He's still there?" Haska put on an innocent face.

We went to the street, a narrow, dirt road. A black body was lying in the middle. We saw woolen stockings like the ones Sonka had brought from her father's for all the comrades. There was something white underneath the stocking — underwear. The body was covered with a long black coat. The face could not be seen, it was covered. Without hat or shoe, the body lay on its back. There were no signs of a wound, and no blood. The body seemed to be sleeping. It was one of those who had attempted to break through to freedom, and who had fled through the opening we had made. He was surely one of ours. The stockings were familiar. Part of the head, protruding from under the coat seemed familiar, too — the hair, the color.

"Haska, I think it is Gedalyahu. The stockings, look at the stockings."

I didn't have the courage to pull back the edge of the coat. I knew that the comrades would break out and most would be killed; what was I afraid of? Of the simple truth about somebody close?

I turned back, resisted. To this day I cannot forgive myself for not having the courage to look at death up close. Time was pressing; in a moment a sentry would arrive. In a little while it would be curfew time.

Haska was white, but with speedy steps she bent down to the corpse. She quickly informed me: no, it is not Gedalyahu. I don't recognize him. I did not know the anonymous face either. I almost felt better.

Stunned, we returned to Haska's room, intent on returning to the neighborhood of the ghetto the next day. That was a frightful night. Only when darkness covered the city was the silence broken. All night long shooting was heard. The grenade explosions made it difficult to hear the cries in the ghetto.

We stood by the window and listened. The horizon turned red. Once again were started fires. They did not cease until dawn. The battle in the ghetto was still going on.

We did not speak that night. We did not close an eye. It was one of those sleepless nights when your hair can almost turn white in a few hours. The shooting shook us out of our shock. When morning came we went out. The streets were empty. Greyness seemed to envelope all the houses and the church opposite, standing high above the city. Dawn came, its light spreading over the ghetto skies.

Mordechai Anielevich wrote in 1942, in the Warsaw ghetto, "Fire burns, but it also warms." The fire of revolt burned the ghetto and thereby seemingly sealed the fate of a Jewish community, the 60,000 Jews of Bialystok. We remained alone, fighting against terror and alienation, we the remnants of Polish Jewry. And a new day came, a day of heroic effort and struggle and new danger.

August 17, 1943.

It was forbidden even to come close to the houses and courtyards bordering on the ghetto. During the night, the German SS were replaced by Lithuanian, Ukrainian and Bielorussian forces; the collaborators from prewar Poland's national minorities.

We were at the Yuroviecka gate. Three uniformed soldiers were standing there and the gate was closed. Only yesterday the big transport had been taken out; where was it now? And how many were still hiding? Who had been shooting during the night? The green soldiers were frightened. They apparently did not enjoy the ambushes set for them by the Jews remaining in the ghetto. It creaked open and revealed all of Yuroviecka Street. I climbed up on the embankment and could see the whole length of the street. Something moved on the empty thoroughfare — horses, pulling wagons loaded with piles of rags. They were living people who shook like dead bodies to the movement of the iron wheels on the stone pavement, there were children in the wagons — live children, all that were left of the living. They were crying. On both sides of the wagons marched the men in green uniforms with their rifles ready. From Yuroviecka Street the road led directly beneath the railway embankment. The wagons moved slowly through the small tunnel; in a moment they would appear on the other side. I jumped down. The wagons were at my side. The sentries were driving one of them away. I went to another wagon; if he drove me from there, I would move aside and come back again.

I made the rest of my way in a mad run. There were many people on the embankment, Poles who had come to look at the Dantean sight. Many of them were inhabitants of the suburb and had strange tales to relate. Since yesterday Jews had been lying here on the giant lot. They had not been given even a drop of water, not yesterday, and not today. The sun was beating down on their heads. There were three rings of SS men with 'storks nest' in each corner, and machine guns on them. From afar the soldiers looked like green dwarfs. It was impossible to get close. The rings were right. Every few meters there was a position. The wind was coming from that direction and blurred sounds reached my ears. The wind stopped at my feet, at the high embankment. The voices, too, reached with their faint echoes. The sun was hot on my head, on their heads. Within the rings of sentries black spots were moving, Jews, people I had seen yesterday on Yuroviecka Street, for whose sake I had fought, together with my comrades, and from whom I had fled.

Inside the armed circles were two tight blocks of black spots. Like a giant swarm of bees, there was one big block from which a thin thread eventually split into two. Where it broke was an empty field, and in the middle was a small group of men in uniform. That was the selection site. There the fate of living people was decided. Who was to die, and who was to live in slavery and die a slow death in a concentration camp. Here they separated families, fathers from sons, parent from children. One end of the thread moved slowly toward the cars on the horizon, and the second end joined the other smaller clump. From afar you could see the death dance, an assembly line on which columns of people moved.

My mother was now among them. I stood and watched.

For a whole day I moved about the area. I walked along the railway and back. Bronka came, too; in the evening Haska came as well. Once again we walked the streets. The ghetto was locked tightly. Only the number of bodies along the ghetto fences increased; they were spread all along the street. Many tried to break through, and fought for their lives.

For three whole days I wandered along the embankment. The sun beat on their heads for all three days. Each day I found the same scene: the big block was growing smaller, thinning out with the thread running from it without stopping. One end went to the other block, the other to the cars.

During every one of those days we searched the ghetto neighborhood. The piles of the dead increased during the three nights, and every morning soldiers collected the corpses of the rebels. In the morning they sealed the holes in the walls and mended the barbed wire. Every dawn the neighbors reported that dozens of Jews in the neighborhood were attempting to escape, that many were shooting at the Germans and killing them, and that the German bodies were being carried away immediately. The neighbors also said that it was difficult to sleep at night, that the houses shook from the many explosions nearby. The battles in the ghetto were continuing. On the third day after the beginning of the revolt, when I came to the railway embankment in the Bialostochek suburb in the morning, I found the field empty. No imprisoned and tortured Jews, and no armed SS soldiers. The area was dead, the history of 60,000 Bialystok Jews had ended.

By the fourth day after the revolt life in the street was back to normal. People in the city still talked about the Jews, about their desperate struggle, and their eventual annihilation. But life went on. The avenues of trees were green, birds chirped and the market behind the avenue hummed with activity of peasants bringing their "black" chickens to the city, and German soldiers looking for a "bargain", among the peasant wagons crowded in the market square.

We were looking for Jews to save, and for some link to our group in the forest. Once again I roamed the city streets. Haska continued to work for the German family and would return only in the evening. All the girls were working. Only I was wandering through the streets without any plan. The battles in the ghetto were continuing. I talked with Olla and her husband Vladek about going into the ghetto. He never ceased talking about the Jews' fighting. I didn't tell him that I, too, had taken part in the battle. He told about Germans killing Jews every night, but tried to encourage me and to convince me that the day of vengeance was not far away. However, when I told him I wanted to search the ghetto for comrades whom I could take outside the city, he argued with me:

"These are only the first days; your friends are not foolish enough to try to break out now. They will wait in the bunkers, and you, too, must wait. You know it is impossible to get into the ghetto. Look at the piles of bodies carried every day to the graveyard on Zabia Street."

Vladek was right, but the ground was burning under our feet. This was the fourth day that we were without any contact with the fighters in the ghetto. We did not know if they were still alive — or if they were with our group in the forest. The sense of isolation crushed us. Our meetings in the evenings were gloomy; we had learned to be silent. We found that if anyone of us spoke of what was in her heart all the others would follow suit, and the bitterness would become a destructive force. We kept quiet to escape despair.

So, I roamed the streets. There was a lot of movement on Pilsudski Street. It was noon, the weather was still fine. We hoped that it would rain, that soon a storm would come and wash everything away. The sun beamed its bright hot rays. Stores were crowded with German buyers.

I crossed Pilsudsky street and stopped. Behind the "Pan" movie house I saw a crowd of people all looking toward the courtyard. The movie house's back yard bordered on the ghetto, on the court of 6 New World Street, where our first apartment had been. Now I stood there all alone a crowd of Poles, among the wise-cracking hooligans who were to be found near the movie house all the hours of the day. They were cheering. What had happened?

"Nothing, there is a Jew hanging there."

A Jew had hanged himself from a beam of his half-destroyed house. On the fourth day after the liquidation of the ghetto. For four days he had fought and hidden, and when he saw no way out, had hanged himself. I heard the nasty whispering, the wild laughter; I could sense their satisfaction. I looked at the crowd. There were Polish faces torn by pain. Someone had turned aside and was saying something to himself. A woman wiped away a tear . . .

Marylka

That evening I went to Bronka's. Bronka had changed her apartment and was now living in a tiny, warm, sunlit room in the home of a rich Polish family. In front of the house was a fine garden, with colorful flowers, and fruit trees shading the court, their branches rising to the windows. Bronka's room had a small window with white net curtains, through which the sun filtered. The room was suitable for a single girl from a "decent" family. Bronka played the role very well. Her landlords respected and admired her for her good Polish "education," her good manners and her aristocratic appearance.

We were talking about the searches we would have to make. Bronka agreed that if we did not find anybody from the fighting group in the city we would have to start looking in the forest. There was no point in just waiting idly until someone from the aryan underground found us.

It was a fine evening, and Bronka walked with me to my home.

I was telling Bronka about Marylka, and suddenly, there was a familiar figure ahead of me. A woman crossed the street. Her back was bent, her gait somewhat unsteady, the platinum hair was smooth and cut short. It was she!

Without saying anything to Bronka I began to run. I caught up with her and embraced her. Marylka was frightened; she was not prepared for this meeting. Her movement in the city always involved risks. When her astonishment subsided, her feelings became evident: her lips trembled as if she was talking to herself. Her bright eyes misted, and the single small wrinkle over her nose seemed to move. She opened her mouth but before she could say anything, was silent again. Once more she tried to say something, but instead grasped my hand firmly. Her own, too, was trembling.

I looked at her. She was dirty, weary, the soles of her feet were sore because her shoes were too large. She was dressed carelessly, I pulled her aside to a nearby alley. Bronka stood by, amazed. I introduced Marylka to her and we decided to arrange a meeting immediately with the other girls. Marylka had been wandering through the streets for days, looking for comrades who might have escaped from the ghetto. They had attempted to organize armed assistance from the forest when they learned about the events in the ghetto, but the effort had failed. They had not been able to come.

Now she was seeking any kind of contact. She knew only about the beginnings of the battle. I learned that on the day of the revolt, even before I had left, two comrades had succeeded in breaking the siege, armed with pistols. They had escaped, and were the only ones to reach the group before Marylka left the forest. Perhaps there were now more comrades there; the group had sent patrols out; they might, perhaps, find some people walking along the road and could pick them up. Marylka herself had been roaming the city for three days. She had many addresses, but had not found even a single comrade from the ghetto at any of them.

All the girls were excited when I introduced Marylka to them. We walked in pairs, along Saint Roch's Cathedral. Marylka was very pleased by the sight of this large group of experienced girls who knew their work, comrades who for half a year and more had stayed outside the ghetto waiting for the day when they would be called to action. That day had arrived. They were all emissaries of the militant movements which had taken part in the establishment of the fighting antifascist front in the ghetto. Bronka was a representative of Dror, Haska, Rivkele and I of Hashomer Hatzair, and Liza and Anna of the Comsomol. There were other Jewish girls who were not acting in behalf of an organized group, but whose help was also certain. My sister was one of these.

I remember them so well: Haska Bielicka was Helenka, and Bielicka her family name was now Stashuk; Rivkele was Maryshka, with her family name remaining Madajska. Ruth was Ania, Liza Chapnik was Marysha Morozovska; Bronka Vinicka had become Yadwiga Skibel. I was Halina Voronovich. Marylka had remained Marylka Rozycka. My sister Miriam was Julia Balchus.

Haska-Helenka worked for SS officers, Rivkele-Maryshka for a German Gestapo doctor and for the police. Ruth-Ania was employed in the kitchen of the Ritz Hotel, the city's most splendid hostelry. Only high-ranking Germans and guests from Berlin and Koenigsberg ate in the restaurant there. Liza-Marysha also worked for an SS family, and together with Helenka also helped in the kitchen of the SS Verkzentrale canteen. Bronka had a job with the "zugfuehrers". My sister also was employed by an SS family. Marylka worked "on her feet", coming into the city and returning to the forest every few days. She was a partisan courier. I was still idle, and I was determined to join the partisan group in the forest.

The group was our family now. To clarify our new tasks, and to coordinate activities between the city and the forest, it was decided that tomorrow after dark I would go to the forest with Marylka.

There they were waiting for her, for information and for the food items they were unable to obtain. She could not return empty-handed. Medicines in particular were lacking. Marylka had Polish friends who helped her obtain all these. Since yesterday the partisans had been waiting for her each evening at the meeting place there. The forest was dense; the paths complicated, and they had therefore chosen a point closer to the main road to meet her, and lead her to their camp.

We were to leave for the forest some minutes before nine, the curfew hour, in order to get past the police station at the end of Shenkievich Street, on the other side of the railway. We wouldn't have anything suspicious in our packages and could, therefore, leave the city by the main exit.

Marylka slept at Marysha's, in a distant suburb on the other side of the central railway station. She had a private room with a separate entrance from the street.

Marysha's landladies were a woman and her daughter. The mother was a widow, a seamstress: the daughter had a position in an office. The mother must have worked nights in order to give her daughter an education, at least six years of high school, so she would not have to be a seamstress but could work in an office.

Marysha's room had a wide old wooden bed, a folding table and some other rather primitive articles, including a table made of boards. In the middle of the apartment was an iron stove. Most important, there was also an opening to the cellar where there were small unnoticeable pits which were excellent hiding places.

Now the cellar would be very necessary for us. Marylka was enthusiastic about her place; it was the most isolated of all our apartments. Her landlords wanted to consider us members of the family, but Helenka knew how to "manage" them, especially the landlady. Usually, she did not lag far behind the young and primitive Polish woman in her (pretended, of course) desire for merriment. Haska decided to introduce Marylka to Misia, her landlady. Marylka made a very fine appearance and spoke Polish well. She came from Lodz, and had one very good trait: she knew how to make friends quickly, and how to endear herself. She did this with natural feminine grace. How natural and fitting that daintiness seemed in contrast to her coarse masculine features, the movements of her somewhat large hands, and her work as a partisan courier, covering many kilometers daily. Still, she was the same Marylka, and these qualities helped her succeed in the city and on the roads among strange people, among gentiles, and under the suspicious eyes of anti-Semites.

We left the city according to plan, our packages divided between us. The streets were almost empty, the last passerby hurrying home. We hurried too. Marylka was apparently thinking of home. I was taking a new road, a beginning that was also a continuation. We were not stopped. Outside the city we passed suburbs, wooden houses and courtyards with dogs guarding them. The inhabitants were still sitting in their doorways enjoying the light evening breeze. This was the dangerous stage: people did not walk about at this hour in suburbs which were not their own. The police stations were still nearby. We had to calculate the time precisely; in another two hours all would be asleep, and then it would be possible to steal through the side paths. It would only be feasible to get to the forest under cover of darkness. We would have to find shelter for the next two hours.

Marylka had some stations along the way. One was an isolated house at the fork of the branching road. It would be possible to wait there until nightfall. We sat silently in a corner of the kitchen. When we left a dog barked close by, but we moved ahead. The path was narrow and led between gardens and fields. From here we had to get quickly to the side road linking with the Volkovisk-Bavanovich road. On both sides were swamps which could not be crossed, and there was a great deal of military movement at night, too. We had no alternative, however, and had to travel some distance without any cover. It was good that many military vehicles did not pass. When they did come, we lay in the ditch on the side of the road, and we were lucky that they did not notice us.

We came to a dark wood. In Poland, with its many forests, this was called only a wood. We could not go in too far; we must not lose sight of the road. In addition, deeper in the wood the ground was treacherous; with moss on top and treacherous bog below. Marylka went ahead, and I after her. I was tense. Every tree seemed to be a figure moving in the night wind, the branches resembled hands reaching out to seize me. Every once in a while the noise of a vehicle came from the road and pale beams of light moved among the trees. The road turned left. Marylka said that it went to a well-guarded German training camp. We had to go around the camp. To the right a dirt path crossed a plowed field. Further to the right was the Polish village of Grabovka.

It was a dangerous village. It was big and it had a police station. The chief enemies were the dogs. When you stole through the plowed field where only a few trees covered you from the left, you were between the training camp and the village. You had to be extremely careful not to go to the right or to the left. Any wrong step to one side would arouse the barking dogs. We stole along moving quietly. The ground was wet and soft and at times we sank up to our knees. Marylka wore high leather boots, while I had only sandals on my feet. The dampness penetrated our bones. From the right we heard the noise of barking dogs, a sign that we were too close to Grabovka. We had to go further left.

We heard the sound of guns. The guards were shooting in the air for encouragement; they were not aiming at us. We were in a bottleneck between the camp and the village; another few hundred steps and we would reach the road leading into the forest, where they were waiting for us. Almost all the danger was behind us. A gigantic black mass loomed ahead, the "old forest", and the main thing was to get to that dark strip. These moments were crucial; if we got to the "old forest" the danger would be over. The Germans were still shooting, would keep on shooting until morning.

We ran the last approach to the black forest at gallop. We leaped among the first trees and breathed freely. Now we felt our weariness. During the journey I tried to hide my excitement and nervousness from Marylka. Until now I had been accustomed to other kinds of underground roles whose success depended upon acting, pretence, shrewdness and experience in enemy territory. Now there was a forest in front of me, a black area, strange and unknown. Here you had to work not by daylight, but in the dark, and you had to go around the enemy.

I knew them. I knew the sentries, the police workers with their stupidity and cunning. I knew how to act in their presence with a gun in my purse. I knew how to pretend and smile while handing over my forged identification cards and permits. Now — I had a new role. No wonder, then, the deep fear veteran partisans, combat soldiers, who knew how to blow up railways and bridges and were not deterred by any combat role, had of the city. No surprise, then, that the Soviet partisan commanders, with whom we worked for some time, had such admiration for the girls working in the city underground.

We rested for a few minutes. It was already after midnight, we had to hurry. The comrades would only wait until three o'clock, since they had to get back to camp before dawn — it was impossible to move about in the forest in daylight.

Our path wound between tall tangled trees. It was a broad dirt road, quite easy to follow. However, you had to know just how to walk, not to leave footprints. German vehicles came through here quite often, but had, thus far, hardly ever come at night. They were afraid of the forest. Still, it was better to be careful when we heard a noise from afar and hide among trees. They were accustomed to shooting blindly as they came along this path.

The comrades were waiting. The "old forest" came to an end, and there was a road separating it from the "new forest". Marylka knew the way; we had to get to a ruined tank, a left over from the 1941 battles. After that we had to turn left 200 steps, lie down and listen. That was the meeting place. But there might also be an ambush. You therefore had to wait patiently. You listened, then you gave the signal. Three times you imitated the sound of the cookoo, and waited again. The reply came in another few minutes, and then — you saw the two armed figures.

It was difficult to make out their faces. One was Sergei and the other — Yaakov, our Yaakov, one of the three Hashomer Hatzair members in the forest. They embraced us hurriedly, took our bundles, and without asking questions took their places one at the head and the other at the rear, with the two of us in the middle. We moved forward.

A tragedy occurred while Marylka was in the city. Not far from the tank, on the highway leading to the forests where our partisan comrades were operating, two members (one of whom had broken out of the ghetto on the day of the revolt and had reached the forest with drawn pistol — the Comsomolite Gryscha Lunskiy) had found an unexploded bomb. As they were examining it, it exploded, and both Gryscha and Yoel Kissler were killed instantly.

On the way Yaakov told me: "Some of those who jumped off the train have come, among them Yoshko Kawa."

"What about our people?"

"Not one."

In the camp I found about fifty people. More than ten of them had leaped from the death train, among them some of the fighters who had participated in the revolt and had been trapped in the transport after breaking the siege. The others were simple Jews, most of them young, who had jumped from the trains and miraculously reached the partisans. Our patrols had picked up some of them, and others had accompanied the fighters they had met on the way.

The bunker to which I was brought was too small to hold everybody. Two tiers of boards, nailed to the walls, did not provide enough room for all to lie down at once, so they took turns. The smoky, sooty stove that coated the whole bunker with its dark ash was the center of life inside. Those who were not lying down napped sitting at the stove or helped the cook prepare the meal potatoes which had been brought from the fields. Food stocks were meager, and if more people came there would not be enough to feed them all. Without security precautions and an armed escort it was impossible to return to a village that had been visited once before, lest the police had already been called; or if not the police, then the villagers who organized their own guard. How many times could you deceive the villagers and pretend that there was a large force behind you? The villagers had eyes, also there were footprints, and it was easy to discover how many fighters there really were. It was, therefore, necessary to go further away each trip. It was also important to move the camp site. So — first, arms, and until there were arms, also food. That was what the fate of the group and of the refugees depended upon. The old work had to be resumed, sources had to be found in the city for arms and food, until the unit could stand on its own feet.

Our instructions were: "Go back to the city; go back and organize the city together with Marylka and the other girl comrades. The city must be at our service. The city, with all its underground forces . . . Arms, information, addresses, connections, bring us all these. Go back to the city. Go back, don't run away to the forest."

Simple humanity moved me to keep silent in the face of their demands and not to pour salt on the open wounds or augment their feelings of pessimism, hopelessness and impotence. Was it heroism that led me to renew the battle that had been shattered on that August 16, with the end of the ghetto revolt? No, it was just a matter of simple human decency and loyalty to my comrades. There is a need for these two qualities in times of trial and distress. No, under no circumstances could I, on that night, in that dark bunker, by the sooty stove, refuse to resume our activity.

There was no room for argument even though going back to the city meant renewing the game of hide-and-seek, the hated pretense of being an aryan in an alien world, the life of unending tension. Still, I think they pinned too many hopes on us, they saw us as too sure a support. We were only six Jewish girls pretending to be Poles, in one way or another working hard for the Germans, without any money or contacts, isolated and alone, always searching, and suspicious of everyone.

We set up a contact system, and decided that Marylka would give us all her addresses in the city. That would also make it easier for her; free her from making the trips to the city too often. We also decided on communications among the people scattered within the city itself. We began the organization of cells; clarified the subject of arms, and planned to renew our ties with Jan. The group command took it upon itself to "do something" to ease the money situation, perhaps carry out an operation against some rich farmer serving the Nazis. We continued with the work we had begun: to watch the exits from the ghetto and to look for ways to get in.

With the morning light my visit came to an end. Everything had been discussed. I would have to spend that day in total idleness, although the ground was burning under my feet. I was in a hurry to get to the city to tell the girls all the news, to share impressions. It was almost unbearably difficult to lie in the bunker until dark. I insisted that the comrades accompany me only to the road, from there I would go to Bialystok alone. They argued that they would all be in danger if the path leading to the camp was discovered. I persisted. It was barely morning; Marylka had to rest for a day or two, at least. I had papers, and my gentile appearance was unquestionable; I would be able to go through the village in daylight. In any case it would be good for me to know the way and the neighborhood by day so that I could come alone a second time. There was no point in demanding that Marylka accompany me. Why should both of us take the risk? That argument convinced them.

When we reached the main forest road there was already a white strip on the horizon. The comrades shook my hand and left. A few steps and they had disappeared, and the sound of their footsteps was lost in the rustling of the trees.

It was still morning when I reached the fork in the road between the training camp and the village. I determined to wait in the bushes for a little while, until more traffic appeared on the road so I would not attract too much attention. The road past the camp was more dangerous at night and it was worth getting to know it. If I passed along it without being stopped it would mean that we would not have to use this dangerous road at night. It would be better to go by day, hide in the nearby woods and when darkness fell, go from there to the partisan camp.

It was broad daylight when I started on this internal way. There were soldiers in the barbed wire-fenced camp, and many parked vehicles. Nobody stopped me. The sentry looked at me indifferently. I was tired and longed for a few moments of sleep. I was picked up by a peasant in a wagon and arrived in the city at noon. I had covered at least thirty kilometers on foot.

One day we wandered, as usual, in the neighborhood of the ghetto. The last night had been noisy with so much shooting, but the morning was quiet. In the environs of the ghetto there was some special movement whose cause was hard to determine. Something had happened, but what? SS soldiers were running around the ghetto borders; there was a great deal of movement along Poleska Street and on the corner near the graveyard on Zabia Street. The *aktzia* had ended some days ago. Perhaps something had happened to the remnants of the fighters in the ghetto? Maybe the battle had been resumed? The night before there had been a great deal of shooting, and many explosions.

For a long time we moved about without seeing anyone we knew. Suddenly we heard shooting again. From Zabia Street there was a tight ring of SS soldiers (who had replaced the traitors from the national minorities). Anybody coming close was driven away. Only toward evening did the news of the affair become clear to us, through fragments of information we heard from the Polish inhabitants of the area, from our landlord who worked near the ghetto, and from Poles working in the textile factory. That day everyone in the hospital on Fabrychna Street had been executed, both the sick and the workers. Women who had given birth, patients recovering from serious surgery, infants who had just seen the light of day, and the mortally ill; all had been taken from their beds. Those who did not have the strength to get up were forced to stand with the blows of rifle butts. Many died on the spot and all, the dead, the dying and the living, were loaded like piles of rags on wagons and taken for execution to the graveyard on Zabia Street. The massacre took only a few minutes, and the graveyard was silent again. There were stories of nurses and doctors who had not been sentenced to die but who did not stomach to watch the execution of their patients, and willingly went to be killed with them. They told of nurses who fell upon SS soldiers and the operation commander Friedl. Some of the hospital's doctors arrived in Auschwitz, and a few survived.

At that same time an *aktzia* was carried out against more than one thousand children, taken from their parents on the pretense that they were being sent to Switzerland. They arrived in Auschwitz and were among the children who died slowly, suffering, in medical experiments, from hunger and hard labor. There were some clever and cunning children who managed to escape from the "transport to Switzerland." People told of one who had been killed escaping; of another who had been wounded but escaped, and one who had disappeared without leaving any trace. They told of one child, who looked "aryan", who fled from the sympathetic people who wanted to take him and shouted that he wanted to go back to his mother. They told of one black-eyed girl, who embraced the German's boots and cried: "Mama. . .give me back my mother." The boot pushed her forcibly and she remained lying on the street until her little comrades picked her up and dragged her with them.[33]

There was one child who looked like a gentile boy that was surely Franck, the son of Marylka's friend. Once he was given to a Polish friend, but ran away from her and returned to the ghetto, to his mother. To spite his new "mother" he walked erect among the neighbors' children and announced: "My name isn't Franek and my mother's name isn't Mania. She isn't in Warsaw, and everything is a lie. My mother's name is Chaya and she lives in the ghetto." They climbed over the fence and jumped into the ghetto.

It was again a summer day. A wide gate opened on Fabrychna Street, long lines stretched through the gate and beyond. They were Jews, well dressed. They walked slowly, with dignity, without children, almost without any packages. I looked closely: Barash was marching in the front row, with his wife at his side. His grey head could be seen from afar. Goldberg, and Marcus, the commander of the Jewish police, the whole Judenrat, and after them more hundreds of Jews, all dignitaries: former heads of the factories, leaders of the Judenrat departments, police officers. There was a wire stretched down the middle of the street. Barash tripped, and almost fell. He bent over, lifted the wire, and threw it aside. Once again he walked slowly, dignified and erect. The company came closer. Sentries walked along the sides of the street and took care that we did not come too close. The company covered the whole of Fabrychna Street and came to the railway, to the industrial station. Barash looked around and did not see those standing on the aryan side of the street, watching. He looked ahead as if his eye had been caught by some distant point on the blue horizon. They marched silently. No one wept, no one cried — no one attempted to escape.

And so were led to Maidanek the last of the Jews, who had lived an illusion. We learned later that all 900 Jews in the small ghetto for Jewish dignitaries and special craftsmen had been taken to Maidanek. There they had been taken first to a work camp near Lublin; Barash had been work manager there, with a ribbon on his sleeve ("Verdienstvoller Jude") until something happened in the work group and the Germans vented their fury on the proud Jew, beat him, and dragged him away to the cruelest of labors. All 900 of the Jewish elite were killed in the gas chambers in Maidanek, together with the last of the Bialystok Jews, some months after arriving in the camp, on November 3, 1943. We learned this later, in the course of our search for contact with the concentration camps and the death camps.[34]

Some days later we were "walking" again near the ghetto. We were waiting for Marylka, who was supposed to arrive from the forest. We thought that it would be better to wait for her outside the city, to take her clothing and give her city clothing before she reached the sidewalks. We walked along Shenkevich Street toward the forest. Today, too, the sun shone. It rained during the night and Marylka was soaked through and through. We put her clothes in a bag, and wrapped her muddy boots in paper. Suddenly a German carriage carrying German officers came up behind us. Finkel, who had been the head of the biggest factory in the ghetto, the Jewish head of Stefan's factory, the textile plant for clothes, chemical products and steel parts, sat in the carriage between the two Germans. He was laughing with them, talking with them as if they were his friends. The carriage passed us and turned into

Yuroviecka Street and stopped near the gate. Finkel jumped out. The Germans remained. They separated from Finkel courteously. All at once one of them drew his pistol and shot Finkel who was standing with his back to them. He fell with his smile still on his face and the words of farewell on his lips. That was the way Finkel died. He had lived as a servant and died that way. He was not sent to Maidanek with the Jews who had been left in the little ghetto. He had been accorded a special honor; he was killed near the ghetto gate, getting out of his masters' carriage.

The hunt for Jews continued every night, and every night the remaining Jews in the big ghetto killed German, Ukrainian and Lithuanian soldiers who were looking for them. At night the Jews came out to collect food and water. The two sides ambushed each other. It was known that there were organized groups in the ghetto. Some said that they were rebels who were systematically attacking German positions. The wagoners (who had escaped to the forest) did not know any of the details. They themselves had arrived in the forest with the help of Volkovisky and Engelman. These two had been in the small ghetto organizing escape groups. Many more might still come this way.

One day Kovadlo, the engineer who had worked with Kuba making the grenades, arrived. The joy in the forest of course, was very great. Especially encouraging was the prospect that still more might come. Kovadlo recalled that Barash had negotiated with Volkovisky and Engleman (the first a Communist, the second from Dror) and offered to give them the Judenrat funds if they would take him to the forest. (His proposal was ridiculous; he should have given the money when the ghetto was still alive and fighting.)

The comrades had agreed to take the funds and scheduled a day for Barash to go. Exit from the ghetto was difficult and demanded great caution. More than two or three persons could not escape on the same day. Nor could Barash be among the first to go, when many fighters were still in the little ghetto and their escape had to be effected. Kovadlo knew that there was a combat unit in the bunker in the liquidated ghetto, composed mainly of the rebels from all the movements who had fought on the front line in Novogrodska, Smolna, Gorna, and Ciepla Streets. They had broken through the siege and reached the bunker. It was known that Velvel and Engelman were in contact with them. The last of the fighters did not want to come over to the little ghetto and organize a piecemeal exit. They still had arms, and they wanted to break out as a fighting unit. They were looking for an organized escape and carrying on their nightly battles in the meantime. Kovadlo did not have any more details. He had been in the small ghetto and only the two, Velvel and Engelman, maintained contact with the rebels and knew their plans.

"Meanwhile Volkovisky and Engleman got out?"

"Last, of course, after they finished organizing the rest of the exit groups of fighters and other Jews prepared to join them." That is what Kowadlo had replied, and what Marylka told us. We, however, knew more than she did. Marylka had been in the forest when Bronka and I wandered in the ghetto neighborhood and had met the latter group, with Barash at its head. The little ghetto had been liquidated, and the group had included Velvel and Volkovisky. They too had gone to Maidanek; they had not managed to get out of the ghetto since they had not finished organizing the escape to the forest.

The fate of the other fighters in the bunker between Gorna and Hmielna Streets was as yet unknown to us. They were still fighting, falling on patrols at night and preparing to leave for the forests as an organized unit, with their arms and ammunition. The days passed, the echoes of the battles inside the ghetto grew weaker each night. Once again "jumpers" arrived, those who had leaped from the death trains. Some more individual refugees came from the transport. One group of fighters that had arrived in the first days after the action and had met Germans on the way had lost some of its comrades near the Chilichanke River, but had long since gone to the forest. We were still waiting for the rest.

The ghetto remained isolated. There was no going in and no coming out. We looked for some way to Hmielna Street and did not succeed. On the day of the revolt the Vultan Iron Casting plant had been destroyed. It stood on the border of the ghetto. We might have gotten through that way, but it was well guarded, even though it had been almost completely destroyed inside. On the day of the revolt, Jewish rebels had broken in and sabotaged it. They destroyed the machinery, blown up everything possible with grenades, driven the workers out and, when they encountered a patrol with a small SS group accompanying a Gestapo commissar coming to examine the ghetto borders, they opened fire, and killed the commissar and some of his company.

The factory was still paralyzed. Armed sentries marched around it; and the Poles were saying that they had already begun to repair the machinery, with the laborers working under guard. The factory was apparently important to the German war industry.

We also gathered information about the break into "Molten Bolt". Who carried out the operations? Who were the saboteurs? Who had commanded? And most important: who had remained alive, and where were they? If they were still alive, still fighting, why didn't they come to us? They had planned to leave, and they hadn't come.

That was the way life flowed. We took our first steps in the city. We were an army of Jewish partisans, planted in the city.

The Factory

My situation in the city worsened. Once again I had to find some legal foothold. My work card was not registered in the labor office, and was actually a forgery. We decided that if it was not possible to change my name and papers I should at least change my looks. I took my sister's dress and altered it, and once again I was dressed elegantly. However, the dress and my sister's fancy hat were not sufficient. The girls decided that I would have to alter my hairstyle. We combed it high over my forehead. A new hairstyle, new hat, and pleated dress — a new woman!

From then on, in many places, I was thought of as a German. In public areas where the danger was greatest, I didn't reveal my "true" Polish face unless it was worthwhile. In the market I had to be Polish, or else they would refuse to sell me the food needed by our unit in the forest, and which the storekeeper-women kept hidden. It was not worth appearing as a German among the neighbors on Saint Roch Street. It was different when an inspection was carried out in the street and the German police or Gestapo patrols stopped passersby and examined papers. It was also good to appear as a German in the only autobus in the city which was only for the use of Germans. In that vehicle you were safe because there were no inspections, and no "kidnappings" to Germany, or to Auschwitz. You could cross the city when you were carrying "contraband". In the forest they needed medicine and compasses. For days we ran through the streets, following Marylka's instructions, and slowly gathered them. Compasses were completely banned. Every fool knew that only people moving in the open, in the forests and fields, and especially at night, needed such instruments. Medicines in too great a quantity aroused suspicion, especially when they were so urgently needed at the front. And we had to have precisely those medicines.

Now Marylka could handle all her contacts in the city, renew forgotten ones and look around for new connections. One by one they appeared, these Poles with whom we established ties. Each had his own task to perform: Felek, Volodya, Hella, and "uncle" Burdzynsky, Vladek and Shchelchik, Yanka and Ada and Buchynsky. They did not come to us all at once. Those who had come found their places in the fighting underground in Bialystok province in the course of time. We gradually expanded our movement. We organized the war prisoners near the city, engineers working for the German industry and the central electric station. We established contact with high ranking Germans, members of the National Socialist party. All this was accomplished by the six Jewish girls.

In Haska's house they began to talk about my not working and not being registered with the police. Perhaps I was a German agent, or maybe I had run away and was in hiding. It was very unpleasant. Suddenly an idea struck me: I would go to the German, Schade. At worst he would be angry but he would not betray me. For over half a year I had been using the forged work card he had given me. During that time he had signed that document almost every two weeks. He was just as much in my hands as I in his.

When I entered his office he did not recognize me. I asked to talk to him privately; he was surprised but agreed. His office was pleasant and comfortable, with wide soft chairs. I sat down. Facing me was the factory director, a typical German, with a shiny bald head, energetic-looking face, bright eyes, a little watery, fleshy fingers, with clean fingernails. Once again the same indifferently courteous question: "Sie wünshen?"

I introduced myself. He began to remember slowly; yes he did recall me. Now he was smiling, the iron mask melted:

"How did you get out? Are you here a long time? Perhaps you have heard something of Mina?"

"I know nothing about Mina. I thought that you would help her and arrange for her to get out."

I had apparently touched a sensitive nerve. He suddenly became edgy. Yes, with all his heart he had wanted to help her, but how could he do it? "Mensch, wie macht man dass?" He had been quite worried about her and her family.

Only after a great deal of time did I learn that he really had saved Mina, and that while I was sitting in his office Mina was hiding in his apartment in the same building. He pretended, and I believed him. He was cunning, and an excellent actor.

Now I disclosed my difficulties to him and explained why I was unable to arrange matters for myself. I did not have any employment; I was not registered in the labor office. No, I would not go to the work office. Schade wondered:

"Why not? I am going to give you a card which will state that you work for me, in Factory No. 4."

"I cannot go there. I have acquaintances among the workers, and I don't know what they are like today. If you are able to arrange the matter without my having to appear there, good; if not I'll have to give it up."

Schade reflected. Finally he said deliberatly, in measured words:

"Yes, I'll do it. Of course it will be easier for me to arrange the registration. Since you haven't worked for such a long time, they are liable to question you. They will not question me. At most, they will ask me for three meters of woolen cloth for a suit . . . Come tomorrow at 4:30 p.m. I'll wait for you in my office. Tell them at the gate that I have invited you."

When I returned the next day a new work card with a new address was waiting for me. He received me with his face shining:

"Everything is in order. They didn't ask questions and they didn't investigate anything. But you will have to work, what do you think?" Once again he smiled.

"That's not good," I said sadly.

"There's no choice. As long as you lived in the ghetto you could get along without working. Now that you are in the city it is impossible for you not to be employed at all. I'll arrange for you to work only six hours, maybe less. You will be able to get away before the end of the work day. You will have to establish some special status for yourself in the factory, so that even though the other workers are not allowed to leave the factory before four, you will be able to do so. I won't be too strict, of course. I'll give you tasks that will free you from constant contact with the other workers."

I thanked him very much and arranged to come to work the following Monday. I left him with my necessary card in my hand. We were all very happy, not only with the arrangement, but also because we had linked a German like Schade to the underground cause without his knowledge. Our landlords also treated me with respect. Tens of thousands of girls my age were not able to find employment in the places where they lived; no institution or office was willing to accept them, and the labor office sent them off directly to Germany when they came to ask for work. Somebody who knew how to manage was worthy of respect.

That is what our neighbors thought; that is what all those living in our house thought. The house manager entered me in his registration book, and I was a legal tenant in 7 Saint Roch Street. I also received a food card, and when I showed my work permit I received the supplement for hard labor.

We found, however, that my identification card had to be extended. That extension was obtained in the commissariat where one was registered. How was I to go to the Vesola St. commissariat? There was no choice. I went to our commissariat on Pilsudsky Street. They asked me if I was a Volksdeutsche. I replied: "not yet", and handed over my papers. I spoke

German; if you spoke a little German, even only a little, you were considered worthy of betraying your own people and becoming a Volksdeutsche. The gendarmes who sat at the table in the dark room behind the barred windows, treated me — or rather my hairdo and painted lips — courteously.

"So, you're moving here? Good, we'll sign your card with the stamp of our commissariat and register you among our tenants.

About 500 people worked in the factory. The craftsmen were Poles and two Volksdeutsche. The "obermeister", who was called the "ober" for short, came from Germany. Schade was the director. In addition to the workers, masters and director, there were office workers. Most of the men and women laborers were veterans in the trade; there were women who had spent twenty years and more at these noisy machines. There was a father and son, both weavers. The son was still young, perhaps 18. It was hard to tell the workers' ages; two women who worked opposite me seemed to be young, but they really weren't. They simply had never managed to develop properly. At their side were two girls; they looked to be about 17 but were only 13 or 14. Both were exiles; their families came from the environs of Bialobuicza. They operated the machines like adults.

My job was not the most important. Schade had adapted the duties to the person. I sat in a corner of the hall with its dozens of windows and looked about. The spindles moved back and forth, the women seizing the loose threads, joining them speedily, catching up with the machines, and following it back and forth. They did that every day, from six in the morning until four in the afternoon. The old master was good-natured, but strict. The terror of the factory was the "ober", short, thin and always shouting. Even before he opened the door to the hall, before his foot was over the threshold, you could hear his loud voice. The smell of alcohol and tobacco on his breath and his hoarse voice filled the air. All the workers feared him, though he seemed miserable to me. He would hit women, men and even the children.

There was a healthy, handsome Polish lad, named Romek in the factory. Once I saw the chief master slap him in the face. Rimek could have knocked him down with one blow, but he controlled himself, and turned his back to "ober".

The two Volksdeutsche masters were also interesting. They were tall, handsome vigorous men. It was amusing to see them bow to the ground in front of thc small, weak "ober". The workers tried not to meet him in the court in the morning. They would walk through other departments, through piles of rubbish, to avoid him. These two, however, as soon as they saw the "ober" from afar, hurried to bow deeply before him and to say "good morning."

Schade, the director, was a special case. The workers were in mortal fear of him. No one dared turn to him with a request or a complaint. The distance between him and the workers was so great that he seemed to them almost super-human. You could hear his voice, too, from one end of the hall to the other, though not often. "Today he is in a bad mood," the rumor passed from mouth to mouth. "He's angry today," workers whispered to each other. I was astonished by Schade's behavior in the factory. Maybe he's only pretending I said to myself. How surprised I was, however, to see him slap a Polish worker.

Schade was strict concerning the quality of the product. He watched his machines, professionally examined every part of the work. A minute or two before four he would appear suddenly in the hall to see whether the workers had already stopped working and left their machines. If they were caught in the act their fate was bitter.

Schade was strict on production and order. He struck workers, and he raised the levels of production. He had an excellent reputation in the central institutions of the textile industry. He was known as a superior professional and a very fine organizer. That is what the office workers said. They knew everything; they had friends in the central office. They had been working together for tens of years. Here it was difficult to keep a secret, despite the distance between the workers and the office employees and the chasm between the factory and its director.

Workers told an interesting story about Schade. He limped slightly. It was said that some workers whom Schade had persecuted had waylaid him in the street when he left his home in the evening, and threw a thick log at him. He tripped, and they disappeared. Since then he limped, but he had kept silent, had not investigated nor looked for those guilty. The workers whispered, and wondered.

I too wondered, and tried to understand the character of that strange man, the typical German who had risked his life to save victims of the Nazis. Yes, Schade was totally German in all his parts, in his strictness, his beatings, his professionalism, his movements and his conduct. Above all, he loved order, and watched over the operations of his apparatus. Apart from that, however, was he anti-Nazi? I wondered. He would beat the workers of the enslaved people, and at the same time he would also help them. How could I understand the complicated nature of Director Schade, member of the National Socialist Party?

Schade generally did not see me when he passed among the machines. He simply did not look my way. Once or twice he approached me in the company of the master to look at my work.

My chore was easy. I had to pull threads through a frame according to a given pattern. I would count: four threads above, four below, two and two and all over again. Opposite me sat a young woman who handed me the threads. Schade stood for a moment and looked at my work without saying anything, without praising or condemning. He turned and left.

The factory workers sensed that I had some special privileges in the plant. First of all, I finished at one in the afternoon, while they all worked until four. Second, the workers were not accustomed to someone sitting off by himself. Every new man or woman immediately entered the workers' family. They all shared the same troubles and concerns. What point, then, in being separate? If Schade hit you, who would comfort you? If the "ober" scolded you, who would help you with some bitter joke? Who could advise you how to avoid punishment for coming late, for being sick, or for a "little" theft?

I would finish my work and hurry home. There was a lot to do, and no time to develop relationships, nor could I establish connections in the factory. I had to keep apart - for better or worse. It was a difficult thing to do. Here were desperate, depressed workers; more than once you wanted to come closer to them, and sometimes you really needed their company; you could use their vitality and simplicity; and then suddenly you remembered: you must maintain the wall, or you would flee.

I asked Schade once to free me for two days since I had to go to Grodno. I also asked him for official permission from the factory so that I could get a travel permit. I told him that I had to visit some village since I had received information that a member of my family had succeeded in escaping from the death car and was hiding there. I stood in the stairway and spoke to him in German. Some workers who passed looked surprised and curious. That was, apparently, a rare sight; a Polish worker talking to the German director.

Schade gave me the permit. He asked no questions. I was free for two days, and even received an official pass. Freedom for a few days was the dream of most of the men and women working in the factory.

There was whispering. Some said that I was a Volksdeutsche, others, believed that I had some doubtful kind of protection.

In any case, all the guessing was unpleasant, since it directed too much attention to me. I heard them, in the main, from my co-worker. Her sister was the chief clerk in the office. She was good looking and intelligent. Her name was Yadzia. From her the rumors passed to her sister, and from the sister to me.

"You know, Halina, many think that you are a Volksdeutsche. I know it isn't so. But why do they say that about you? True, you speak German, you comb your hair like a German, and you are . . . hm . . .close to the director. No, don't be sorry. If only I could talk to him the way you do, face to face, without lowering my eyes. Even if I knew German, I couldn't talk to him that way! Yes, you are a little different from all of us. But I don't care; meanwhile I am benefiting because of you; I also work less."

There was no end to my flow of talk but I could always learn something from her. She was an honest woman. I learned from her mostly, how not to behave; what not to do. She told me who the decent Polish masters and workers were, and who the traitors and the loose-lipped. Her name was Hella. She trusted me. Did she suspect something? Did she guess my origin? Perhaps. But she never even hinted.

Once she told me that her sister had Jewish friends. She had studied with them in the gymnasium. "I don't know what she saw in them but she always sought their company; she said that they were more cultured, more intelligent."

Hella was not afraid to tell me of her sister's liking for Jews and her relationships with them. Hella had her own ideas, about Jews as well as about Schade: Schade was a good man; he was only pretending to be bad.

The Wall of the 71

Something happened. Marylka found one of her acquaintances from the pre-war Communists, a shoemaker. She visited him and learned something about the possibilities of buying weapons in the vicinity. One day she brought important news. A group of Jewish craftsmen were imprisoned in the Gestapo building no. 15 Shenkevich Street. The shoemaker had received a note from a friend, Shatzman, who was one of those being held. They were both shoemakers, and both had belonged to Communist circles.

We tried to establish direct contact with Shatzman. It was not easy. The Gestapo building on Shenkevich Street was notorious, a synonym for horror, fear and torture. It was comprised of a large block of buildings.

The cobbler, a simple, honest man, looked us over and decided to do what he could to help. One day he notified us: tomorrow, between seven and seven-thirty in the evening we must be on Zamenhof Street, not far from Biala. We would meet Shatzman there.

Zamenhof Street was crowded with people. There were no vehicles moving. The street was closed at one end, where the barbed wire fences were, and gendarmes guarded the little bridge over the Bialka River. The dead ghetto was on the far side of the river.

We walked slowly. No one paid any attention to us. It was already past seven. If they had not come to arrest us by now it was a good omen. I crossed the street. We had decided to act with caution. I stood on one side of the road, Marylka on the other. Shatzman was supposed to arrive with a big pitcher in his hand. That was the signal. Minutes passed, and no one came. Suddenly, from behind the corner of Biala, a pitcher appeared, and behind it a figure: not very large, thin, wearing a winter coat buttoned to the neck, and boots. The clothing surprised me; it was clean without the visual signs of damage from torture or beatings. We gestured to him. He looked around, and when he saw that nobody was following, he came closer. His talk was fragmented and his eyes darted about constantly. He wondered how we had found him, and was surprised that we had dared to meet him here. Every day he went from the prisoners' block to the kitchen to bring supper for the twelve Jews. They were all craftsmen and their situation was not bad, except that any day their work might come to an end and they would be liquidated, like many before them. They wanted to escape. They could go out, as he had gone today, and simply not return. Of course they would reach him within a few minutes. However, if the matter were well organized they might manage to get away. Marylka and I looked at each other. Perhaps we would take him with us now; he was here. We immediately realized that we might save Shatzman, but what about the other eleven? We had to get all of them out. We would have to organize their escape.

Some Jews had already tried to flee and had been caught and shot. This happened, however, because the way beyond the Gestapo wall had not been secured. They did not have any address or any organization to care for them. They were caught outside the city.

We told Shatzman to consider the possibilities of the whole group escaping. We promised to organize their flight from the wall and beyond and arranged to meet again at the same place two days later. The entire meeting took only a few minutes. At the end Shatzman blurted: "I have a lot of news from your comrades. Your name is Chaika, isn't it? I was in the bunker with them." He pressed my hand strongly and wanted to leave.

I wished to stop him to make him tell me whether they were living, and if so, where they were, but he moved away swiftly and disappeared around the corner of Biala Street.

Night was falling. I stood and watched the figure disappear behind the Gestapo building wall. That evening we learned nothing about our comrades and the bunker. We returned home close to curfew hour. Haska and Liza were waiting for us, and had already begun to worry. It was difficult for them to believe that we had met one of the Jewish prisoners of "no. 15," and had found it necessary to send him back to his prison.

The meetings on Zamenhof Street were repeated. At every one I wanted to ask him about the bunker, but matters were pressing and the late hour prevented us from asking questions. I didn't dare endanger the complex preperation awaiting us. But I already knew; the comrades were no longer alive.

At the last meeting we finished working out all the details. Every one of the twelve Jews had been given an address by Shatzman, and a well thought out plan of how to get there. Our people would be waiting for them at night. They would remain dispersed in the city for two days and when the searches ended, would be moved to the forest. We warned Shatzman against revealing the plans and addresses before the very last minutes. According to Shatzman, some would bring arms with them. The plan for them to arm themselves was ready, and the escape through the wall was almost a certainty.

On the agreed night we waited for them. We had found appropriate apartments, in Polish homes. Of all our own places only Lizka's was fit to shelter them. Each of us waited for them in one of the Polish apartments. Shatzman himself was supposed to come to Lizka's room.

It was a long night for all of us. In the morning, before leaving for work, we met. It seemed that no one had come, except Shatzman. Lizka reported what he said: he had gone out toward evening, after the others. All of them said that they were afraid to leave. He tried to convince them that their safe days in the Gestapo building were numbered, that the Germans would kill them as they had their families, their relatives and all the Jews in the ghetto. The Germans were keeping them alive for the present, because they wanted good shoes for their wives and fine suits for themselves. All his words, however, had been to no avail. They were afraid, and he decided not to wait, but to leave as usual, with his pitcher, and get away. He had not, of course, given them the addresses; he had detroyed them. The Jews had also been against his escaping; they were afraid that they would all be punished because of him, and tried to force him to remain with them. He had therefore gone out, supposedly only to bring their supper, and had promised to return. He threw the pitcher into the first courtyard and had gone to his shoemaker friend. Some minutes before curfew he arrived at Lizka's.

His story sounded a little strange. We suspected that he had chosen the safest way, had not even attempted to organize the others, but saved only himself. Shatzman had been one of the revolt fighters and had even gone with our comrades into the bunker.

We received him well, took care of him and hid him, but our joy in the great action was marred. We looked again for a way to the Gestapo prisoners, but in vain. We learned from Shatzman that in the prison ther were also Jews who had been caught in the ghetto a long time after the action, and that the Germans were sending them to Novosolky, where they were exterminated. Only the best craftsmen were kept alive.

That evening we all listened to his story. After the revolt he had found himself in the bunker on Hmielna Street. It was spacious and had both electricity and water. There were 72 comrades, all fighters who had participated in the revolt and had succeeded in breaking out of the encirclement. Most had arrived with their weapons. In the bunker there was also a large quantity of arms that had not yet been used, since there was no time to prepare them before the revolt. These were arms from the last shipment to reach the ghetto, some days before August 16.

The main entrance to the bunker was through a well in the court of no. 7 Hmielna. There were additional side entrances. There had been activists from all the movement in the bunker. He remembered Zorah and Gedalyahu, Avremel and Yentel, Hershel from Yashinovka, Henech Zielazogura from Dror, and many of his Communist comrades. He remembered following the revolt. They were returning from the action in the "Molten-Bolt" iron casting plant on the evening after rebellion. Zerah had headed that action. The sabotage activities had succeeded, and they also were able to kill a German commissar and his company. The stories of the tenants of Gorna and Poleska Streets were true.

"That last night, groups went out to attack Germans moving about the neighborhood. Every evening small groups of two or three people ambushed the patrols. Every night they returned bringing new weapons arms and food with them. It was unanimously decided by the command and ratified by all the fighters that they would not move to the small ghetto but would proceed directly from the bunker to the forest. Preparations were made and a tunnel was dug from the bunker under Smolna and Poleska Streets, to the aryan side. The plan itself was not revealed to all the comrades, but it was assumed that implementation was close.

"Every night comrades went out on actions. The mood was good. Everyone was sure that he would get to the forest. Their arms had encouraged them; the command had instilled confidence. There was no feeling of lassitude. The bunker was transformed into a battle base. Meanwhile, the Germans were looking for Jews in the ghetto, in the attics and cellars. At night they would ambush Jews coming out to seek food, and thus were uncovered the hiding places of dozens of people.

Some of the Jews who had been caught did not reveal their hiding places. Some had even defended themselves. There were also other armed Jews wandering about in the dark. We were no longer the only fighters in the ghetto; we were just the first. Other Jews followed us with firearms, and all kinds of weapons, axes and sticks; the Jews' war for survival had entered a high stage, one of battle. Only during the day were the desolate streets still; the patrols in the ghetto continued their action up to the last minute. Fighting continued for a week after the revolt.

"One day we were informed that this was to be our last night in the bunker. Everyone was to clean his weapons, and prepare his clothing; that evening we would leave the ghetto.

"On this final night we were very busy. Comrades left and returned from patrols and preparations were being completed. Before dawn the men were divided into groups and given their exit plans. Commanders were appointed for all groups. During the day we were all supposed to rest, to try to sleep. In the early morning, Gedalyahu and his group returned from their last patrol. On their way they had found food in one of the open houses. We hadn't managed to close the entrance behind them when suddenly the bunker was encircled. The Germans had apparently followed in the footsteps of the last group to return, since they had been able to seal all the entrances so quickly.

"The Germans' cries of 'raus' were answered first by silence. When we found that they had covered all the entrances to the bunker and that there was no way out, our comrades replied with fire. Germans descended into the well and began to shoot into the bunker. The comrades retreated to the other side and shot from there. From there, too, came a rain of bullets. There were no victims, but there was no way out either. Comrades attempted to break out under a rain of fire, but could not. The Germans were waiting for them. They fell upon each one separately, tied his hands behind him and took his gun. A thorough search was made of the bunker. Two wagons arrived, and the guns were loaded in them. Were there victims among the Germans? It is hard to say; nobody saw them. Only in the Gestapo building they said that they suffered many losses. The Germans apparently had obtained the plan of the bunker."

It was treason. Who the traitor was we shall never know. Of the 72, only Shatzman had remained, the single witness to that black day. We were told about the bunker by others who had come to the forest earlier. Barefoot, they were brought to Yuroviecka Street, to the long, thick wall of a German factory there, one by one, under guard. The Germans were afraid to bring them all together. Opposite, on the corner of Ciepla and Yuroviecka Streets, sat the company of SS commanders, commissars and high officers, Dibos and Friedl, who had carried out the ghetto liquidation and put down the revolt. They supervised the execution. Dawn came. There were 71 of them, all young, all with their hands bound, all barefoot but with their heads raised proudly. No one begged; no one pleaded for mercy, and no one revealed any sign of weakness. Proudly they went to their death. Jews who were hiding in the neighborhood watched the heroic tragedy of the martyrs. Their shouts echoed in the air, and will be heard forever . . . Shatzman said that Gedalyahu had been one of the first; he did not remember what he said. All the cries had merged: one had called out "long live the Soviet Union" and fell; another shouted "Israel, forever", and yet another died with Eretz Israel on his lips.

How had Shatzman survived? One of the commissars had recognized him as an expert craftsman who had worked in the ghetto for the Gestapo officers. He pulled him out of the line, whispered something in Friedl's ear, and left him standing on the side. His comrades had been shot before his eyes. From there he was brought to the prison, and from the prison transferred, as an experienced shoemaker, to the Gestapo building.

For a long time we tried to discover what had happened to Mordechai and Daniel. We heard many rumors, but one recurring version, that Shatzman, too, had heard, that Mordechai and Daniel were in the hospital; they had not arrived at the bunker. One of the nurses who fled from the hospital told about two men, one young, called Mordechai, and an older one, who had come to the hospital armed. As long as the hospital remained in existence, the doctors and nurses had tried to keep the two of them there. They had suggested that the two men move to the small ghetto, but they refused. They argued that there was no point in saving their own lives when there were no prospects of continuing the war. When the Germans arrived to liquidate the hospital, they both committed suicide.

That is how Mordechai, the commander of the revolt in the Bialystok ghetto died, and that also is how Moshkovich, the veteran fighter, met his end.

We moved Shatzman to the forest, and he joined the partisans.

Rivkele

Our searches for Jews in the city did not stop. One evening we passed by the Saint Roch Cathedral. Suddenly a large, dark figure appeared; it seemed to have leaped out of the ground. We whispered in Yiddish. The figure stopped. It was a Jew who had been hiding for more than a month in one of the Cathedral crypts. We brought him to one of our underground apartments. He was bearded, unkempt, tall, and broad-shouldered. He was hungry, and looked at us in surprise. We appeared so small and weak compared to him. He stared at us but did not speak. We brought him shaving materials, fed him, and washed him. He was a young blacksmith, only 35, and his name was Rubin. He had escaped from the transport and found refuge under the Cathedral. He used to come out at night and eat the grass which grew in the churchyard; sometimes he would eat the leftovers of meals brought to the church by the faithful Catholics who came from afar.

During the day he lay in his cave. We found him shelter in the home of Ada Liskovska, a Polish woman. She provided food. The fugitive had to lie quietly all the time she was absent, since the neighbors on the other side of the wooden wall could hear every sound in the room. Shatzman, too, had lived in her apartment for a few days until we organized his escape to the forest. We had had to move him somewhere else first, because his coughing would attract attention to Ada's apartment; the blankets and pillows in which he buried his head did not help. Ada's apartment was also used for other purposes; we could leave packages there for a little while; even arms were sometimes hidden there. That came later, however; at first we brought people only.

At a few minutes before nine I would burst into my courtyard. All the neighbors would still be sitting outside since the weather was fine. I would enter happy and laughing, breathing hard, pretending that I was returning from a rendezvous. If the evening was rainy it was good and bad: good because the streets were empty and patrols were rarely seen, bad because one's feet were wet, and the wornout coat was wet, and the bundles on one's back were wet, and so much heavier.

The number of unarmed non-combatants in the forest grew. There was not enough food or medicines. At that time we also carried sacks of food — bread, and beans and medicines — on our backs almost every day. Daily, messengers from the forest waited for us, generally in the graveyard to carry the sacks back, in the dark.

We had to steal our way into the graveyard: it was guarded day and night. The cemetery, however, was large and there were many holes in its high wall. You could hide something there and find it in place the next day. We found a shelter near the graveyard, about thirty meters away. Between the graveyard and the camp of the 42nd regiment was a small house lived in by a Polish woman named Bronia. Her husband was killed by the Germans. He had been a Communist. Bronia lived there with her aged, deaf mother. All her life she had been a worker in the textile factory. She was still young and fresh, her hair was smooth and she wore it in braids wound around her head. Her house was open to us; even in her absence we could leave our packages on the floor, behind the big stove, and lie down on the creaky iron bed.

The availability of Bronia's house made it much easier for us. We could stop there for as long as we had to. We could even lodge "Chechs". The "Chechs" were Jews who could not be mistaken for anything but Jews.

Autumn was beginning to cause trouble for us. Rain fell constantly, and it was cold. One of those who had leaped from the cars and reached the forest was Aryeh Wainstein. His clothes had literally fallen apart, the lice ate at his flesh. He did not have the strength to stand. Eaten by the lice and by despair, he had given up on life, and was totally apathetic.

Under his rags, however, he had hidden the poems and memoirs he had written in the ghetto. They were all that was left of him, and he guarded them zealously. We asked him to give them to us so that we could hide them in a secure place in the city but he refused. His poems still pulsed with the will to live. He was a living corpse. Day and night he lay on the boards in the bunker and wasted away.

We continued to entrench ourselves in the city. Each of us looked for additional underground work. Rivkele was the youngest. After the liquidation at the ghetto she changed. Her world had turned black. For a long time she had hoped that a miracle would happen and that many would return, among them her Yandzia. When all hope was gone, she became mentally unbalanced. Rivkele fought with courage, but her will to live and her concern for life had been undermined. In vain we spoke to her; in vain, I more than once raised my voice in reproaches and even insults. Rivkele wasn't listening; perhaps she didn't hear what we were saying. Rivkele was going her own way.

She was working all along for the same German doctor, who was certified by the Gestapo as a specialist in racial examination. Haska would visit there quite often to steal medicines for the partisans. She used to joke with the old doctor, the expert on the facial and body structure of the Jews. She once asked him to examine her face and determine her racial purity. He looked into her eyes, measured her nose and brows, and the lines of both, made his calculations, and declared: "Yes, you are a pure aryan."

Rivkele told many amusing stories about the old fool. In the end she laughed at him not only with us, but to his face. She "took" from his infirmary everything she could. We warned her to be careful, but she kept taking.

"You don't want me to? Good, I'll bring them to the forest myself." That was how all the arguments ended. Every day she returned from work with her pocket and bags bulging with bottles, creams, bandages and serum. She began to neglect her housekeeping duties, but the old doctor liked her. Once he remarked jokingly:

"What are you going to do when you get married? Who'll cook for you? What will your husband say about your carelessness, about your not knowing how to run a home?"

"Don't worry. When I get married I will be able to hire a German servant. German girls are the best and most loyal servants. It will be better for me and for my husband."

We saw Rivkele running blindly toward death but we were unable to stop her.

She lived with an old Polish lady, a Mrs. Kopolova, on a dirty street close to the city market in an old, red brick house. The staircase was filthy, the steps were twisted and worn. Children played in front of the house and it was always noisy. To the right of the entrance was a tiny, dark room, without a window — Rivkele's room.

The house was filled with articles that were no longer of any use. The landlady was old, and so was everything in the house. But she loved Rivkele as if she were her mother, worried about her, fondled and petted her. Only to Rivkele did she pour out her heart, and it was very bitter indeed. For decades she had lived among Jews. The teachers of the Hebrew gymnasium had been her neighbors and she had thought them to be the best, the most cultured, the best-mannered people in the world, and now they were all dead. How could she, an old lady, go on living? She kept their photographs as she kept the many icons in her house. Only to Rivkele-Maryshka could she unburden herself. Why only to her? Simply because she was a gentle soul. She once told Rivkele not to befriend me any longer because I was most certainly an anti-Semite.

"Your friend Halina is a Jew hater, I don't want to see her in my home any more."

After that Haska or Bronia used to go there when necessary instead of me.

That was the way Rivkele lived — between the Nazi doctor and the old Jew-loving Polish lady.

The rain did not stop. Rivkele found a young Jew in an abandoned cellar in the ruins of the rubbish-filled field between Sosnowa and Piasky market. We went to meet him, in the evening and brought him some food. He was a young man about 19 or 20, tall, dark, and typically Jewish. He had come out of the ghetto to find food for the members of his family hiding in a bunker. We suggested that he go to the forest, but he could not do so immediately; his family in the ghetto was waiting for him, and for the food. He had a little money, and a Polish acquaintance had promised to find him a gun for that money. He did not want to go to the forest empty-handed.

We offered to help him obtain a weapon, and we promised to provide him with food whenever he came out of the ghetto. We asked him to take one of us along and to show her the way he went in. We also agreed that we would wait for him the next day at the same place, and if he did not succeed in leaving, to wait the following day as well. We would do this for a number of days, after dark. We suggested that he give us the money and we would obtain the gun for him and for the other members of his family capable of bearing arms. We explained that he could not wander about the city during the day because he would be recognized immediately. He agreed.

A few days later we met again. He had been in the ghetto all the time; it had been more difficult than usual and he had had to wait until the way was clear. He was prepared to go to the forest but his family had decided to remain in the bunker. They had a comfortable and well-hidden hiding place, and only wanted weapons. Perhaps he would go to the forest alone.

We were very much disturbed by all this. The Germans might discover them at any moment; in the forest they would be free. He agreed with us but was unable to change their decision. We arranged that the next day we would provide him with everything he required, and ordered him not to move from his hiding place during the day. We even forbade him to go to his Polish acquaintance about the arms. Rivkele stayed another few minutes with him to get his money and the address of his Polish acquaintance.

The next day brought fine autumn weather. We dispersed to our work. In the afternoon we met in our room.

Suddenly Bronka, with tears in her eyes, burst into the room. Something terrible! Rivkele was no more. The fellow from the ghetto had gone to the market and shopped around. He held his shoes in his hands, when two gendarmes stopped him and began to question him.

The gendarmes asked where he got the shoes. He said that he had had them repaired.

Didn't he know that aryan citizens were forbidden even to repair Jewish shoes? He answered simply that a Polish woman had taken his shoes to repair them."Where is that Polish woman?"

He gave Rivkele's address. Rivkele had taken his shoes to have them repaired, and told him to come to her house to get them. She had given him her address. When Rivkele came home during her noon break she saw two gendarmes at the entrance. She began to run. She did not want to fall into their hands alive. They did not try to shoot at her; apparently they wanted to take her alive. One of them, however, almost caught up with her and thrust his bayonet at her, hitting her in the back. She ran, bleeding and stumbled, and the second one lunged with his bayonet and he, too, stabbed her in the back. Bleeding, profusely she was caught and taken to the hospital, mortally wounded. Her clothing was searched but nothing suspicious was found. Her work card certified that she worked for a Gestapo doctor. They set a guard at her bed.

Bronka said that immediately after the encounter the gendarmes had gone to question Rivkele's landlady.

"But why did she run away? We didn't want to hurt her," the gendarmes insisted.

They expressed their sorrow to the landlady. She said that she would go to the hospital to visit Rivkele. We were stunned, and decided to establish contact with the nurses in the hospital. The landlady helped. The news we received was horrible. Rivkele was fighting stubbornly for her life, suffering terrible pain, and the guards did not budge from her bedside. They listened to every groan and sigh she uttered but she did not lose consciousness. The guards were not able to get a word out of her. The hours passed; night came and went; daylight returned. Rivkele continued to fight off both death and the questioning of the Gestapo sentries. When we came again to ask the nurse about Maryshka, we were met with downcast eyes. We understood Rivkele had died.

With great emotion and tearful eyes the nurse told us, "Your friend died like a saint. Some minutes before the end I asked her if the pain was very bad, and if I could help her. She replied, 'Don't worry nurse, Jesus, too, died for others; maybe my death will decrease the suffering of others.'"

The nurse wept. We stood terribly shaken and moved in the hospital corridor and looked at the nurse, wiping the tears from her eyes. We knew that it was only for our sake, to remove any suspicion from us, that Rivkele had mentioned the name of Jesus as she expired. She died a hero's death.

The funeral took place the next day. In the morning Bronka and I went to the hospital. The mortuary was at the end of the large courtyard. Rivkele lay there alone. We had brought her clothing, following the Christian custom of dressing the dead in their most splendid clothes for burial. She looked so little lying there on the floor; so transparent. Her eyes were wide open as if she were still fully conscious. Her bright braids were spread across her shoulders to her breast. Her wounds were not visible; they were in her back. We brought flowers. Someone had bound a wreath to her head. A little later the old landlady came with two neighbors. She lifted the covering and stood petrified.

"Look, look, Christian people, God's angel is lying here." The women wiped their eyes and new tears flowed. Bronka and I watched the funeral service. Only we two did not weep. Some other neighbors and acquaintances of the landlady were there and some of the hospital workers also came. We walked in the middle. The women spoke of Rivkele's sainthood. One whispered to me:

"You know, at first I thought she was a Jew. The Jew who gave her his shoes to repair, and in general . . .the running away, the guard at her bed . . . But now I am angry at myself for thinking that of a Christian child, so pure and holy as she was. God will punish me for the evil I did to her."

I let her chatter on and even nodded my head in agreement. In the Catholic cemetery I listened silently to the priest's prayer. I saw them digging the grave, I saw them all genuflecting. I saw the big cross being planted on the pile of dirt, the only sign of her grave. How ironic, a big birchwood cross on the grave of Rivkele, the Jewish fighter.

Bronka also visited the old woman, Rivkele's landlady. Old Mrs. Kopolova told Bronka of the many talks she had had with the girl. "You know," she told Bronka, "Maryshka was apparently a Jew who had converted."

"How did you reach that conclusion?" Bronka asked.

"You know, Maryshka used to sigh so much at night, turning from side to side, always sighing. That was the Jewish spirit that did not leave her in peace! *(To ten duch Zydowski nie daje jej spokoju)*."

A month later Bronka was invited, along with Rivkele's other friends, to a service in Saint Roch Cathedral in Rivkele's memory.

It was Sunday. We dressed in our best and appeared one by one in the Cathedral. We scattered among the congregation. When everyone kneeled, we kneeled, we muttered, said "amen" and kneeled again. We even gave our pennies to the priest, in accordance with their custom. The congregation was not large, but more than we had expected. We listened to the priest who prayed, mentioning the name of Maria Madeiska a number of times and praying for her eternal rest. Sunday festivity prevailed in the church, the light of the candles in Rivkele's memory, the singing and the organ music made us feel isolated and alien. This was beyond our realm of comprehension, it was unreal, and almost unnatural. Silence was best; better to go on in a life that was understandable and normal. For us, this had become a life of war.

Fraternity in the Underground

Felek Lorek headed a cell. He was a Communist and had been a worker. He came from Poland's industrial area, the region of coal mines and the steel industry, Zaglembia. The first cell he established was composed of textile factory workers, a second of all kinds of offices and institutions in the city, and a third of persons who had succeeded in avoiding labouring for the Germans and by using fictitious names, had moved from petty trade to smuggling. Then railway workers were organized, bakery people, airfield personnel, tobacco and others. We did not maintain direct contact with these cells; that was Felek's job. We only supplied political material and instructions for projects to be implemented. In the course of time the cell provided precise plans of various installations, charts of the railway lines and sidings in the area; information about developments on the Polish street; about arrests; the bitterness and the living conditions of the workers. They also provided medicines and explosives, collected money and looked for arms in the city. Their work expanded; Felek ran around the city all day long; his meetings with us increased, at least once every two days, all over the city.

In Felek's cell there were people in whom we were particularly interested. One was an engineer in the electric power plant, Dimidovich, and one was a guard at the punitive camp near Bialystok. In addition, there was "uncle", Burdzynsky, and Ada Liskovska, whose apartment was at our disposal. With these we maintained direct contact.

We were no longer an intimate family; the early organizational tools were no longer appropriate. We had to appoint ourselves as a central committee, and divide the responsibilities. One was to concentrate the work of the Polish cells through Felek for which Lizka was chosen. She also maintained direct communication with the three persons mentioned above. Each of these filled a special function, but also contributed to the overall operation. Buchinsky, for example, the policeman in the punitive camp, hid arms over night at his apartment. When we had to find out where the military units around the camp were situated and where their arms stores were, Buchinsky told us. When we wanted to get someone out of the camp — someone who had been sent there because he had left a factory or fled from compulsory labor, or had been caught smuggling "goods" from the village, Buchinsky would help. He would prepare the escape plan, and stood guard during the escape. He also supplied weapons. Not a great deal — one "piece" at a time, but how valuable each one was!

I didn't know Dimidovich. Lizka maintained contact with him, and his main task was to supply us with plans of the industrial areas.

We had known Ada previously. We relied on her strength and her wisdom.

Finally, "uncle". We called him that because he looked avuncular. We also introduced him as our uncle to our landlords. "Uncle" Burdzynsky was the only one who visited us in our home. Underground laws and organizational frameworks did not apply to him. He, too, was a veteran Polish Communist, behind him were tens of years of struggle against Polish reactionaries, prisons and revolutionary activities among the workers. He was elegant, and looked like an aging intellectual. He had grey hair, walked slowly and deliberately without a touch of nervousness or impatience. He was always neat and clean, his clothes pressed and brushed. He gave us respectability and gave security. Such an "uncle"! So intelligent and aryan looking! He could easily be introduced as a gymnasium professor, a former government official, or the owner of an estate. He was a good cover for our isolation. A lone person without family was suspect in those days, but he could be Haska's uncle, and mine, Lizka's, and Bronia's. It could be assumed that our various landlords, scattered in all parts of the city, would never meet, barring some unforeseen accident. There was no such danger.

"Uncle" Burdzynky had a number of responsible contacts readily available. He was a pure Pole and it was easier for him to make new connections. Most of his contacts were outside the city. In one village he had a "daughter", a Jewish girl whose name was Hanka. He had saved her and now she, too, was a link in the underground. She worked as housekeeper in an estate held by Germans, but there were many Poles there, and Hanka became a link in a wide periphery. Our partisans were able to go there. They knew where the Germans' arms were, where they slept, and where the guards were. They also knew exactly where the large food supplies that the Germans were accumulating for the army and for Germany on the whole were kept. Hanka took care of a child, not hers, a Georgian boy. With the German invasion Hanka had wandered eastward. She was taken into a Soviet Army bus. The vehicle was bombed and the boy's mother, the wife of a Soviet officer, was killed immediately. Hanka was severely wounded and the child lay at her side, also hurt. Hanka picked him up, and since then was never separated from him. She became his mother, and "uncle" Burdzynky, his grandfather. He was four years old when we formed the underground links. Burdzynsky was thus at once father, grandfather and uncle. Above all, he was a member of the committee, controlling underground links, the only older person among us, the six Jewish girls of the committee, one of whom had already sacrificed her life. We were thus five left, with "uncle" the sixth.

Among "uncle's" contacts was a Jewish woman, Hella, a former Communist, and engineer by profession. She lived on a rich German estate which housed an experimental station. The Germans living on the estate were soldiers whose job it was to supply produce from the land to the army. They also ruled over the poor villages in the neighborhood. Hella worked there as manager and translator. From time to time she would come to the city to receive instructions from us and to transmit information about the neighborhood that became, in time, the target of constant partisan attacks. After a number of successful raids upon the estate, and the expropriation of weapons and food, the Germans remembered that Hella was the only Pole who knew all the secrets of the arms and supply stores. She was the only one who could have given the information to the partisans. The Polish woman and translator whom the Germans had respected and who had always shared their secrets, and whom most of the peasants considered a traitor, was suddenly arrested and vanished, without a trace. Hella was the wife of the engineer, Kovaldo, who had fallen in partisan battle. She carried on after him until she was murdered.

The workers of the "Roberg and Fink" factories appeared — veteran, heavy-footed, workers in a heavy industry. Their representative was Loninkin.[35]

A completely different underground group and with different functions was headed by Volodya Orlov, a Bielorussian who had been a militiaman with the Soviets and lived with his large family in the city's eastern suburb, on the way to the Volkovysk road. Since the arrival of the Germans he had been in hiding, going home rarely, and then only at night. He found refuge with Soviet citizens who had not managed to flee or who had turned back when the German army sealed off the road in front of them. From his hiding places he would check on the people, discover who had changed his allegiance, who had simply turned his back in despair and given up, who it was worthwhile to include in the underground or whom to give some task to perform.

In that way Volodya organized a cell, and he was wary of anyone who went to work for the Germans instead of finding some way to the underground. In his own suburb Volodya had also found Bielorussians, veteran inhabitants of Bialystok, who were prepared to take on any dangerous mission. Volodya also had a brother who lived in his house, and like Volodya, he too knew the forests.

The cell that Volodya established was also mixed. There were partisan couriers, who knew the neighborhood well and were excellent guides. More than once Volodya or one of his people led us by new paths when we found that the old one was dangerous. We could also go to his house, leave a package until evening, as in Bronia's, or leave suspected persons there, until they were moved to the forest. Volodya and his people watched over the eastern entrances to the city and maintained contact with various underground people. The electric power station on the site supplied a wide range of industries.

Volodya armed people from the suburb who were waiting until the central committee decided that the time was ripe for them to go to the forest. Volodya's task, however, was not over. Not all of his people were properly armed, and the partisan units could not absorb them until they were. The cell also had to prepare and train its members, and to carry out a number of important actions.

In the same suburb, three houses away from Volodya, lived Anela, a Jewish woman from Lodz. She had fled the ghetto during the first *aktzia* and had hidden in a small, filthy room in the suburb. Her husband, a Communist, was killed in the ghetto. As long as it existed he used to slip out occasionally and go to her. After the revolt Anela remained alone, in her sixth month of pregnancy and with a five year-old son. She looked stereotypically Jewish — the long nose made even to look longer by pregnancy and hunger, and her curly black hair.

The landlord from whom Anela had rented the room was also poor, a crude and drunken shoemaker. When Anela could not manage to pay the rent (only with difficulty did she find bread for her little son), the neighbor informed on her to the Gestapo. They came and asked for papers, and questioned her and the child separately. Her papers were in order, but her face was a Jewish one. The boy saved her. He stood up to the investigation, convinced the Germans that he was not Jewish, that his father had deserted them and that his mother was pregnant. They freed the mother and child, but afterwards gave them no rest. The drunkard persecuted her unmercifully. It was then that Volodya had appeared with his drawn pistol. He placed the weapon in front of him on the table, looked at the members of the family and told them: "If one of Anela's hairs falls, or her son's, or if you tell anyone of my visit, your life won't be worth anything."

After that it was easier for us, too; we had another underground apartment near the city.

The contact with Volodya and the transmission of instructions to him and his group were left to Haska. It was difficult to walk the five or seven kilometers to the suburb and back after a day of tiring work. Haska therefore learned to ride a bicycle. It was her landlady's. She agreed to lend it only to Haska. The development of our relationship was quite interesting.

By accident, Haska had found a room with a young couple. They were completely alien to us in body and spirit, representatives of a distant and hostile world. It was good to live with them. Our status depended upon one thing alone: our conduct. That behavior cost us a great deal, in taut nerves and added secrecy, but it had its rewards.

He was tall, strong, with a face that was primitive and even a little ugly. On Sundays he dressed up and looked like a prosperous grocer. He worked at the pumping station of the water system near the ghetto fence, between the end of Yuroviecka and the entrance to the Bialystocehek suburb. He worked for the Bialystok municipality and was always talking about his connections with the city clerks and officials and boasted about his relationships with the notables. When he was drunk he lost control of his senses: he would curse and shout. When his besotted anger increased and his wildness became unrestrained, he would shatter dishes, break furniture, overturn the pots on the stove, and sometimes seize a kitchen knife. He wielded the knife over his head, scared his family, and threatened everyone. His hand shook and he could not hold it firmly. It was said that he needed only one drink to be as drunk as Lot.

However, even when he was sober, there were times when his anger erupted like foaming whitecaps on a stormy sea. It was his wife who angered him most. He was madly jealous, and always suspected that he was being betrayed, whether there was reason or not. His wife was young and pretty, a refined country beauty. She was gay and full of life, dancing and singing. She wanted everybody to admire her, to love her, for her world to be filled with light and joy. She did not care very much who was the provider. She might just as easily be captured by the pleasant voice of a chance acquaintance, some old man captivated by her beauty as by some young lad, a relative, who would write her sentimental poems. The romantic music that the phonograph played for many hours of the day spoke to her hastyheart.

Her husband was jealous when she sang, when she dressed, and even when she bathed. There were always quarrels and there were always some apparent reasons for arguments. If she was in a good mood, it was a sign that she was happy with her lovers. When her affairs were bad, she decided that she was tired of her husband, and wanted to be rid of him. In short, they were perpetually at odds with each other.

We were caught in the middle. Each of them actually looked to us, and especially to Haska for moral support. Each shared secrets with us and wanted us to be both detectives and mediators. When he was drunk there was only one place in the house he respected: our room. Despite his drunken stupors, he never touched us. She would run to us when the storm broke; then she was sure he would not beat her. Misya, the landlady, had many secrets, and they were all known to Haska. Haska kept them. Sometimes she saved Misya from unpleasant situations, when she was in "someone's" company and her husband was unexpectedly free from work that day. Haska fulfilled small missions, delivered a note, or fixed a date for another day. Then she was given the bicycle, which served us for a long time. I used the autobus "Nur fur Deutsche" (For Germans only).

Our room had become a partisan center in the city. People came and went, couriers arrived. Marylka lodged there almost regularly when she was in the city; packages were brought in and taken out, arms were hidden and no one suspected. Marylka came in her dirty, dusty boots; we went out for whole nights, men from the forest sometimes arrived for operations and stayed with us. All this without anybody seeming to notice. Haska was an actress, really an artist. Even her mistakes in Polish did not bother her. Sometimes the landlords argued in the kitchen over some Polish expression, he wanting to show off his knowledge and she, to show her superiority, and in the end they came to ask Haska to mediate.

Becoming enthusiastic about his Polish loyalty, he would boast of his brave stand before his German superiors, and would begin to believe that he actually was a brave warrior for his enslaved country. He cursed the Germans and believed that he was spitting on them and rebelling against their rule.

Behind his patriotic pretentions, there was nothing, of course, but empty words.

One day Misya burst into our room with a smiling face. "Look, today he brought me cloth for a suit, light cloth for a summer suit."

"Who brought it? Where did he get it?" we asked.

"Oh, my darling" Misya laughed, "Look what kind of a suit I'm going to have sewn. I'll go to the best seamstress, the one who lives on the next street."

"But where did he get it from?"

"Do I know? Apparently, from the ghetto."

Our landlord also tried his hand at looting, did "business" with the police and the SS soldiers, stole into the ghetto at night and thereby won his wife's heart. Peace reigned for a day or two in their home. After a few days, other articles appeared, old bedding, a woman's dress, a coat, shoes and furniture. Yes, our landlord had looked around in a deserted apartment, waylaid a fleeing Jew, and took his coat.

Germans Lend a Hand

It was a sunny Sunday. Haska and I were not working because it was Sunday, Haska because she had managed to get out of working in the SS man's home. She could no longer abide the brutality of the Luchterand family, their Nazism and racial arrogance, and the many demands that prevented her from devoting herself to the underground. She had therefore decided to rid herself of that job at all costs. Her employer, Luchterand, once slapped her on her hand. She took her coat and fled directly to the labor office, and managed to get as far as seeing the manager. She broke into tears and showed the marks of her beating. (On the way, she had pinched her hand and hit it so that marks would be visible.) The labor office decided that she was freed of her employment with Luchterand and would have to appear at the office during the coming week, to be sent either to other employment, or to Germany.

We felt that Haska had fallen from the frying pan into the fire; if she were sent to Germany she would be even worse off. We decided that I should speak to Schade about her.

It was quiet in the room. Suddenly the door opened and an unknown man appeared in the doorway. He greeted us courteously in German and asked to be excused for daring to come to a strange home without an invitation.

"My name is Busse. I live in the next house. I am looking for a room for one of my workers who has just been married."

Busse? A German begging pardon of Poles? Who was he? I knew the name but could not recall from where.

We replied in German. He was surprised at the speaking of German and at the young Polish women who did not go to church on Sunday morning. He asked us if we lived here, since he was going from house to house looking for an empty room. God forbid, he did not want the room for nothing, as did others . . . (apparently referring to other Germans). He was sorry for his Polish worker: a decent, lonely person. Now he had the chance to settle down, but had no place to live.

This was a strange German; one who was walking his feet off looking for a room for his Polish worker. He was tall and straight, dressed in a coat that matched his dark hair. He was very handsome and intelligent looking. He had deep set eyes, framed by dark brows, and black hair. He wore large glasses and he looked like a Jew from a good family, a scholar. He conducted himself courteously and good naturedly. He was really a charming man. We knew, however, that we could not allow ourselves to be captivated by some German's looks. We had met many whose faces were pure but whose hands were stained with blood. Perhaps he was a provocateur or a detective; otherwise why was he so interested in us? Why was he asking where we worked and wondering why we did not go to church on Sunday?

Busse? Suddenly I remembered. He said that he employed many workers, that he had a contracting office for house painting and a studio for artistic pictures. I recalled one of my acquaintances in the ghetto, a young woman, black haired and good-looking, who had worked in his office as a bookkeeper. Bluma was the daughter of one of my mother's friends, and she had said a great deal about her employer, how he had taken risks to help her and his other Jewish workers and had smuggled food for them to the ghetto. He would accompany them and hide their contraband in his pockets.

She had also said that Busse had informed the Labor Office that he would pay his Jewish workers the same wages he paid the Poles despite the explicit ban on doing so. When he did not receive official permission he paid the Jews the difference out of his own pocket "off the books." So this was that German, Busse. I had been thinking of him in our search for "different Germans" of Schade's sort. Chance had brought him to us. I hinted to Haska that I knew who he was. I decided to become provocative:

"Are you surprised that we didn't go to church today? No, we never go to prayers. There are also different kinds of Poles. You know, I have heard about you. A Jewish woman worked for you, her name was Bluma. We studied in the gymnasium together and in the ghetto days I used to meet her in the city sometimes. Who knows where she is now?"

Busse was stunned.

"Yes, she worked for me. She was an excellent clerk."

Now, I was more confident:

"My friend here is a real artist; she paints wonderfully well. Until now she has worked as a servant; a waste of her talent. Perhaps you can take her into your employment?"

"Why not?"

"But what will the Labor Office say?"

"Come to my office tomorrow, I think I can arrange the matter. I have some contacts there."

That was how Haska began to work in Busse's office. She took Bluma's place as a bookkeeper. From time to time she also painted portraits. The job was pleasant; not far away, easy office work, an excellent attitude on the part of the employer, and complete freedom. Haska could leave her work for an hour or two, she could also stay away for a day or even longer. Busse kept his silence. He began to visit in our home. On dark, rainy fall evenings he used to come to us for a "little chat." His wife would accompany him. Our landlord wondered at our new acquaintances and did not hide their surprise. Our prestige was enhanced. Haska would also sew in her spare time; she was a wonderful seamstress. The pictures she painted and the dresses she sewed saved us from hunger more than once.

Our chats with Busse were interesting. He talked a great deal about Jews, about the Bible and the Talmud. From those books he had grasped the greatness of that people, so persecuted and oppressed. From them he had learned that they were the chosen people and that their Torah was the true Law. Yes, there was no doubt about that and this was the reason Hitler was killing them. Once, he cried out:

"I am so ashamed I am German; if only I could be a Jew!"

He apparently regretted his outburst because he was silent for the rest of the evening. He visited us almost every night and we always had the impression that he was groping for answers to questions that were bothering him. He spoke about God and wanted to know why such criminal acts were not punished. He believed in a Supreme Power, in a high morality, independent of time and place and eternal. That morality, that spirit — was God. He was educated, and he quoted the great philosophers. Many times he spoke in condemnation of the abominable acts committed against the Jews. Hitler was the evil devil dragging the German people behind him. The Germans had allowed themselves to be seduced; he was therefore ashamed of them. He believed that there were still Germans who thought as he did. Yes, Nazism too, was a philosophical question for him and war against it (those were his very words) also belonged in the sphere of the search for absolute truth. Of the Soviet Union he knew nothing. He was convinced that Russia was intent on taking Hitler's place, to fight him with the very same means which he used. In the beginning we attempted only to shake his pacifistic outlook founded on humanitarian views and did not demand deeds. We were cautious until the work of the underground required his aid.

It happened at the end of the fall season. Rain mixed with snow was falling. That day two men who had fled from Maidanek, Stasiek and Roman, came to us. They were two young Jews who, in the ghetto days, had belonged to the underground periphery. They had escaped from Maidanek while they were being led out to work. They said that many Jews from

Bialystok were still in Maidanek. They told us about Bluma; one of them knew her.

At about the same time, Felek came from the camp near Radom, in Blizin. Felek had not fled by himself. His wife, Lotka Debrovolska who was also living in the city as an aryan, had gone to the camp and organized his escape. She was a Warsaw woman with an aryan face. She had courage and intelligence, and she belonged to the underground. Lotka's friends, Bronka and Krysia, hid the two refugees from Maidanek in their home. Lotka's action led us to think that if she had been able to get to Blizin and get her husband out, we could organize an escape from Maidanek.

We turned to Busse. More than once he had said that he would give up all his property if he could only save Bluma. We seized upon that. Haska disclosed to him that a certain Jew, whose wife was Polish and whom we knew well, had fled Maidanek and had known Bluma there. We wanted him to obtain a permit there for himself and for one of us as his secretary or translator. We introduced Busse to Lotka and Roman. He questioned them, and finally believed that Lotka really was Polish, and that Roman was her Jewish husband.

Then he began to make the rounds of the German institutions, to obtain a travel permit to Lublin. Just when he was about to receive what he wanted we suddenly learned that on November 3 all the Bialystok Jews had been murdered. The workcamp near Maidanek had been liquidated. There was no longer any purpose to our trip. Busse however, remained an ally. Once he said to Haska:

"You are different. I have not found your like among the Poles. No, don't tell me stories, you are keeping a secret, not only about your past but also about the present."

Haska was quiet, then blurted unintentionally:

"We are Jews."

Busse was stunned. Then he smiled, and finally he could not restrain himself. He embraced Haska and kissed her on the brow. He was so upset that he stammered in a whisper:

"I knew, I knew that you represented a different world. So, you represent that people, that people that has suffered so much and is still doing so that the world may be redeemed. You will remain alive, you must live; you represent a completely different experience, a much higher one. Now I understand, you are helping Jews, and trying to save them. That is why you wanted to go to Maidanek. Let me help you as much as I can. Here is my money. I will give it all to you. Don't pay any attention to the books and the report. Take whatever you need; I don't care if I'm caught forging accounts; I'll manage."

When Haska told us what happened we were quite upset. We thought that she had acted hastily. A few days later Busse came to visit us. He sat silently. Suddenly he began to talk. He asked our forgiveness for having burst into our lives in such a way. Perhaps he was not desirable at all. He was a German, and maybe we hated him just as we did all Germans. For three whole days, however, a thought had continued to bother him. He suffered sleepless nights. How could he help the Jews?

Since he knew our secret we spoke to him openly: We have to fight the Nazis.

"How fight?"

"With arms," we replied.

He had been a wealthy inhabitant of an East Prussian town. He was an amateur artist and musician. When Hitler came to power he had believed that Hitler would bring liberty and justice to the people as he had promised. He joined the National Socialist party. After a time he found that the Nazis had lied. In 1935 he returned his party card with a letter explaining his action.

He had been naive. He wanted to satisfy his own conscience passively, and had honestly believed that he had done his duty.

After that, his affairs developed as expected. He was saved thanks to his family's respectable status, and the whole matter ended with his business being closed. When the war broke out he returned to the party, otherwise he would not have remained alive, and obtained a permit to open a business in occupied Bialystok.

We convinced him that his anti-Nazi conscience would not be clear unless he actively fought against fascism.

He began by contributing financial aid and by hiding people in his home. He also helped a German woman whose Jewish husband had been killed in the ghetto. She remained with their half-Jewish son. Busse adopted the child. The Nazis would take such children out of school, supposedly for medical examinations in a "sanitorium." That place was a concentration camp where the children served as guinea pigs for medical experiments.

Busse had adopted the child and taken the mother into his employ as his housekeeper. He brought us the maps and compasses. He brought Haska a pistol. That was the dream of every one of us, to replace the cyanide with a gun.

And so Busse became a fighter. By the time he was integrated into the German cell, he had already been involved in many underground activities.

We never asked him to join the partisans or to blow up bridges and railroads. He was a militant who was needed in the city, among his German "brethren", the Gestapo, the police, industrialists and businessmen of whose actions he was so ashamed. In fact, we always tried to dampen his enthusiasm. We urged him to return to the National Socialist party, to their clubs; we encouraged him to pay his membership dues, to continue his friendships with the Germans he hated. We calmed his stormy spirit and convinced him not to react negatively to his comrades' Nazi behavior, but to agree with their views, to behave like a loyal member of the underground.

We also learned important things from him. We smuggled in all kinds of contraband, such as secret millitary maps and the anti-aircraft plans of the city.

Schade was different from Busse and our ties with him developed in other ways. Toward the end of the fall Schade was transferred to another factory, Combinat No. 5. His replacement was the former director Factory No. 2, a typical German, vicious and full of hatred. He did not have Schade's expertise. In his previous job he sent dozens of workers to concentration camps, and even had three of them hanged in the factory courtyard, supposedly because of sabotage. The factory workers said that the sabotage had been totally imaginary.

When he was transferred to us my situation worsened. I could no longer leave my work early, I received no leave and every day I was moved to a different job to work on machines I did not know. Once the new "chief" said to me:

"Why are you working in the factory? You know German, and in general one can see that you are educated."

"Simple. I want to learn the trade, and you can't learn one from books."

"Very good. Maybe we'll send you to Germany to learn a trade. Would you like that?"

I saw that my situation was becoming serious. The suspicions and the time restrictions did not please me at all, but I finally found a way out. The factory office needed someone who knew German, and so I was taken out of the factory and brought into the office. I worked at night at the telephone switchboard, and received information, especially about the approach of "enemy aircraft". Soviet aircraft were as yet very rarely seen, but there was a great deal of fear because the front was coming closer. It was my task to transmit the information promptly so that the workers would have time to stop the machines, turn off the electricity, and go down to the shelter. I had all the night hours for myself, and the daytime ones I could also use as I liked. In the evening I enjoyed the solitude in my office. The typewriters were at my disposal and there were no overseers present. It was then that the propaganda material, including information from the front, was prepared and printed.

The winter had come and our links with the forest became tenuous. We had to intensify our work in the city, to strengthen the cells and to intensify our political work within them. It was then that Schade appeared. After he left the factory he disappeared completely. We were looking for practical people and wanted to recall Schade, but I did not know how to contact him. That same night, the telephone rang.

"Who is speaking?" the voice asked.

"One of the employees," I replied.

"I know all the workers. Who are you? My name is Schade, the former director of the factory."

It was midnight but the voice from the other side was live and a little merry. When I told him who I was, he was happy. "How are you?" he asked, "how is your work?" I told him that I had something about which I wanted to talk to him.

I went to see him the next day toward evening. I had only an hour; then I had to get back to the telephone. Our talk was direct and to the point. He told me the news from the front and I pressed him to tell me what he intended to do to participate in the war against the Nazis.

"I've saved Jews," he replied.

"Are you satisfied with that?"

"I don't know; what more can I do?"

I asked him to reflect. We arranged for a second meeting. He told me that he had been a member of the Nazi party and wore a swastika in his lapel, and had come here from the heart of Germany. He was an engineer and a textile expert. He had devoted his whole life to that profession. He had not taken part in political life. His life had been difficult and it was only through willpower that he became an expert. During the crisis years in Germany, after World War I, he had been unemployed for some time until Hitler came to power. Then he understood that if he wanted to succeed he had to join the Hitlerite party. After that, his life became easier and he had swiftly risen in the ranks of the professional and social hierarchy. When the Germans conquered these regions he had been sent as a specialist with a very honorable and responsible position that he could never have attained were it not for the war.

Here, however, his eyes were opened. Two matters especially had affected him: the annihilation of the Jews and the war on the eastern front. He had seen the racial doctrine implemented, and Nazism at the beginning of its collapse. He had been aided in this by the Jew, Mina, who had been with him and who taught him a chapter in the life of society and revealed the laws of social development in peoples and regimes. She explained to him why Nazism was doomed to defeat, and made him see the true nature of his masters.

Here, he declared that he had always been a working man, and from time to time even had expressed some sympathy for the Soviet Union. In Schade, without his awareness of it, you could see the German school, the appreciation of everything that was German, order, professionalism and education. He was the pure professional, and he had made his own reckoning. I suspected that his aid to Jews and his anti-Nazism were calculated, the result of his seeing reality as it was: the Soviet Union would triumph, and one had to prepare for the change while there was still time.

Actually, the whole issue was not important. We needed Schade in our work. However, before we decided to recruit him, we questioned him extensively.

I finally informed Schade that I represented the partisans in the forest and a political anti-Nazi underground movement in the city. Schade declared his readiness not only to help but also to join the active organization. I demanded that he recruit other Germans like himself; he refused at first. He was not prepared to take that risk. In his opinion Germans could not be trusted.

"Why not? How about you?"

We did not press him. At first we asked him to provide us with a radio receiver, and keep it in his house. He agreed. He replaced his own radio with a larger one. He bought it with his own money, of course; we had no funds. From then on I was able to sit at the radio every evening and listen to broadcasts from Moscow and London.

During that same fall Schade supplied us with arms. The first acquisition was a German rifle. Marylka, Sergei and I organized its transfer from Schade's home in a suburb behind Mickewicz Street to the forest.

The news from the front was very encouraging. In Bialystok the Germans were distributing . . . "Pravda." The masthead, the print, even the style were remarkably like the real "Pravda" that appeared in Moscow. People obtained the paper and passed it from hand to hand, hid it under their clothing and rushed home to read it in secret. But this "Pravda" was strange.

Small hints, without any hatred, were infiltrated between the lines. It was very subtle work, not blaring propaganda, and it was very effective. Not everybody grasped the truth that this "Pravda" was fostering sophisticated German propaganda.

We had to publish the truth about the fake "Pravda" and information about the advancing Soviet forces had to be distributed to reinforce the German-haters. The radio in Schade's house, and the typewriters in the offices of factory no. 4, helped us bring the news to the cells. From then the truth spread to wide circles of the population.

The office's three rooms were located in a building in the factory yard. The windows facing out were closed and barred. One wall was near the watchman's shed, a second close to the director's apartment. The inside room looked out on the courtyard and its walls touched the two others. The telephone was in the inside room, where I sat. By the time someone reached my office I could hear his steps in the corridor, and the creaking of the first and second doors, before he entered. I had time to pull the paper out of the machine and hide it. The noise of the typewriter was drowned out by the hum of the motors and machinery in the factory. For nights I worked that way. First, I had to compose the text according to the notes I had taken down from the radio. I also had to decipher every name and every place. For that I needed a map. Not all the names were known to me, even less so to the readers. I had to explain, for example, where Komsomolsk was, Derzinsk, Krematorskaya and Slaviansk, which had been taken in September, and where Dogorobazh and Komarici were situated. Reading that the British had dropped 1,000 tons of bombs on Berlin would encourage people and show them that there was a just reward for their patience. I had to list the German losses accurately, and not publish false information that would appear unbelievable not to encourage the illusion that the war was ending. People might be disappointed, and were only one step away from despair. We had published the truth and that would strengthen weakening hands and destroy the myth of the invincibility of the German army.

The month of September drew to a close, and we learned what was happening in Italy. The British army had taken Torento; the American Fifth Army had captured the port of Salerno; Mussolini had been arrested, and the National Executive committee of "Free Germany" was operating in the USSR. The Soviets took Briansk, and every day announced the conquest of hundreds of places. The Russian front was advancing from day to day, and I followed it and took notes, and the machine printed them. At night there were no visitors to the office, except for the watchman, who came to wind the clock. Five minutes before the hour I would pull the paper out of the machine; when the watchman left, I put it back in again. The director completed his last round at eleven; after that he went to the toilet. When I heard the water flushing and the bang of the door, I knew that he would not return that evening.

One night, midnight, the door opened suddenly and the director appeared on the threshold; I had not heard his footsteps in the corridor. The typewriter noise had apparently covered his steps.

"What are you doing here?"

I was frightened and wanted to hide the paper. I had copied down the exact figures of the German losses: 5,729 planes had been hit . . . Unthinkingly, however, I pulled back my hand. If I hid it he would realize that something was wrong.

"Nothing. I'm bored, and I am afraid of falling asleep."

"What are you typing there? Let me see!"

"I'm . . ., I'm just learning to type. Maybe I can get better work during the day."

He believed me. I looked into his eyes. He drew close and stood over me. I jumped swiftly and to my surprise asked him innocently:

"Is it forbidden to do this, sir Director? I am trying not to damage the machine."

"Good, good! Stop. Watch the telephone and in case of an alarm wake me by knocking on the wall."[36]

A Jewish Sigh

It was during those fall days that Marylka brought us the frightful and tragic news that on November 4 the entire dugout in which Aryeh Weinstein, Yoshke Kawe and others had hidden had been blown up. The dugout was in the forest where the fighting unit had been. For greater security the non-combatants were dispersed throughout the forest. Most of those in the destroyed dugout were people who had jumped off the railroad cars, and were not yet armed.

Marylka was so upset by the news that she found it hard to speak. The men had lost their will to fight; they had gone to sleep without taking any security measures. It was not only by arms that men in such a situation survived but also by their spirit. Weapons could not compensate for carelessness and indifference. When men from a dugout in another part of the forest came to bring food and maintain contact, they found only a deathly silence.

Only one man had not been killed and had hidden among the trees until the Germans went away. How had the Germans gotten to the dugout; who had shown them the way? The partisans groped their way the next day in the villages and in the more distant farms from which we took food. It immediately became clear that the Germans who had carried out the action had been a new SS unit stationed in Suprasl to fight the partisans. The Germans were known for caution. They never traveled a road they did not know, especially not in the treacherous forest: how had they discovered the way? We found out, two days later.

They had not yet managed to move the camp to another area when early one morning shooting was heard near the partisan dugout. The guards alerted the partisans who were always in a state of preparedness. When they emerged from the dugout they could distinguish approaching Germans through the fall mist. A battle ensued. Sasha (Yezhi Suhachevsky) commanded the partisans. There was no point in continuing a face-to-face confrontation when dawn came and it grew light. Sasha ordered the retreat, as planned, covering the retreat with his machine gun. They all succeeded in falling back, thanks to Sasha's successful cover, but Sasha himself died in the battle.

The Germans destroyed the dugout. They searched the whole neighborhood, going right past comrades hiding behind the trees and bushes scant meters from them; they fired at random. The Germans did not find anyone. Sasha was taken away by his comrades, along with his machine gun. The Germans retreated leaving their own dead behind them.

The comrades knew that the Germans would return to gather their dead. In the meantime, they took all the guns and searched among the German documents. Among those killed was the forest keeper from Suprasl, Karpovich, a traitor. He knew every path, every part of the forest, every spring and every cave. He lived in Suprasl in the Gestapo building and never moved without a guard. He had been a great treasure for the Germans and they had guarded him because he was the apple of their eye. It was he who led the Germans to the Jewish partisan camp. Sasha had fallen, but before he died he had succeeded in killing Karpovich the traitor.

At the end of autumn Natek Goldstein came to us* to show us the road to the new camp. Natek was a young man, blond and broad-shouldered.We had already heard of him in the ghetto. He had been one of the arms smugglers, one of the executors of the sentence against the Yudkovsky traitors, and a courier to the forest. He had a broad face and light eyes. He was to return to the forest with one of our girl comrades but there was frost that night and afterwards snow covered the roads and paths outside the city. He was compelled to remain with us and wait until the snow melted. We introduced him as our cousin from Grodno.

Those were bleak days. We were busy organizing the cells, publishing the radio reports, distributing material and gathering information and various articles, and searching for arms. We had only a little money, and we were hungry and cold. We also had to feed Natek and conceal him for at least 12 hours a day.

We were in a bad mood. Every day we went to work; every day we went on with our activities and fulfilled our tasks, but the lack of weapons in the forest and these first days of separation from our comrades there depressed us.

One day that fall Lizka was on the way home. The rain had stopped and crowds were coming out of the cinema on Pilsudsky Street. It was already getting dark and Lizka was bitter. Without thinking she sighed, an ordinary Jewish sigh: "Oi."

---

* His name was mentioned in one of the Judenrat announcements as having been punished for some crime during work. In the announcement he appears to be 16 years old.

Suddenly someone grabbed her by the hand.

"You're Jewish!"

Lizka tried to free herself, but without success. The fellow went on:

"I know that sigh. Only Jews sigh that way. Come with me."

Lizka shouted vulgar curses and insults.

"You son of a bitch! What are you bothering me for? You're a good Pole who likes the Germans, hah, you son of a bitch? Let go of my hand. Phew . . . you should be ashamed . . ."

He let go. Her nerve and her vulgar manner helped her escape, her aryan looks, whose validity had been damaged by one human sigh, also helped. We had learned another lesson in underground living.

Natek returned to the forest and the news from there was encouraging. The unit had recovered from the blows it had suffered. We were encouraged by the reports and by the receipt of arms and other materials we sent. With the help of the underground apparatus a number of impressive actions were carried out. The results of one of these actions I saw for myself.

Bronka and I were hiding on the railroad to Grodno, to renew our contact with Jan. This time we were traveling without special travel permits. The manager, Grimm, Bronka's employer, put us in the mail car. We were approaching the Charmoviesh station. Suddenly the train stopped. The brakes screeched and we were thrown forward.

An extraordinary sight greeted us: shattered cars, twisted rails uprooted. We got off the train. Some cars that had not been shattered were lying on their sides far from the tracks. The wounded were being dragged away. Weapons, bones, soldiers packs and helmets were strewn about. People were jumping out to see the sight. Gendarmes standing among the twisted tracks shouted at them to get away immediately. Most did not obey, and looked at the wounded unemotionally. The gendarmes hurried us across the tracks to another train. We had to rush to find places; the Germans were in a hurry to continue the trip. We moved to the second train, stunned by excitement. Bronka naively asked her "Zugfuehrer":

"What happened? Did the locomotive break down or did the train go off the tracks?"

"Oh, you little fool! You don't understand anything. The partisans sabotaged the tracks, and shot at the train. You are lucky they didn't attack the one in which you were riding."

"Why should they want to kill me?" Bronka wondered; "I'm not a soldier, nor a German."

"Ha, ha, ha," he laughed at her, "true they destroyed an army train but they could also have sabotaged this one too."

"No, I don't believe it. According to you, we mustn't ride on the train at all; it's dangerous."

He smiled at Bronka's naivete and refreshing youthfulness — believing that nothing bad could happen to her!

We still did not know what had happened to the saboteurs who had perpetrated the action, but we rejoiced. The world was suddenly very bright.

A second action that deserves mention was the blowing up of the electric power station in a surprise attack that had been planned down to the last detail.[37] We had assembled the information from the underground cells in the city. We were especially aided by some people in the Bielorussian-Soviet cell, headed by the power station engineer, Damidowich. The Germans who guarded the plant were so surprised, they threw away their weapons and attempted to flee. The station was blown up and destroyed, the weapons were taken from the Germans, and anyone who resisted was killed. The partisans succeeded in withdrawing to the forest in the darkness. The next day we read large posters on the walls of Bialystok, the regional capital: "Yesterday a criminal act was committed. . .(etc.) Since the guilty persons have not yet been found, two hundred hostages, former Soviet citizens, have been imprisoned because of their connection with the partisans. If those guilty of the criminal act are not turned in by tomorrow, all the hostages will be shot and their property confiscated by the German authorities. Signed: the head of the police and security services."

It was difficult to read the announcement with indifference. We knew the 200 Soviet citizens would be killed, but the Germans would not have allowed so large a Soviet community to remain in the heart of the forest in any case. Most communities of this kind had already been liquidated. It had been that way in Vilna, and in Grodno. Still, it was hard to accept the fact that the Germans would kill whole families, women and children, and use a partisan action as an excuse. Two days later 200 Russians had been executed.

In the meantime we had invaded new territories in the forest. Occupying an area was a unique concept for the partisans. It included the forest and all its paths, villages and inhabitants, including the private farms (Hwtors) within it, the shepherds and forest workers, the foresters and their families. Occupation meant, first of all, knowledge. Knowing a forest was not the same as knowing a road or city. The forest was treacherous; each tree looked like every other. The trees and the paths were treacherous, misleading and deceiving to the eye and ear.

In the areas we occupied there were no other organized partisans. We took positions in the villages and in the farms. We knew all their inhabitants; we knew who was a traitor and who a friend, where the police stations and the mobile SS units were, where the rich farmers lived, and where the poor were. We knew the forest in all its parts, where springs flowed and where the rivers were that had to be forded. We were few and our arms in meager supply. The Germans still moved securely in the forest. Partisans had not yet attacked them from the rear. The information we gathered could not be utilized in a practical manner. Of what good was information about the city of Bialystok's anti-aircraft defenses or about military units stationed in and around the city, when we had no communication with the front? Moreover, would we be able to hold out without some larger partisan base? Winter was closing in and it held many dangers for a small and isolated fighting unit. Treacherous snowfields would surround us and deepen our isolation. Would we be able to control the area with our meager manpower and weapons? Would we be able to hold on to our conquests?

These doubts moved the command to send two of the best of the partisans to the Bialovez forests. We knew that the road was difficult and that they would have to move stealthily and seek shelter in villages they did not know, and forests they did not recognize. We knew they would have to find their way with the aid of maps and compasses; that they would have to cross well-guarded railway lines and ford rivers whose depth they could not assess. It was vital however; we had to establish contact at all costs with the partisan base in Bialovez. Eliash and Marek set out on the dangerous road. We heard nothing about them for a long time.

Jan promised us a machine gun and 600 bullets. We saw the gun; it was not modern, but it was in good condition. There were no parts missing, and did not even had a stock. It was a German gun that had to be operated by two persons. We did not yet have that kind of gun in the forest. Of course we jumped at the opportunity. We decided to go to Grodno and bring it from there to Bialystok by train. We promised "Zugfuehrer" Grimm a fine present if he helped us bring in the "shmuggle." We went without permits. From time to time he came into the car in which we sat. When an inspection came close to the car, Grimm would immediately appear, sit with us and cover our lack of permit by pretending to engage us in intimate discussion. Bronka exploited his presence to gain status among the travellers. Her ringing voice filled the car packed with Poles: peasants and smugglers. Her height seemed to fit her elegant face, reflecting security and even arrogance. Bronka held on to her chamois gloves and she waved them about in front of the gendarme like an important document.

It was still early when we arrived at Kuznica. We had to go another nine or ten kilometers by road from there to Jan's house. We had chosen to get off there to avoid the inspection at the central station before Grodno. We arrived at Jan's house at noon. Jan put a bottle of beer on the table and ordered his wife to feed us as quickly as possible. Outside, the skies were clearing. The rain had stopped.

Jan hitched his horses, put the suitcase with the weapon and ammunition under the seat and we set out on the dirt road to the small station of Todrkovce. At the beginning of winter the sun begins to pale by noon, the air is cold and damp. We sat on the suitcase, bobbing to the tempo of the wheels that sank into the mud from time to time. We passed villages on the way and Jan made short stops at acquaintances' homes so as not to arouse any suspicion that he was going in an unusual direction. He drank a bit of liquor, made some secret deal in a whisper, bought tobacco and sold the devil knows what, and once again pulled the reins, pursed his lips and the horses moved forward.

The station was empty. Two uniformed Germans in front of the building were walking, one of them leading a large dog on a long chain. A Polish railway worker appeared after some minutes. The train was apparently due soon. We noticed the two Germans in time and were still able to retreat. However, what was the point in retreating; the suitcase would not get to the forest by itself. Jan became quite tense but continued to drive. We stopped some ten meters from the station, and Jan helped us unload the suitcase. We placed it behind the station building and said goodbye. We entered the station with empty hands. I stayed near the suitcase and Bronka went to the platform. She opened with a broad "guten Abend," and, with a smile, asked the Germans when the train was supposed to arrive. The two were happy, apparently, with the company.

"The train will arrive right away, but you will not go away from here yet; the train doesn't stop here, only slows down a little. You won't be able to jump on."

Bronka joked, showed her nimble feet. She would certainly manage, she promised them. "And if I don't, maybe you will help me; maybe you can influence the Zugfuehrer to stop for a moment."

I listened to the conversation. I stood some distance from the suitcase and from time to time looked toward the tracks. Bronka returned, and we exchanged roles. Now I went to the platform, rubbing my hands and stamping on my feet.

"Oh, another cutie; where's your friend?"

"She'll be back right away."

"Where were you until now?" He looked at me, half with a desire to flirt and half with suspicion. After all, what were two city girls doing in that desolate station between fields and villages, in the twilight of a cold and wet winter evening?

"Come, let's look for your friend," the one with the dog said. Bronka, however, had apparently had heard the discussion. She burst out laughing from behind the station. The noise of wheels was heard. Would Grimm, "her" Zugfuehrer be on the train or not? What if he did not stop the train?

I disappeared behind the building. Bronka would have to keep them busy up to the last moment; I had to drag the suitcase to the mail car.

I heard her voice. She talked loudly without stopping.

The train entered the station and slowed down. Now I heard Bronka's voice again:

"Oh, guten Abend; wie gets, Herr Grimm?"

Grimm was on the train. It was still moving. Patience. Don't rush. Grimm would wait. The train came to a complete halt. Bronka seized the suitcase and with deliberate steps walked toward the mail car. The Germans looked at her. One of them wanted to help, but stopped:

"Oh you tricksters, what do you have in this suitcase?"

The suitcase, however, was already in Grimm's hands. He made a face. He had not been thinking of such a large and heavy piece of "goods". But we didn't care. The valise was inside, and we behind it. Bronka waved her glove at the Germans standing on the platform and smiled. It was good they were not travelling with us. It was cold in the mail car. Grimm put the case to one side and suggested we move to the passengers' compartment; we might catch cold.

"We've brought a lot of 'good things'," Bronka laughed.

We moved to the passengers compartment. It was cold and dark there too. The suitcase remained in the mail car. It was locked, and Grimm would not open it to see what was inside. He was afraid. He would watch it. We had no travel permits. If we were caught, it would be better for us to be caught as far away as possible from the bag. But no one came to examine the travel permits; they had apparently already done this between Grodno and the small station where we boarded. We still had to get out of the train and to the city, from the central station. There the danger was great, because they generally conducted inspections.

We reached the main Bialystok station at dark, between seven and eight o'clock.

The train stopped. There was a long queue near the exit. We took the suitcase and turned toward the exit. A sentry stood behind the partition. We saw Haska and Marylka waiting for us. Travel permits were examined beyond the exit; near the narrow passage, two or three meters long, two railway policemen were stationed. One of them was stout; I recognized him from previous trips. His job was to catch smugglers. He looked at every passerby, and anyone who did not seem "kosher" in his eyes was taken aside. He also had a big dog. How were we going to get through without travel permits? The examination was very strict that day.

Bronka returned; she was looking for Grimm. I waited. In a little while my turn would come. I pushed myself toward the rear, to the tail end of the queue. The line kept growing smaller. Finally, Bronka came, with Grimm. He took the piece of luggage from me and turned toward a side exit limited to the use of German railway workers. Bronka and I walked behind him. A sentry was standing at the exit: Grimm went ahead and passed. I did too; Bronka was stopped; she would have to go back to the main exit. They might arrest and question her, and send her to a work or even a concentration camp. Grimm ran ahead; I stopped him and asked him to take me home.

"Don't be afraid, Bronka will return right away. I have a little liquor. We'll heat up the electric stove and fry some of the goodies you've brought. We've succeeded, haven't we? We must celebrate."

"But, Herr Grimm, when will we get home? It's late. And what about Bronka?"

He insisted. The suitcase was in his hands and he turned toward his house.

"Under no circumstances. My brother is waiting here and he will take the valise. I will go to look for Bronka. It's late. Tomorrow we'll bring the delicacies to you and have a feast. Then we won't be tired." I took the case from him almost by force. I thanked him and promised to let him know what happened to Bronka. I found the girls easily. Lizka was also there. Marylka and Lizka immediately took the suitcase and moved away from the station. Haska and I went to look for Bronka. Finally we saw her being led away in a group of women to the house opposite, where the railway police were stationed. Haska tried to talk to Bronka. The stout gendarme with the dog grabbed her hand and pushed her into the line. In vain Haska tried to explain that she had not come on the train.

"No, you did, I saw you. Where is your travel permit? You don't have any? Come with me."

I decided not to push myself forward. The heavy gendarme was watching Haska. She went to the station. Bronka, on the other hand, slipped out of the line and disappeared in the crowd. Bronka and I waited for Haska. Finally she returned. She had been asked to pay a fine for travelling without a permit, but she insisted that she had not been on the train. The other women smugglers were examined carefully, their bundles, baskets, and even their bodies. Haska had no bundles.

"You threw away your bundle," the gendarme charged. Haska, however, did not intend to pay the small fine at all. "Even ten marks is money," she argued. "I am not a smuggler, I work and I don't have money to pay fines for crimes I did not commit."

In the end they let her go. The women wondered at the strange girl who did not think it worthwhile to pay such a small amount to escape the claws of the gendarmerie. The Germans, too, wondered. Every Pole paid ten marks out of fear alone, even if he or she was innocent.

Because of the way she carried on, they did not even examine her purse or her clothing. They simply let her go.

Bronka hurried to Grimm, to mollify him. She arranged to meet him the next day for a fine meal. She told him all about her adventures, how she had escaped and how they had caught Helenka instead, until Grimm was satisfied. The girls returned home happy and encouraged. I boarded the German autobus near the station and rode directly to the factory. That night I would do no typing. That night I had earned the right to sleep restfully by the telephone in textile factory no. 4.

The next day Bronka and I hurried to the market. We brought two kilograms of excellent ham, eggs, and a piece of lard. We wrapped them well and brought them to Grimm. Bronka fried the meat, salted the lard so that it would last a long time, set the table and the two of us waited for Grimm to return from work. The glasses gleamed, the white tablecloth was immaculate. The liquor on the table glowed richly. Grimm returned from work and when he saw the spread his face lit up. He decided to send the lard we brought him to his family in Germany. We were all elated. Our comrades in the forest, however, would be the happiest of all: Marylka and Haska were going to bring them the weapon the next night.

The evening of the next day was dark and damp. A heavy mist covered the forest. It was a good night to go and it was only too bad that Haska's shoes weren't suitable for the damp ground. We brought the weapon part by part during the day and hid it in a nearby grove. Leaving the city would therefore be easier. Marylka and Haska left early; they did not have to wait for curfew. The forest was dark by six in the evening. If everything went well, if they waited for us in the right place and at the right time, Haska would be able to get back on the same night. But Haska could not be relied upon. She would always exploit the opportunity to spend a day in the forest with the comrades. She loved being with them. Nothing disturbed her, neither the bone-chilling cold or the wetness or even the danger of being hunted. She always came back with dozens of intriguing stories. She took an interest in the problems of all of the unit's members and knew all of them; their names and their past activites, their states of mind and their combat capabilities. For her, the fighting partisan unit was a group of individuals.

Haska returned, beaming, two days later. For a whole day she had enjoyed an atmosphere of freedom, without Misia and her anti-Semitic husband. She was especially happy that the weapon had been delivered safely in the forest. They had assembled it and found it to be in working order. How they had rejoiced! They did not let her leave without taking some gift with her for the girls in the city. They searched in their pockets and bags and found something from their past — a beautiful small comb, a gold ring — and gave them all to her as gifts. A strange and beautiful relationship was entered into between the forest and the city. It was odd because it was not symptomatic of our difficult, harsh lives, and close because we wanted it so much. There was also another gift! For the first time we received food from the forest. A good portion of meat. "In one of our recent actions the meat was seized from a rich farmer who collaborated with the Germans. For the girls to enjoy and not go hungry," said Haska.

In the forest they were now talking about going into the ghetto to look for people who might have remained, and also to search through the hiding places. In one of them there had been an excellent radio receiver. It was worth bringing it to the forest, so that they would not have to wait for the news from us. The ghetto was still tightly closed. Only isolated groups of municipal workers entered, under German guards, to take care of the sewage and electric systems. A rumor spread that in a few days work groups would go in to pack and classify all the Jews' belongings and prepare them for shipment to Germany. We would have to try to enter with the municipal workers or with the conscripted work units. We looked for an opportunity, and once again Busse helped. He obtained a permit from the police and the civilian authorities responsible for abandoned property, as a house-repair contractor. The permit was valid for him and his secretary.

Haska took a large portfolio, put in it all kinds of old sketches and plans she had found in Busse's office, and went with him to the ghetto. In the afternoon, Haska returned. We crowded around her to hear what she had to say. Haska, however, was silent; she sat at the table, apathetically chewing her food. She showed no signs of emotion. Her eyes were fixed and expressionless. She did not sigh, or weep. She said not a word. Had she really not seen anything there worthy of mention? We envied her and wanted to see the Jewish ghetto again, to look around, to find something worth saving. Haska remained silent. In the end, we learned from her fragmented remarks that they had reached the place where the radio was hidden, but they did not find it. They met no one. That was all.

After Haska left for work I suddenly noticed a package near the bed. It was not large, and it was wrapped in a sheet torn from an old newspaper. I picked it up and trembled: an old dress, which belonged to my mother fell out of the newspaper. I recognized it at once. I had not asked her to bring anything back. And what else was I seeing? A skirt of Zila's, Haska's Grodno friend, which was worn and torn. There were other small valueless articles, left by comrades and by her younger sister. That was what Haska had stolen from the ghetto.

I held the articles, my hands shook and my heart pounded. Haska was late returning from her job. She came into the room and did not ask about the package, did not even mention it. She sat at the edge of the bed, silent. I handed her her supper, but she did not eat. With difficulty, I took off her coat. She did not move. All at once she got up, stretched and fell helplessly on the bed. She suddenly started to cry, sobbing in Yiddish: *Zila, Zila . . .kumt . . . geht nisht avek . . . Chaika . . ."** The Yiddish was clear. On the other side of the thin wall, in the adjoining room, our landlords were eating their meal. Haska's crying grew louder. I was sure it was heard not only in our apartment but in the whole court. A chair moved on the other side of the wall, and I heard heavy footsteps walking toward the entrance. In another moment they would be here, and Haska did not stop crying:

*"Zila . . . Chaika . . . kumt, geht nisht avek . . . geht n. . ."**

Without thinking I began to fondle her face, her soft, dishevelled hair. She was silent, but after a moment opened her mouth again. She shivered again, pushed my caressing hand away, and tried to free herself. I held her chin and stuck my fist into her mouth. Her crying was choked-off. It was late, and I had to go to work in the factory right away. There was nobody else in the house. Like an angel from heaven, Marylka suddenly entered the room. She did not get excited like me; she seized Haska's hand, stuffed a handkerchief into her mouth and asked me to bring cold water. When the neighbors came to our room Haska was lying still, and breathing heavily. Broken words came from her mouth, unclear and not understandable by our Polish neighbors. We asked them to leave because something bad had happened between Helenka and her betrothed, and her heart was broken. Marylka explained:

"When she becomes accustomed to the thought that her betrothed has left her she will be embarrassed that all of you witnessed her emotional reaction."

Misya felt that she was an expert in these matter. She also considered her-

---

* "Chaika . . . come here . . . don't go away . . ."

self Helenka's closest friend, and therefore decided to remain in the room. Marylka then had a stroke of genius.

"Misya, maybe you'll go and call Busse. It seems to me that he has a good influence over her."

Misya was pleased that she had been entrusted with so important a mission, and she hurried off to Busse. We remained alone. By the time Busse came, Haska was already completely quiet. Under her open eyes one could detect dark black rings. Pale as a sheet and shivering from the cold, she lay in the bed weak and silent.

When I returned from work the following morning at six o'clock, Haska and Marylka were sound asleep. In the courtyard a door creaked; a neighbor was going to work. There was the sound of water flowing from a faucet, and the sirens of the factories. I fell asleep. When I awoke Marylka was standing over me unbuttoning my coat. It was already bathed in light. Haska dressed to go to work. She did not speak about the previous evening.

The Soviet Partisans

Winter came. There were beautiful, bright days, wonderfully tranquil. It was a winter without storms. The snow cut us off from the forest. A white carpet seemed to cover the tens of kilometers between us and the partisans. We could not go to the forest because the snow was deep and our footprints would have disclosed the whereabouts of the partisans.

Marylka was rooted in the city without any possibility of returning to the forest. From time to time we received vague information, from Volodia's contacts, about battles in the forest, and large-scale searches by the Germans. Every additional day of separation was an imminent death sentence for the partisans. Now we discovered how isolated we were. A large partisan unit controlling some forest area and the villages within it would not be bothered by the snow to such an extent. The Germans, however, were camped behind our weak unit; in every nearby village there was a police station. Ours was not a typically "partisan" area, like those in the Bielowicz region. There, entire villages were controlled by the partisans.

We had no choice; we had to concentrate all our activities within the city, completely cut off from our partisan base. We had to initiate activities and carry them out alone. We operated without instructions and without realizing the immediate combat value of our city actions. We gathered secret information without having any direct contact with those who could use that information. We organized new cells without knowing when we could direct them to the forest.

In that way, we organized a new cell of "aryan" Jews. We found our candidates one by one. The first was Janka Malevska, a young woman of courage. She was from Lodz; tall and beautiful, talented and impudent. It was thanks to that impudence that Janka had managed to pass as an aryan in the city. Without any acquaintances or connections she had made her own way. She worked in a German office responsible for fuel distribution in the city. It was a highly respected office among the Germans in wartime and many sought the favor of the office's directors and workers.

Through her office she organized arms shipments from the villages. An office car travelled frequently to the provincial towns. Janka "made a deal" with the Polish chauffeur, promised him part of the "profit" from the smuggled goods, and wrote the travel order herself, stealing the stamp and forging the director's signature. The gasoline tank had many hermetically sealed hiding places. The cost was small; we would buy two kilograms of lard and a piece of meat for 100-150 marks. We smuggled a rifle and grenades and the chauffeur thought he was carrying meat and bacon. We hid the rifle and grenades in Lizka's cellar and waited for the first thaw.

We also began to press our new acquaintances in the city to cooperate with us. They included Lotka, Krysha, and three men: Felek, Lotka's husband, whose escape from Blizin she had organized, and Stashek and Roman, who had fled from Maidanek. We demanded that they come out of hiding and join the fighting unit at the first opportunity.

We did not receive clear answers. The men promised to discuss the matters as soon as the snows melted. Also, they said, they had no weapons. We informed them that we would obtain guns; one gun was already waiting for one of them in the city and at the first opportunity he could take it and leave for the forest. The women, who were endangering themselves guarding the men, could also obtain weapons with our assistance.

They were divided in their attitudes. Lotka said that Felek should go to the forest, Stashek was silent, Roman developed his theories:

"You don't understand anything. You weren't in a concentration camp, you didn't see men degraded, life as it is. The Soviet front is rapidly coming closer, the Red Army is winning; why should we go to the forest, so few, so miserable, unarmed? What value does such a group have from the historical point of view, and in relation to the scope of the war?"

The debate with Roman went on for a long time. The women who were hiding him and his friend Stashek were simple and honest. They did not want to drive him out of their home in the cold, treacherous forest, and thought that they were saving the men. Roman knew how to defend his wish for comfort with dozens of arguments. Lotka, however, joined in our work and became devoted to it with courage and enthusiasm. Felek, too, who was less "intellectual" than Roman, immediately agreed. At the first opportunity he would go to the forest.

In January 1944, we suddenly received a pleasant surprise. It was cold and the snow was deep. One morning I brought from my office night work a typewritten slip of paper: the Soviet Army had crossed the former Polish border and a tiny but well-known town in Volynia had been taken by the forces of the First Ukrainian Front. It was Rokitno, our little Jewish Rokitno, a place so close and well-known, on what had been Polish soil.

In the very midst of winter a bit of spring came for us. After Rokitno, Klosov, with its quarries and its large chalutz Zionist training farm, was captured and then Kamienitz-Podolsky. The Sluca River appeared on the map of Russian conquests. Then came the city of Sarni, and Lutzk and Rovno. February came turning sorrow into joy, sadness into hope. The world was marching toward liberation. We thought we might hear the thunder of Moscow's cannons celebrating the liberation of Leningrad, and see the beams of the searchlights cutting across the sky. These rays of light broke the suffocating siege of snow.

Far to the the rear of the enemy, other liberating forces were also operating. There was a revolution in Italy, and people were struggling for freedom in Greece. In France arrests were increasing, a sign that the French were also fighting against the fascists. Polish soil was shaken day and night by exploding railways, bridges and police stations. The forests were filled with partisans, arrests were increasing, and the terror was intensified. Day and night German cities were being bombed from the air: 2,300 tons of steel were landing on Berlin; 1,300 Ameican planes raided military targets in Pas de Calais; Braunschweig was bombed, and Hanover, and Cologne. Every day thousands of tons of explosives were destroying German cities, industries, and the inhabitants' morale and their ability to continue to resist.

My sister Miriam's landlady, the rich and aristocratic wife of an SS Obersturbenfuehrer, cried all day long and did not hide her fears even from me, the "Pole". Her husband wrote to her from the east asking for warm clothing and instructing her to prepare large packing boxes. She could not understand: her high-ranking officer was asking for clothing from home. "Is it possible that our army, the German army, is not providing clothing," she asked her servant Julia (my sister Miriam). And why did he want her to prepare boxes? What did it mean? Were they really unable to drive the enemy planes away from German soil before the Russians dropped those terrible bombs? The German woman, however, gradually became inured to the situation, to the puzzling effect of her husband's letter and to those she was receiving from her family in Cologne. As usual, she looked for inexpensive chickens to buy, baked cream cakes, and ate sandwiches at four o'clock tea. "Frau Gudmeier" was a nice woman who did not understand her world. But she was getting used to it, just as she had to the murder of the Jews.

At the beginning of March the snows melted and a strong spring wind blew into the city. Sergei came with that first wind. The news he brought with him was both so dreadful and joyful that we did not know whether to cry or laugh. There had been heavy losses during the period of our separation. The deep snow and the fine weather had been death traps; the partisans had not been able to move. The slightest activity attracted the attention of the Germans stationed in nearby villages. For a long time the partisans had existed on a little dry flour sometimes mixed with snow. When that ran out they ate the remains of the dry beans and lentils. Many were ill, and were without even minimal medical aid. Comrades lay powerless, unable to move hand or foot. Some few who still held out were doomed to suffer a slow death, from hunger and disease. The Jewish partisan unit was dying. It had been decided to send those comrades still able to stand to the neighboring village to obtain food, at any cost. The remaining comrades were put on alert should the Germans discover some traces of those leaving. Sergei, Yaakov and Natek went, and when they left the camp area they were ambushed. After a short battle, Natek Goldstein was killed. They determined to draw the attention of the Germans to themselves, to save those left in the dugout, but they did not succeed. The Germans followed their footprints to the dug-out. The comrades fought with their last ounce of strength, escaped, hid and disappeared. After every battle and withdrawal, when the scattered fighters met again, one or two more were missing.

Every step left traces and these brought on renewed chase. "Oblawa" hunted. The true meaning of that word cannot be fully understood by anyone who has not lived in the forest with the partisans. That winter of 1943 was a terrible ordeal for them. They ran tens of kilometers every day in knee deep snow. They escaped, hid and shot desperately. They were consumed by despair; ammunition was lacking as were other essential means for survival. They lived that way for weeks and months, burying their dead, eating the bark of trees and sometimes frozen potatoes dug out of the icy fields. They also cared for their wounded: Riva Woyskowska's hand was seriously injured, and they could not help her. Her wound became infected and her life was in danger. They had no way of treating blood poisoning.

It was then that the Soviet partisans arrived, healthy, dressed in warm clothing, well-armed and full of vitality. They were young in body and spirit. They had reached us after covering hundreds of kilometers through villages and forests, rivers and railway lines, in constant battle and against German ambushes. Many messengers had been sent to us during that winter but most had fallen along the way, encountered ambushes or died in battle. Benk, the second secretary of the Communist Party's regional committee died in this manner on his way to save Jewish partisans. A few had reached our area. They came to the old camp, and when they did not find anyone there, returned. Marek and Aliash* had reached Bialoviez made their report. The command immediately sent messengers to help. More than 100 men

* Marek Buck and Eliyahu Warati, today Vered, a member of kibbutz Eilon.

had died searching for our unit while we were beaten, dispersed and compelled to wander from place to place. Aliash, too, had roamed the forest for a long time and had been compelled to return when he could find no one.

Finally, however, the Russians succeeded. The eastern front was nearing the Soviet partisans but had not yet completed their task. It was not only their desire to help us that had brought them here. The need to infiltrate behind enemy lines had encouraged them to leave their strong base in the dense Bielorussian forests. Those who came were mostly Russian paratroopers who had been sent to the Bialoviez area about half a year earlier. They were General Kapusta's men. When they reached the Bialystok area where we met, we were the only organized force there. Without us there would not have been any serious anti-Nazi partisan activity or any effective urban political underground. We were the only base they could depend upon. We knew the area, the forests and the villages, and behind us we had a well organized underground.

They brought help; medicine, food and arms. They also brought a breath of spring. Our meeting with them was so sudden and so unexpected that for a long time both sides did not want to speak about it. Coming as it did when all hope seemed lost, it was hard to believe that it really happened. One girl had come with them. She was their radio operator, and she carried her set on her back. Her comrades said that she had jumped with it from the plane.

Sergei said that the first assistance received from the young paratroopers was tendered with so much love and concern that many thought they were dreaming. The weak received special treatment. Our doctor seemed to have been born again; he forgot his own weakness, took the medicines that had been brought in his shaking hands — the bottle of beer that was opened, the rations of bread and meat — weighed them and apportioned them to each according to his ability to digest them. He administered injections, bandaged wounds, fed, warmed, and issued instructions. Many had fallen, but those who remained slowly returned to life. Once again they took their weapons in hand, refilled their ammunition belts, and a few days later were unrecognizable. The Russian guerrillas were aided by the Jewish partisans' knowledge, their remarkable orientation and their connections in the neighborhood.

The number of Soviet guerrilla fighters grew daily. One unit after another arrived. According to them, about 200-300 fully equipped men were coming. Their aim was to base an entire partisan brigade in the neighborhood. In the spring, we would be partisans asked to help in establishing their group; that is to form units, and further expand into the region. The brigade commander and his staff were due to arrive within a few days.

Sergei came to give us all the news and to take one or two of the girls back to the forest. The Russians very much wanted to meet the girls about whom our partisan comrades had spoken so much. The brigade commissar had expressed his strong desire to meet the Jewish women who lived in the city as aryans and held all the threads of the antifascist underground of the whole region together. Political and educational work as well as preparing people before they left for combat activity was our job, and he understood that we would be his main support.

Lizka went first. When she returned we met in her room and listened to her story.

"From now on we are the official antifascist committee for the city and its suburbs. Our authority in these matters will be unlimited. The activities we carry on will be coordinated only with brigade headquarters in the forest. In all matters concerning the city and its environs the brigade will make no decisions nor execute any action without our recommendation. From now on we will be in direct contact only with brigade headquarters."

We listened, with conflicting thoughts in our minds.

"How can they decide all this without talking with our Jewish unit in the forest? Our fate is the same as theirs. It was the ghetto underground that sent us and we are its extension. We are part of the Jewish unit and it is not possible for us to make any arrangements with anyone else apart from it."

Lizka, however, continued:

"Wait, the matters have been discussed. You make me so nervous that I am skipping the main parts. First, we had a discussion with Riva, the brigade commander, and myself . . . "

"What, you saw the commander and did not tell us?"

"What is he like?"

"The discussion with the commander," Lizka continued, "was at the request of the Jewish unit. The unit cannot continue to function as it now exists, it cannot remain an independent unit. Most of its members need to recuperate, and those remaining are too few to form an autonomous regiment. If they leave the unit as it is, with its sick and wounded, it will have to remain non-combatant for a long time, with even the healthy members not participating in combat activity.

"The solution, then, is to divide the unit between the two existing regiments, to arm those fit for immediate duty, with the remainder recuperating within the combat regiments. In the commander's opinion, we must not leave any partisan force, and particularly a Jewish unit that has suffered so many losses, outside combat, and that is important, he thinks, even if some of the comrades, meanwhile, do not go out on operations. The debate over this was painful many of our comrades were against disbanding the fighting Jewish organization.*

"Of course I stipulated a condition concerning ourselves, too. I said that our decision would depend upon that of the Jewish force in the forest. Actually, the debate has not yet ended, but it is clear that the unit will accept the brigade commander's proposal."

Meanwhile, a number of important joint decisions were made. First, the command agreed to accept any Jew hiding in the forest, whether he was capable of bearing arms or not; old or young, man or woman; any Jew as Jew and a victim of Nazism. The second one concerned the Germans. Until now they had apparently not succeeded anywhere in recruiting antifascist Germans for organized action. This was undoubtedly a great innovation in the history of the antifascist underground. The commander admitted that he had extremely positive instructions on this matter and wanted first to meet one of them, one of the most courageous among them, to decide together with him, and with the comrade who would deal with the Germans in the future, about the formation of a special German cell on the order of the existing Bielorussian and Polish ones.

After Lizka, I went to the forest to meet the brigade staff. I went with Schade. He had immediately agreed and was so excited by the proposal that he apparently forgot how dangerous it was for any German, a member of the Party and the head of a large war industry, to be caught in the forest in the middle of the night, stealing his way to the partisans. He would be tortured and killed. I did not recognize Schade that night. He was very excited. Suddenly he left me, and disappeared. A few moments later he returned, with Mina Kiselstein. She was the girl who had worked for him and through whose agency we had established our contact with Schade, and from whom I once received a forged document. We embraced each other and did not speak.

On the next day I led Schade to the brigade commander. We moved slowly and carefully, through the mud. I led with Schade walking a few steps behind. He drew his pistol and moved forward.

At the rendezvous, 50 meters to the left of the path, two men were waiting for us. I looked at the new, strange faces. They were young, wearing canvas hats on their heads. They carried short, wide-barrelled automatic guns with full bullet-holders. They had slightly snub noses, wide faces and small eyes. Schade was confused but went with them. One of them was in the lead, we

* Later we discovered that at that time most of the Jewish national units in the various partisan regions had been disbanded.

were in the middle, and the second brought up the rear. The road was secure, groups of partisans were guarding it from among the trees.

Sergei joined us on the way. Schade was very happy; he had apparently been a little troubled in this strange, silent, armed and alien company; he was among the "Bolsheviks", and he had never seen a Bolshevik. Sergei he recognized; he had seen him in his home when he had given him the rifle.

We reached the camp after midnight. A partisan removed his sheepskin and spread it on the ground for us to sit on. "At least you won't get wet this way," he said. I translated for Schade and Schade laughed. He wanted to express his thanks but did not know how.

The Combrig (brigade commander) let him wait, perhaps deliberately. He let him look around, be impressed, adapt. It began to rain, and the partisans brought us canvas cloth with which to cover ourselves. They lit a fire in the bushes so that we would be warm. Some tried to converse with me. Surprisingly, they knew everything. They knew that I had participated in the ghetto revolt; that I had been a member of the command, that my name was "Galina" not Galutchka, what I was doing and how I had "found" this German. Their words did not warrant any special note, no shared sorrow, no pity for the ghetto that no longer existed. They talked to me the way men spoke to a young woman they both respected and liked.

He wore a sheepskin hat, tall, shining boots, a short, warm coat and a wide belt on which hung a large automatic pistol in a wooden holster. He appeared suddenly, walked with long, swift strides, with his company behind him. All jumped to their feet and greeted him with a short military salute. He motioned with his hand, partly as an order and also as a comradely gesture:

"Sit down, please."

I looked at Schade. This short ceremony had apparently been to his liking. I didn't know whether it had been staged or whether it was entirely natural. Sergei introduced us: this is Gala, and this is director Schade. The Combrig rose, approached Schade and pressed his hand. Voichehovsky was clever. The discussion began; Sergei translated part and I interpreted another portion.

"I welcome all of you as Germans who seek freedom and oppose fascism!'

Schade was moved. He admitted: "This is not how I imagined the 'Bolsheviks.'"

"Why not?"

"I admit, propaganda is effective. We were taught to look upon Bolsheviks as barbarians, and here I see cultured, esthetic people, who know what lies ahead of them, and are nevertheless fighting for the benefits of others."

The Combrig asked some questions about Schade's work and how much he knew about Soviet industry. We had heard that Schade was an expert. Schade replied that he did not know very much about the Soviet industries. He was entrusted with the management of the factory after the Soviet retreat and had noticed their effective organization of the production system. The Combrig said something more about the famous German order and quoted Lenin about combining American tempo, German order and Russian initiative in building a socialist country. Schade's face lit up. He was especially pleased that he had not been received as an enemy but as a representative of the other, future Germany. He had probably been quite fearful. After that, a practical discussion ensued. Voichehovsky asked about the possibilities of organizing Germans like himself into a cell that would take its orders from someone appointed for that purpose.

Schade hesitated, but agreed to organize the cell. In the end he announced that he was prepared to fulfill all instructions in a manner expected from a member of the underground. Of course he wanted to know who would be in command of the Germans. Finally, he asked if they did not think that he should join the partisans. The Combrig smiled, pressed his hand and told him:

"That day will also come. But before you fight with arms you will have to fight on another field; and as for the authorized person, here she is." He pointed to me and smiled. It was obvious. That was the task I had filled up to then, and I would be expected to continue in a more concentrated and organized fashion.

The rain did not stop, but we felt warm. The fire burned out, the canvas cloth was soaking. Schade sat among the comrades, enjoying the quiet singing. I went with the Combrig to discuss plans for the Germans and for our work in the city. He listened more than he spoke.

I informed him that in a few days we would send some people to the forest. "Remember, one is sick and will have to be cared for."

"No matter. Send them, send them. We'll manage. My staff is already complete. Instruments, arms, everything is in place. In another few days two more regimental commanders and commissars will arrive. We'll enlarge our force to at least 1,000 people. Nu, I depend upon you. We'll welcome anybody you send. I have decided, in general, not to accept anyone from the city without your recommendation. Examine the people in the cells and send us the best of them, or the most urgent cases, those who no longer have any place to hide. And Jews, Jews; send as many as you can. I have received explicit instructions to accept any Jewish candidate — because he is Jewish."

We spoke further about organizing an intelligence service. It was clear to both of us that the Germans would have to serve as our main ally in that field. It was also worthwhile receiving arms from them, not particularly because of the need but because of the test it set for the German. If he was ready to provide weapons with which to sabotage the Nazis, then he was working against German solidarity and nationalistic sentiments embedded deep in their hearts. "Did you see how Schade's eyes shone when I spoke of German order; how I bought him with that banal compliment?"

The Combrig also wanted to know about other Polish organizations, which were not in contact with us. He listened very attentively when I told him about the A.K. ("Armia Krajowa" — National Army — Polish armed underground).

"Yes, I want contact with them."

I wondered what he wanted with the A.K., the chauvinist group which fostered hatred for the Germans, the Jews and the Soviet Union. They were satisfied with their patriotic education that did not lead to any real combat actions, because of their calculations for the future. I did not understand what benefit could derive from any contact with people for whom a Communist was a kind of monster without a homeland, the enemy of culture and private property.

Voichehovsky insisted. He wanted that contact, especially with one of their leaders, through whom he could reach the rank and file.

"But they will sense that you want to influence their soldiers over their leaders heads; it will be a dangerous game."

"Perhaps, but worthwhile. The problem is not only a military one. It possesses political and historic value. If you succeed in discovering anyone let me know immediately. Wait, I'll introduce you to the commissar; actually that is his job."

The discussion ended. The rain stopped. The first rays of light broke through the trees. Suddenly it was quiet. The Combrig said goodbye and disappeared, and the two partisans urged us to follow them. They took us out to the main road, but not by the path on which we had come. We zig-zagged through the trees, scrambled among the bushes until we reached the edge of the forest. It was daylight.

We leaped into a nearby grove and waited until we could hold hands and go for a "stroll" to the city. Schade was delighted.

The Oath

Once again we were in the city. The information we gathered now had new meaning. The German cell was established. At the first meeting in Schade's home were Schade, Busse, the director of Factory No. 1, whose name I do not recall, and Bolle. The first two I knew well. The third was a German who had spent many years in Czechoslovakia. He hated Germany and the Germans and particularly loved Czechoslovakia and the Czechs. He was fabulously wealthy, growing old and fat, and was a typical bourgeois liberal. He was Schade's friend and he had connections, and all doors were open to him. He could place his splendid many-roomed apartment at our disposal. His radio was one of the better ones. He also had excellent wine in his cupboard. His wife and family were in Bilitz. He could give us money and cloth for clothing for the partisans. We no longer needed money; Sergei had brough us a first package. Lizka and I had also brought packages of new money, genuine looking marks, produced somewhere in the heart of Russia. The cloth for the partisans we gladly accepted. The essential matter was information about army units stationed in the city, their movements, numbers, names, strength; high ranking personnel in the Gestapo, the party, the police. We wanted to know where they had come from, how they had attained their rank, their families, wages and activities during work and after, how many rooms they had, where the entrances to their apartments were, who worked in their homes, and so on.

The fourth German in the cell was Bolle. He had left Germany a long time ago, and since then had lived in Bialystok. He was a city notable, an engineer. He was young and vigorous, very well educated, and had even absorbed some political education during the Soviet period when he had a respectable job in the textile industry. The Germans had sent his Jewish wife to the Ghetto but he had succeeded in saving her before the liquidation, and now he was hiding her behind a wall in his home. He could operate in the Polish sector among the many workers who were his sworn friends.

Busse felt uncomfortable in this company of Germans. The other three knew each other. He did not trust the Germans, and had agreed to come only because I was there. But he left the meeting pleased. When Schade told us about the meeting with the Combrig and his staff, Busse's eyes shone. He drank in every word as though he had been waiting a long time. He was bothered by only one question:

"Why had they invited Schade and not him?" I promised that he would be invited to the next meeting.

In the days that followed information was accumulated, sorted and coordinated. We were able to make our first full and comprehensive report based on facts and sources. After every report we received the thanks of the Combrig and his staff.[38] Spring came and our work expanded. We took turns visiting the forest; each time a different girl was sent carrying documents and new information. The Germans did not disappoint us; our cells were organized and our contacts multiplied. Among the documents that Haska once took with her to the forest were our "oaths". The first to take the oath was the "committee". Each of us wrote it out and signed it. It was brief:

> "I swear by this vow to fight and to give my life if necessary in the war against the German occupiers, until the liberation of all of our country from the fascist plague. I will keep secrets and obey all the battle orders of my officers. If in this I fail or betray, may I be overtaken by the vengeful hand of my comrades in the antifascist underground."

The oath was then administered in every one of the cells, and undoubtedly helped to unite our people more solidly.

Meanwhile the regiments in the forest had been filled out, organized and dispersed in various parts of the Azovs, Suprasl, Krinki and Budiski forests. Isolated groups of Jews wandering in the forests were added to the regiments. There were already 500 to 600 fighters in the brigade, and it was still growing. In the spring we decided to move the Jews still living in hiding places to the forest. Felek, Lotka's husband, was the first to go. The messages he sent back were very encouraging.

Then we sent a Jewish girl whose aryan name was Regina Rasina.[39] She had worked in the home of a village priest for a long time, until she was discovered, and then she fled to the forest. We brought her to the brigade and in a short time she became a courier among the regiments operating in the forests. After her, Stashek and Roman, the two men who had escaped from Maidanek, came to the forest. Stashek brought a gun with him, and Roman was armed immediately upon his arrival. His camp was stationed in the Azovs forest.

Spring arrived, but the ground was still wet. The first days in the forest are difficult for city people, especially the first bath in the morning dew and the spring cold. The camp moved from place to place, without any permanent site, without bunkers. Yet we were convinced that anyone coming to the forest and experiencing hard life in a partisan regiment might curse the day he came but would eventually become an integral part of it. He would become a member of a fighting company, accepting everything that came with clear will and firm determination.

We made a mistake with Roman. We had always fears about him. We never liked the philosophizing of the all-knowing intellectual, who covered his weaknesses and desire for comfort with "objective" arguments. But Jewish sentiment, the desire to save an additional person, prevailed and we failed.

This is what happened. One day Roman disappeared, with his rifle. That same afternoon, our guards warned that German units were moving toward the camp from several positions. The alarm given, and they began to retreat, shooting. The fighting continued for a number of hours. The regiment eventually broke through the encirclement without any losses, but disturbing thoughts troubled the commander. The matter was transferred to the brigade staff for investigation. When Lizka came to headquarters she already knew the results of the investigation. Contacts in the nearby villages provided some details about a tall partisan, apparently a Jew, who had been caught in the village of Grabowka. He was handed over to the gendarmes and had broken under torture. He described the site of the camp gave the number of partisans, etc. Then the Germans came.

Voichehovsky told Lizka the story, without comment. He was gloomy, and did not joke as he usual did. Lizka felt that she had to assume the blame: we had sent him, and we were responsible. That was partisan law. Why was the Combrig silent; why did he not accuse her, at least demand some clarification?

Roman had done something for which a fighter would have to stand trial before a military court: he had deserted. And then, when he was caught, he had endangered his partisan regiment and even brigade headquarters. He had been apprehended and probably shot by the Germans; we, however, were alive and therefore we should be judged in his stead. We decided to bring the matter to the brigade staff.

We wanted a direct and definitive clarification. Lizka and I went to the Combrig. He listened to our arguments, at first coldly and politely, but finally the stolid mask fell. The commissar was also present, listening. We were insulted when the commissar tried, at the end, to turn the whole thing into a joke. We were also offended by his paternal attitude, even a little by his unconcealed admiration. That was not in keeping with his task as commissar, and we told him so.

"Yes, girls, you're right. I confess that this commissar standing before you is a hard man and has very often been harsh to good fighters who failed. However, facing you, your many misfortunes and disappointments, your great strength in overcoming them and fighting the way you have until now, your difficult lives as aryans in a strange and alienated city, I cannot maintain my tough stance, I have to consider any mistake of yours as only an error . . ." He spoke seriously, thoughtfully. It was the first time I had seen him moved. Finally he added:

"You know, I am Ukrainian. Until now I have tried to hide my origin from you. Before you I am chagrined that I am Ukrainian. I, the commissar, am suddenly ashamed of my Ukrainian origin, as if a people, as a people, can make a man ashamed. Still, I am. There are many Ukrainians, believe me, who did not collaborate with the Germans and did not mobilize to help annihilate your people, and still I am abject."

The Combrig summed up the commissar's remarks simply and unemotionally:

"True, if he had not been a Jew, if it were not for the fact that you sent him to us with the desire to save some poor remnant, you would have to face judgment. Certainly you are responsible for anyone coming with your recommendation. That does not apply to any organized unit that you send. Such a group will have its special officer and will be kept in reserve for a little time. Even here, however, there must be at least one man in the unit whom you know well. You can also express your reservations, and then we would adopt special precautions. However, in the case before us, you would have to face judgment were it not, I repeat, for the Jewish aspect of the affair."

That is how the clarification ended.

Spring was splendid that year; or perhaps it only seemed so to us. The streets were bathed in sunlight and outside the city was all in bloom. Our ties to the forest had become much closer. There were all kinds of people among the partisans. Sometimes even a patrol or regiment commander, or a commissar, might go astray; sometimes something from the past was reawakened and he got drunk and began to say offensive things, to dredge up anti-Semitic memories and tell vulgar jokes.

It was then that the Combrig showed that he could punish unmercifully; remove the man from his position, take away his arms and assign him difficult and dangerous tasks. In that way the transgressor atoned for his sins. This was what maintained the brigade; discipline was of course stronger than human weakness. After all, not everyone was strong enough always to be able to keep you from committing robbery, getting drunk, becoming anti-Semitic and even raping.

The Combrig could be likable, comradely, but also hard. How far that trait went, we experienced personally.

It happened at the end of the spring. Lizka and Haska went to the forest to report to Voichehovsky on a contact we had found with the A.K. through a Pole, Lisovski, a former teacher who was one of the most honest of the anti-German fighters in the A.K. From Lisovski we also received arms when we were still an isolated Jewish partisan unit in the forest. He had given us the weapons despite the A.K. leadership decision not to give them to Jews or any other group fighting the Nazis.

We applied to him now in our search for some contact with the A.K. fighting units. The organization's combat officers did not want to meet a Soviet partisan commander even though they, too, were very much interested in such a meeting. They hesitated a long time, and put it off on various technical grounds. Finally, however, something influenced them, perhaps the speedily approaching front or perhaps they truly came to the conclusion that they had to fight against the Germans and that their leaders were misleading them. In any case, Lisovski brought us into contact with one of the combat officers and hinted that the political leadership in the city did not know anything about the meeting. Haska and Lizka reported the time and place.

Toward evening the girls met with some of the headquarters staff, including two of the youngest. One of them, incidentally, a young Comsomolite, had been appointed as the Combrig's deputy, and was apparently to be the contact with the A.K. The girls were talking about Lisovski, when suddenly one of the partisans began shouting, and ran amok. The partisans had returned toward morning from an operation. They had succeeded in blowing up a German equipment train on the railroad to Volkovysk. They drank a little and fell asleep. This man, however, became drunk.

The Combrig had warned him a number of times, and took away his bottle, but the drunk went to the nearby village, robbed a farmer, at gunpoint, of a full pitcher of "bimber" (homemade beer) and returned completely intoxicated. Then he began to annoy the city girls, and when the Combrig drove him away he returned, shouting and creating disturbance. The drunken partisan was not afraid even of the Combrig. He took a sleeping partisan's pistol, shot into the air, and again began to bother the girls. Only with difficulty did the Combrig restrain his anger. Blushing, he sat and talked. Suddenly, he asked the girls' pardon, nodded to two staff members, and before the girls knew what was happening they saw the drunk led to one side. Two shots rang out and the drunk fell. He was buried on the spot. The Combrig returned, silent for a moment, and then said:

"Excuse me, I am very sorry about the whole affair. For a long time I have wanted to do that, but I wanted to spare you the sight. He was not a bad partisan, he was a good fighter, but this wasn't the first time that he endangered the whole camp by his excessive drinking. He went to a neighboring village and robbed a farmer. From the village it would be easy to follow his footsteps, and the farmer who was robbed was also likely to call in the Germans. At night he blew up a railroad train, and now he risked himself and his whole unit because of too much vodka. The Germans are certainly looking for traces of the saboteurs. And in addition, what was most unpleasant for me, was the way he pestered you." Here he turned to his comrades. "The son of a bitch, didn't he know that the girls come to us to relax from the tensions in which they found themselves day and night in the underground. Here they have to rest, to feel themselves free of worry or persecution. Here we have to instill in them the feeling of a home and freedom. It's just a shame for all of us that there was a traitor like that among us, someone who did not grasp such a simple matter. Yes, comrades, it is a sin not only not to fight the fascists; it is also a terrible thing to waste the war efforts and the daring and courage."

The Combrig's Victory

The contacts with the A. K. combat forces were made. The Combrig himself dealt with them. After a number of meetings with their commander, the Combrig decided to move with part of his headquarters staff to the A. K. area of operations. Our pleas and those of our group were of no avail to his staff. We explained that the A.K. could not be relied upon; that they were liable to betray and execute him and his comrades at any moment. There had been such cases. He insisted that he would succeed in utilizing the true antifascist struggle. The road was long and involved many risks; the A. K. units were situated in the distant Augustov forests. The Combrig decided to first consult with the regional partisan command in the Bialoviez Volkovysk area. And then he had an idea.

"The girls, those all-powerful girls! You only have to drop a hint, and they are already carrying out the operation. They will get me there. The trip will take a short time and I will be able to return according to plan."

Sometimes his exaggerated trust in us was amusing but also decidedly pleasant. The "dyewchata" (the girls) became an entity not to be questioned or doubted. We were not only the official antifascist committee, we were "the girls". That was much more than a matter-of-fact organizational term.

We began to look for a way to get the Combrig to the Bialovicz base. We told Busse that we were looking for such a way. Two days later he showed us a travel pass to Koenigsberg, and a permit to purchase a private car. We never found out from where and how he was able to get the car permit at a time when the Germans were confiscating all automobiles for the front.

Before his trip to Koenigsberg we decided to give him a pleasant surprise: we told him that the Combrig himself wanted to meet him.

The meeting was held in the nearby forest. The Combrig and his staff took the risk of coming close to the city to enable Busse and Schade to return to their affairs and homes that same evening.

Busse returned happy as a child. He related details, was enthusiastic over every word coming from Voichehovsky. The elation of this 40-year old man had its special charm. He was especially impressed with the staff members, their courtesy, their clean clothes. The last detail was very important for our Germans. Schade pretended, of course, that he had not been too excited; it was already nothing new for him and in that way he emphasized his superiority over Busse. Each one wanted to prove that he was the most trusted, that he was treated with greater confidence, that he shared more secrets.

Busse went to Koenigsberg, and the Combrig determined to move immediately to the Augustow area. More people had arrived, and he received broader authority to act as he saw fit.

One of the reasons for this was the fact that the front was coming closer. All the existing forces had to be mobilized for the war behind the enemy lines. The closer the front came, the more effective the partisans were in sabotaging the rear and the greater the importance of unifying the fighting forces. The danger was also very real that the Polish A. K. fighters would persist in their hatred and after the liberation return home with their weapons. Now it was no longer enough to be concerned about the war itself; there had to be a care for the time after victory. It was impossible to leave armed forces outside the victorious armies, without discipline and military coordination.

The Combrig left, and only faint echoes reached us about fierce battles between the Polish A. K. members and the Germans. After a while we also learned the details. The Combrig faced many tribulations in the Augustov forests, had combatted both treason and the refusal of the A. K. commanders to fight. Only by miracles were he and his men saved from the traps set by A. K. opponents and traitors. He finally won over the soldiers. They trusted and followed him. He did not invoke their nationalist sentiments, or speak with them in a language they could not understand, or tell them things which were foreign to them. With wisdom, deliberation and courage he conquered their hearts.[40]

Germany Collapses Before Our Eyes

In the city we now had to be more careful than ever. Arrests became an everyday affair, deportations westward were of massive dimensions. Tremendous areas of the Ukraine and Bielorussia were emptied of their population, cattle and grain, by the Germans. The city prisons were filled and emptied and then filled. One night they arrested Lisovsky. He had apparently been on some list given to the Gestapo by one of the prisoners. From now on every one of the girls had a signal for her window: if the shade was raised it meant danger.

We had to continue to be very careful in the way we conducted ourselves. We must seem happy, to give parties, to invite "decent" guests, and most important — to celebrate saints' days, like good Catholics.

One day, soon after we heard that there were rumors in the courtyard. It was being whispered that strange girls were living here, and one who visited them was certainly Jewish.

We had no idea how it all had started, but suddenly we felt the ground burning under our feet. Then something else happened that hastened our decision to move.

Marylka and Haska had gone to the market to buy articles for headquarters with the forged money, when a Polish woman recognized Marylka from when they were neighbors in the Soviet period, and knew her as Jew and a Communist. Before they could get away two gendarmes appeared. Haska turned the whole affair into a joke.

The gendarme held her arm and she kept laughing. The gendarme became angry:

"It's too early to laugh, you fresh Jew."

"Why shouldn't I laugh? They'll laugh at you too if you tell anyone that I'm Jewish."

The gendarme held on to her. After handing the Jewish Communist over to the police, the Polish woman left, and the Gendarmes had not stopped her. They had not even asked for her address. At the police station all the policemen crowded around them and Haska began:

"So, tell me; he says," and she pointed to one gendarme, "he says that I'm Jewish. Look into my eyes, look well, ha, ha, ha, am I Jewish?"

The chief himself came from behind his desk, placed Haska in the light coming through the barred window and looked intently into her eyes. The gendarme turned red with anger. He brought in a Jew and here they were daring to question his decision. The chief himself was examining the girl as if he were an expert on Jews.

"No, how can it be? See what beautiful blue eyes the girl has," the chief said, in good spirit. Haska joked, laughed, and Marylka stood aside and watched the game. When the girls were asked for their papers they showed them with a big, confident "please." Haska's address, Saint Roch Street, was registered with the police.

When they returned from the police station they decided to move immediately. Busse came to our assistance. His studio was on the main street, where only Germans lived. Above his place were some dilapidated homes. He would repair them quickly in a week we could move in. Haska would live there as the firm's employee, since Poles were generally forbidden to live in German houses. I, of course, would join her. There we would not have any neighbors and could act as we liked.

We accepted Busse's offer. The apartment was rebuilt in a few days; a large room with a stove and a toilet in the yard. The entry was through a separate side entrance. It was an ideal apartment. It was also an excellent cache for all kinds of contraband. Busse carried on, too. He brought his information as he had been instructed, arranged all kinds of difficult matters and afterwards would pull a bottle of good wine from under his arm, place it on the table, and disappear. Once we sent wine and German cigarettes to the forest, a gift from Busse. A second time we delivered bolts of cloth in Busse's car, the product of Combinat No. 5. It was cloth intended for pilots and high ranking officers. That was Schade's gift.

It was a hot summer. The cells were about to send most of their members to the forest. The time had come.

Incessant consultations and clarifications were held in our apartment. Felek left and Volodya arrived. Some people had to be hidden for a day or two before they could go to the forest; the Gestapo was looking for them.

There was a prisoner camp west of the city. We had sought some contact with the inmates for a long time. Their situation was extremely bad, and we feared that as the front drew near they would be killed. Felek, Volodya and Kurillo were mobilized for the operaion. One of Felek's men worked nearby, Felek visited him every day and every day he brought information. The camp was very well guarded, with no possibility of attacking it from the outside and freeing the prisoners. It was too close to the provincial capital. The partisans had no foothold in the area, in the forest or in sympathetic villages. It was also close to the main thoroughfare, the highway leading westward.

There was no choice but to organize a gradual escape of the prisoner from their places of work. That kind of escape could succeed only at the beginning. We decided to go ahead, and to arm those prisoners whose lot it would be to escape last. Kurillo who worked in the neighborhood was put in charge. We knew that the prisoners would be more likely to trust someone who spoke Russian. We would have to arrange for them to be hidden in one of the suburbs until dark. They were to arrive during the day in groups of two or three.

The escape succeeded, the only one ever from that prison camp. Only a few dozen escaped, and hundreds remained. They were not taken out to work after the escape. Two men who seemed to the Germans to be prisoners' leaders were shot on the spot. However, in the course of the following days we succeeded in smuggling in light arms, grenades, pistols, and at the end, when the Russians began to bomb the city and to come closer, we smuggled in small magnetic mines. The prisoners would be able to use these mines in the event of an evacuation. If they were moved by car or train they could blast a wall or some part of the vehicle and escape.

Several more prisoners from the camp reached us. In the forest they were organized into a special reserve battalion. Slowly they returned to normal life, slowly they recovered from the nightmare of the camp, the hunger, fear and beatings. Their dry bones were fleshed and they soon were on their feet. When they received weapons they became good fighters.

Another group of escaped prisoners brought to the forest was from the Todt labor army, composed of many peoples, including Bielorussians, Ukrainians, and even Cossacks, Georgians and Armenians. They had been mobilized by the Germans. We decided, with headquarter agreement, to move them to the forest. First, they would have to atone for their sins, and then fight. After victory, justice would be done unto them. Their escape was easier because they enjoyed greater freedom of movement. On the other hand, it was more difficult to organize them; it was not clear which of them were traitors. We decided to move all units of members from the minorities. The escape was planned in our room, over the studio. The operation went off well.

Liberation was approaching with giant steps. On July 3 Minsk was taken, and the cities of eastern Poland fell one by one into the hands of the Red Army. After Minsk, Kovel was liberated and after Kovel-Baranovich

Osmiana, near Vilna. It was very difficult to believe that we had come this far, that we were still alive and that victory seemed closer. Somewhere on the Normandy coast of France the allied forces had invaded Europe. The second front for which we had prayed so much in the Stalingrad days had finally been opened — a good sign that the end of the war was near. Signs of victory were already evident in the city streets, first in the incessant night bombings. To maintain our legal status to the last moment we all continued to work as usual, though at times I would receive night leave and go to the forest. I continued to work in the office, at the telephone. The factory was still operating though from time to time the work was interrupted for long hours because of the bombing. The shelter in the factory courtyard was too small to hold all the workers. The women would burst into tears and the men would quiet them. The fear was very great. I remained alone in the office, and waited for the all-clear.

Tension in the factory increased. Discipline broke down and even the Germans with the director at their head, could not enforce order. The director would run back and forth as though he was still in control, even then.

Once a bomb fell very close to us. The building actually shook. The Germans' anti-aircraft defense returned tentative scattered fire. We heard a prolonged shriek and the German anti-aircraft cannon once again opened fire. Small fragment fell in the factory yard. I went out there and hid under a large steel tank. The director ordered the workers to be sure to come back tomorrow. Let no one dare be absent for fear of the bombing! He made a long and boring speech: German cities are also being bombed without let-up and their workers are working without fear. Our workers listened indifferently.

Before morning the telephone rang. "How are things with you?" "Everything is in order," I replied. The voice on the other side was angry: "How in order? What's in order? The power station opposite you has been destroyed."

When I left the factory, the city was engulfed in flames. The central electric power station opposite the factory was a heap of rubble. Many buildings had been destroyed, among them the splendid Hotel Ritz, which had been only for high-ranking Germans. I hurried home. The girls were looking out of the window. After the first bombing, Lizka had moved in with us. It was better being together, should we have to leave the city in a hurry.

I decided not to go back to work. The bombings continued all night, and we already knew that between 11 and 12 o'clock we had to dress and wait for the alarm. We had to go down into the cellar of Busse's house. It was not far away; we could get there in time. We were always ready. Each of us had a small hand bag containing linen, stockings, and important papers.

In those days all our calculations were upset. We knew that the front was close, we knew that liberation was near, but we did not know exactly when it would come, or just where the liberating army was. During the day there were meetings, and running about the city; at night — bombing. The heads of the cells came, people who had worked for the underground, Felek, and Busse, Schade, Demidovich and Buchinsky. Some had children and were concerned for them. Their move to the forest had to be arranged. We had to be strict on security, and take any documents they had from them before they left. One brought arms, another brought plans. No one knew if we would have time to use them.

The city took on a new look. The Germans were organizing an evacuation; it was dangerous to walk in the streets. They seized people and pushed them into cars and trains. Soldiers were running about the streets, going into shops and taking whatever they liked without paying. The shops emptied swiftly and were soon locked. Now they were breaking into the shops at night. The city was in confusion; there was no order, no government, chaos and terror prevailed. Every day it seemed as if the end had come, but the situation dragged on for weeks. The Germans were going westward, but were still there. Big crates of furniture, clothing, machines, long caravans moved westward. The Germans apparently still had enough time to confiscate anything that could be moved. There was the German neighborhood; living in it were the respectable families of SS officers and the Gestapo, directors and "chiefs". Boxes were piled in front of the houses. A lady came out of the house with a little dog behind her: she was taking him for his last walk. There was a porch coverd with greens and flowers; a German family was taking pictures; they carried small suitcases. The little dog was with them.

We decided to act. A courier from the forest brought a large quantity of magnetic mines. They were small and looked like little wooden boxes. Inside was a clock. One set the clock for a specific time and left the mine in front of a moving car. The mine would cling to the car, and explode at the time set. The mine was only strong enough to disable the car. In that way we could impede the German flight for a little while and sabotage their moving operation. The courier brought specific instructions: only two or three girls were to remain in the city, the rest were to go to the forest. We hesitated; which of us would go? No one wanted to leave her comrades, or wanted to give up the privilege of seeing the Soviet army enter the city.

There was, however, no way to avoid going to the forest. Some girls had to leave in any case: Mina, who had hidden in Schade's home, could no longer remain there. There was an imminent danger that the Germans would blow up Schade's house. Her friend, who had been hidden by the director of factory no. 1, also had to leave for the forest. And the same for my sister Miriam. They informed us from the forest that we cold bring along anyone we felt needed a hiding place, including the Germans. The Germans came to us one by one, their faces fallen, their eyes misty. They listened to what we had to say and asked us to help them. Now, however, the choice was theirs. They had to decide, and that was difficult. It was hard even for an anti-Nazi German to be in a city which was being emptied of Germans, a city which the Soviet army would enter at any moment.

German commando units had begun to set fire to the city. They started with military targets and went on to every building that had housed a German institution of any kind. Time was pressing; the arsonists were doing their work methodically. It was forbidden to try to extinguish the fires. Anyone coming close to a burning building was shot.

The discussion in our house continued. The first to come was the director of factory no. 1. He waived the right. He was too old for this adventure. He was also not strong enough in body or character. This was a revolution and he was not prepared for revolutions. He was leaving his keys and left everything in his house in our hands. He knew they would burn his home on the very day he left the city and turned westward, to his family in Bilitz. He was the first.

The second was Busse. Even on that day he remembered to bring something from his cellar so we would not be hungry, and we were. He was thinking very seriously. He had been sleepless all night. It was hard to look into his sad, weary eyes. No, he would not go to the forest. Perhaps his decision was not correct, but it was not in his nature to ask for a reward for his insignificant assistance to the underground. He had no right to ask for that privilege when his people deserved the most severe punishment. All Germans were responsible for the actions of the Nazis, and of the German army; all had to be punished. He did not believe that the Russians would treat him with preference. Those in the forest would join the army or go home. Representatives of the local administration would come, begin an investigation and ask questions. "You would have to defend me; I would be a burden to you. I have no right to make it harder for you. The world is open to you and why should I interfere in that?"

Busse finished, and he seemed to have tears in his eyes. It was difficult to convince him; it was not easy to say to him, openly: stay with us, we promise you a future bound with our future. And still, we talked to him. Perhaps our promises were not convincing; in any case, Busse too left that very day. Bolle, the local German, went with his Jewish wife to a village, to one of his Polish friends. He could not remain with his Jewish wife until the Russians arrived; nor could he go to the forest.

Schade remained. He appeared toward evening, shaved, dressed in sports clothes, high boots, riding a bicycle. He was prepared to go. Mina would leave first; he could not let her remain in the house. We moved her to our apartment, and that evening Schade appeared on the bicycle, with a Soviet gun in his bag. Schade and Haska left the city that evening for the forest.

The next day was a sad one in our home. Most had already left; Mina and her friend, my sister Miriam, the Germans, the couriers, and the heads of the cells. We cooked cereal and sang the latest partisan song: "Dark Night." The house was empty, the street was deserted. Red flames leaped at the sky from all directions. We wandered through the streets. A drunken soldier offered to sell us his rifle for fifty marks. We gave him the money and took the rifle home.

Fifty — counterfeit —marks for a good, almost new rifle, with ammunition.The soldier went away singing and weaving on his wobbly feet. He was no longer a soldier, just a man in rags.

The commando unit was continuing its methodical torching. They had sent the equipment and machines to Germany; they emptied the city, and now they were burning it. That was their order. We continued to plant more mines, and distributed them to those of our people who remained in the city, to use at any opportunity. In the afternoon Bronka and I said goodbye to the remaining comrades — Lizka and Ania, and we, too, left the city. It was hard to give up the rifle we had bought for fifty counterfeit marks, and we decided to come to the forest with our own weapons, Bronka with a pistol and I, a rifle.

It was a fine, warm July day. The road was dusty, and the sun beamed its rays abundantly. We were at the cemetery, on the edge of the city. A few more isolated houses, and the road was ahead. We heard the sound of a motorcycle; perhaps they were coming after us! Bronka stood in the middle of the road and raised her hand. A marvelous idea! The motorcycle came closer, ground to a halt. A German officer asked Bronka what she wanted.

"I want to get home to say goodbye to my parents. I want to get the transport going westward today."

"Get on. Where are you going?"

"To Suprasl."

He looked at Bronka. From her his glance shifted to me.

"Nu, get on, you too. What are you carrying, is it heavy?"

We placed the wrapped rifle behind the officer. I held on in back with difficulty. He drove with great speed, covering us with a cloud of dust. He talked to Bronka, and she was keeping him "interested." Near Grodnichka he stopped. If we wanted to return with him, we would have to wait here. He would return soon.

"No, thanks. We have to get to Suprasl —it's another five kilometers.'

The officer raced away.

Once again we were standing on the road. Again there was a loud rumble.

This time a truck appeared from behind the turn. Who could be driving? The Germans were all going in the opposite direction. This time I lifted my hand. The truck stopped. It was loaded with soldiers, armed, and with steel helmets on their heads. We wanted to get away but the soldiers invited us on. There was no way out. I got on first, a soldier helped me lift the "package."

We came to the railway leading to Charnovies in the forests nearby where one of our units was operating. We were on a forest road. The Germans became tense, picked up their guns. One of them leveled the barrel of a machine gun. What had happened, we wondered, pretending to be afraid.

"Little fools, what do you know?"

We emerged from the forest area and the soldiers sighed with relief; the danger from the partisans had passed. From afar we could see the big Suprasl bridge. The truck turned left; we said we wanted to get off. The soldiers laughed. Bronka and I banged on the driver's compartment; he stopped the truck and we jumped off. I threw the rifle ahead of me. The soldiers looked at us. One of them wanted to come after us but the truck began to move slowly on the dirt road.

We stood on the empty road, bathed in sunshine. The bridge was ahead of us, with sentries on both sides. I waited and Bronka went ahead. She asked the soldier if he would allow us to go by since we worked in the textile factory here in Suprasl. The combinat here was not no. 4, as my work card said, but would he notice that? Bronka returned and took my card. I watched. Apparently the many stamps made a good impression. Bronka called me. We came to the middle of the bridge; the package had not been checked. On the other side it was easier. The sentry looked at the work card, shook his head and said:

"Foolish girls! You're going to the Bolsheviks. They'll kill you; leave your homes and come with us."

"Yes, yes, we only want to say goodbye to our parents," Bronka said.

We continued on our way until we reached the cemetery. We did not know what was taking place in the town. We decided to hide the rifle in the cemetery, and enter with empty hands. We would return later. There was a well in the graveyard in which we washed our faces and hands. We arranged our clothing, shook off the dust. It was almost evening. We came to the center of the town; the daughter of a Polish partisan lived there. She would be able to show us the way and perhaps even accompany us; she was in constant contact with her father.

We gave her the password and she let us into the house. She was a beautiful young woman; blonde, tall, erect and healthy looking.

Her home was a room in an attic, though she actually lived with her aunt below. She suggested that we wait until she could cross with us. We refused, and told her that we had left something in the nearby graveyard. At dark the three of us went to the cemetery. We found the package and brought it to the attic, and asked her to show us the way that same night. She disappeared, and after a little while, returned and informed us that for the time being it was impossible to move along the road. "They are fighting there and the Germans will arrest you as spies, or you will be hit by a bullet. There is a side road from the highway, and from it, along the forest, you will be able to get to your destination. But it is forbidden to walk there. I walked to the courier. He is not returning either. I would show you the way through the fields but the area is flooded, and if you don't know the path you are liable to drown." She concluded: "You don't have any alternative; wait until tomorrow. If by morning the situation doesn't change, we'll convince the courier to take you through the fields."

We slept in Suprasl. We had hardly fallen asleep when we were awakened by many tremendous explosions. The house trembled, and every blast threw me to the floor. I dressed with difficulty. The girl was already knocking at the door and hurrying me to get down quickly to the trench behind the house.

Bent over, we ran to the trench. Overhead, cannon fire lit up the sky. There was fire from the east and from the west. The attack from the east grew stronger. I saw ribbons of flame twisting over our heads. The air thundered and the ground shook. Fragments fell in the untilled field behind us. Infants in the trench cried. Women nursed them, to quiet them.

In the morning, light cannons ceased to fire. Greyness appeared behind the dark horizon. Behind that drabness the fort surrounding the town was still black. Strange figures appeared from the side streets; stealing their way, limping, torn and ragged. Could these be the invincible soldiers of the Third Reich? They moved slowly, one by one, knocked at doors and pleaded for a drop of water. Frightened, unkempt, they kept looking back. They were no longer an army; they were refugees, or perhaps deserters.

At noon we learned that the road was still crowded with retreating German troops. Bronka had returned to the city after many adventures, and together with the girls who had remained there, prepared a welcome for the liberators. The partisan's daughter took me to the courier and he toward evening brought me to the partisan headquarters camp. We had crossed flooded fields, wallowing in mud up to our knees. I had my rifle on my shoulders. For the first time I was carrying a weapon openly.

Eternal Glory for the Fighters

We spent a few days in the forest, attached to brigade headquarters. The front came close to the city of Bialystok, and the partisans were busy cleaning out the remnants of Germans from the city. I heard the German prisoners' replies: every one had been a worker; every one had gone to fight because he had been mobilized against his will, and every one was an anti-Nazi. We were together, Haska and I. One day the staff decided to conduct a survey in Suparsl. I was added to the survey group. We walked along the road, rifles on our shoulders. Haska had given me her belt and pistol. I was dressed in long trousers and a short coat. For the first time I did not look like an elegant city girl. No more underground. It was a strange feeling.

One of our tasks was to uncover and arrest collaborators in town. We met crowds of Red Army soldiers camped on the outskirts of town: soldiers and officers, armed, dust-covered and sweaty. They had come a long way. They were very weary. Hundreds of vehicles passed with mobile kitchens and field pieces. I saw the "katyusha"* for the first time. The soldiers looked at us and their glances fell on me:

"Partizanka, hah?"

"Yes, partizanka," I replied with childish pride.

We went through the town. People were standing on their doorsteps, looking at us. One shook our hands, another greeted us, and still another just looked without speaking.

We gathered the needed information and returned. The road to Bialystok was open, and we were promised a meeting with a liaison officer to exchange information and to coordinate our operations with the local authority.

The officer arrived that same evening. The following morning we returned to the city, back to liberated Bialystok.

We passed villages. Peasants stood, dazed, in their doorways. Everywhere they told of fleeing Germans. From one village they fled that same

* A multi-rocket weapon used by the Soviet forces.

morning, and we immediately seized the schoolhouse where they had been stationed. We cleaned out the filth they left behind and lay down to rest. It had been a very hot day. We were hungry and thirsty, but we had been ordered not to ask the peasants for food. Our food ran out during the last few days; everyone received a slice of smoked meat, a ration with which we would have to be satisfied until we arrived in the city. Traveling on the road had been tiring; tens of kilometers in the heat of the day. We obeyed orders and did not accept any food from the peasants. Only a few days ago we forced them to supply us with food. Now our partisan existence ended. We were marching on liberated soil, parading as victors.

We entered the city at the head of the partisans. The Kostucio Kalinowski Brigade led the way. The city was in flames. The streets were desolate. No one came to greet us with drums and cymbals. No flowers were presented to us. The city was dead. Sad victors.

A figure appeared from the corner of Warshavska Street. A single human figure on the whole street. It ran toward us madly. Beneath the brows of the ragged dark figure were two burning black eyes. The face was only bones, the skin waxlike. The nose was exceptionally long, the hands and feet thin. Only the eyes, the eyes burned. She was the only Jewish woman we found in the city; one who had hidden for a year in cellars and holes, a Jewish woman half-demented from her sufferings and the unexpected relief.

We came to the quiet suburb behind Mitzkevich Street. Factory No. 5 was in front of us, in flames. A small group of factory workers pushed out of the gate. I recognized one of them; he was a member of a cell. I had not known that he worked for Schade. His comrades were standing at his side, astonished, as though they did not believe their eyes. My acquaintance clapped his hands and laughed. He pulled his comrades by their sleeves; they stood riveted to the ground and looked at us. He tugged at their sleeves; "We can still save something from the factory," he shouted, and they disappeared into the gate.

That is how we entered the city that lost tens of thousands of its inhabitants. We came as mourning victors, into a city bereft of its Jews.

Behind the corner of the street, between Sienkewicz and Yuroviecke in front of the big gate, extending over the whole length of the street, was a red cloth with these words emblazoned on it:

Eternal Glory to the Fighters

We wondered who had raised that banner. It was red, as the fire burning all around us, and as the embers falling at our feet.

We crossed the city and looked for our girls. In the German section beyond Mitzkevich Street, where Haska, Lizka and Miriam had once worked as servants for the SS families, there were some buildings that had been saved from the conflagration. A sign in white letters read: "Danger — Epidemic".

Those buildings had been saved: factories, Becker's factory, and from behind the burning fire our girls were running toward us, sooty and excited, the Jewish girl fighters who remained in the city without any other Jews. They had saved these buildings by posting the warning of an epidemic, and the Germans were afraid to come close enough to set them on fire.

They received us with "Eternal Glory to the Fighters!" but the dead will not rise from their graves. We are too few to redeem the memory of so many.

Epilogue

This book is based upon facts as they remained in my memory. In 1949, seven months after coming to Israel, these memories were still fresh in my mind. During those first years after the war on the soil of liberated Poland we still lived the experiences of the Nazi occupation and the extermination. Our return to life did not mean cutting off the past. It was part of our being, not as traumas or as phantoms we were dragging behind us but as an organic part of our very lives: our feelings, concerns and fears. We still could smell the ghetto odors. Our hands felt the walls of its ruins and our feet trod the cobblestones on which we had walked together with the Jews being led along their last road.

There was no need to reconstruct the events or bring them to life again; I still lived them, without any intention on my part to do so.

This book was written as a testimony. I have avoided going into detail about events in which I did not actually participate. Though I was a partner in the activities of the main underground and played a considerable role in some of the branches, they do not always reflect their relative importance. Thus, for example, the chapter dealing with the history of the partisan units in the Bialystok region is inadequate. Members of movements other than Hashomer Hatzair, who also worked in the underground then, may feel that their names and places have been omitted and that they were neglected in this memoir.

They may be justified. In 1949, I did not think it was the time for exhaustive research, but only to relate the information as it was indelibly etched in my mind and heart. I had no documents, nor could I have had any. We may assume that not too many new ones will appear. Additional testimony, to our sorrow, will not appear. Those facts which have not been written down so far, will probably never come to light.

Since I was in the center of the underground activity in Bialystok, and for some periods in other ghettoes, it was my duty to serve as a source for information of this kind.

The book is replete with descriptions of and facts about the activities of the Judenrat in the Bialystok ghetto. I have included these as background for the life of the ghetto, and in any case they should not be overlooked. The underground came up against that institution at every step. The Judenrat's importance was not limited by the walls of the three-storied old age home on Kupeicka Street, where its offices were; it dominated the spirit of the ghetto Jews and roused them to revolt, but under no circumstances did it remain outside of their lives. The facts determined by the Judenrat were physical, and their implications were complex.

In writing The underground "Army" in 1949 I had not seen the Judenrat records uncovered many years later by Nachman Blumenthal, in his *The Path of the Judenrat*, published by "Yad va'Shem" in 1975. These records not only do not contradict what I have written, but are even more shocking in their dry, formal statements. The nature of the Judenrat, as I examined it in the light of my own knowledge and experience, receives even more frightful significance from the documents themselves.

The Judenrat records were official, and could not include, for example, Barash's discussions with the underground representatives, Mordechai Tenenbaum and myself. From this standpoint the memoirs are preferable to official documents whose general historical trustworthiness is limited. Under ghetto conditions not everything could be written down. Members of the underground themselves were careful not to leave any traces behind. Very few kept continuous diaries. The pages of Mordechai Tenenbaum's diary that were preserved in their cache and were published in Israel a few years ago are invaluable. Even they, however, could not reflect all the facets of our life.

I knew of these pages while they were being written. More than once Mordechai called Edek and me to his room and read to us what he had written, before it was sent with Bronka Vinicka (today Klibansky) to be hidden outside the ghetto. I knew that these words were written in moments of tension, when the writer wavered between hope and despair over the future of the ghetto, the people, political leaders, institutions, movements, and the Judenrat. They were penned in fragments, hurriedly, feverishly, almost automatically, without any real opportunity to balance, analyze or summarize. That is perhaps the great historic value of Mordechai Tenenbaum's entries.

The last date in the Judenrat records is November 11, 1942, that is, four months before the first *aktzia* in the ghetto. The Judenrat records omit a number of decisive events in the life of the ghetto: the first *aktzia*, in which 10-12,000 Jews were sent to Treblinka; they do not include Barash's talks with the underground, as I have noted. I also have reservation about some of the marginal comments provided here and there by the editor as, for example, his statement in the introduction: "Every single Judenrat had to face its fate . . . alone and abandoned by God and man. In every ghetto events started from the beginning . . . They were never told how the liquidation of hundreds of other communities had been effected nor explained clearly what was in store . . . No one turned to the Judenrat on this subject . . ." All the facts prove that the Judenrat members knew about Ponar as early as December, 1941; Barash heard the truth from me. He knew about Treblinka, and he himself testified in his speech of October 11, 1942 (item 50, p. 252, Records): . . . "everybody knows what happened in Warsaw, in Slonim . . . (It is) Better to go to Volkovysk* than to Treblinka . . ."

This is to say, it is not a lack of information we have here but a policy that was the direct opposite of that adopted by the underground.

Undoubtedly, the same known facts led to two contrasting lines of action: that of the Judenrat on the one hand, and of the underground on the other. To ignore that fundamental fact (for the Bialystok ghetto too) is to deny the basic truth and ascribe exaggerated importance to secondary facts.

* Where Jewish girls were taken to work. After the liquidation of the Volkovisk ghetto, after many tribulations, they returned to Bialystok.

Notes

1. On Friday, June 27, 1941 there were pogroms against the Jews, under the protection of the Wehrmacht and with the participation of the Grossdeutschland Waffen SS. Jews called that day "der roiter Freitag" (red Friday - tr.). Jews were also kidnapped on Thursday, July 31, 1941, and on Saturday, July 12, 1941.

2. Only the Judenrat Chairman, Rabbi Dr. Rosman, was appointed by the authorities. The other Judenrat members were volunteers. Rabbi Rosman turned to Barash, Barash to Sobotnik, and so on. The Judenrat's presidum included Rosman, Barash, Goldberg, Glikson, and Sobotnik. There were 24 members in the Judenrat council, The Path of the Judenrat.

3. Four or five thousand Jews were deported between September 18 and October 21, 1941. The facts of protectionism during the deportation to Prushany, and also the use of bribes, are verified by the Judenrat records (no.13) of October 3, 1941. According to these entries, "lower ranks" were deported; the aged, the poor, and social welfare cases. The Judenrat gave special protection to the intellectuals. The alphabetically arranged lists prepared for the deportation did not include Judenrat workers, professionals and their families, the wealthy, etc. (item 9, 10 of September 12, 1941, p. 34-6 The Path of the Judenrat). The property of those deported to Pruzhani was transferred to the Judenrat.

The Judenrat had 2000 employees, 100 percent more than was required. These workers did not receive salaries but only benefits, and supposedly, "life insurance." The Judenrat had 200 policemen at its disposal.

4. The Judenrat records and the placards posted in the ghetto streets include the details of all the German demands: various home articles, furniture, etc. An announcement of that kind appeared on September 10, 1941 (item 92, p. 330-332, Path . . .).

5. On November 23, 1941, he told a public meeting in the "Linat-Zedek" (item 21): "We must act without mercy against those workers leaving their work or changing their employment by themselves. There is a danger to the ghetto in that . . ."

At the Judenrat meeting of November 29, 1942, he said (item 22): "Our status in the eyes of the city authority (Bialystok-Regierungspresident Magonie and afterwards Landrat Broks, in September 30, 1941) has improved so much that he displays the ghetto products under glass in his office . . ."

At that same meeting, Barash warned against some things that had happened, "when a truck was repaired and it did not have a lamp, brakes, wheels . . .mattresses did not fit the beds . . ," acts of sabotage that would lead to catastrophe.

The records are full of such warnings, and they testify that the Judenrat wanted to produce well and faithfully, and only the masses committed sabotage.

An exhibition of 500 ghetto products was displayed in the offices of the Ghettoverwaltung in Warsawska Street. That exhibition was Barash's pride. (Judenrat meeting of March 22, 1942.)

6. On January 18, 1942 (item 27) Barash told a Judenrat meeting: "Recently we have been caused a great deal of trouble by the actions of irresponsible persons, Bialystok inhabitants, who have returned from Vilna." I had "returned from Vilna" exactly at that time. What was Barash inferring? We can assume that it was the warning against underground activity that he repeated over and over again. At that time Barash had a talk with me along the lines I have described in the book.

7. The records of the Judenrat meetings of January 18, 1942 report that Barash told that same meeting that "The Judenrat has given the army a winter gift: 3,500 pieces of clothing, 500 winter coats, 500 pullovers, 500 pairs of gloves, 500 hats and socks. In addition, our industry will produce canvas boots, leather boots, shoes . . . 500 tailors will work."

8. The Zelikovich affair is detailed in The Paths of the Judenrat (pp. 186-8, 196). According to this, he was a member of the police who, together with five other policemen, carried out searches; on his own initiative, relying upon the authorities, they stole, robbed and extorted even from the Judenrat's own financial department. Zelikovich's loyal henchman was Fenigstein, commander of ghetto police station no. 1. Zelikovich also mediated between the Gestapo and Jews and was an informer. The Gestapo executed him. Barash attacked him openly at a general meeting in the "Linat Zedek" hall on June 21, 1942.

A reorganization within the police followed, with its commander, Marcus, turning his back on Zelikovich, despite their former good relations.

9. The refugee problem continually troubled the Judenrat, which considered the ghetto's growth a danger to its existence. Record no. 37 of April 4,

1942, quotes Barash: "We have spoken against the ghetto's growing population. Now we are being warned by the Gestapo, and the situation is dangerous. Because of the additional refugees from Vilna and other places, terrible things occurred in Lida (why had they also occurred in Vilna? Barash knew the answer, from us, but ignored it. - C. G.). We are doing everything possible to remove the evil decree from the ghetto but, as is well known, the Bialystok ghetto has a relatively large population and the matter is liable to end tragically. Here we must adopt measures."

The murder in Lida is pictured here as punishment for the flow of refugees. At that time Barash knew explicitly about Ponar. Barash had also witnessed the liquidation of ghettoes smaller than that of Bialystok. The authorities demanded lists of Jews who had registered after September 1, 1942. Because of this the Judenrat decided to apply sanctions against the refugees and to severely punish not only the refugees but anyone giving them shelter (announcements no. 237, 248, 249).

"The list of names of the non-registered Jews was transmitted . . . to the police command and to the Gestapo," Barash says in his report of May 2, 1942 (item 39). The decision was taken on April 4, 1942 (item no. 37).

Barash reported on the murders in Baranovich at a general meeting in the "Linat Zedek" hall on April 5, 1942. He said that "2500 Jews had been put to death because they did not want to work." Of course that was not true. On March 4, 1942, 1500 "useful" Jews were also killed there, and it does not seem possible that Barash did not know this. We provided him with authentic information.

10. In a Judenrat announcement of December 3, 1941, we find that Leib Weinstein, with eight others, did not report for work and were punished with hard labor (no. 173 of the Judenrat announcements). We can assume among them was Aryeh Weinstein, a member of Hashomer Hatzair. We knew that he was expressing his revolt in this way, something that generally resulted in personal suffering.

11. "The ghetto's welfare and security depend upon each of you" Rabbi Rosman said at a general meeting in "Linat Zedek (item 44 of June 21, 1942.). "If you fulfill your obligations, if you obey the instructions of the authorities, everything will be in order," Barash said at that same meeting.

Then Barash listed the dangers lying in wait for the ghetto: 1. (the greatest danger) the ghetto was large and numbered 35,000 (there were more Jews than that in the ghetto at the time but they feared to appear too "large" in the enemy's eyes. — C. G.); 2. the danger of the illegal migration from Prozhani; 3. many were not working. To this list he added:

"Our security is in direct relationship to the achievements of our work.

We already have 20 factories. Recently we have added a canvas factory, a brush factory, a barrel factory, in which Gauleiter Koch has shown a personal interest. Still to be opened are factories for ropes, horse-shoes, wagon-wheels, and clothing, that will employ up to 2,000 women workers."

The ghetto was visited by military delegations: Gestapo heads from Koenigsberg and Berlin, heads of the trade office, and Gauleiter Koch, who was in charge of East Prussia and Reichscomissar for the Ukraine. The Bialystok region had been annexed as Regirungsbezirk to East Prussia, and Koch's title was oberpresident.

Among the dangers to the ghetto Barash also listed smuggling, enjoying luxuries, currency exchange, and the like. According to the records of the Judenrat meeting of August 1, 1942 (no. 48), Barash declared that:

"I know that political work is being carried on in the factories. I do not want to talk here about ideas. If anyone thinks it right to risk his own head for his ideas, we can acquiesce. However, to endanger the lives of 35,000 Jewish souls — that is a kind of hooliganism and can lead to very bad results."

The Bialystok ghetto administration, an authority of the Bialystok city administration, sent a letter to the Judenrat on October 1, 1942:

"Subject: Production of padded clothing and winter clothing in the ghetto factories.

The military clothing office in Koenigsberg (Prussia) in its report of September 21, 1942 pointed to the receipt of articles of clothing produced in the ghetto with such serious faults as to be viewed as acts of sabotage against the arms production of the military authorities. The samples were indeed satisfactory, but the product as a whole was so bad that if the matter is repeated the military authorities will be compelled to refrain for issuing further additional orders.

"I have today personally warned the Judenrat very seriously and I impose upon it alone the responsibility for all such cases in the future. There will be very dire punishments and the Jews, because of their irresponsible actions, will have only themselves to blame if there are other, similar transgressions."

12. The gate on Kupiecka Street was locked on July 2, 1942, following the orders of the authorities (Judenrat announcement no. 295).

13. On March 16, 1942, the bread ration was reduced by 25 percent. At first the ration had been 250 grams per person for two days. At the end of 1941, and at the beginning of 1942, the two-day ration was 200 grams, at a cost of 15 pfenning a kilogram (later 30 pfenning). After that, it was only 100 grams and in the spring of 1942 it was reduced to 150 grams for two days. Workers received additional daily rations.

14. In May 1942 the ration was cut by 20 percent for all the population and by 25 percent for the workers.

15. Barash headed the industrial department; Melnicki was his deputy.

16. This figure conflicts with the figure Barash announced publicly, 35,000. First, Barash did not want to reveal the truth for fear of a German "evil eye." Second, the ghetto population had been augmented by many refugees from the region that had been "cleansed" of Jews, beginning in October-November 1942.

17. "This is a terrible picture of 7,000 persons returning after a hard day's work trying to bring food in, and having it confiscated. Friends of the Jewish police, standing near the gate, buy it from them, and then sell the seized articles in stores they opened. They are therefore interested in having the things discovered, so that they may steal what the poor laborers bought with their blood."

These remarks by Barash at a meeting of the Jewish police on June 20, 1942, demonstrate the moral level of the police. Barash, of course, ignored other aspects of police service because he shared them with the police. In any case, there is no reason to wonder that members of the fighting organization assumed the task of police service against their will. To encourage the policemen in their harsh functions they were told that they were fulfilling a national mission. "If a book is ever written about the ghetto, we shall be remembered with honor," they were told by Berman, the deputy commander of the Jewish police in Bialystok.

18. Dr. A. Kanaris, representative of the Sicherheits-Politzei and the Sicherheitsdiensl for East Prussia. His office was in Koenigsberg and he often visited Bialystok.

19. a. On September 30, 1941 Magunia was appointed Regirungspräsident for the city of Bialystok. Landrat Bricks succeeded him. The city was governed by an Oberburgermeister, first Schwandobias, and later Nicolaus. His title was Staatskomissar.

b. The ghetto was managed by the Ghettoverwaltung. After March 1, 1942, management was in the hands of the authority for the city. From November 1942 it was headed by SS Obersturmfuehrer Klein who had worked previously in Refarat YVB, the Gestapo department dealing with Jewish affairs: compulsory labor, health, supplies, etc. He was supposedly the sole authority in the management of ghetto events, but other institutions intervened. Sometimes the interests of the various bodies clashed, with those of the Ghetto paying the price of the conflict, or in some situations benefiting from them. Barash did everything he could to exploit these conflicts for the benefit of the ghetto. According to Fritz Friedl's testimony written in the Bialstyok prison on June 12, 1949, he had received the Judenreferat JVB on October 1, 1942, and then had come from Allstein to Bialystok. Friedl was sentenced to death.

20. The Wirtschaft and Rustungsamt was an organ of the OKW — the army. Its commander was Krieger. The inspector for the Bialystok region was Froese. The ghetto *aktzias*, arrests and investigations were commanded by Fritz Friedl.

21. On November 2, 1942 all the Jewish communities in the Bialystok region, except for Bialystok itself, were liquidated. The towns of Yashinovka, Sokolka, Prushany, Krinki, and part of the Jewish community in Grodno were razed. Altogether, 150,000* Jews were annihilated.

22. The ghetto was reduced. Zamenhof, Zydovska and part of Biala and Branska Streets were excluded from that area. 5,000 Poles were settled there; peasants from the partisan areas in Bialoviez were to take the place of the Jews who were doomed to death, or to work in the ghetto factories. This order was not carried out because most of the factories were destroyed at the time of the revolt. The Poles were sent to work in factories in the city.

23. The address which I quoted from memory is in the spirit of the following quotation from the Judenrat records (no. 30 of October 10, 1942). According to the records, Barash said that "there are a number of signs and secret information that the *aktzias* against the Jews will start in the Bialystok region and in Bialystok itself . . . " Jewish police commander Marcus said that "the center of gravity is in the problem of work." Lifshitz said: "The ghetto inhabitants do not grasp the situation at all. All our announcements and requests fail to convince them. The same is true for the workers."

We know that at that time there was a great deal of preaching about labor. In view of the dangers, people were urged to work and not to resist. They did not understand that it was precisely because of the dangers, and because Jews knew their critical situation that they began more and more to evade the work. This proved ineffective and did not provide safety.

On October 11, one day after the Judenrat session, a public meeting was called in the "Linat Zedek" (item no. 50). Rabbi Rosman said there: "We have called this meeting to provide information about the 'bacchanalia' beginning to run riot in the ghetto; not obeying orders; avoiding the obligation to work; hiding the shirkers." (These things caused dissatisfaction on the part of the authorities, and since Bialystok had previously been a model of which we were proud, he had decided to speak to the people — C.G.).

Barash added: "Recently real dangers for the Bialystok region and city

* German archives later cited a figure of 400,000.

have appeared. We must try to find ways to eliminate or delay the danger and *at the least, to limit its scope* (that is, to sacrifice some Jews for the sake of others — C.G.). To our sorrow, Bialystok has recently become the largest of the ghettoes, after the Lodz ghetto, and there is a great danger in this." Barash knew that the smaller ghettoes had been destroyed throughout the province at just about that time, when:

"The consuming fire is burning in the east up to Derechim and to Malkinia. In order for the conflagration not to spread, everybody, especially in Bialystok itself, must adopt special measures. The people in our ghetto, however, conduct themselves in a completely opposite fashion, as if they were deliberately seeking to provoke a catastrophe. Most recently, our ghetto has become wild and unbridled. If, of the 25,000 inhabitants only 14,000 are working, even those authorities who might favor us will be inclined to (? — C.G.) inevitably ask themselves where are the rest of the people." That was Barash.

Back in August 1942, after the beginning of the *aktzia* in Warsaw, and after Barash had been told about Slonim and Vilna, he made a speech (item 48) as follows: ". . . We want to live. We have women and children. There is no mercy; there is only one path: deeds! To make the ghetto an element they will regret destroying because it is useful, and that is what we are doing."

On October 11, 1942 Barash read aloud the letter from the city authority concerning Jewish acts of sabotage "in the production of supplies for the military authorities." This referred to the production of the clothing factory (see note no. 11). Barash added: "If there is real sabotage the workers will be the first to be shot. I ask the brigade leaders to tell this to the workers, and especially to the shoemakers." We realized that the ghetto institutions wanted the work to go well, but that the people refused.

At the celebration of the Judenrat anniversary, on June 29, 1942, Barash said (*The Path of the Judenrat*, p. 216):

"When weak people pay compliments to the strong, that is known as flattery. We, however, the weakest of the weak, are hearing compliments from the strongest (the Nazis — C.G.) and from the authorities. That change is the result of our creative work . . . There is no room for optimism in the ghetto, but when I survey the road we have travelled, and our resources, I am sure that we will bring the Bialystok ghetto to a happy end . . ." Barash always complained that the Jews were ungrateful, saboteurs, as compared to some of the Nazi authorities who lavished compliments on us for our work. The complaints against "such" Jews were made by Judenrat members on every occasion.

"If you fulfill your obligations, if you obey the instructions of the authorities, everything, God willing, will go well," said Rabbi Rosman on June 21,

1942. "Don't talk about political affairs, don't deal in Russian currency, don't smuggle commodities into the ghetto; if we are in earnest about keeping your houses, courtyards, and streets clean, and if we are consistent in paying our taxes; if the workers are obedient then, God willing, there will be peace for Israel."

24. At all the Judenrat meetings Barash would speak of the "orders," German orders for goods, as the key to the ghetto's existence and future.

25. The canvas factory produced 100 pairs of boots daily; according to Barash's plan, as presented in his report of May 2, 1942 (item 39) production was to be increased to 250 pairs.

We have also found a warning to the shoemakers not to sabotage the product (item no. 49). Such warnings against sabotage and imperfect goods were also issued previously. See notes 23, 24, 29, 34.

26. The Grodno ghetto was completely liquidated in March 1943. The process took several months to accomplish.

27. According to the Judenrat records (*Path of the Judenrat*, no. 427, p. 540), 1148 Jews were moved to Bialystok from Grodno.

28. We find a superficial comment on the February *aktzia* in the testimony of Fritz Friedl who, beginning with October, had been responsible for the Jewish "Referat." This testimony was given in the Bialystok prison in June 1949 in his own handwriting, and a copy exists in the 06 office of the Israel Police.

". . . At the beginning of February Sturmfuehrer Ginter appeared before Dr. Altanalo. Mr. Ginter explained to him that he had instructions to investigate the Bialystok ghetto to uncover the sabotage organization, and also the ones responsible for counterfeiting money and forging passports. The Bialystok command unit knew nothing about units of that kind. This was undoubtedly intended as an excuse for the partial evacuation of the Jews, and it was necessary to separate Altanalo from this because of his stand in favor of the ghetto's existence. I know nothing about the success of Ginter's investigations. He had independently arrested and deported 10,000 Jews, and it was not known where he sent them. There was a great deal of unrest in the ghetto. Heimbach instructed Barash to pacify the ghetto, and to announce that there was no intention and no order for any further evacuations. There was a very gradual relaxation of tensions. The Jews continued to work, but a certain measure of disquiet remained . . ."

29. In the Judenrat records and announcements are to be found "trustworthy evidence of these acts of vengeance which were, apparently, directed in part by the police and the Judenrat. An official Judenrat statement (no. 388) reports that three persons were hanged "for the crimes of robbery and theft from homes of families who were deported."

Another public announcement condemns 35 traitors:

"Those listed below are condemned and put to shame for having in these sad days (during the February *aktzia* — C.G.) robbed evacuated apartments, and those left unattended."

The archivist (according to Blumenthal in *The Path of the Judenrat*, page 514) adds:

"Under the heading of thieves the bloody record lists informers, who revealed hiding places to the Germans during the *aktzia*. Many of them were killed by the people."

After the February *aktzia* the police, according to the records, removed Jews and arrested them. That was always Barash's approach: to deport the worst elements. In keeping with that principle, he exploited the matter of the informers to rid himself of those elements he considered bad. In my estimation, this action served a double purpose, to utilize the matter of the informers to get rid of these elements, and the reverse. Since there was mass anger and sharp spontaneous reaction against the traitors, the Judenrat desired to disguise this public reaction, which could be interpreted by the Nazi authorities as an organized underground activity, by putting the official stamp of approval on the killing of the informers in the street by labelling them thieves and criminals. The Judenrat also wanted to re-establish its own good name in the eyes of the Jews by sanctioning this act of punishment, especially since the Jewish police, too, had "revealed" Jewish hiding places to the Germans.

30. This incident was publicized in a Judenrat pronouncement (no. 391, pp. 516, 517 *The Path . . .*) on the *Pogorelsky* affair of February 17, 1943. The announcement declared: "5000 marks will be paid as a prize from the Judenrat to anyone informing us of the whereabouts of *Pogorelsky Tanhum*, born in 1923." The writer of the records added: "Two men with weapons were arrested outside the ghetto. They declared that it was *Pogorelsky* who had supplied them." The same affair is mentioned in Mordechai Tenenbaum's diary, *Pages from the Fire*, p. 85.

31. The fence straightening and the changes in the ghetto borders were reported in announcements nos. 418, 419 (*Path . . .*, p. 534). They also include a statement on the "transfer of a portion of the population from some streets."

32. The small ghetto remained in existence for approximately three weeks after the final liquidation. The activities of the armed units in there, continued as long as there were still people in hiding. The Nazi units looked for hidden Jews until September 16, 1943 (*Path . . .*).

33. 1200 children were returned by the Nazis to the Bialystok ghetto, and on August 22 they were sent, accompanied by a doctor and 30 teachers, to

Theresienstadt and from there, two or three weeks later, to Auschwitz. According to N. Blumenthal's comments (*Paths of a Judenrat*), the evacuation of the children and the sick from the ghetto continued for a few days.

34. The following is a portion of Fritz Friedl's testimony on the liquidation of the ghetto, and Jewish resistance:

"I knew Globotznik when he appeared at about the end of July or the beginning of August 1943, before SD and SIPO Commander Oberregirungsrat Dr. Zimmermann. I saw him once. He had a service rank of an SS Obergruppenfuehrer, comparable to the service rank of general. I was not present during his conversation with Dr. Zimmerman; I do not know whether Heimbach was there. After that, Heimbach told me that Dr. Zimmerman informed him that Globotznik had been ordered by Himmler to evacuate the Jews from the Bialystok ghetto, that he, Dr. Zimmermann, at the meeting of the bureau heads of the State Police that took place in July 1943 in Berlin, had attempted to leave the Jews in the Bialystok ghetto because they were working solely for the Wehrmacht, and that the evacuation had to be implemented by bypassing the commander, Dr. Zimmermann. Globotznik was to assume overall command of the ghetto, and he would also maintain the necessary police forces. Immediately after that, a delegation ordered by Globotznik and headed by Hauptsturnfuehrer Megel came from Lublin to Bialystok and surveyed the ghetto factories in detail. Megel did not mention that he had been given the task of evacuation, but did say to Heimbach that the ghetto enterprises were really model ones. The delegation returned to Lublin that same day, and on August 15, 1943 another delegation headed by Megel came once again to Bialystok. A secret talk took place in Dr. Zimmermann's office, in which Heimbach also participated. After that meeting, Heimbach told me that the ghetto evacuation would commence on August 16, 1943, and that the police forces were already arriving. I was ordered by Heimbach to invite Barash, a member of the Jewish Council (Judenrat). Heimbach informed Barash that the ghetto with its machinery would be *transferred* (emphasis in original — C.G.) to Lublin by the police forces; that he was to inform the Jews in the ghetto of this, and to tell them that they were to take their families, and that they would continue to work in Lublin in the same manner as in Bialystok. The Jews were to conduct themselves quietly; nothing would happen to them. Barash was very much (*sichtlich*) impressed. The evacuation began on the morning of August 16. Globotznik also appeared. The police brought in one German police regiment and two police regiments comprised of members of the minorities (Ukrainians). The evacuation was directed by Megel. He had with him a number of SS Obersturnfuehrers, including, I think, one by the name of Wagner. The evacuation, however, did not go smoothly. There was shooting on both sides, and both suffered killed and wounded. I know that Globotznik sent in an armored car to break the Jewish resistance . . ."

The translation of this document in the 06 bureau of the Israel Police is listed as no. 1505, page one of four pages. The place and date of this testimony is Bialystok, June 12, 1949.

35. Some of the names of the members of the "aryan" underground, like that of Loninikin, Demidovich, and others, appear in the report by Liza Chapnik, responsible for the urban underground in the name of the Kalinovsky Soviet Partisan brigade operating in 1944 in the Bialystok region. That report was written immediately following the liberation of the city of Bialystok in August 1944, for the officers of the High Command of the Soviet Partisan movement. (See appendix.)

Not all the details in that report are accurate. As a Comsomol member, Liza Chapnik was made responsible to the partisan brigade commanders, for the work in the city. She did not actually take part in all stages of the formation of the Jewish partisan movement.

36. This propaganda activity is described with many inaccuracies in a report composed in 1944 "On the Activity of the Bialystok Antifascist Organization". The original is found in the archives of "Moreshet", and the report includes names mistakenly listed in this context.

The chapter on the Germans is reported by a third person, who did not take a direct part in this activity. The report, as a whole, was hurriedly composed during the march from the forest to liberated Bialystok. The writer did not have the time to examine and check the facts. She was also motivated by the desire not to leave out any known name among those who remained alive, so as not to diminish their rights and achievements, and therefore she included names that do not belong to the report.

37. The above report includes a description of this action, among others.

38. There are details on this operation in the above report.

39. Her name is mentioned in the above report.

40. The links with the A.K., which we helped to establish, in many cases, led to catastrophic results for many Jewish partisans. More than once they were ordered to give up their arms because this was a condition of the A.K. people in certain units. Soviet partisan officers more than once yielded to the pressure and accepted this condition, if only in order to obey their instructions concerning ties with the A.K.

At that time, our ties with the Jewish partisans were more tenuous. Our connections were transferred to brigade headquarters. The facts about Jewish arms being taken by some Soviet officers became known to us only after the liberation.

Appendix

The Postcard Sent to Vilna Describing the First Action and the Loss of Edek and His comrades

Halina Stasiuk
1/4 Puliver Street
Bialystok
June 14, 1943

Abroad
A. Kommar
12/3 Pilies Street
Vilna

My dear,

I understand your anger at my silence but it happened, and we don't always write.

I know that you would very much like to know how your son died. I will try, then, to the best of my ability, to describe it, though it can only be truly understood by someone who was a witness. He was asked to pay 6,300 rubles. He and his partners decided not to pay, and to prepare their defense (even) before the indictment. His situation was very miserable, because most of the furniture (almost all) had been taken by one of the cousins, who had sold them for money and prepared a vegetable garden without taking the other cousin's opposition into account. At the last moment it became clear that the advocate had not prepared the defense properly on some points of the charges. At that time they began to speak of duty of 2100 RM (marks). All this happened on the first day. Our son then had forty bundles (pieces) of goods in his possession. After that there was again talk that they were demanding 6300 RM, and he decided to wait until the storm passed. He decided to pay the sum demanded but not one penny more. He and his comrades were prepared for this. He was completely cut off from his cousins, who were in another place. Zigmund, too, with 13 pieces of goods was, during the last days, in another place. In the end they turned (informed) our son in. From that point of view the place was . . . . . . very good. Each piece of goods was taken out separately, one by one and collected in the street, and in that way he was destroyed. He was helpless! That is how things looked; you can imagine his tragic situation. Everything needed was there . . . . and Edek perhaps (thought) that he would succeed, but what good are illusions, that is what happened. You know that I don't know how to write. In order to know truly . . .it was necessary . . .together with him, and that was impossible. About other things happening here in another letter.

Greetings to all of you. I press your hands! Halina sends greetings from the bottom of her heart. She will write.

Hold out.

I, too, am trying Ganiek is going to begin to work in the vegetable garden tomorrow.

Geniek

Explanations:

Halina Stasiuk is Hasia Bielicka, who was already living outside the ghetto at the time of the first *aktzia*. The postcard was written on June 1943, four months after the first *aktzia*. During all those months there had not been any appropriate address on the aryan side in Vilna to which the situation in Bialystok could be reported.

Geniek, who signed the postcard, is Gedalyahu Shayak.

Furniture is arms; *son* is the fighting organization; *RM — marks*, the Jews evacuated in the *aktzia*; Zigmund was Zerah; *goods* were guns; *cousins* - partners in the organization. *One of the cousins* refers to Dror. Halina is Chaika Grossman.

A German Document on the Revolt in the Bialystok Ghetto

The following document (copies from "Yediot Yad Va'shem," December 31, 1963) is the only official German document on the Bialystok ghetto revolt. It was written by the Koenigsberg branch of Dr. Goebbel's Propaganda Office in Berlin, on September 24, 1943.

The document reached the Propaganda Office in Berlin, as we can see from the stamp, on September 26, and was stamped to be filed as just another paper. It was discovered by the historian Yosef Wolf, and a photostat was sent to "Yad Va'shem."

Reich Propaganda Office
East Prussia

(stamped) Reich Office for Information and Propaganda
September 26, 1943

Koenigsberg, September 24, 1943

Re: Jewish Operation

To Sir

Reich Minister for Information and Propaganda
Williamsplatz 8/8, Berlin

In accordance with the order of SS Reichsfuehrer and Head of Police, Himmler, there began, in the early morning of August 16, 1943, the operation of clearing the Bialystok ghetto that still contained 30,000 Jews, directed by Gruppenfuehrer Lokocnik.[a] The operation was so unexpected and sudden that, in contrast to the general rule, the Jews were surprised. The ghetto was cut off by 43[b] persons of the police regiment who had arrived the previous evening and who also served during the following days in searching the ghetto. On the night before August 17, 1943, the first fires set by the Jews broke out and were extinguished by the local firemen and region firemen who were called in. It may be determined that about five thousand Jews hid in the sewage pipes, [c] cellars and also in previously erected bunkers, and they put up considerable resistance. In one place a group of Jews had built a bunker eight meters beneath the ground. These armed Jews attempted again and again in the course of this operation to break through the encircling chain during the night and to escape from the ghetto. Except for some isolated breakthroughs, these attempts were repulsed every time. In general, these rebellious Jews were equipped with a great deal of food, arms, hand grenades, rifles, etc. It may also be affirmed that there was a certain amount of automatic arms of Russian and German origin. During the course of the general operation, fires broke out from time to time. These were intended in the first days to create panic among the Jews, but afterwards were intended to cause damage to the Germany economy and especially to the war economy. With the aid of the firemen it was possible to prevent great damage to the buildings. At the time of the transport, about 200 Jews fled; most were shot, the rest - except for three, were captured. The operation clearly showed that there was a live link between this ghetto and Warsaw. Transmission equipment was not found but a number of radios were. The armed resistance resulted in the wounding of nine Germans on their side, among them were two officers.[d]

The region is now free of Jews, except for a number of hoodlums and isolated groups of Jews among the bandits.[e] The latter are mostly the same ones who fled the ghetto during the February *aktzia*. On September 8 the clearing of the ghetto was completed, and it was transferred for further management to the "Treuhand"[f] in Bialystok.

With the completion of the police action we must estimate the damage caused as quite considerable. The Jews' sabotage was responsible for extensive damage to most of the plants. The hospital too will have to be completely re-equipped.

Notes

a. Intention is to Globotznik, of course.

b. Here there is certainly a mistake; the real number was in three figures at least.

c. Jews could not hide in the sewage, since Bialystok's sewage system was not adaptable for it.

d. If the report admits that two officers were wounded, the real number of losses was undoubtedly much higher.

e. The German term for the partisans.

f. The guardianship authority (Notes according to N. Blumental's explanations of the document in "Yediot Yad Va'shem" above cit.)

Report on Activities of the Antifascist Organization in Bialystok

This report was written immediately after the liberation of the Bialystok region by the Soviet army in August 1944. It was the work of Liza Chapnik (now in Moscow). She was responsible for the command of the Kostuchi-Kalinowsky partisan brigade, and for the activities of the antifascist committee working in the area of urban Bialystok and its environs.

The report was written for the representatives of the High Command of the Soviet Partisan Movement, and appears here in its original form.

The report is composed of two parts:

1. The underground in the Bialystok ghetto and the city as a whole up to the suppression of the revolt and the liquidation of the ghetto.

2. The partisan period after the ghetto's liquidation, and the antifascist committee.

The first part was written by Liza Chapnik with the help of Riva Wojskovska (now in Poland), a Communist who left for the forest with the first of the Jewish partisans, to serve as the unit commissar. Liza Chapnik did not participate in underground activity in this stage. We can therefore understand her comment that the report on that period would be made by Ryva Voiskovska, M. Buch and Chaika Grossman. It contains information only about the activity of the Communist group in the ghetto underground. It does not include the wealth of material on the underground as a whole, with its various nuances, movements, and groupings.

The second part includes most of the material, though it, too, is not exhaustive, and contains a number of inaccuracies:

In October 1941, under the direction of a member of the all-Soviet Communist Party, Yakubovsky Tadeysh[1], Voiskovska, Ryva[2], Roshicka[3]; Masha (Mazyla)[4], the "NIURA," which was called the "Workers and Peasants Organization for War Against the Invaders," was established. The above organization's activities included, primarily:

1. Propaganda activity in every ghetto factory in which action cells were established, and conducted under the committee's guidance. The committee printed the despatches of the Soviet news agency and distributed them to the factories and the local population.

2. Mobilization of people for armed struggle against the invaders and organizing the ghetto's self-defense. The arms were obtained in various ways. Once members of the organization succeeded in taking 30 rifles from Gestapo stores. Grenades and explosives were prepared in the ghetto under the direction of the engineer, Farber (a member of the committee).

Eighty members of the organization were sent to the forests (the Azovien and Suprasl forests). Close ties were maintained with these partisans in order to guide them in their struggle and to provide material aid. Of those sent to the forests, some fell in battle, and the rest were attached to units of K. Kalinovsky Brigade commanded by Major-General Kapusta.[5]

In 1942 comrade T. Yakubowsky was killed on his way to Warsaw, where he had been sent to establish a liaison with the PPR underground organization which already had links to Moscow. In his possession were forged documents (large quantities of these were prepared in the ghetto); he was arrested by Gestapo agents in the Malkinia railway station. Another, a

1. Murdered by the Nazis; represented the Communist underground on the "aryan" side and maintained close links with his Communist comrades in the ghetto.

2. Now in Poland was active in the Fighting Jewish Organization, and commissar of the Communist Jewish partisan group, "vpierod."

3. Now in Poland; a courier between the fighting Jewish organization, and the forest and the "aryan" side; a Communist.

4. Was murdered by the Nazis. A Communist, she too represented the non-Jewish underground.

5. The above brigade was organized around Bialystok only around April 1944. Its commandos came mostly from Soviet paratroopers. A good part of the Jewish partisans who functioned for over a year in that area were integrated into that brigade.

"Niura", a woman committee member who fell into the hands of Gestapo agents as a result of provocation, died after being tortured.

Realizing that the date of the ghetto's liquidation was coming closer, the members of the committee intensified preparation of the Jewish population for resistance, and also provided assistance to the masses of ghetto inhabitants who were unable to leave for the forests.

According to the information contained in the Moscow "Einikeit" no. 24, the self-defense groups conducted battles against large SS units, as well as tanks, and in the course of one month killed 1,000 Germans.[6]

The most active section of the organizers of the antifascist activity were equipped with forged documents and sent to work within the Bialystok ghetto walls.[7]

(Comment: Detailed material on the activities from 1941 to July 1943 will be presented separately by comrades R. Voiskovske, M. Roshicka, M. M. Buch [8], C. Grossman.)

The group listed above, composed of: 1. M. Rishicka, 2. Liza Yosipovna Chapnik, 3. Chaya Yudilovna Bielicke[9], 4. Anna Agramovna Rud[10], 5. Chaya Grossman, 6. Bronia Vinickaya [11].

Bialystok ghetto in January 1943. These comrades survived. Others, like Ryva Medeiska (Vilna)[12], Chanka (Bialystok)[13] and others, were discovered by Gestapo agents, and killed after torture, suffering, but they did not betray their organization. The six comrades organized the antifascist committee under the leadership of M. Roshicka and expanded their activities. The illegal conditions hindered their activities, but despite the difficulties the committee succeeded in estalishing contact with a group of antifascist Soviet patriots: Budinsky[14], P. Lorek,[15] V. Niesmialek,[16] E. E. Orlov, M. Barborin.

Fundamental Lines of Activity of Antifascist Committee

A. Mobilizing members for antifascist committee.

6. The number published in "Einkeit" was exaggerated.

7. This detail, too, is not exact; it is correct to some degree for the first stage of the underground organization.

8. Now in Poland; one of the activists in the ghetto underground, a Communist.

9. Now a member of kibbutz Lehavot Habashan. Her name is Hasia Bielicka-Bornstein.

10. Now in Moscow.

11. Now in Jerusalem; worked for the Fighting Jewish Organization on the "aryan" side; a member of "Dror."

12., 13. The girl members of Hashomer Hatzair were tortured and killed by the Gestapo. They died heroes' deaths. Rivka Madeiska is the Rivkele mentioned in the book.

14., 15., 16. Poles active in the underground after the ghetto liquidation.

After meeting with a series of individual comrades and groups in secret apartments, the problem of the growth of the anti-fascist organization was raised in detail, in order to adapt it to conditions of heavy fascist attack. The structure of the antifascist organization into cells of two to four members each. The group was composed of three or four cells; the leader received his instructions from the committee and reported directly to it. The members of the individual cells did not know the members of the (other) cells, nor their leaders. In the month of May 1942, the antifascist organization grew to 80 members.

At the end of April 1944 the headquarters of the K. Kalinovsky Brigade, commanded by Colonel Voichetovsky, reached the Bialystok region. The head of the antifascist underground organization of the city of Bialystok, Comrade Liza Yosipovna Chapnik, was invited to the forest to meet commander Voichehovsky. That first meeting officially ratified the composition of the antifascist committee that included: Chairman L. Y. Chapnik, and committee members E. E. Rud, M. Roshicke, C. Grossman, B. Vimicke, C. Bielicka, B. Budzinski.[17] They divided the tasks among themselves and drew up a program of action for the coming period. In May 1944 the antifascist committee established contact with two other antifascist groups:

1. A group numbering 30 persons, headed by A. G. Loninkin, according to the antifascist committee's instructions in Votkovisk and,

2. A second group, numbering 15, headed by Z. Peshkov, worked independently. By the end of May the Bialystok antifascist organization grew to 125 members.

The antifascist groups (cells) worked in the following plants:

1. The textile combinat
2. The railway
3. The bakery workers
4. The airfield
5. A foundry
6. A tobacco factory
7. As Gestapo servants
8. Ruberg's factory
9. Fink's plants
10. The war prisoners' camp
11. D. A. K. number 14

---

17. All of the members of the committee, except for the elderly Pole Budzinsky, were comprised of Jewish girls between 20 and 24 years of age.

B. Propaganda activity

Propaganda was directed against the measures adopted by the fascist invaders and was expressed in the following:

a. dissemination of leaflets and newspapers prepared by the underground committee of the Bielorussian Communist Party, the League of Communist Youth in Bielorussia and the antifascist committee;

b. dissemination of news from the Soviet News Agency;

c. talks with individuals and small groups exposing the true face of the fascist invader and describing Hitler's goals for the European peoples. Imparting concrete information about the annihilation of the Russian people, the Jews, the Poles, etc.

The material, printed or handwritten, came from comrades who listened to the radio in the homes of German members of the antifascist organization (at night). Comrades Mina Kizelstein[18] a member of Soviet Communist Youth organization, Chaya Grossman, and Maryla Roshicka transferred radio sets that had been hidden in special basements from the ghetto across the barbed wire.

Vasibolod Demicotufca and a number of other comrades brought partisan literature published by the Underground Committee of the Bielorussian Communist Party and the Bielorussian League of Communist Youth from the press at night. Comrades L. Y. Chapnik, M. Roshicka, E. E. Rud, C. Bielicka, A. Loninkin, L. Posuk, E. Orlov, brought this material to the cells and groups to be disseminated among the population.

By propaganda activities directed against the measures adopted to transfer the population to Germany, they succeeded in saving a number of comrades from German hands, by directing them to underground work or taking them out to the forests.

1. Baruch Shatzman's escape from the Gestapo was organized, and he was transferred to the "20 Years of October Revolution" partisan group.

2. Persons who fled from the death camps of Treblinka and Maidanek, like Felix Rosenblum, were transferred to the Matrosov partisan units.

The escape of 25 comrades being moved by the Gestapo to the Koenigsberg camp was organized by a special contact and, as a result, 12 arrived with their weapons and transferred to the Zablodovo unit; 13 died in battles on the way.

C. Surveys and assistance to the partisans

The city of Bialystok was divided among members of the antifascist

18. Now in Israel.

organization into a series of lookout areas. It was the task of these persons to watch over important operative and strategic German military objects, as well as all such features as construction, the camouflage of defense installations, the concentrations and sites of airplanes, bomb stores, fuel, ammunition, the numbers and locations of military units, the Gestapo, the SS police, gendarmes, the location of industrial plants, etc.

The information gathered was drawn on special maps which were transferred to the headquarters of the Kalinovsky brigade to be carried across the front.

In addition to the special scouts for the various regions of Bialystok a number of comrades also operated as scouts: comrades Bielicka, C. Ruda, M. Roshicka, E. M. Orlov, F. Lorek, V. Aksinovich, V. Demidovich, A. Loninkin, Akimova. some of these comrades obtained their information through ties with the Germans.

By means of discussions seemingly on other subjects, comrade Bielicka was able to get a complete count of the numerical composition of the antiaircraft guns that arrived from Minsk and Bzest, and their locations. By means of "advice" of an ostensible artistic nature, they discovered the location of the apartment where Erich Koch, the German authority for Bielorussia and East Prussia, was to live.

As part of their provocative measures in their war against the partisans, the Gestapo organized raids and sent German, Ukrainian and Bielorussian police, in partisan dress, in to the areas where the partisan units were working. Through the Gestapo service workers and other technical apparatus the committee was able to discover their goals, numbers and time of departure. This information was immediately transferred to the partisan units.

The Gestapo also sent provocateurs to the partisan unit. Through our agents we gathered information about the activities of these persons and immediately informed the partisans. In this way, Captain Mazal, a Gestapo worker, came to the A. Matrasov unit and was exposed by the antifascist committee.

In the same fashion the committee learned through Nicolai Bakunovich, of impending mass arrests in certain sections of the city. At the time when the Red Army units were approaching Bialystok the antifascist committee members scouted the mining of houses, streets, roads and other objects. This information was conveyed to the antifascist committee, and from it to the K. Kalinovsky partisan brigade.

On July 20, 1944, for example, a map of the city noting the places mined and the defense positions, was delivered to and sent by the Partisan Brigade to the commander of the Third Army. The plan was checked by scouts from the front.

Special energy, initiative and courage were displayed in this scouting effort by comrades M. Roshicka, A. Y. Chapnik, E. E. Rud, C. Bielicka, C. Grossman, Vinicka, R. Rasina, F. Lorek, V. Aksinovich, V. Demodovich, A. Loninkin, R. Dobrovolska.

Help to the partisans was demonstrated in obtaining and supplying arms, ammunition, medicines, paper, batteries, radio tubes, topographical maps, compasses, rifle oil, grenades, sulphuric acid, etc.

Some very poorly equipped partisan units were supplied with such vital necessities as soap, linen, etc which came from the city.

All these materials were provided or bought with the money of the members of the antifascist committee and transferred to the forest by couriers. Especially outstanding in their work were comrades M. Roshicke, A. Y. Chapnik, E. Rus, C. Bielicka.

As an example, by pretending to be food speculators travelling from Grodno to Bialystok, they were able, in September 1943, to transport a machine gun in a large suitcase. It was only comrades B. Vinicka and C. Grossman's skillfulness, precision and resourcefulness that made it possible to move the machine gun safely to the "Kadima" Jewish partisan unit. They camouflaged a rifle, and carried it through the city to a partisan unit. It was the camouflage, and especially calmness and quick thinking that made the move successful. Comrades M. Roshicka, and E. E. Rud carried a machine gun and rifles wrapped in blankets through the city in broad daylight.

Because of these and other facts in their antifascist activity, they were not caught by Gestapo agents or by the police. Totals were transferred:

20 rifles
4 machine guns
more than 22 pistols
30 compasses
more than 60 grenades

In addition, they supplied a large and quite adequate quantity of medicines, surgical instruments, topographical maps of the partisan areas of operations, and other materials.

D. Activity among the Germans

With the help of antifascist organization comrades M. Kiselstein and C. Grossman, who worked in a textile factory and were fluent in the language, German, very careful discussions were held with the German director of that factory, A. G. Schade. They succeeded in discovering his antifascist views and in recruiting him into the ranks of the active antifascists. In a similar fashion a second German, a painter by profession, Wenturi, was also recruited by Hasia Bielicka. During the period of the liquidation of the ghetto the German Schade hid nine Jews from the textile factory in his apartment, gave his arms (a pistol) to the partisan C. Pachinsky (a member of the Communist Party), obtained a rifle from the police and gave it to Berkner, a scout in the headquarters of the K. Kalinovsky brigade. He obtained four pistols and a great deal of ammunition for that Brigade. The chairman of the antifascist committee arranged two meetings among the Germans Schade and Wenturi with the headquarters of the K. Kalinowski Brigade, and according to its instructions established a German antifascist cell that transferred information of great value (secret decisions of the Gestapo and the Hitlerite party) to the headquarters of the A. Kalinovsky brigade. With great difficulty Wenturi obtained a license to drive a small car. He often placed the car at the disposal of the committee to move arms, medicines, city plans, etc., to the forest and to the partisan units.

They frequently prepared railroad travel permits for the antifascist committee couriers. Benishek then gave the A. Matrasov unit a rifle and six grenades.

With the Red Army's approach and the German evacuation of Bialystok, the committee succeeded in moving one German, Schade, with full equipment — an automatic rifle and pistol — to the A. Matrosov unit. The German, Bolle, hid with his wife in a village, and there welcomed the Red Army. The other two Germans were compelled, because of their poor health, to go to East Prussia. Before leaving, they declared; "We will welcome the Red Army in Prussia."

E. Activities against informers and traitors to the homeland.

The activity among the traitors was conducted by comrades N. Bakonivic, I. Gaponin, Kurillo, A. Savicki, E. E. Orlov, Toropachu. N. Bakonivic directed the efforts in the Bielorussia National Union, and obtained systematic information about the main events. B. N. O. K., together with others received lists with addresses, information from the questionnaires, and photographs of members of the Bielorussian National Union. Some members of the B. N. U. were recruited by them and helped them in their activities.

M. Toropchin and A. Rud obtained the membership lists of the Ukrainian National Union and also information about the composition of the Ukrainian police. This material was submitted to the director of the special department of the partisan force commanded by Major-General Kapusta, comrade Patrichenko.

Kurillo, Savicky and Gaponin conducted activities among the Ukrainian policemen guarding the lumber storehouse near the railway line, and six of them were brought with their arms to the A. Matrasov partisan unit.

F. Sabotage Activities

The antifascist group regularly stole parts from the Ruberg factory and there were, as a result, five to ten-day stoppages in production, since replacements had to be supplied from Koenigsberg. At times they intentionally broke drills and other tools, and as a result, products remained unfinished for from four to ten days. During assembly screws were filed, and lacking threads, they closed with difficulty and caused a great deal of damage during shipment. Seven times in the course of three months three drills were put out of operation and thus completion of production was held up for fifteen days. Two lathes were damaged by dropping nuts between the gears.

For these actions a number of workers, sometimes innocent ones, were punished severely, either by the directors or by the police, who tortured them to death. However, German oppression did not stop them. Comrade A. Loninkin, together with the technician of the municipal electric power station, prepared and implemented large-scale sabotage. On July 16, 1944 he blew up a 15,000 volt electric power station, which supplied current to the railroad and the railway shops. As a result, the following installations were put out of action; the Bialystok station, the station and shops in the city of Lapy, the shops and station of Staroshelec. Especially devoted and courageous antifascists among the group of workers in the Ruberg factory were comrades A. Loninkin, A. Akmalev, E. Ibvon. Activities to impede production were considered by many antifascists as important daily obligations. "The lower the production and the poorer the quality — the better for us." Our people worked diligently only when a German stood at their side with his whip; when he moved away, they either stopped work entirely or took apart what they had previously assembled, and mutilated the parts.

R. Rasina and Ada Malevska, on July 20, 1944, with the help of magnetic mines, blew up four trucks loaded with barrels of fuel. With the help of an acquaintance who worked in the dining room, Ada Loskovskaya succeeded in penetrating the SS kitchen, putting poison in the cooking pot and killing 50 Germans and eight Poles who worked there.

Zina Salinniva took part in this poisoning. Antifascist committee members Chapnik, Rud, Bieliecka, and Dobroviolska concealed arms and couriers from the partisan units in their rooms. Two partisans belonging to the

Rokosovsky scouts were provided with an underground room and were also supplied with passports. A member of the partisan intelligence was moved to Warsaw on a special mission and his trip made secure. Important roles in concealing arms were filled by comrades Kurillo, Sovicky, Bielicka, Grossman and Demidovich, who placed their rooms at the disposal of the committee of the antifascist organization.

G. Activity among the Poles

In keeping with the instructions of brigade commander, Colonel Voichehovsky, comrade Chapnik, Chairman of the antifascist committee, and antifascist committee member B. Vinicka, went to the Polish national organization of the city of Bialystok. These comrades conducted activities within this organization and gathered illegal literature, which was transferred to the headquarters of the K. Kalinowsky partisan brigade.

Polish partisans were operating in the Bialystok area, but were hostile to the Soviet partisans. Brigade commissar comrade Voichehovsky made it his aim to coordinate the activities of the Polish partisans and his brigade for the sake of unity in the war against the fascist invaders.

After tremendous efforts and after overcoming many difficulties and a lack of trust, comrades Chapnik and B. Vinicka arranged a meeting among Brigade commissar Voichehovsky and representatives of the Polish partisans. As a result, we were witness to the joint struggle of Polish partisans and the K. Kalinowsky Brigade in the Kryshim Ossowich region 8.

H. Welcoming the Red Army

With the approach of the Red Army, the Germans began to evacuate the population and certain members of the organization were directed to the partisan units. Committee Chairman Chapnik and committee members A. Rud, M. Roshicka and B. Vinicka remained in the city. These comrades organized intensified watches against mines and thanks to their heroic efforts, four houses, one textile factory and one storehouse of that factory were saved from destruction. Knowing that the Germans were very much afraid of infectious diseases, they posted signs which read: "Achtung! Sehuengefahr!" ("Beware! Plague Danger!") and added the picture of a skull. The German sappers and engineers were fearful of entering and ordered all the tenants of the neighboring houses not to enter them for three weeks.

Preparations to receive the Red Army had begun in March although the enemy was still in the city. In A. Rud's attic we wrote slogans and made placards. All the members of the antifascist committee prepared bouquets, decorations, etc. All this activity was conducted to the accompaniment of roaring cannons. On July 26, 1944, we met the first scouts of the Red Army and organized a warm reception.

The soldiers of the scout unit and their commander thanked us warmly for the welcome. On the 27th of the month, at seven o'clock in the morning, the antifascists went out to the Volkovisk-Bialystok road, outside Bialystok. The army organized a concert and a lecture for us on the international situation.

Before their trip to Grodno the members of the antifascist committee and organization, who remained, were presented to the National Committee for the Liberation of Poland and were assigned to responsible duties in the city of Bialystok.